· THE WARRIOR AND THE PRIEST ·

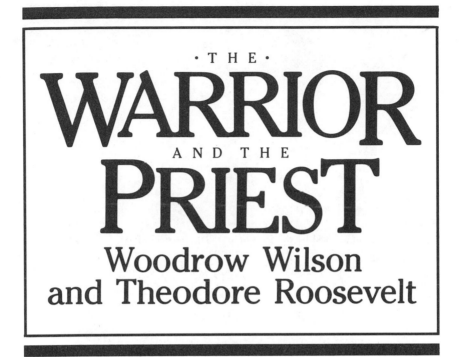

·THE·
WARRIOR
AND THE
PRIEST
Woodrow Wilson
and Theodore Roosevelt

JOHN MILTON COOPER, JR.

THE BELKNAP PRESS OF
HARVARD UNIVERSITY PRESS
Cambridge, Massachusetts
and London, England

Copyright © 1983 by the President and Fellows of Harvard College
All rights reserved
Printed in the United States of America
10 9 8 7 6

This book is printed on acid-free paper, and its binding materials have
been chosen for strength and durability.

LIBRARY OF CONGRESS CATALOGING IN PUBLICATION DATA

Cooper, John Milton.
The warrior and the priest.

Bibliography: p.
Includes index.
1. Presidents—United States—Biography.
2. Wilson, Woodrow, 1856–1924.
3. Roosevelt, Theodore, 1858–1919.
4. United States—Politics and government—1901–1909.
5. United States—Politics and government—1913–1921.
I. Title.
E176.1.C7919   1983   973.91′1   83–6021

ISBN 0–674–94751–7

Designed by Gwen Frankfeldt

To my father,
who introduced me to
the greatest sport in the world,
American politics

Contents

Preface   xi

I The Dude and the Professor

1   Knickerbocker and Gray   5
2   Manse and World   15
3   Paths of Glory   27
4   Groves of Academe   44
5   Acquaintances   59

II Two Presidents

6   Public Performer   69
7   Academic Reformer   89
8   Stalemate and Departure   109
9   Spokesman and Critic   119
10   Adversaries   130

III The Great Campaign

11   Insurgent   143
12   Frontrunner   164
13   On the Hustings   187
14   The New Nationalism versus
     the New Freedom   206

IV The Warrior and the Priest

15 Party Leader   229
16 Crossroads of Politics   248
17 Designs of Diplomacy   266
18 Facing War   288
19 The Decision to Intervene   303
20 The End of the Conflict   324
21 Legacies   346

Notes   365
Acknowledgments   424
Index   431

Illustrations

following page 136

Theodore Roosevelt in 1884

Woodrow Wilson, circa 1885

Portrait of Roosevelt by John Singer Sargent,
  1905

Portrait of Wilson by Sargent, 1917

Roosevelt in Colorado, 1905

Roosevelt at the University of Washington, 1911

Roosevelt in Massachusetts, 1905

Wilson at Princeton, 1910

Wilson and Tumulty, 1912

Wilson campaigning, 1912

Roosevelt and Wilson "debate," 1911

"Professor Wilson Visits Congress," by Max
  Beerbohm, 1914

Cartoon of Wilson by Rollin Kirby, 1915

Cartoon of Roosevelt by "Ding" Darling, 1916

Cartoon of Roosevelt by Darling, 1916

Cartoon of Roosevelt by Kirby, 1916

Cartoon of Roosevelt by Kirby, 1916

Wilson in Paris, 1919

Preface

WOODROW WILSON AND THEODORE ROOSEVELT shaped the American presidency and altered the course of politics in the United States. Following a line of lackluster chief executives, they reinvigorated the office and thereby redefined the contours of political life. Both men were exceptionally gifted and resourceful; both were learned in theory and accomplished in the practice of democratic government. Their deep and sophisticated understanding of major issues and their success in bringing those issues before the public enabled them to leave a lasting imprint on history.

As presidents, they seized upon and expanded three powerful aspects of the office—public dramatization, education of the people, and party leadership. Theodore Roosevelt made himself the first truly contemporary American president by dramatizing himself through the mass journalistic media. He owed his rise to the fame he had gained through well-cultivated press coverage of his exploits as a reformer, rancher, hunter, police commissioner, war hero, and engaging personality. Exuberant and expansive, he epitomized the enjoyment of power. Roosevelt exploited the public dimensions of all his roles and offices with zest and skill. He capitalized upon the opportunities for public persuasion afforded by the presidency, which he called a "bully pulpit." More important still, his overwhelming personal popularity gave him a power base apart from his party and other more traditional sources of support and restraint. That feat made him the progenitor of what has since been labeled the "imperial presidency."

To contemporary observers and later interpreters, Woodrow

Wilson as president appeared to offer a sharp contrast to Roosevelt. Disciplined and controlled, he seemingly embodied a less joyful exercise of power. He pursued a more conventional style of politics with resourceful single-mindedness. Yet Wilson greatly admired Roosevelt and imitated some of his practices, especially in public persuasion. No president has spoken more often to Congress, and few have made more frequent direct appeals to the people. Fittingly for one who had been a professor and university president, Wilson regarded education of the public as the most important ingredient in political leadership. Further, acting as what he called a "prime minister," he worked through his party organization to draft, implement, and defend legislation. No president since has wrought such legislative and administrative achievements within the first term of his presidency. His accomplishments in educating the public and leading his party made Wilson one of the ablest practitioners of the dynamic presidency.

Roosevelt's and Wilson's most significant contributions lay in shaping the major ideological dimensions of twentieth-century politics. They lived in a critical period of partisan and ideological conflicts over issues arising from a newly industrial society and from involvement in power politics abroad. Roosevelt inherited from William McKinley a pro-capitalist Republican party, which he tried unsuccessfully to redirect toward a more nationalistic, less materialistic brand of conservatism. His failure had major consequences for Republicans and conservatives. Wilson inherited from William Jennings Bryan a reformist Democratic party, which he refined and solidified as a coalition of less advantaged groups seeking to advance their interests through the welfare state. His success had lasting consequences for Democrats and liberals. The criticism and dissent that the two men generated stimulated the development of other ideological positions. Pro-business and limited-government conservative doctrines at home and resistance to commitments overseas, often dubbed isolationism, developed apart from and largely in opposition to Wilson's and Roosevelt's policies.

In world affairs Theodore Roosevelt became the first president to act self-consciously as the leader of a great power, and he was a tireless evangelist for international activism. Woodrow Wilson also became an advocate of international involvement and world leadership, but he pursued a more pacific vision. He enlisted his party's overwhelming support and led the Democrats in a direction on foreign policy that they almost certainly would not have taken otherwise. In foreign affairs the conflicts between these men established durable but complicated patterns of support and opposition. Although Wilson and Roosevelt both favored greater international involvement, their personal and philosophical differences ruled out cooperation during their lifetimes. Only a generation after their deaths, with the renewed international crises of World War II, did advocates of their respective views join forces to advance programs of world leadership and collective security. In the 1930s and 1940s Franklin Roosevelt gained much of his success at home and abroad because he could draw upon and partially fulfill the domestic and foreign policy legacies of both Theodore Roosevelt and Woodrow Wilson.

These presidents were uniquely gifted to preside over the greatest transformation in American politics in the last century. In their early careers there was an uncanny congruence in their attitudes toward contemporary issues and approaches to politics, but by the time Wilson entered active politics in 1910, the two men had become rivals for leadership. When they ran against each other for president two years later, they were formidable antagonists. Over the next seven years—until Roosevelt's death and Wilson's physical and political collapse—their conflict engaged them so deeply and ranged so broadly that it has been compared to the clash of Friedrich Nietzsche's philosophical embodiments of the Will-to-Power, the Warrior and the Priest. Like Thomas Jefferson and Alexander Hamilton a century earlier, neither Wilson nor Roosevelt could have developed fully in his politics without the other as a foil. Out of their confrontations—first principally over domestic reform and later increasingly over foreign policy—emerged a series of passionately intense, wide-ranging, and philosophically rich debates about the purposes and directions of American and world politics. Except at a few points during the pre–Civil War controversies over slavery and sectionalism, the United States had not witnessed such a conflict since the days of Jefferson and Hamilton.

The apparent contrasts between the political personalities of these two men have made it tempting to ascribe their beliefs and actions mainly to psychological factors. Inner drives did have major effects on their public careers, but the two men and their conflicts should not be viewed solely or primarily in terms of psychological compulsions. Social background, party circumstances, and political thought were more important influences on each of them. Two labels frequently applied to them—Roosevelt's affirmation of national self-interest, or "realism," and Wilson's pursuit of transcendent ideals, or "idealism"—are misleading and require further refinement. In foreign affairs Roosevelt often did welcome strife, and he frequently stressed practical limitations on diplomatic commitments. By the same token, Wilson did strive to reform international affairs in a more peaceful direction, and he justified his policies with exalted rhetoric that appealed to moral and religious values. But categorizing Roosevelt as a realist and Wilson as an idealist is a half-truth. In domestic affairs the two men professed to reverse these positions; in foreign affairs they were by no means polar opposites. In both realms Roosevelt continually proclaimed himself an idealist, appealed in even more exalted terms than Wilson to transcendent values, and scorned Wilson as the opposite of idealistic—as narrow, timid, and selfish. In both realms Wilson extolled what he called "expediency," argued for patience and caution, and rejected Roosevelt's approach as wrong-headedly and excessively idealistic—as quixotic and deluded. Wilson and Roosevelt were fathers of opposing schools of domestic and foreign policy, but their conflict was much more complicated and ran far deeper than a clash between realism and idealism. Their thought and actions exposed the deeper meanings behind their contemporaries' responses to the chief issues of the industrial age and shaped American and world politics for generations to come.

The stakes involved in understanding these men and their places in history are high. They brought a depth and sophistication to the exercise of power and to public debate that have had no equal in the United States in more than a century. Altogether, their contributions and conflicts made Woodrow Wilson and Theodore Roosevelt the most significant presidents and political leaders since the Civil War.

· I ·

THE DUDE AND THE PROFESSOR

The idea that a Harvard-trained dude could make a career in the rough-and-tumble of politics appeared ludicrous, and it seemed equally unlikely that such a plunge could be taken by a middle-aged professor with no practical experience in government. Yet such was the force of each man's personality and such the force of his vision that each somehow made men and events serve his purpose, and the dude and the professor became respectively the twenty-sixth and twenty-eighth Presidents of the United States.

Henry W. Bragdon
Woodrow Wilson:
The Academic Years

THEODORE ROOSEVELT AND WOODROW WILSON followed different but parallel paths during the first forty years of their lives. They were born within two years of each other, Wilson on December 29, 1856, and Roosevelt on October 27, 1858. Each grew up in a family that felt the strain of divided loyalties during the Civil War. Those strains and the aftermath of the Civil War had profound effects on each man's later political views and career. But the most profound influence of their early lives on their engagement with politics was a shared personal circumstance.

Both Roosevelt and Wilson had heroic childhoods. As boys, they struggled to overcome handicaps that threatened to bar them from the adult roles they longed to play. For each youth the strongest outside influence toward overcoming his handicaps came from his father. Those struggles helped shape their views toward politics. The two young men received bachelor's degrees from leading colleges in succeeding years, Wilson from Princeton in 1879 and Roosevelt from Harvard in 1880. Each subsequently tried his hand briefly at the law. During the 1880s both drifted a bit before beginning their ascents, which took them to the peaks of their respective professions shortly after the turn of the twentieth century.

The peaks they climbed exposed the biggest divergence in their lives before 1900. Roosevelt became president of the United States in September 1901; Wilson became president of Princeton University in June 1902. Roosevelt went further sooner, and he triumphed at the calling that had originally attracted Wilson. From the time of his graduation from Harvard, Roosevelt was in the thick of politics with almost no interruptions. His career had a few fits and starts, but he sought and held ever-higher offices and won growing fame and honor. In contrast, Wilson renounced his youthful yearning for active politics and entered academic life. He established himself as a renowned analyst and commentator on politics and government and a widely regarded public speaker, but he remained essentially a spectator and bystander. The divergence in their careers and the differences in their sectional backgrounds and party allegiances were obviously significant, yet the two men differed surprisingly little in their views on major public issues and in their basic approaches to politics during the first four decades of their lives.

·1·

Knickerbocker and Gray

BY THE TIME HE BECAME PRESIDENT in 1901, Theodore Roosevelt had already begun to enjoy the legend of the most famous childhood in American history. Like Abraham Lincoln's, his boyhood served as a legendary example to American youth. He, too, had overcome adversity and in the process had built the character that led him to achieve the world's greatest honor and success. Unlike Lincoln, however, Roosevelt basked in his legend during his lifetime and played the main part in its creation. As his friend and sympathetic critic Lewis Einstein observed, Roosevelt consistently skewed accounts of his early life to make himself appear as much of an ordinary person as possible. Although he did not magnify his handicaps or disadvantages, he did downplay his special gifts and advantages. Roosevelt acted in part to inspire the nation's youth. By insisting, as he always did, that his accomplishments had sprung from effort and perseverance, not from inborn or inherited superiority, he could urge others to emulate him. The Roosevelt legend did provide an inspiration to American youth, particularly boys, and it also proved politically profitable for him. [1]

Roosevelt needed to make himself seem ordinary because he plainly was not. Two glaring distinctions, one intellectual, one social, marked him from birth. Abundant evidence attests to his gifted, capacious mind. From earliest childhood he showed a voracious, intense appetite for learning. After learning his letters, he became a reader of awesome speed and trancelike absorption. By all accounts, too, his memory bordered on the phenomenal. His parents evidently approved of and indulged their son's studies, and their wealth and position allowed him the advantages of travel and education and assured him a level of cultivated taste. The boy demonstrated his intellectual bent by the time he was nine by becoming a dedicated amateur zoologist. His original ambition, which he did not abandon until midway through college, was to be a scientist. Clearly, Roosevelt had a mind that set him apart from his contemporaries and even from most presidents.

His other inborn distinction was social. On both sides his family had occupied positions of eminence for several generations. The Roosevelts were Knickerbockers, descendants of the early Dutch settlers. His father, Theodore Roosevelt, Sr., a successful importer and glass merchant, belonged to the innermost circle of New York society. He became a millionaire when he inherited his share in Theodore's grandfather's estate when the boy was twelve. Theodore's mother, Martha, or "Mittie," Bulloch Roosevelt, came from one of the leading families of Georgia. The Bullochs had long supplied their state and nation with military officers, judges, and legislators, and they had owned vast plantations worked by hundreds of slaves. In the Civil War the Bullochs' Doric-pillared mansion near Atlanta was looted though not destroyed. The family had already lost its fortune, and two of Mittie's brothers, who had fought for the Confederacy, went into exile in England. In contrast, Theodore Roosevelt, Sr., continued to prosper after the Civil War. In 1873, when they returned from a second extended tour of Europe, he moved the family into an elegantly appointed new home just off Fifth Avenue in Manhattan's most fashionable neighborhood.

But Theodore Roosevelt's childhood also had a dark side, which provided the occasion for his heroism. None of the four Roosevelt children, two boys and two girls, escaped some form of physical disability. Theodore, the older son, suffered from severe asthma and a nervous digestive system. He was nearsighted and belatedly began wearing glasses when he was thirteen. Weak and sickly, bookish and bespectacled, the youthful Roosevelt was almost a caricature of the pampered, protected rich boy. "I was nervous and timid," he later recalled, and he might have remained so except for a remarkable personal transformation. Starting when he was eleven, he pursued a five-year regimen of exercise and outdoor activity that made his body strong and robust. His asthma, which almost certainly had psychosomatic aspects, gradually subsided, and aside from a few injuries and a nearly fatal tropical fever contracted when he was in his fifties, he remained in vigorous health until a few months before his death at the age of sixty. More immediately, the young Roosevelt began to exert what he called his "prowess." He came out of his shell, made friends, became sociable toward girls, and showed the first signs of leadership. Even without embellishment, his boyhood did lend itself to an exemplary tale of self-improvement.[2]

Such an experience could hardly have failed to leave a lasting imprint. Its most important effect was in causing Roosevelt to regard himself as a self-created character. His metamorphosis from a scrawny, shrinking boy into a strong, masterful man furnished a lifelong model that he not only applied to himself but also used as a standard of judgment for other men and, with special adaptations, for women, as well as social groups and nations. The two most noticeable aspects of his self-created character were an openly avowed obsession with physical matters and a spirit of perpetual youthfulness. Roosevelt's physical obsession manifested itself most clearly in his pursuit and promotion of sports and fitness. But he did not like or recommend all sports, by any means. Every one of his favorites—boxing, hunting, rowing, football, horseback riding—featured exertion, bodily combat, danger, or some combination of those. For him, only sports such as those served to build strength and character. The other main manifestation of his obsession was a readiness to inject physical considerations into almost any subject. Later, when he battled big business, Roosevelt sneered at the rich as physically soft, and he always scorned opponents of wars as physical cowards.[3]

That obsession with physical "prowess" betrayed an obvious insecurity, as did the other outward sign of his self-created character—his youthfulness. Almost no one who knew Roosevelt failed to comment on this trait. To some it seemed charming boyishness; to others, irritating immaturity. Both assessments contained a measure of truth. Roosevelt's nervous intensity and sheer physical joy of living gave him inexhaustible high spirits. Yet in a sense he never fully matured. Throughout his life he showed an adolescent's incessant need to prove himself. While president he repeatedly took ridiculous personal risks on hikes and hunting trips. In 1914, at the age of fifty-five, after nearly losing his life on an expedition to the Brazilian jungles, he explained, "I had just one more chance to be a boy, and I took it!" In 1913 in his autobiography he recalled reading as a boy in a novel of Frederick Marryat's about "how to acquire the quality of fearlessness. He says that . . . the course to follow is for the man to keep such a grip on himself that he can act just as if he was not frightened. After this is kept up long enough it changes from pretense to reality, and the man does in very fact become fearless by sheer dint of practicing fearlessness when he does not feel it . . . This was the theory upon which I went." Fearlessness never did become completely natural with Roosevelt.[4]

In his struggle against physical inferiority, the youth owed much to his father. According to several recollections, Theodore Roosevelt, Sr., provided the impetus by challenging his son, "You must *make* your body." That story, like other parts of the account of his childhood, had apocryphal adornments, but the elder Roosevelt did act as both a model and a prod to his son. Strong, handsome, industrious, upright, Roosevelt, Sr., seems to have been an ideal father—"the best man I ever knew," his son repeatedly called him. Warmth, gentleness, and a sense of fun saved him from being overbearing, but he did not accept his older son's physical shortcomings. He built a gymnasium in the family's new mansion and consulted doctors about the best exercise programs. "He not only took great and loving care of me," Roosevelt remembered in 1900, ". . . but he also most wisely refused to coddle me, and made me feel that I must force myself to hold my own with other boys and prepare to do the rough work of the world."[5]

The father also set the directions that the son took when he emerged from his youthful struggle. Roosevelt, Sr., was the strongest influence on his son's life. His mother, though loving and refined, faded into the background of the family by the end of the Civil War. Once a strong, vivacious young woman, Mittie became almost a stereotype of the helpless southern belle. The leading female role in the family fell upon Theodore's older sister Anna, who was called "Bamie." Perhaps in part to fill the gap left by his wife's abdication, Theodore, Sr., came to stand as a paragon of masculine virtue at the center of the family. His death from cancer in February 1878, during Roosevelt's sophomore year at Harvard, therefore fell as a particularly cruel blow. For a while his father's death threatened to devastate Theodore, who went through a troubled, often violent nine months before regaining a measure of emotional stability the following fall. For years afterward he sought to emulate his father. When he entered the New York legislature in 1882, he told a family friend, "I honestly mean to act up here on all questions as nearly as possible as I think Father would have done, if he had lived." On his first day in the White House after becoming president in September 1901, he reminded his younger sister Corinne that it was their father's birthday. "I feel as if my father's hand were on my shoulder," he confessed, "and as if there were a special blessing over the life I am to lead here."[6]

The senior Roosevelt's death had opposite effects on his two sons. The younger, Elliott, who had once seemed strong and capable, never got over the experience. He had already shown symptoms of epilepsy, and after his father's death he began a long slide into self-indulgence, alcoholism, and extramarital dalliances. By the time of his own death in 1894, Elliott had become the perfect picture of the upper-class wastrel. For Theodore, his father's death provided a liberation that capped his self-transformation. After his stormy period of mourning, he emerged as the man of the family and swiftly made two major shifts in his life to prove it. First, in November 1878, he met and fell in love with Alice Lee. The young Harvard swell pursued the beautiful Boston debutante with characteristic intensity and determination, and he triumphed with their engagement during his senior year and marriage shortly after graduation.[7]

Roosevelt's other shift was to renounce science for another career. Several factors apparently entered into this change in ambitions. One was intellectual. With his love of the outdoors and his talents as a naturalist, he chafed at the German-inspired emphasis on laboratory work and microscopic analysis that was coming to dominate biological studies at Harvard and other universities. His studies implanted an abiding distaste for what he regarded as the "scientific" ideal of tedious, unimaginative collection of facts in all fields of inquiry. But in abandoning biology Roosevelt did not suppress his intellectual inclinations. He soon turned to historical research and writing, and in his senior year he began work on what became his first book, *The Naval War of 1812*.

Probably more important in his renunciation of a scientific career was his father's influence. During his freshman year, Roosevelt recalled in his autobiography, his father had advised him "that he had made enough money to enable me to take up such a career and do non-remunerative work of value *if I intended to do the very best work there was in me*"; he had also cautioned that "if I went into a scientific career, I must definitely abandon all thought of the enjoyment that could accompany a money-making career, and must find my pleasures elsewhere."[8]

Inasmuch as his father had "from the earliest days instilled into me the knowledge that I was to work and make my own way in the world," the hint of discouragement was hard to miss. In fact, Theodore Roosevelt, Sr., had already underscored his point. At the beginning of his son's freshman year, on Theodore's eighteenth birthday, he had written, "I have worked fairly hard all my life and anticipated passing over to you many of my responsibilities as soon as your shoulders are broad enough to bear them. It has always seemed to me as if there was something so peculiarly pleasant in the relations between a father and son, the enjoyment of the father is so great as he cares for the boy and sees him gradually become a reasoning being, his mind and his physique both developing under his care and training, and above all his religious views becoming more fixed." Then he reiterated: "As he approaches manhood the boy enjoys relieving the father of part of the responsibilities which he has borne until that time, and these cares prepare the boy to take the father's place in the great battle of life."[9]

Ironically, his father's death provided the means by which Roosevelt could have comfortably pursued a scientific career. His inheritance brought an income of about $8,000 a year, a handsome sum in those days; another $4,000 a year came to him from a trust fund upon his mother's death six years later. Roosevelt never did work for a living, and he did not become fully self-supporting apart from his inheritances until he was president. His rejection of moneymaking was conscious and persistent. Sometimes he apologized for it as a personal failing, and he later worried about not being able to leave his children as much as his father had left him. At other times he maintained that his interests in literature and politics simply led him elsewhere. But his attitude toward wealth went deeper than personal quirks and preferences. One of Roosevelt's fundamental political views was rejection of "materialism," and upon that attitude he increasingly based his efforts to elevate public life. His antimaterialism was not just a patrician disdain for newer wealth. Early in his young manhood he began to express contempt for the social upper crust as well. Roosevelt regarded his father's occupation and his own social class with at least a measure of disdain.

The young man's ambivalence about his paternal legacy was most clearly demonstrated in the career he chose. In August 1879 Roosevelt wrote in his diary that after college he might "study law, preparatory to going into public life." That was his first reference to a political career. Until his junior year at Harvard he had taken little interest in public affairs. The new interest undoubtedly sprang in part from a desire to emulate his father, who had carried on a family tradition of civic involvement and good works and whose last illness had occurred just after a stinging political defeat. In a move to clean up corruption and trim the power of the New York Republican machine, President Rutherford B. Hayes had nominated the elder Roosevelt to be collector of the Port of New York, one of the richest patronage-dispensing positions, but the state boss, Senator Roscoe Conkling, had blocked confirmation of the appointment. The son may well have warmed to politics, as Carleton Putnam has suggested, as a way to avenge his father's humiliation.[10]

Two other aspects of his choice remain noteworthy, however. First, Roosevelt was attracted to the one field in which his father had conspicuously failed. Second, his spirit and manner in entering politics smacked of a desire to strike out on his own. "My whole career in politics," he explained privately in 1901, "is due to the simple fact that when I came out of Harvard I was firmly resolved to belong to the governing class, not to the governed." That statement, which Roosevelt often repeated publicly, showed contrarily both how much aristocratic assumptions permeated his thinking and how uncomfortable he was with his own class. In 1880, when Roosevelt had announced that he was joining the local Republican organization in New York, he told Jacob Riis ten years later, people in his own social circle had derided him. He would meet no gentlemen there, they had scoffed, only grooms and saloonkeepers. "Then, if that is so," he said he had answered, "the groom and the saloon-keeper are the governing class and you confess weakness.

You have all the chances, the education, the position, and you let them rule you. They must be better men." Roosevelt soon showed that he was no renegade, since he became an antimachine good-government man. But if he sought to beat the politicians at their own game, he was playing by their rules, not his friends' or his father's.[11]

Mixed attitudes toward his background also shaped an important component of Roosevelt's politics. During his nearly forty years in politics, his name was associated conspicuously and consistently with one issue above all others—war. He became the most prominent militarist in American history. Some interpreters have accounted for the origins of his militarism in the parades, the war news, and the war games of his childhood during the Civil War. Others have found its source in the fascination with manliness instilled by his body building and the fondness for firearms acquired through hunting. Yet thousands of young Americans lived through the Civil War and enjoyed hunting without acquiring a similar outlook, while some outstanding exponents of physical fitness, such as David Starr Jordan, became pacifists. The deepest root of Roosevelt's compulsive, often frenetic militarism lay in his father's having failed to answer his most important challenge in "the great battle of life"—he had not fought in the Civil War.

Roosevelt's biographers have been oddly reluctant to draw many inferences about the impact on him of his father's lack of war service. Roosevelt never mentioned the matter publicly or, it seems, privately, but he did leave a trail of clues to his attitude. In his autobiography he explained his enlistment in the Spanish-American War: "I had always felt that if there were a serious war I wished to be in a position to explain to my children why I did take part in it, and not why I did not take part in it." Roosevelt, Sr.'s, reasons for not fighting had been honorable. As Theodore's older sister Bamie recalled, their father had wanted to join the army, but their mother had been in frail health and he had feared that his fighting against her brothers might kill her. When Roosevelt went to war himself in 1898, his wife and his oldest son both lay gravely ill. Yet, he told his presidential military aide in 1908, he decided "that it was my one chance to do something for my country and for my family and my one chance to cut my little notch on the stick that stands as a measuring rod in every family. I know now that I would

have turned from my wife's deathbed to have answered that call."
His father had aided the Union war effort in several civilian capac-
ities, including making long tours of army camps with the Sanitary
Commission, but he had also resorted to the practice under the
Civil War draft of hiring a substitute to take his place in the ranks.
In a speech at Harvard in February 1907, recalling his joining the
National Guard directly after graduation, Roosevelt declared, "I
did not intend to have to hire somebody else to do my shooting for
me."[12]

An influence from his mother's side of the family filled the
emotional breach left by his father's not having fought. Whatever
her other failings, Mittie Roosevelt imbued her children with a
strain of southern romanticism, much of which attached to her two
brothers, who had served as Confederate naval officers. Young
Theodore had met his dashing seadog uncles, James and Irvine
Bulloch, on the family trips to Europe, and it was almost certainly
from them that he acquired the interests that led him to write *The
Naval War of 1812*. "It was practically a civil war," Roosevelt noted
in the book, in which he acknowledged the assistance of Captain
James Bulloch, "formerly of the United States Navy." That book,
which he began while still at Harvard and finished during the year
after graduation, expressed many of his later political views, including advocacy of a strong navy, neo-Federalist scorn for Thomas
Jefferson and his followers, and a nascent imperialism in his depiction of white settlers filling empty lands and subduing backward
races. He also showed detachment in praising British seamanship
and the generalship of Andrew Jackson. Indeed, his praise for
Jackson's "master spirit" and "his cool head and quick eye, his stout
heart and strong hand" suggested that his uncles had awakened him
to not only new interests and views but also to an alternative
masculine ideal. Besides writing about military affairs during the
year after he left Harvard, he began practicing them in a small way
by joining a mounted unit of the New York National Guard.[13]

Graduation from college, marriage, and entry into politics in
1880, at the age of twenty-one, completed Roosevelt's emergence
to manhood. At Harvard he had enjoyed the best of several worlds.
He had belonged to the most fashionable social set and had been
elected to the most prestigious club, the Porcellian. Academically,
he had finished just below the top tenth of his class and had been

elected to Phi Beta Kappa. His unusual intensity had not diminished his esteem among his social peers, and his changing interests and romantic and athletic involvements had scarcely detracted from his intellectual attainments. He had overcome not only physical frailty and a timid disposition but also family tragedy to become a man among men. Yet behind his accomplishments lay deep insecurities and painful, barely acknowledged conflicts. Those insecurities and conflicts ensured that heroic struggle would become his permanent way of life.

Roosevelt's heroism received a stern reinforcement in the spring of 1880. When he underwent a routine medical examination at Harvard, he later recalled, the physician told him he had a weak heart and must avoid exertion if he wanted to live more than a few years. The young man promptly replied that he had no intention of following the doctor's advice. If he had to lead that kind of life, he would rather die young. This story sounds like one more addition to the legend of Roosevelt's youth, and in a way it was. He kept the doctor's warning secret from everyone until the last year of his life, when he revealed the incident for inclusion in *The Boys' Life of Theodore Roosevelt*. Both the event and its revelation provided a fitting end to his legendary youth. It was fitting, too, that his original commitment to politics and the germs of his most important views emerged from his youthful struggles and crises. At least twice again in his career, he took crucial steps and shaped critical attitudes in response to personal trials and tragedies. For Theodore Roosevelt even more than for most people, the child was father of the man.[14]

· 2 ·

Manse and World

WOODROW WILSON'S CHILDHOOD never became famous. Little about his early life seemed extraordinary, much less heroic. Born in a Presbyterian manse in Virginia, he grew up in medium-sized towns in the South, where his father, Joseph Ruggles Wilson, held pulpits and seminary professorships. The life of a successful minister was secure and comfortable. Even the Civil War did not directly upset routines or cause hardships. Joseph Wilson did some civilian work in support of the Confederate cause and periodically went to the front as an army chaplain. His church in Augusta, Georgia, was converted for a time into a military hospital. Although the elder Wilsons had come from the North in the 1850s and still had close relations there, family divisions because of the war did not greatly affect them. Soon after the war ended, visits resumed with his mother's family in Ohio. Contacts might have recommenced on his father's side, too, if a trip by Joseph Wilson to Ohio in 1866 had not resulted, evidently, in a quarrel and a break. The young Wilson grew up unaware of his father's relatives, whom he did not meet until many years later.

The greatest influence of his early years was not war or politics but religion. Woodrow Wilson was the son, grandson, and nephew of Presbyterian ministers. Nearly everyone who has written about him has commented on how the pulpit and the manse left unmistakable marks on the style, direction, and content of his political career. A clerical background was hardly unusual among politicians of his time, but Wilson's experience with such a background introduced the first element in his early life that was out of the ordinary.

Thanks to his forebears, Wilson was also born with social and intellectual distinctions. Although the South festered in poverty following the Confederate defeat, and ministers did not earn large salaries, Wilson's family enjoyed prestige and comforts. Nor did his family come from the common run of preachers. After Episcopalians, Presbyterians stood higher socially than any other denomination in the South, and Wilson's relatives moved near the top of their church's hierarchy. Joseph Wilson rose steadily to bigger and better churches. In 1870, when he became professor of theology and rhetoric at the Columbia Theological Seminary in South Carolina, while also holding the pastorate of the First Presbyterian Church of Columbia, he had seemingly attained the pinnacle of his profession.[1]

Status also devolved upon the boy from his mother's side. He was christened Thomas Woodrow Wilson, after his Scottish-born grandfather. The grandfather had been educated at Glasgow University and had occupied a pastorate in England before emigrating to Ohio, where he settled and held pulpits. Wilson's mother's younger brother, James Woodrow, had carried the family banner higher by studying at Harvard and in Germany, where he had earned a doctorate at Heidelberg, and then by joining the Columbia Seminary faculty. In addition, James Woodrow headed the Confederate Chemical Laboratory during the Civil War and afterward augmented his seminary duties by teaching at the state college and editing the southern Presbyterians' denominational magazine. In 1884 James Woodrow lost his seminary post through a heresy trial, because of his efforts to reconcile Charles Darwin's theory of evolution with the Bible. Soon thereafter, however, he became president of South Carolina College, now the University of South Carolina. In the close-knit social world of the southern Presbyterian clergy, the Woodrow connection counted heavily. As a young man, Wilson was commonly referred to as "Dr. James Woodrow's nephew."[2]

It was hardly surprising that Wilson showed intellectual inclinations. His background was almost as much academic as clerical, and his father played a large role in nurturing his interests. When Wilson later counted his father among his three great teachers, more than filial piety prompted his judgment. Whatever his shortcomings, Joseph R. Wilson seems to have been a gifted teacher of his specialty, rhetoric. The elder Wilson devoted probably his best pedagogical talents to his older son, who was known as "Tommy" in his youth. The two were a devoted pair from the time the boy was eleven or twelve. The father spent his free days walking and talking with him, assigned him subjects for essays or speeches, and then evaluated his performances. The clergyman's imposing presence and taskmasterly role did not preclude joking and fun, and his surviving correspondence makes clear that he balanced tough criticism with warm encouragement. The stress in his teaching fell always on clear thinking and expression. Despite the poverty and provinciality of his native region, Wilson received an enviable early education. [3]

What does seem surprising in view of his family background is that he did not become a minister. Some family recollections indicate that his father hoped he would follow in his footsteps and that when the youth was sixteen or seventeen he may have felt a call to become a minister. As Wilson himself remembered it, however, he had never had any inclination toward the ministry. In fact, he was already showing an interest in politics at the time he supposedly experienced his call. The ministry may have seemed less attractive to both father and son, as John Mulder has suggested, after Joseph Wilson left Columbia in 1874 because of a bitter dispute over his duties and accepted a better-paying but less challenging ministerial post in Wilmington, North Carolina. Yet even without the paternal troubles, young Wilson might not have wanted to enter the pulpit. [4]

The religious environment of Wilson's youth was neither narrow nor oppressive. The Wilsons and the Woodrows adhered to the liberal camp of Presbyterianism in both senses of the term—they were both intellectual and worldly. James Woodrow's educational accomplishments and his defense of Darwin placed him in the line of Presbyterian scholars that had come from Scotland and had found its leading light in the United States in James McCosh, the president of Princeton from 1869 to 1888. Joseph Wilson did not belong in their intellectual league, although he did spring to his brother-in-law's defense in the heresy controversy. Rather, Joseph Wilson embodied an approach to religion that accepted the world in word and deed. In his sermons the handsome, heavyset man preached pursuit of success and happiness through faith and active involvement in secular affairs. In his life he pushed the limits of behavior then permitted to ministers. His taste for pleasures ran to vacationing at fashionable resorts, smoking, playing billiards, and even occasionally drinking whisky. When the elder Wilson advised his son, he repeatedly advocated not merely accepting but embracing worldly standards and success—so much so that his letters read like elaborations of Polonius's advice to Laertes in *Hamlet*.[5]

Young Wilson's temperament and inclinations developed in response to influences from both sides of his family and a certain tension between them. His mother, Janet, or "Jessie," Woodrow Wilson, played a critical role in his childhood. More retiring and sedate than her husband, she pampered and protected Tommy, the third child and older son among her four children and obviously her favorite. The boy resembled her physically, with gray eyes, high forehead, and slender build. From his mother he also seems to have inherited or acquired two of the traits that later struck his contemporaries most. One was a tendency toward solitary habits. Although he liked people, Wilson never became naturally sociable and always had to work at personal relations, apart from his family and intimate friends. Probably also from his mother and two older sisters Wilson acquired his lifelong liking for female companionship. The other trait Jessie Wilson instilled in her son was self-confidence. Unlike his father, who suffered from depressions and swings of mood, Wilson had his mother's more equable disposition, together with an unshakable belief in his own abilities and prospects.[6]

Tommy Wilson was his father's son, too. Although he did not inherit his father's good looks, a lack that always bothered him, he did share his most prominent feature—a large, strong jaw. He also acquired some of Joseph Wilson's high spirits and aggressiveness, which made an often-volatile combination with his own solitariness and self-confidence. That combination might have made him self-righteous, as many people mistook him to be, if he had not imbibed his father's worldly, tolerant religious outlook. For Wilson, Presbyterianism was a faith and a way of life. At no time did he entertain doubts about basic Christian precepts, and he considered religion a closed subject for discussion. As an adult, he prayed several times a day; he led family Bible readings, and he persisted in strict observance of the Sabbath, always attending services and eschewing both work and entertainment on Sundays. But in early manhood Wilson shed most sectarian concerns, joining a Congregational church in Connecticut in 1888 and the newer, more liberal of Princeton's two Presbyterian churches in the 1890s. In all, he remained a devout but rather conventional American Protestant of the late nineteenth century.

Despite what many interpreters have contended, specifically Calvinist doctrines and viewpoints had comparatively little impact on Wilson. He never took any interest in theology or metaphysical speculation, although exposure to ideas about predestination probably reinforced his personal fatalism. More generally, Calvinist views on the reconcilability of material interests with the pursuit of God's will contributed to Wilson's political views later, as did the Calvinist synthesis of faith and reason and the Presbyterians' long-standing commitment to education. But such views came naturally to large numbers of nineteenth-century Americans raised in reformed but not highly evangelical Protestant denominations. Wilson's clerical family background almost certainly insulated him against any delusions he might have had about becoming a messianic crusader in politics. He resembled other American Protestants in holding strong views about personal and social morality, and he believed that life was a serious business, to be lived according to God's purposes. But he always remained humble about presuming to know what those purposes were. Similarly, although he believed that Christians must combat injustice and work to improve the world, Wilson had little patience with crusades against vice, and he dismissed regard for one's own character and virtue as "priggish." Thanks mainly to the sophisticated, tolerant influences of his ministerial family, particularly his father, Wilson proved to be far less of a moral uplifter and self-righteous reformer than such prominent figures among his contemporaries as William Jennings Bryan, Robert M. La Follette, or, at times, Theodore Roosevelt.[7]

Most significantly, Joseph Wilson made his son the vehicle for his own disappointed ambitions. From the time Wilson was seventeen, as John Mulder has shown, the emotional balance between father and son shifted. The older man lived more and more through the youth's achievements and prospects. In part, the father's search for fulfillment through his son reflected his having married upward in Presbyterian society. The Woodrow connection, combined with his beliefs in worldly success, left him with an urgent need to vindicate himself. Increasingly after 1874, he sought such vindication through his son. One sign of the family competition came after the young man's graduation from college, when he started signing his name T. Woodrow Wilson—"at my mother's special request, because this signature embodies *all* my family name." A few months later, when he decided to drop "Tommy" altogether, his mother was delighted: "I always wanted to call you Woodrow from the first."[8]

If a clerical and intellectual background made Wilson's childhood unusual, the boy himself supplied the heroic character. The handicap he had to overcome was potentially more debilitating than Roosevelt's, and he had to struggle virtually alone because it went unrecognized. His family thought Tommy was slow to read. According to his own recollection, he did not learn his letters until he was nine and evidently did not read with any facility until he was eleven. Wilson never did gain much speed at reading. "I wonder if I am the slowest reader in the world," he once remarked to his brother-in-law. His parents reacted to the problem with a mixture of defensiveness and embarrassment. Jessie Wilson made excuses for Tommy's slowness, and the situation almost certainly heightened her indulgence and protectiveness toward him. Joseph Wilson discussed the boy's difficulties with Grandfather Woodrow and Uncle James, and though he maintained hope for his son's abilities, the rest of the family appear to have dismissed the boy as not too bright. Wilson later told his wife that he had been "always a slow fellow in mental development—long a child, longer a diffident youth."[9]

As Edwin A. Weinstein has speculated, Wilson probably suffered from a form of dyslexia, which may have stemmed from a congenital brain defect. Over a century later, dyslexia remains a difficult condition to treat, yet Tommy Wilson cured himself of a condition that no one recognized or understood. His parents' encouragement must have helped, but he really achieved a lonely triumph. As an adult, Wilson adapted to the aftereffects of dyslexia and compensated for them. Because reading never came easily to him, he developed a fierce concentration and a near-photographic memory. Friends and relatives noted that he never became a wide reader but preferred to reread favorite books and poems. Wilson made that preference the basis of his scholarship and educational philosophy, both of which emphasized intensive rather than extensive study. Writing presented equal trials, which he met with ingenuity and application. When he was sixteen he began teaching himself shorthand, and when he entered Princeton he took notes and kept a diary in a difficult system of shorthand. He bought a typewriter in 1883, when the machines had been in use only nine years and featured cumbersome nonstandard keyboards. He began using the typewriter for most of his correspondence and papers. Most important, Wilson composed his writings and talks in his mind. "I write in sentences rather than words," he told a friend in 1897. "They are formed *whole* in my mind before they begin to be put upon the paper, usually." He wrote out speeches on only the most formal occasions, preferring to speak from brief outlines, often in shorthand and sometimes only jottings on small cards, or with no notes at all.[10]

Wilson's youthful struggle was less spectacular than Roosevelt's but no less heroic. In conquering his disabilities in learning and communicating, Wilson liberated a powerful intelligence from what could have been withering bondage. This self-transformation also left a lasting set of imprints, one of which was clearly a reinforcement of his solitary tendencies. His handicap went unrecognized in an otherwise healthy boy, who played sports well though not strenuously and did not wear glasses until after college. As a result he almost certainly got little sympathy or encouragement except from his parents. The experience most likely isolated him from others, and that isolation, abetted by his mother's protectiveness, probably helped push him further toward being a loner. His struggle also helped build his self-confidence. Overcoming dyslexia, even without fully appreciating the feat, must have taught Wilson unforgettable lessons in relying on his own powers and believing in his abilities. Altogether, his childhood could have served as another exemplary tale of surmounting odds and rewarding compensations.

The struggle against his disability played an important part in directing his interests and ambitions. From adolescence on, politics absorbed Wilson. Except for an earlier fascination with ships and the sea, he never seems to have had any other interest. His father most likely influenced his political inclinations, both by providing an example of swaying people through oratory and by directing him toward worldly involvement. Another influence came from his southern environment, where, Wilson told a college friend, "as usual, politics is the all-engrossing topic of conversation. Southerners seem born with an interest in public affairs though it is too often of late a very ignorant interest." But the timing of his interest in politics disclosed that it also sprang from his newly gained confidence in his own powers. When he was sixteen or seventeen Wilson began envisioning a statesman's career for himself. Above his desk in his room in Columbia he put up a picture of the British prime minister, William Ewart Gladstone, and he joked with friends about one day serving in the United States Senate. By the time the family moved to Wilmington in 1874, Wilson was practicing oratory in his father's church and reading on his own about history and government.[11]

The youth's newfound prowess expanded his horizons. As Wilson remembered it long afterward, he experienced an intellectual awakening during his freshman year at Princeton in 1875. But his memory seems to have been faulty. His realization of his interests and abilities was more gradual and occurred particularly during the two years before he entered Princeton, when he attended Davidson College in North Carolina, the South's best Presbyterian college. He apparently recognized there that he needed greater educational challenges. Princeton provided such a challenge, and it became Wilson's home for half of his adult life. The College of New Jersey, as it was formally called, was enjoying a renaissance at the hands of James McCosh. Although himself a leading Presbyterian divine, McCosh was loosening the college's sectarian ties, upgrading the library, faculty, and curriculum, and making it attractive to sons of wealthy businessmen and social leaders.[12]

Young Wilson found his stimulation at Princeton less in his class work than in his own reading and in his friends and activities. His academic performance was hardly spectacular. His class standing gradually declined until he ranked barely within the top third at graduation. His grades mirrored his interests; the best came in history and the worst in the sciences, which bored him. Wilson cared little about grades, his friends also recalled, and devoted his energies to his own reading and participation in campus activities. He became a campus leader and, within decorous limits, a bit of a rebel. After a lonely start, he joined one of the more desirable student groups, which lived in the best dormitory and included talented young men of serious, independent mind; Robert Bridges became a renowned magazine editor, and Charles A. Talcott served in Congress before and during Wilson's presidency. Wilson's college activities centered on public speaking. He took a leading part in Whig Hall and founded the Liberal Debating Club. He also edited the student newspaper, *The Princetonian*, which he used as his platform for boosting athletics and criticizing the curriculum. [13]

Behind his happy immersion in college life lay both deepening reflections and conflicting interests. Politics continued to dominate Wilson's thought and provided an outlet for his own embryonic ideas. His background as a southerner and a minister's son meshed neatly with the disdain that prevailed in educated and respectable northern circles for corruption and machine politics, which were Republican at the national level. From the first, Wilson's political writings shared the two most common assumptions of the time. One was that current American politics needed vast improvement, and the other was that it suffered by comparison with politics abroad in Britain as well as at home in the pre–Civil War era. In view of his own growing talents as a speaker, it was hardly surprising that the young man began to commend debate as a remedy for the country's political ills. Most of his *Princetonian* editorials criticizing college studies urged the introduction of opportunities for genuine, not contrived, debate on important questions. In an essay written probably in January 1878, during his junior year, he carried the argument further by urging the reinstitution of meaningful debate on the floor of Congress as the way to get better men to run for office, reduce the influence of parties and factions, and restore politics to bygone glory. [14]

That essay, written shortly after Wilson's twenty-first birthday, formed the beginning of his real intellectual awakening. In it he broke with the prevailing conviction among critics of current politics, namely that blame for all ills could be laid at the door of universal manhood suffrage. Wilson countered by comparing American and British experiences with universal male suffrage to argue that the fault must be found elsewhere. That essay marked both an assertion of intellectual independence and an embarkation on a continuing line of reflection. A year later Wilson expanded those arguments in his first article in a national magazine, "Cabinet Government in the United States." The article was accepted for publication in April 1879, during Wilson's senior year at Princeton. It appeared soon after his graduation in the August issue of *International Review*, a Boston-based journal edited by a young Harvard instructor and aspiring politician, Henry Cabot Lodge.[15]

In "Cabinet Government" Wilson reiterated his arguments that universal suffrage could not be made "the scapegoat of all our national grievances" and that "*debate* is the essential function of a representative body," and he concluded that the United States must imitate British practices by appointing cabinet members from Congress and allowing them to speak on the floor. Dismissing separation of powers as "not in accord with the true spirit" of Anglo-American institutions and mocking "the alarm-bell of *centralization*," the young man maintained that his plan would encourage "responsible leadership" and thereby arrest the "marked and alarming decline in statesmanship" in America. Although "Cabinet Government" owed much to other writers, the article was a remarkable performance for a college senior. It was also an intellectual breakthrough for Wilson. Four years later he recounted that around the end of his junior year, before he wrote the article, he had discovered the writings of the English editor and writer Walter Bagehot. Those writings had demonstrated to him the need for "a comparative examination of our own constitution as it exists outside of the books and stripped of 'the refinements of literary theory.' "[16]

Wilson was describing the first of his two moments of profound scholarly insight and what was really the beginning of his career as a political scientist. For the next fourteen or fifteen years, Wilson followed Bagehot in studying and writing about how politics actually, rather than formally, operated. His debt to Bagehot meant that his work was not completely original, but that hardly detracted from his scholarly accomplishments. Wilson's attraction to Bagehot was an example of inspiration coming to a prepared mind. He had already formed the concern over parliamentary debate and the comparative perspective that made him receptive to Bagehot's viewpoint. Wilson likewise showed discrimination in appreciating Bagehot's realism, as opposed to the formalistic, juridical perspectives that dominated most European and American political writing. In all, his use of Bagehot's approach represented the kind of creative borrowing that has advanced most disciplines more than completely original thinking. The Englishman also inspired the young American to sound new notes of unsentimental detachment and even iconoclasm in his thinking and to introduce a spare, pungent style into his heretofore florid writing. Woodrow Wilson had found his second great teacher.[17]

For the immediate prospects of the young man who still called himself Tommy Wilson, however, these new insights and inspirations created two potential conflicts with his first great teacher. One conflict concerned his political views. Joseph Wilson deplored universal manhood suffrage so strongly that his son felt obliged to withdraw from Princeton's senior prize debate because he drew the side approving its retention. Though Ohio-born, the elder Wilson espoused the southern Democratic views of state rights with a convert's zeal. "Cabinet Government" showed that his son was already repudiating that viewpoint. The second potential conflict involved the young man's career plans. From the time he entered Princeton, both father and son assumed that he would become a lawyer. Joseph Wilson pushed the choice. "To a lawyer—to a *judicial* mind—*logic is everything*," he wrote in one of his letters of advice and criticism, "—and true oratory, whether of the bar or the pulpit or the hustings, consists in the statement of connected thought (i.e., logical statement) uttered with the energy and courage of *conviction*." With his deeper reflections on politics, the son was beginning to doubt the attractions of a legal career and perhaps, without admitting it, to question the adequacy of his father's teaching.[18]

By the time he was graduated from Princeton in 1879, at the age of twenty-two, Wilson felt troubled about his vocational choice. Politics remained his consuming interest and statesmanship his aim, but as he approached a career in law, he wondered whether it would serve his ends. A month after graduation he warned Charles Talcott that they "should leave nothing undone to keep ourselves fresh from the prejudices and free from foolish inaccuracies of those with whom we will constantly be thrown by the necessities of our law practice," all the while preparing themselves for the political tasks "which, it is to be hoped, will raise us above the *pettiness* of our profession." Wilson's disquiet stemmed both from his taste for political reflection and from an interest in writing. His college diaries and notes contain more references to literary style than to any other subject, even politics. Those jottings marked the beginning of twenty years of a growing, sometimes almost obsessive, concern for literary expression and style. Wilson was being drawn to an activity that flew directly in the face of his childhood disability. Heroic struggle became a way of life for him, too. [19]

Within a year after leaving Princeton, Wilson ratified his passage from youth to manhood by his metamorphosis from Tommy to Woodrow. The change of names epitomized his self-transformation from a seemingly slow-witted boy into a man of promise and accomplishment as a speaker and writer, with firmly established political interests and ambitions. Yet ambivalence shadowed the end of his youth. If his political inclinations were set, his attitudes and views were not. Rather, the dawning of political insight promised to transport him away from some of the strongest elements in his background. The problem of finding the right path to pursue his inclinations vexed him still more. Wilson already felt torn between intellectual and worldly callings, and efforts to combine them consumed the next several years. It was fitting that he left his youth in a state of flux, for change and metamorphosis characterized both of his adult careers. For him, youth was less a course setting than a prelude.

· 3 ·

Paths of Glory

THE TERM "DUDE" WAS COINED at almost the moment Theodore Roosevelt began his political career and his association with the West. It seemed tailor-made for him. His foppish dress and refined manners drew snickers in the Republican club, which the new Harvard graduate and society bridegroom joined in the fall of 1880. His cultivated, squeaky voice, eyeglasses on a silk cord, and the name Theodore aroused derisive laughter when he entered the New York state legislature in January 1882. His glasses earned him the nickname "Four-eyes" in the Dakota Territory, where he alighted in a fancy buckskin-fringed hunting outfit during the summer of 1883 and proceeded to buy into the cattle business. Both politicos and cowboys came to respect him, however, when he showed that he could hold his own in caucuses and conventions and on hunting trails and cattle drives. Except for combat in the Spanish-American War, the most emotionally satisfying experience of Roosevelt's life was his initiation into professional politics and the Wild West during the first half of the 1880s. He advanced his youthful self-transformation by proving himself in two of the roughest environments in America, yet he underwent these rites of passage without altering his social and intellectual identity. Far from a handicap, being a dude was the source of some of his immediate success as a politician and a westerner and later became an essential element in his attractiveness as a national figure.[1]

Like the exemplary tales of his childhood, most accounts of Roosevelt's early manhood contain distortions. Much as he liked to claim that he worked his way up from the bottom in politics, he did not. Attending Republican meetings during his first year out of Harvard was just another diversion sandwiched among studying at Columbia Law School, clerking in his cousin's law office, writing *The Naval War of 1812*, participating in the social whirl of Fifth Avenue, and taking a four-month European honeymoon in the summer of 1881. Upon his return to New York that fall, Roosevelt found himself nominated for a seat in the state Assembly and won the election in November without an extensive campaign. His speedy, almost effortless rise owed something to luck, inasmuch as a minor revolt in the Republican club had thrown open the Assembly nomination. But a more important element in his success was his social position. As he recalled, the club's regulars had felt flattered at "the idea of a Roosevelt joining them." They had also recognized that he would appeal to voters in his own silk-stocking neighborhood and to students and faculty at Columbia College. He benefited in the election from private advice and public endorsement by such family friends and professional associates as the eminent lawyer Joseph H. Choate.[2]

In three tempestuous years as an assemblyman at Albany, Roosevelt continued to enjoy advantages because of his background and demeanor. His name and appearance may have seemed amusing, but they gained the young man an inordinate amount of attention in the press. One political condition Roosevelt never knew was obscurity. New York newspapers and weekly magazines at once touted him as a rising star, and during his second year in the Assembly, the *New York Herald* assigned a special reporter to cover and coach him. Roosevelt reciprocated by providing good copy, as he battled corrupt influences and flouted his party organization, but the chief reason for his receiving so much attention derived from his social standing. Nineteenth-century newspapers and magazines had learned that their largely middle-class readership devoured material about the rich and well born, while aristocrats could be counted on for dash and color in their doings. Roosevelt had the added advantage of operating in politics, a field that since the Civil War had been dominated by a drab lot of humdrum professionals. His experience in the New York legislature marked the beginning of a long, mutual love affair between Roosevelt and the press. It also opened the first major career in American politics to be conducted

wholly within the era and under the influence of modern journalistic media.

Roosevelt best characterized his early political views when he
recalled in 1911, "When I left college, I had no strong governmental convictions beyond the very strong and vital conviction that
we were a nation and must act nationally; I had not thought out, or
been given the opportunity to think out, a great many questions
which I have since recognized as vital." He devoted his main energies in the legislature to combating corruption, promoting civil
service reform, and advocating a higher tone in politics. He also
claimed in his autobiography to have learned "the invaluable lesson
that in the practical activities of life no man can render the highest
service unless he can act in combination with his fellows, which
means a certain amount of give-and-take between him and them."
The legislature did introduce him to the ways of politicians, especially when party cohorts cut him out on several matters of
importance, but he had by no means committed himself to their
calling. After being reelected in 1882 and 1883, he decided not to
seek a fourth term in the Assembly. Roosevelt was still a political
amateur, torn between upper-class distaste and professional adaptation. He reached the crossroads of his early career in 1884, when
fresh personal tragedy and an important new friendship coincided
with his first plunge into national politics.[3]

Tragedy struck early in the year. In February his wife Alice
died after giving birth to their first child. Only hours later his
mother died in the same room where his father had died six years
before. The blows devastated the twenty-five-year-old Roosevelt.
His ranch in Dakota provided a refuge from sorrow during the next
two years. The main impact of Roosevelt's western experience
came during this period. Wilderness camping and hunting had
formed part of his adolescent physical regimen, and he had bought
his herd of cattle a year earlier. Yet his only extended stay in Dakota
came after the summer of 1884. Leaving his infant daughter Alice
in the care of his older sister, he threw himself into hunting and
ranching with the same fury he had shown after his father's death.
"Black care rarely sits behind a rider whose pace is fast enough," he
wrote four years later. Roosevelt reveled in the solitude, and the
austere beauty of the Bad Lands rekindled his earlier interest in

nature. He does seem to have been purging himself, as Edmund Morris has suggested, of the memory of his wife, whom he never mentioned again, not even to their daughter.[4]

His endurance of long hours in the saddle and his willingness to stand up to bullies with fists and firearms gradually converted local opinion of Roosevelt from contempt to admiration. Even his physical appearance altered. Friends and acquaintances who saw him after his first year in Dakota all remarked on how his tanned complexion, thickened neck, and greater weight gave him the look of a different person. The West seemed to complete Roosevelt's self-transformation. But the dude had not really changed. His commitment to western ways was neither permanent or deep. Between the summers of 1884 and 1886 he spent a total of fifteen months on his ranch. He did not stay for an entire winter in either year; his longest stretch there came between March and July 1886. The rest of the time he shuttled back and forth to the East Coast.[5]

Before Roosevelt retreated westward in the summer of 1884, he made his first plunge into Republican presidential politics. In the process he forged lasting personal bonds with a fellow Harvard man from Massachusetts, Henry Cabot Lodge. Although the two young patricians in politics had met earlier, they did not become close friends until they joined in an effort to prevent the nomination of any Republican presidential candidate tainted with the jobbery and machine methods of the post-Civil War era. James G. Blaine was their special nemesis. His nomination confronted them with a painful choice between party regularity and their social peers' demands that they bolt in protest. Whether Roosevelt would have stuck with the Republicans in 1884 without Lodge's friendship and influence is open to question. It is clear that the calumny heaped on them in their own circles and from journalistic organs that had previously lauded them hardened them in their choice of party regularity and political professionalism. The whole harrowing year helped wean Roosevelt from any remaining tendencies toward lighthearted dilettantism. He did not abandon his concern for respectable government, but he grew less tolerant toward his social peers and their disdainful attitudes. "Mugwump," the name given to high-class bolters in 1884, remained his choicest epithet.[6]

In the fall of 1884 Roosevelt campaigned in New York and in Massachusetts, where Lodge was running for Congress. He visited his relatives regularly, and he fell in love with Edith Kermit Carow, a childhood sweetheart. In the fall of 1886 he ran a losing race as the Republican candidate for mayor of New York. Immediately afterward he sailed across the Atlantic to marry Edith in London and to honeymoon once more in Europe. He visited his ranch only for hunting trips, never longer than two weeks, during the next decade, and he sold his cattle after losing over half the herd in the disastrous winter of 1886–87.

Roosevelt did not adapt completely to the western environment while he was there, either. "Mr. Roosevelt" to everyone but fellow cattle owners, he brooked no undue familiarity. Books accompanied him everywhere—even when he pursued outlaws—including Matthew Arnold's essays on a cattle drive and a French translation of *Anna Karenina*. Once, immediately upon returning from chasing horse thieves, he wrote his sister Bamie about "desirable additions to our limited list of 'intellectual' acquaintances, and further material for that far distant salon wherein we are to gather society men who take part in politics, literature and art and politicians, authors and artists whose personal habits do not disqualify them for society."[7]

In his subsequent career on the national scene, no aspect of Roosevelt's life except his war service made him more of a popular figure than his western sojourn. Nothing did more to make him appear a man of the people. He himself liked to recount how ranching had augmented politics in ridding him of all snobbish inclinations. Actually, his experience was more complicated. In going west, Roosevelt was following a well-beaten track among the upper crust on both sides of the Atlantic. One of his Dakota neighbors was a French marquis, while two others maintained dude ranches for scions of the best British and American families. His closest friend after Lodge was still another Harvard patrician, from Philadelphia, who took a similar fling at adventure and self-discovery out West—the novelist Owen Wister. Thanks to their inherited wealth and assured social positions, the three shared an old-fashioned gentleman's way of life. They rejected working in business to pursue more elevated callings—literature for Wister and a combination of literature and politics for Roosevelt and Lodge. Roosevelt had gladly dropped his law studies upon election to the legislature in 1881 and had invested in the firm that published *The Naval War of 1812.* One attraction of ranching for him had been the prospect of an agreeable way to earn additional income for his political and literary pursuits.[8]

Ironically, an old-fashioned gentlemanly way of life conferred two great advantages in newfangled politics. One outward advantage was that, as Roosevelt's experience in the New York legislature had shown, his patrician status and manners ensured attention from the press. By pursuing such leisure-class adventures as hunting and ranching, he added to his glamor. Roosevelt capitalized on his attractiveness to the press by granting frequent newspaper interviews and by writing magazine articles, illustrated with his own photographs, about his western experiences. It was no accident that his career coincided with the rise of the upper-class adventurer hero in popular fiction. The first of these emerged in the 1890s as the favorite dime-novel character, Frank Merriwell, a wealthy, clean-living, super athlete at Yale. Poor lads who made good might embody what young people were supposed to value, but, as one observer has recounted, Frank Merriwell "approximated the young god that almost every boy in the United States actually wanted to be." By the late 1880s Theodore Roosevelt was on his way toward becoming the real-life equivalent of Frank Merriwell. Between his social position and his shrewd instinct for publicity, he was laying the groundwork for his later stature as a popular idol. Only a war was needed to finish the job.[9]

A second political advantage in being a gentleman of leisure was that he had opportunities to develop his views. Although he liked to dwell on what he learned in the hard school of experience, he learned at least as much from books. Roosevelt remained an omnivorous reader on a galaxy of subjects, and he also became a prolific writer, publishing seven books during his first ten years after graduation from Harvard. Some were slight pieces, such as collections of his western magazine articles and a pair of brief biographies in a series edited by Lodge. But he also wrote the first two volumes of his four-volume history, *The Winning of the West.* Dedicated to Francis Parkman, Roosevelt's history took up where Parkman had left off in the story of the white settlement of North America. Although Roosevelt lacked Parkman's genius for narrative—curiously, narrative was one of his weaknesses as a writer—he shared his predecessor's feel for the great social and geopolitical forces that had shaped the conquest of the continent. He likewise seized upon the insights of newer professional historians such as Frederick Jackson Turner to interpret the impact of the frontier on American politics and society. By the time he had completed the fourth volume of *The Winning of the West* in 1897, Roosevelt had established himself as a distinguished historian. He was an amateur in the tradition of Parkman, and he rejected the German-inspired "scientific" model exalted among university-trained scholars. Yet he dug deeply in original sources and probed the past with insight and imagination.

If nothing else, Roosevelt's reading and writing brought breadth and cultivation to his developing political views. His twin starting points were the prevailing upper-class disdain for politics, which he combated but did not entirely reject, and a strongly felt but vaguely defined nationalism. Biographers, historians, and other writers have long argued whether Roosevelt should be called a conservative. His later championship of far-reaching reforms and his self-designation as a "radical" prevent easy classification. Yet the origins of his views make it clear that a deep-seated conservatism formed his basic political outlook. Not only did he approve of and seek to uphold the existing distribution of power and privileges in society, but he began with the aristocratic assumptions of one who believed he was or ought to be part of the "governing class." Throughout his life he viewed power from only one perspective— the operating end. He could sympathize but could not identify with people who were on the receiving end. A belief in nationalism was a logical projection of his affirmation of power, which plainly had roots in his youthful self-transformation. Nationalism likewise came naturally to one of his family background, which had been Federalist in the early days of the Republic and staunchly Unionist and Republican during the Civil War. Roosevelt chose as his first political heroes Lincoln, the savior of the nation, and Alexander Hamilton, the architect and prophet of its centralized power.

From the beginning, Roosevelt differed in his energy and his imaginative grasp from others who sought to uphold the existing order in the United States. His nervous, dynamic temperament would probably have unfitted him under most circumstances for the calm quiescence normally valued by those who want to maintain things as they are. Moreover, his inescapable yearning to make

politics important did not sit well with the soon-to-be-con-
summated alliance between leading segments of the Republican
party and dominant American business interests. The ideological
stress in that alliance was on the primacy of economic issues and
governmental restraint. But Roosevelt's personal inclinations ensured only a level of activity, not its direction. His main concerns
during the late 1880s and early 1890s, when he became succes-
sively a United States Civil Service commissioner and New York
City police commissioner, remained honesty and decency in government, and his interest in foreign affairs was growing.

His learning and vision, more than temperament, distinguished
Roosevelt's emerging political outlook. His historical studies informed his nationalism by placing the growth of the United States
in a two-thousand-year context of the movement of peoples and the
development of social and technological processes. Sweep and
imagination characterized Roosevelt's views more than depth and
criticism, inasmuch as he used his intellect mainly to fortify his
inclinations. He built what John M. Blum has called "an eclectic
intellectual home, its parts connected, but the whole more comfortable than integrated." Yet for a politician, especially in America
after the Civil War, it was a remarkably well-furnished home,
which afforded broad and clear vistas of his field of activity.[10]

The two greatest issues of Roosevelt's career were the response
of government to the growth of big business and the role of the
United States in world affairs. Both issues started to attract the
young man's attention during the late 1880s and early 1890s. He
learned about discontent over new economic conditions in the New
York mayoral race in 1886, when he not only lost to a Democrat but
also placed third behind the radical spokesman Henry George, who
headed a coalition of dissident labor groups. Predictably, Roosevelt
condemned their radicalism as destructive and impractical. He also
decried expressions of farmers' discontent in the 1890s, such as the
rise of the third-party Populists and the seizure of the Democratic
party by the free-silverites in 1896. However, he showed almost
equal distaste for business-minded spokesmen. In a magazine article written just after his 1886 defeat, he asserted that "an individual
in the bourgeois stage of development . . . [is] not unapt to be a
miracle of timid and short-sighted selfishness. The commercial
classes are only too likely to regard everything merely from the

standpoint of 'Does it pay?' " As economic issues such as the tariff and the currency became increasingly prominent, he confessed to Lodge in 1894 that he had "a tinge of economic agnosticism" in him. As polarization of a dispossessed poor and a bloated plutocracy seemed to threaten, Roosevelt's distaste grew. "I know the populists and the workingmen well, and their faults," he told another friend in 1894, "I like to see a mob handled by regulars, or by good State guards, not over-scrupulous about bloodshed; but I know the banker, merchant and railroad king well too, and *they* also need education and sound chastisement."[11]

Foreign affairs became a concern for Roosevelt during the same period. Starting with *The Naval War of 1812,* historical research had familiarized him with American expansion. His urge to fight in a war had led him to offer to raise a cavalry regiment from among Dakota cowboys during the Mexican border troubles in 1886. Both when he visited Great Britain at the end of 1886 and when he lived in Washington from 1889 to 1895, he moved among a cosmopolitan set of intellectuals who helped to broaden his acquaintance with international affairs. Roosevelt soon began to advocate that the United States modernize and expand its navy, dominate the Western Hemisphere, and play a generally more active and aggressive role among the great powers. His international activism reflected both a long-run reckoning of the currents of world politics and a personal itch to see military action. In 1890 he gloried in America's part in "the grandeur of the movement by which the English-speaking race was to spread over the world's waste space, until a fourth of the habitable globe was in its hands, and until it became the mightiest race on which the sun ever shone." At the same time, no diplomatic dispute of the day, no matter how minor, failed to arouse his belligerency. Recalling an incident with Chile in 1892 over some American sailors' misconduct, his wife later asked a friend, "Do you remember how we used to call Theodore the Chilean Volunteer and tease him about his dream of leading a cavalry charge?"[12]

Comic though it sometimes seemed, Roosevelt's personal belligerency was fundamental to his political outlook. American disputes in the mid-1890s, first with Britain over the Venezuelan boundary and then with Spain over the Cuban revolution, confirmed and deepened his alienation from businessmen and his upper-class peers. In January 1896, during the Venezuela dispute, he lashed out in a public letter against the "stock-jobbing mentality, the Baboo kind of statesmanship, which is clamored for at this moment by the men who put monetary gain before national honor, or who are still intellectually in a state of colonial dependence on England."[13]

Roosevelt's attitude went deeper than the desires of some fellow conservatives for involvement abroad as a distraction from economic and political discontent at home. Nor did he necessarily rate foreign policy higher than domestic concerns, as some writers have contended. Rather, Roosevelt was applying his personal philosophy to the nation. He believed that belligerent nationalism offered a cure for what he saw as the degenerative materialism of advanced industrial nations. He shared the view of his friends Henry and Brooks Adams that civilized peoples were growing flabby and timid and therefore prey to attacks by primitive and warlike ones, but he countered their pessimistic conclusions by arguing that the United States could prove an exception by reasserting its "barbarian" qualities. At the time of the Venezuela dispute he told Lodge, "The clamor of the peace faction has convinced me that this country needs a war."[14]

Before the country got its war, however, Roosevelt saw extensive service in domestic affairs. The four-year hiatus after the 1884 campaign marked his only time out of office. Although chance affected him as much as any politician, the succession of positions he held between 1889 and 1898 added to his preparation for high office. The Civil Service Commission appeared a dead end, since the body had only limited authority and was engaged in constant conflict with party professionals. Yet frustrating and thankless as the commission's work seemed, Roosevelt realized that it taught him much about how the federal government operated. He also formed a circle of cultivated friends in the capital, who included Lodge, Henry Adams, John Hay, and the young British diplomat Cecil Spring Rice. In his own way, Roosevelt became a Washington insider.

He felt glad to return to New York in 1895 as police commissioner, in order to engage in what he considered real work and to get back in touch with his home political base. The police department provided him with the urban equivalent of his ranch. The dude proved himself in another rough environment, and he once more basked in the attention of the press. Although his fights against corruption and for strict law enforcement were newsworthy in themselves, his manner and appearance accounted for much of the publicity. Roosevelt's wide-brimmed western hat, glasses, and prominent teeth made him the cartoonists' delight and gave him instant recognition. He also made friends with several rising reporters, including Jacob Riis and Lincoln Steffens, and acquired skill in handling the press. The police commissioner presented the public character that needed only the Rough Rider's war as a stage.

Roosevelt later claimed that those two years in New York, particularly his late-night rambles through the slums with Riis, helped open his eyes to social and economic inequalities. That is another apocryphal embellishment. Sensitive and observant though he was, Roosevelt was never basically humanitarian or compassionate. He was already worried about problems of wealth and poverty, but he cared about their effects less on the victims than on the nation's strength and unity. As police commissioner, Roosevelt learned more about how business interests and political rings intertwined on the local level to provide the power base for an organization like Senator Thomas C. Platt's New York Republican machine. That venerable machine and its Democratic opposite number had been in a slump during Roosevelt's earlier terms in the legislature, but now they had come back to compete and cooperate with renewed vigor. Roosevelt first clashed with Platt over his law enforcement activities, and the two men took each other's measure.

Roosevelt committed himself to the urban environment no more than he had to the western one. "It is absorbingly interesting," he told Lodge at the outset of his police work, "but you need not have the slightest fear about my losing interest in National Politics." He maintained his ties to the national Republican party. He campaigned energetically for William McKinley against William Jennings Bryan in 1896, and he continued to write and speak about foreign affairs. After a year as police commissioner, he admitted to his sister Bamie that he missed Washington: "I see but little of the life of the great world," and his work had "nothing of the purple in it; it is as grimy as all work for municipal reform over here must be for some decades to come."[15]

In 1897 Roosevelt rejoined his friends in the capital and got his hand into foreign policy through appointment as assistant secretary of the Navy under the McKinley administration. The appointment came partly as a reward for his campaign services, but it owed more to lobbying on his behalf by Lodge, who had become a senator from Massachusetts and a powerful figure in the party, and to the acquiescence of Senator Platt, who then and later preferred to have Roosevelt away from New York. The Navy Department post permitted Roosevelt to continue agitating for war with Spain and to play a part in the preparations for it by increasing the Navy's readiness and by ordering the Pacific squadron to stand ready to attack Manila. The naval post also gave him his first experience at administration of a large-scale organization, for which he showed a decided flair.[16]

The Spanish-American War answered Roosevelt's prayers. Friends and family tried to persuade him to stay on as assistant secretary of the Navy. "That he is making a terrible mistake I cannot doubt," Lodge told Roosevelt's younger sister. Everybody in Washington "thought that he deserts his post & sacrifices country to self." Roosevelt saw the matter the other way around. "But if I am to be of any use in politics," he asserted to a friend, "it is because I am supposed to be a man who does not preach what I fear to practice, and who will carry out himself what he advocates others carrying out." That reasoning showed how central the personal element was to his thinking. Despite his exuberance, he had no illusions about the squalor and misery of war. Those grim prospects attracted him. He resembled Francis Parkman not only in his choice of historical subject but also in his desire to test and discover himself in a dangerous, primitive environment. Like Ernest Hemingway, he believed he would find the best such environment on the field of battle. Fighting in Cuba evoked the same sentiments in Roosevelt as had ranching in Dakota a dozen years earlier. Both at the time and in his memoir published the following year, Roosevelt gloried in how well his regiment, whom reporters dubbed the "Rough Riders," mixed tough westerners with upper-crust characters, like himself, from Eastern cities.[17]

The war furnished his golden opportunity. Within six months he was a popular hero, governor of New York, and a rising star on the national scene. Indeed, except for the acquisition of the Philippines, the political making of Theodore Roosevelt looms as the most significant consequence of the Spanish-American War. Without the war experience, he probably would not have reached the top rank of elective politics, much less become president. Yet as Lewis Einstein has argued, his part in the war was not merely a lucky break. No other American profited so much politically from the war. Roosevelt became its principal legatee because of his social background and previous career. The press headlined him from the moment he announced his enlistment. Stories about the Rough Riders stressed the same feature he did—the mingling of cowboys and blue bloods. Roosevelt did not leave publicity to chance, either. He made special provisions for reporters and photographers to accompany the regiment, including a pair of men with motion-picture equipment. He proved his heroism by risking his life, and he had every right to glory in exorcising any youthful yearning or family stigma that plagued him. But his part in the war hardly went unsung. For the rest of his life he was fondly known as the Colonel, and the charge of the Rough Riders up Kettle (not San Juan) Hill remained the best—though usually inaccurately—remembered event of the Spanish-American War.[18]

The war had both outward and inward effects on Roosevelt. The office he won in November 1898 and the circumstances of his victory projected him a long way down the road to the White House. Governors or former governors of New York had run as major-party candidates in five of the seven presidential elections between the Civil War and the Spanish-American War. No sooner was Roosevelt elected governor than he began to be mentioned for a place on the national ticket in 1900. The crowds and their responses as he hit the campaign trail revealed his drawing power. Without him the Republicans could not have won their narrow victory in the wake of state scandals. When the vice-president, Garret A. Hobart, died in 1899, pressures mounted for Roosevelt to run. He did not want the vice-presidency, and he might possibly have spurned that crown but for the intrigues of Senator Platt, who wanted him out of New York. Platt's maneuvers would have gotten nowhere, however, without Roosevelt's glaring popularity. His westward journey to the Rough Riders' reunion during the summer of 1899 turned into a whistle-stop tour with inescapable presidential campaign overtones. A near revolt on the floor of the 1900 Republican convention might have nominated him even without

Platt's skullduggery. Aside from the candidate's own reluctance, the only objection to his nomination came from Senator Mark A. Hanna of Ohio, who reportedly protested, "Don't any of you realize that there's only one life between this madman and the White House?"[19]

By the time he became governor of New York in 1899, Roosevelt had enjoyed a varied exposure to politics from the local to the international level. The governorship simultaneously broadened and tested nearly all of what he had gained from his previous exposure. His chief immediate problem lay in his relations with Platt. When he had returned from Cuba in 1898, Roosevelt's first offer of a gubernatorial nomination had come from a group of clean-government independents, whom he had strung along but then had dumped when he received the Republican nomination. Yet although he had again chosen party regularity, Roosevelt in no way became Platt's man. Throughout his term as governor he maintained a prickly but correct relationship with the senator-boss, observing diplomatic niceties, listening attentively to advice, never hastily refusing demands, yet always maintaining his distance and independence.

Roosevelt's dealings with Platt involved more than just their respective power. Public agitation over large corporations and their political influence had not evaporated with Bryan's defeat in 1896; disquiet seemed to be growing. Roosevelt gingerly referred to the "trust problem" in his first gubernatorial message and supported a tax on state and municipal franchises granted to businesses. In May 1899 Platt responded by accusing him of being "a little loose on the relations of capital and labor, on trusts and combinations"—in effect, a closet Bryanite. Roosevelt pleaded his soundness, but he asserted that a measure such as his franchise tax was strengthening "the republican party among the mass of our people and making them believe that we do stand squarely for the interests of all of the people, whether they are or are not connected in any way with corporations."[20]

The governor's answer did not mollify the boss, who soon began his vice-presidential machinations. What might have happened if Roosevelt had stayed in New York is interesting to speculate on. His remarks about the trusts and the franchise tax expressed a deep concern. "We have serious problems abroad," he declared in May

1899, "but more serious ones at home. Ultimately no nation can be great unless its greatness is laid on foundations of righteousness and decency." Americans must especially "believe that we have more to do than simply accomplish material prosperity" and must uphold "the honor of the State." That concern for national unity and spiritual elevation became his departure point as president, and it almost certainly would have underlain any future state administration. Roosevelt might have vied with such middle western governors as Robert M. La Follette of Wisconsin and Albert B. Cummins of Iowa for the honor of spearheading the reform drives that were later lumped together under the label "progressivism."[21]

Roosevelt would have brought a different perspective toward large corporations and other questions, as he showed in his subsequent dealings with La Follette, Cummins, and other middle western and western progressives. Building on his social background and intellectual cultivation, he had developed a broad political outlook from his original aristocratic conservative base. He could defend the existing social order in America while appreciating the validity of some of the criticisms of the disaffected. He never pretended to be other than a product of the upper classes, yet he accepted the need for the broadest popular participation in politics. As early as 1887 he had argued that the Hamiltonian legacy of strong central government must be united with "the one great truth taught by Jefferson—that in America a statesman should trust the people, and should endeavor to secure each man all possible individual liberty, confident that he will use it right." He had praised Lincoln for showing "how a strong people might have a strong government and yet remain the freest on earth."[22]

Even more remarkable was the way Roosevelt maintained and strengthened his combination of aristocratic outlook and acceptance of broader democracy during his first twenty years in politics. His accomplishment can best be appreciated by comparing him with a pair of fellow Harvard men from distinguished Eastern seaboard families, who also brooked their social peers' disdain to pursue political careers. One was his friend Lodge, who was eight years older and sometimes served as Roosevelt's mentor. The two men shared a contempt for mugwumps and an ardor for American empire, but they began to part company over domestic issues toward the end of the 1890s. Lodge disliked big businessmen as much as

Roosevelt, but he seldom overcame his distaste for the lower orders enough to support much in the way of reforms. In part, their difference lay in the contrast between Roosevelt's exuberant and Lodge's reserved temperament. But more of their difference sprang from the breadth of perspective each brought to bear on national problems. For all his gifts and character, Henry Cabot Lodge remained critical and often negative in his views. Increasingly, he and Roosevelt made a political odd couple. That they never broke was a tribute to the regard they had formed for each other during their early political trials and to the similarity in their basic assumptions and in their views on international affairs.[23]

The other patrician in politics offered a different and still greater contrast. He was Boies Penrose of Philadelphia, who finished Harvard with honors a year after Roosevelt and entered the city and state arena on the side of cleaner government. Penrose grew comparably disgusted with the anticorruptionists' shrillness and ineffectuality, but his response was to defect from the clean-government forces. By working his way up through the ranks of the Pennsylvania Republican machine, he gained a Senate seat in 1897 and coleadership with the other senator, Matthew S. Quay. After Quay's death in 1904, Penrose became the undisputed boss of Pennsylvania and a major power in the national Republican party. He publicly maintained an attitude of disdainful cynicism, and he frequently boasted that he provided the kind of government that people wanted and deserved. Wealthy and a member of one of the leading Philadelphia families, Penrose apparently remained personally honest. Later, however, he became a debauchee in his habits, and he delighted in manipulating the moral shortcomings of his followers. Lodge and Penrose represented the Scylla and Charybdis of aristocrats who made their way in American politics after the Civil War. One maintained rectitude at the price of negativism. The other went slumming and got addicted to low life. Far more than he had among slum dwellers or cowhands, Roosevelt proved his worth by escaping the political fates of his fellow dudes.[24]

The vice-presidency was a comedown for Roosevelt. As he had feared, there was little to occupy his time. He made plans to resume his law studies privately under the tutelage of Chief Justice Edward Douglas White. He also hatched a scheme to involve professors from Harvard, Yale, and perhaps Princeton in enlisting promising students in politics. The office did have the compensations of putting him in touch with foreign affairs and giving him time for reading and reflection, although he had done plenty of both while governor. During 1899 and 1900 he had spoken out repeatedly on foreign policy issues, particularly the Hay-Pauncefote Treaty with Britain concerning an interoceanic canal in Central America, and he had written a book on Oliver Cromwell during the summer of 1899. One critic reportedly laughed off the book as "a fine imaginative study of Cromwell's qualifications for the governorship of New York," but it was perhaps Roosevelt's best single work. It contained a probing inquiry into leadership in a time of upheaval and a careful consideration of the competing requirements of order and change. Roosevelt was once more using historical interpretation to shed light on his own time. He also reflected on the balance between intellect and action in statesmen. "Cromwell, like many a so-called 'practical' man," he wrote, "would have done better work had he followed a more clearly defined theory, for though the practical man is better than the mere theorist, he cannot do the highest work unless he is a theorist also."[25]

By the time he became vice-president, Roosevelt's political bearings were set. The assassin's bullet that made him president in September 1901 was an accident, yet, as with all vice-presidents who succeed, there was little accident in his being in the line of succession. Even without the vice-presidency Roosevelt would have stood an excellent chance of becoming president. His advantages, gifts, and training had put him in a position to grasp and wield the greatest power in the land.

· 4 ·

Groves of Academe

WOODROW WILSON'S ACADEMIC CAREER has attracted more subsequent attention than any other such career in American history,
possibly in all history. Part of the interest in his academic years has
derived from his significance as a scholar, teacher, and university
president. Of far more interest, however, is that those years served
as a prelude to his political career. Although the larger reason has
led interpreters to draw distorted pictures of those academic years,
the concern for political preparation reflects Wilson's own priority.
When he finished Princeton in 1879, he did not choose an academic
career. "The profession I chose was politics," he stated four years
later to his fiancée; "the profession I entered was law. I entered the
one because I thought it would lead to the other." But he realized
that without private income, the years of narrow, grinding toil at
the bar would have rendered him unfit for political service. "A
professorship was the only feasible place for me," he concluded,
because it would allow him to study and write on politics. "Indeed
I knew very well that a man without independent fortune must in
any event content himself with becoming an *outside* force in politics, and I was well enough satisfied with the prospect of having
whatever influence I might be able to exercise felt through literary
and nonpartisan agencies." In short, academic life appealed to Wilson as a parapolitical career.[1]

Actually, his brief trial and abandonment of the law were more
complicated. Entering the University of Virginia Law School in the
fall of 1879 quelled neither his literary yearnings nor his misgivings
about a legal career. He spent much of that summer and fall writing

essays in the vein of "Cabinet Government." Those essays, only one of which was published, marked a further stride down young Wilson's road to intellectual and emotional independence. In one of the unpublished pieces, entitled "Congressional Government," he maintained that the Constitution was a product of growth and adaptation: "It is a corner-stone, not a complete building. It is a root, not a perfect vine." He also took the unfashionable position among educated people of defending political parties. In the published essay he not only obliquely criticized his native region's rural torpor, he also declared, "But *because* I love the South, I rejoice in the failure of the Confederacy." Its defeat had helped the South by eliminating slavery and by preserving a single, strong nation. At the same time Wilson complained continually about the dullness and technicality of his legal studies. He occupied himself increasingly with outside reading and writing, debating, and falling in love with his cousin Harriet Woodrow, who was in school nearby. The young man's complaints heightened the evident tension with his father, who scorned "a mere literary career such as you seem to dream about now and then" and admonished him to "conquer the law, even through all its wretched twistings of technical paths of thorn."[2]

Wilson's involvement with the law, first as a student and then in practice occupied a miserable four years. He disliked his studies. The romance with his cousin ended when she rejected his proposal of marriage in September 1881. His health began to bother him. Recurrent colds and stomach upsets caused him to leave Virginia in December 1880, midway through his second year of study, without taking a degree. Wilson continued to read law at his parents' home and in May 1882 he was admitted to the Georgia bar and joined another young lawyer, Edward I. Renick, in practice in Atlanta. That city was the bustling commercial center of the "New South," of which Wilson approved, but he found Atlanta unattractive and his occupation unrewarding both financially and intellectually. As before, he busied himself with reading about history and politics and with writing. That, too, proved a source of frustration. In 1882 Wilson expanded his earlier comparison of British and American political practices into a book-length study entitled "Government by Debate." Despite the aid of his friend Robert Bridges, who had become a writer for the New York *Evening Post*, several publishers turned the manuscript down, although G. P. Putnam's Sons offered to bring it out if the author would put up a subsidy. "If I had the money, I should not hesitate to close with Putnam's offer," Wilson told Bridges, in March 1883 ". . . but, as things now stand, I have no choice."[3]

The encounter with Putnam's highlighted Wilson's underlying predicament. That firm, in which Roosevelt had invested, had published *The Naval War of 1812* the year before; in effect, Roosevelt was subsidizing his own book. Wilson desired above all what Roosevelt had—the wealth and position that would allow him to be a gentleman writer-politician. As he correctly noted, lack of private means was the nub of his problem. "No man can safely *enter* political life nowadays who has not an independent fortune," Wilson wrote Bridges in May 1883, "or at least independent means of support: this I have not: therefore the most I can hope to become is a speaker and writer of the highest authority on political subjects." Wilson had evidently decided on an academic career even before he began his law practice. He and Bridges discussed the change at a Princeton reunion in June 1882, only a month after Wilson had joined Renick in Atlanta. He seems to have hung out his shingle mainly to satisfy his father.[4]

Wilson's abandonment of the law bore an ironic relation to his growing independence. His decision early in 1883 to enter academic life through graduate study at The John Hopkins University meant that he would continue to be financially dependent on his father. Wilson did not become self-supporting until he assumed his first teaching position in 1885, when he was twenty-eight. Moreover, a professorship would mean a partial return to the family fold. His father and uncle had both taught at the Columbia Seminary, and in 1885 his father assumed a chair of theology at Southwestern University in Tennessee. The first suggestion of graduate study at Johns Hopkins came from James Woodrow, who wrote a recommendation for his nephew. Family influences may have played a part in Wilson's choice of an academic career, which was by no means his sole alternative to the law. It seems surprising that he did not choose journalism, since a newspaper or magazine post would have allowed him to write and keep in touch with politics. Some of his closest friends were journalists, including Bridges and Albert Shaw, whom he got to know at Johns Hopkins, and Wilson later did much of his writing as a political scientist for general audiences in preference to academic specialists.

Yet Wilson deliberately rejected a journalistic career, both when he was casting about for an alternative to the law and when he was offered a job with a weekly magazine during his second year at Johns Hopkins. If family influences made a professorship appear more respectable, Wilson himself doubted his aptitude for journalism. Whenever he described journalist friends, he invariably commented on their quickness and cleverness, traits in which he believed himself deficient. In contrast, he believed his own strengths lay in detachment and reflection. "If you understood the practical side of government and extracted a bit of its philosophy as a college pupil," Wilson later recalled saying to himself at the time of the magazine offer, "there's no reason why you should not hope to do more and better of the same kind as a professor, if only you keep out of scholastic ruts and retain your sympathetic consciousness of the conditions of the practical world." Besides this self-assessment, career calculations underlay his choice of academic life. A professorship appealed to him almost entirely for the leisure it would afford for writing. In considering his first academic position, Wilson confessed to his fiancée, "After all, it's my *writing*, not my teaching, that must win me reputation." Teaching entered his thoughts only incidentally, mainly as an opportunity to practice oratory. Despite all his later criticism of German-derived research ideals and his advocacy of undergraduate teaching, Wilson unmistakably cast his lot with the new academic professionalism and its emphasis on publication and usefulness to society.[5]

Choosing an academic career climaxed the young man's assertion of independence. During his four-year entanglement with the law, his writings showed a growing detachment from his southern Presbyterian background. In addition to applauding the Confederate defeat, in other published pieces he commended Negro education and welcomed looser southern ties to the Democratic party. In "Government by Debate" he once more defended parties and advocated making them more responsible through imitation of the British cabinet system. Wilson still showed no fear of centralized government, and in 1889 he claimed, "Ever since I have had independent judgments of my own I have been a Federalist(!)." No religious references intruded into his writings, for he separated personal faith entirely from political analysis. Wilson was obviously following his own inclinations, but none of these expressions constituted acts of rebellion against his family, particularly his father, whom he loved and respected. In 1893 he published an essay in defense of "mere literture"—a phrase he used as the title of both the essay and the book in which it was later collected. Perhaps his clearest sign of standing on his own came toward the end of his year of law practice, when he met and fell in love with Ellen Louise Axson, the daughter of another Presbyterian minister from Rome, Georgia. The couple became engaged in September 1883, just before Wilson left for Baltimore to enter Johns Hopkins, and they were married as soon as he finished his studies in June 1885. The young man's ardor for his fiancée fueled his desire to get on with his career.[6]

The Johns Hopkins University tested Wilson's academic resolve. He disliked the institution and the professors from the start. In its eighth year of operation when he entered in 1883, "The Johns Hopkins" was in its heyday of propagating the gospel, imported from German universities, of academic professionalism. The professors with whom Wilson studied in the Seminary in Historical and Political Science—Herbert Baxter Adams and Richard T. Ely— epitomized the university's promotion of research and specialization. Adams struck Wilson as "insincere and superficial" and Ely "stuffed full of information but apparently too full to have any movement which is not an impulse from somebody else . . . I should be much discouraged," he told Ellen, "if it were not for the compensation of splendid library facilities and of the opportunity of learning a great deal from my fellow-students." Fortunately for Wilson, Adams permitted diverse work under the banner of "institutional history," and after a frank exchange in December 1883 the professor encouraged him to proceed with his study of American government. Wilson began writing in January 1884, and by September he had finished the manuscript, again entitled "Congressional Government." This time the first publisher to whom he submitted his work, Houghton, Mifflin & Company of Boston, speedily accepted. At the end of January 1885, the book appeared in print, attracting widespread immediate interest and lasting acclaim as a classic of American political analysis. The book represented another remarkable performance by Wilson, who had just turned twenty-eight and was in his second year of graduate study.[7]

Although *Congressional Government* appeared to herald the explosion of a prodigy, the book had unfolded only after long germination. Its approach and most of its ideas dated back to Wilson's college essay, "Cabinet Government," six years earlier. These had undergone reiteration and refinement in "Congressional Government" and "Government by Debate." The book repeated such earlier points as suggestions for maximizing debate in Congress through imitation of British cabinet practices, defense of political parties, and acceptance of centralization. What was new in *Congressional Government* were the form and tone. As Arthur S. Link has observed, a fresh reading of Bagehot's *The English Constitution* during the summer of 1883 seems to have provided Wilson with a model. "His book has inspired my whole study of our government," he told Ellen when he started writing. Wilson kept his attention focused on how American government really worked and purposely soft-pedaled reform proposals. "I have abandoned the evangelical for the exegetical—so to speak!" he informed Bridges, "—and the result is something very much more thorough and more sober, as well as most valuable and likely to be acceptable if published." The book was also clearer and livelier. Rather than suffering from an academic approach to politics, his writing benefited from the introduction of greater realism through detached observation. Wilson had found his literary vehicle.[8]

The main contemporary criticisms of *Congressional Government* were that Wilson too readily accepted popular participation and parties and, contradictorily, that he wished to imitate undemocratic British practices. The main subsequent criticism by political scientists has been that he overrated the power of Congress and underrated the actual and potential powers of the president. Only the first of those criticisms has much validity. Wilson did depart from the prevailing disdain among intellectuals and the better classes for popular involvement in politics, although he shared their dismay at the existing levels of leadership and practice. "The natural, inevitable tendency of every system of self-government," he argued, ". . . is to exalt the representative body, the people's parliament." Any practical reform must therefore recognize that condition.[9]

The charge of Anglophilia does not stick. As a youth, Wilson had admired British politics, but by the time he wrote *Congressional Government* he viewed all parliamentary institutions solely through comparing their efficiency. The chief comparison in *Congressional Government* came in what later generations of political scientists would call a "case study" of financial policy. Wilson found that the House of Commons functioned in a better-coordinated and more accountable fashion than the House of Representatives. Edward S. Corwin, who became his departmental colleague at Princeton and was himself a leading political scientist, later asserted, "I don't think W.W.'s regard for the British system was pietistic, but chiefly pragmatic." It was also a manifestation of his newfound intellectual autonomy. [10]

The most serious criticism of the book has been that Wilson misread the distribution of power in American government. Although that criticism has some validity, it is largely beside the point. Wilson's greatest weaknesses as a scholar lay in his lack of curiosity and distaste for research. "The fault of my mind is that it is creative without being patient and docile in learning *how* to create," he confessed to Ellen in February 1885. He not only balked at the library research touted at Johns Hopkins, but also, as several critics have noted, he never made the short trip to Washington to visit Capitol Hill while he was writing *Congressional Government*. The departmental colleague at Princeton who knew him best later recalled that Wilson disdained accumulation of facts and made his way as a scholar "rather by direct intuitive insight than through any process of laborious induction." In view of Wilson's childhood dyslexia and his continuing difficulties with reading, such a preference was understandable, but overreliance on intuition later detracted from his work as a political scientist. [11]

In *Congressional Government* that weakness did not seriously diminish his accomplishment. The inspiration from Bagehot led him to center the book on two questions. First, where did power actually reside? Second, how might power be exercised more efficiently and in ways that were more readily accountable to the electorate? Wilson did not care whether the executive or the legislative branch had more power. Rather, he criticized the diffusion of power not only among the branches of government but also within them, especially in Congress. Both the committee system and the more generally "businesslike" methods of caucuses and behind-the-scenes dealing made senators and representatives less account-able to their constituencies. Wilson related both kinds of diffusion to the changing nature of political issues, particularly since the Civil War. Such great earlier concerns as the establishment and preser-vation of the Union had given way to less exciting and less pressing matters. The country's current displeasure with politics stemmed from Americans' perplexity "at finding ourselves denied a new order of statesmanship to suit the altered conditions of govern-ment."[12]

In keeping with his previous advocacy of maximizing oppor-tunities for debate, Wilson again recommended bringing the real business of Congress out of the closet and onto the floor for open and responsible discussion. More important, he once more urged some form of fusion of legislative and executive power. Such fusion was particularly needed because the present political doldrums would not last. The social and economic challenges of industri-alization would soon demand stronger and still more centralized government. "As at present constituted," Wilson noted toward the end of the book, "the federal government lacks strength because its powers are divided, lacks promptness because its authorities are multiplied, lacks efficiency because its responsibility is indistinct and without competent direction." *Congressional Government* was hardly a perfect book, least of all as a portrait of American politics in 1885, but its shortcomings pale in comparison to its insight into the problems of American government and its prophecy of the revival of political concern to meet industrial problems.[13]

Wilson never again matched the scholarly achievement of his first book. None of the six books he published during his academic career had either the grasp or the impact of *Congressional Govern-ment*. In 1889 Wilson published *The State*, a textbook that con-tained incisive analyses. All governments rested, he argued, "in all cases ultimately on *force*." Their functions he divided into two categories: "constituent functions," such as the police and armed forces, were necessary for the preservation of the government it-self; "ministrant functions," which might include a variety of pro-visions to promote public welfare, were optional activities to be judged according to their "expediency." Wilson closed *The State* with a call for "conservative adaptation, shaping old habits into new ones, modifying old means to accomplish new ends." But he also took a relativistic attitude toward governmental actions, commenting at one point that law "plays the role neither of conscience nor of Providence. More than this, it follows standards of policy only, not absolute standards of right and wrong." Wilson would undoubtedly have resented being called a political agnostic. Yet he eliminated overt references to religion and to moral preferences so completely from his political writings that some of the Princeton trustees' doubts about his Presbyterian orthodoxy almost prevented his appointment to a professorship there in 1890.[14]

Wilson also later blazed a major new trail in the study of government—inquiry into how legislation was carried out after being passed. But Wilson never followed up on his own initiatives. After *The State*, he published only one other book and a few articles in political science. All his other work went into two histories, a biography, and two collections of essays mainly on literary and general topics. In 1893 he published *Division and Reunion*, a history of the United States from 1829 to 1889, which contained well-wrought interpretations but rested upon thin research. He completed his historical work with the five-volume *A History of the American People*, which appeared as a popular-subscription set in 1902 and which Wilson himself later dismissed as a high-class potboiler. His biography, *George Washington*, published in 1897, was a warm-up for that glossy effort. The essay collections, which appeared in 1893 and 1896, brought together writings that belonged to a class later dubbed "middlebrow." Wilson's only subsequent work in political science resulted from a series of lectures he gave in 1907, after he had become president of Princeton. Published in 1908 as *Constitutional Government in the United States*, the lectures resurveyed, some twenty years later, the terrain of *Congressional Government*.[15]

Wilson failed to repeat the triumph of his first book in part because he succumbed to temptations to make money. He attained a genteel style of life for his family, which came to include three daughters as well as several of his and Ellen's live-in relatives. He consistently augmented and sometimes doubled his Princeton pay, one of the highest academic salaries in the country, through non-scholarly writing and off-campus lecturing. But Wilson was not just moonlighting to raise his family's living standard. In keeping with his original desire for political influence, he wanted to reach beyond academic specialists. "I want to write books which will be read by the great host who don't wear spectacles—whose eyes are young and unlearned!" he asserted to Ellen in 1884. His obsession with literary style grew, and he often wrote on subjects other than politics. Nor did he forsake scholarly goals. By the end of the 1890s, Wilson was laying plans to write a major work on the nature of political life, which he called the "Philosophy of Politics" or "P.O.P." In January 1902 he explained to Frederick Jackson Turner that he must decline further historical writing "if I am to do the work I really seem to have been cut out for." The following May he wrote an analytical memorandum on the meaning of leadership, apparently intended as a beginning for "P.O.P." A month later, however, he was elected president of Princeton and shelved the work.[16]

"Philosophy of Politics" might well have surpassed *Congressional Government*. By 1902 Wilson had gone through the same process as with his first book of initial insight, reinforcement, and long germination. This time the inspiration came from Edmund Burke, whom he had long admired but whom he had now come to appreciate with deeper understanding. Sometime early in the 1890s, Wilson reread Burke's *Reflections on the Revolution in France* and grasped its vision of anti-ideological politics. In his essays and lectures on Burke during that decade, Wilson uncannily foreshadowed mid-twentieth-century proclamations of the "end of ideology." He lauded Burke in 1893 as the philosopher of a politics which "has never been speculative; it is profoundly practical and utilitarian. Speculative politics treats men and situations as they are supposed to be; practical politics treats them (upon no general plan but in detail) as they are found to be at the moment of actual contact." Burke's thought hewed, Wilson added in 1898, "to the slow pace of inevitable change and invents nothing," yet such thought also had "the power of life in it,—and, if the power of life, the power of growth." That conception of organic, nonideological politics was the basic insight on which Wilson planned to build "Philosophy of Politics." He later used a few gleanings from his Burkean vision in *Constitutional Government*. He rejected what he called "the Whig theory of political dynamics," based on a Newtonian model, and he declared that "government is not a machine, but a living thing. It falls, not under the theory of the universe, but under the theory of organic life." If Wilson had enjoyed the opportunity to use that insight the way he had used the Bagehot approach in *Congressional Government,* "P.O.P." might have been a masterpiece. [17]

Wilson's unfulfilled promise as a political scientist should not be overrated. He recognized his limitations. A younger colleague at Princeton recorded him as saying in 1903 "that his mind was not philosophical—that as soon as he felt that, in pursuing a thought[,] his mind was leaving the solid basis of fact, he at once 'shied off,' as he expressed it." Wilson remained an inspired observer rather than a theorist or philosopher of politics. Despite the title, his "Philosophy of Politics" probably would not have rivaled the general works of such European contemporaries as Max Weber or Georges Sorel. Wilson could also have profited from more research of his own instead of relying heavily on the observations of others, as he did with Gamaliel Bradford in *Congressional Government* and Henry Jones Ford in *Constitutional Government.* [18]

Yet Wilson's stature and promise as a scholar were much greater than has usually been appreciated. The work he produced made him the finest American political scientist of the period of his academic career, from the mid-1880s to 1910. His depictions of government and politics in the United States delved deeper and comprehended more than the English writer James Bryce's longer and better-known treatment in *The American Commonwealth.* His understanding of the basis of politics and his use of organic metaphors gave him a more incisive framework for political analysis than anyone else in the United States. Only with the work of such different men as Charles E. Merriam and Harold Lasswell would American political scientists begin to operate on Wilson's level of inquiry. Withal, he developed a homely lucidity in expression and retained a common-sense outlook that academic writers, particularly in the social sciences, have increasingly lacked. His true successor among political writers in those qualities was Walter Lippmann. If Wilson had either stuck to his political insights earlier or gone ahead with "P.O.P.," he most likely could have become what he originally aspired to be—the American Bagehot. [19]

Such scholarship could not help but prepare Wilson for his later political involvement. Yet the utility of his academic political science to his public career was not simple or direct. Many who have written about Wilson in these years have sought to account for either the origins of specific policies or, more often, the reasons for his emergence as a leader of progressivism. Those writers have missed the main point about Wilson's years as a writer and professor. His career as a political scientist turned out differently than he had planned. Rather than using his professorship as a handy perch from which to be "an outside force in politics," he became more of an academic commentator. In most of his writing and lecturing about politics he followed the pattern set in *Congressional Government*. He treated the actual operations of government and offered little advice to citizens and statesmen. Wilson did not read avidly in newspapers and magazines to keep abreast of current events. His notes and correspondence during the 1880s and 1890s rarely betrayed concern or detailed knowledge about major domestic issues like the tariff, currency, or regulation of business. The single exception came after 1898 with foreign affairs. He, too, became an ardent advocate of American expansion, and his enthusiasm probably sprang in part from personal circumstances.

Wilson's detachment from public affairs reflected his detached political views. The upshot of that detachment was a highly permissive attitude toward the use of public authority to help solve social and economic problems. In *The State* he argued that the "ministrant functions" of government could include almost anything that a community found "expedient"—from sanitation and education to ownership of railroads and telegraph lines. The concept of "expediency" held a lasting fascination for him, and he in no way repudiated it when he became attracted to Burke in the 1890s. Wilson did not grow more conservative in response to the turmoil of that decade, as some writers have concluded from his attraction to Burke and his dislike of Bryan and free silver in 1896. Far from joining the standpat ranks, he supported certain reform efforts, particularly at the municipal level, and he occasionally voiced sympathy for farmers' discontent. Wilson's attraction to Burke owed almost nothing to contemporary issues and actually reinforced his belief in governmental permissiveness. "Burke is the apostle of the great English gospel of Expediency," he wrote in 1893. In Burke's thought he found in 1898 "visions of the future in it, as well as of the past,—and the future is bright with a reasonable hope of healing change." In short, Wilson gained from his reflections on Burke and from all his academic studies not so much specific views as a broad, dynamic perspective on the purposes and methods of politics. That perspective served him better than anything else when he entered politics.[20]

Another side of his academic career also served him well in politics. Teaching, the part of professorship that at the outset had concerned him least, lived up to his expectation that it would provide a platform for oratory. His seventeen years of teaching from 1885 to 1902, first at the newly opened Bryn Mawr College, then at Wesleyan University, and after 1890 at Princeton, witnessed Wilson's emergence as one of the nation's most renowned college lecturers. As important as oratorical skill to his success was the gift for lucid explication that he showed in his writing. That gift also stood him in good stead in politics. Wilson's effectiveness in the classroom varied inversely with the level of instruction. Introductory lecture courses, which he organized largely according to his own interests, were his forte. Advanced undergraduate and graduate courses, which usually required him to cover bodies of less congenial material, elicited competent performances but far less sparkle. Although Wilson taught part of each year from 1887 to 1898 at Johns Hopkins, he never conducted a graduate seminar of his own and directed few theses or dissertations. His one real failure as a teacher came at Bryn Mawr when he was supposed to guide the research of two or three graduate students in history and politics. Instead, he gave extended monologues, which filled one of the auditors with a lifelong distaste for him.[21]

For a decade academic success contented Wilson, in no small measure, perhaps, because repeated job offers advertised his fame and boosted his pay. In 1898 he was invited to become faculty chairman, in effect president, of the University of Virginia, but a group of wealthy Princeton alumni pledged a $2,500 annual supplement to his salary to keep him at Princeton. After 1896, however, Wilson showed signs of restlessness. In February 1898, when he finally did observe Congress in action, he told Ellen, "The old longing for public life comes upon me in a flood as I watch." Around the same time, according to his brother-in-law, Stockton Axson, he snapped, "I get so tired of a talking profession."[22]

Some of Wilson's discontent may have had a physical source. In May 1896 he suffered what was probably a small stroke, which partially incapacitated his right hand. That small stroke seems to have prefigured and formed part of a clinical pattern of larger strokes that he later suffered at roughly ten-year intervals. A more severe stroke occurred in 1906, and in 1919 a massive stroke left him partially crippled. The 1896 illness apparently affected Wilson's personality. According to Axson, he relaxed less after that illness and seemed more driven in his work, which would have been in line with the effects of a small stroke. Another sign of a hardening in his personality may have been his forming the first of a pair of intimate friendships with men who were also stooges. The first was with his Princeton faculty colleague John Grier Hibben. The second, with the wealthy Texan and amateur politician Edward M. House began when he ran for president. At all events, Wilson, who turned forty in December 1896, was receiving his first unwelcome reminders of mortality.[23]

His political views also changed somewhat after 1896. As John M. Mulder has noted, Wilson began to inject more personal notes and value judgments into his writings and lectures, and he allowed some of his religious views to creep into his academic work. The clearest change in his public utterances was advocacy of a more assertive foreign policy. In the Venezuela controversy with Britain in 1895, he initially disapproved of American actions, and in 1898 he viewed the acquisition of the Philippines with skepticism at first. But Wilson soon changed his mind about the Philippines, and he warmed to a larger role in world affairs as a tonic for American politics and government. "We cannot govern an empire with disintegrated [governmental] bodies," he affirmed in November 1898; "there must be unity of action in order that there may be efficiency and responsibility." In January 1899 he stated, "As long as we have only domestic subjects we have no real leaders." When Filipino nationalists revolted against American rule shortly afterward, Wilson applauded the "young [American] men who prefer dying in the ditches of the Philippines to spending their lives behind the counters of a dry goods store in our eastern cities. I think I should prefer

that myself. The Philippines offer an opportunity for the impetu-
ous, hot-blooded young men of the country to serve their country
according to the measure of their power." If only he could have
been one of them himself, like the Rough Rider colonel who was
now governor of New York.[24]

A lesser source of Wilson's discontent was his academic institution. By the late 1890s Princeton had reached a critical point in its
long evolution, initiated by McCosh, from denominational college
to modern university. An elaborate sesquicentennial celebration in
1896 symbolized the transition. Wilson was the principal speaker at
the main ceremony, at which the institution officially changed its
name from the College of New Jersey to Princeton University.
Four years later the university established a graduate school, with
Andrew F. West as dean. Behind those changes lay several years
of ferment among the younger professors and alumni. The critics
chafed at slow progress in curricular reform, in upgrading of academic standards, and in faculty recruitment, and at the dilatory
ways of McCosh's successor as president, Francis Landey Patton.
Although Wilson at times acted as spokesman for the discontented
faculty, for the most part he occupied himself with his writing and
lecturing. The leading critic and intriguer against Patton was not
Wilson but Wilson's later antagonist, Dean West.

Equally because of his fame as a writer and lecturer and because of his relative detachment from the campus conflict, Wilson
became the beneficiary of a trustees' coup that toppled Patton in
June 1902. Wilson was their unanimous, first-ballot choice to be the
new president. He had known something about the plots against
Patton, but he professed genuine surprise at his own election.
Although he regretted shelving "P.O.P.," Wilson was pleased at
the change. At the end of June 1902 he wrote his cousin Harriet,
who had rejected his marriage proposal twenty years before, that
although he and Ellen were sorry to be leaving their home for the
president's house, "we shall be public personages." A university
presidency was not what Wilson had originally wanted, and during
the 1890s he had turned down other offers of presidencies besides
the Virginia post. Yet he knew that the challenges and opportunities at Princeton in 1902 could bring some of the practical
involvement in the world that he had found lacking in his life.[25]

· 5 ·

Acquaintances

THEODORE ROOSEVELT AND WOODROW WILSON almost certainly
heard of each other early in their respective careers. Roosevelt's
exploits and writings figured prominently in the journals read by
socially respectable, better-educated people. People in the same
circles read and discussed Wilson's *Congressional Government.* In
1888 both young men had their impact confirmed when James
Bryce published *The American Commonwealth.* The Englishman
handsomely acknowledged and freely quoted from *Congressional
Government,* as well he should have done. Bryce's reliance on
Wilson's assessment of the diffusion of power and his comparison
with the British system bordered on plagiarism. "How remorse-
lessly 'Congressional Government' (a small volume by myself) is
swallowed up in Part I of Bryce!" Wilson commented privately.
Roosevelt had met Bryce early in 1887 while honeymooning in
England, and he had read and criticized page proofs of the book
before it appeared. Bryce quoted Roosevelt several times on municipal reform and shared his hope that reformers could work successfully within party organizations. He also identified Roosevelt as
"one of the ablest and most vivacious of the younger generation of
American politicians." For one who sought to bring intellect and
respectability to his political calling, that was akin to a junior officer's being mentioned in his commander's dispatches.[1]

In view of the differences in their backgrounds, careers, and
personalities, Roosevelt and Wilson could easily have become rivals and critics. Professors occupied a place of special scorn in
Roosevelt's denunciations of doctrinaire, impractical mugwumps.

In 1892 he scoffed at "the various plans to have Congress made into a 'responsible' body like the British Parliament." Such schemes showed that "the college-bred man of scholarly traditions and little practical experience who writes about our politics often seems to know next to nothing of the subject." Wilson evidently sometimes found Roosevelt comic and yet envied him. Ellen Wilson remarked, after seeing Henry Cabot Lodge's house, "He seems to be, like Roosevelt, one of fortune's all round favourites!"[2]

In fact the two men became, if not close friends, warm and mutually admiring acquaintances. They first met in March 1896, when they shared the speakers' platform at a meeting in support of a municipal reform movement in Baltimore. They dined together in January 1897, when Roosevelt visited Princeton. Wilson corresponded with Roosevelt later that year in an effort to help his former law partner, Renick, keep his government job. After Roosevelt was elected governor, he invited Wilson to confer with him about politics at Albany, and Wilson solicited his advice on a faculty appointment at Princeton. Roosevelt's response showed, Wilson told his wife, "a very sane, *academic* side of him—not known by everybody so much as to exist, but constituting his hope of real and lasting eminence." Publicly the professor praised the governor as "this gifted man" who was "too big a man to have it make any difference to him whether he was in office or out of office." After Roosevelt became vice-president, Wilson joined in his project to interest college students in politics, and he spent part of a weekend at Roosevelt's home at Oyster Bay. When Roosevelt first succeeded to the presidency, Wilson was so pleased that his brother-in-law Stockton Axson suspected him of contemplating a switch to the Republican party. Roosevelt reciprocated the admiration. "Woodrow Wilson is a perfect trump," he told a mutual friend when Wilson was chosen president of Princeton. "As an American interested in that kind of productive scholarship which tends to statesmanship," he wrote Wilson, "I hail your election as President of Princeton."[3]

Neither man was being sentimental. Their admiration had a realistic basis in their mutual perception. They had arrived at different destinations, having started from dissimilar backgrounds and chosen divergent paths. Those differences would remain important in their careers and in their relations with each other. But in their views of such issues as trust regulation, the currency, and the tariff and, more important, in their convictions that men of refinement and learning should involve themselves in the political arena, little separated them. Both men had pursued intellectual callings. Roosevelt remained an old-fashioned gentleman amateur writer and historian. As a political scientist and commentator, Wilson belonged to a new breed of academic professionals. Yet Roosevelt practiced rigorous research and, of the two, was far better versed in "scientific method." Wilson likewise eschewed the fact-grubbing research ideal of his own training. Appropriately, one historian they both admired deeply was Parkman.

In politics Roosevelt was an insider and professional, Wilson an outsider and observer. Yet Roosevelt, for all his fuming at mugwumps, valued theory and outside expertise. Wilson sometimes sounded almost pathetic in his admiration for the statesman's calling. Despite belonging to opposite parties, their major issues were often virtually interchangeable in content, if not in degree of involvement or emotional temperature. On the issue that both considered paramount—American expansion and a larger world role—even their passionate engagement was nearly the same. "There is no masking or concealing the new order of the world," declared one of them in October 1900. American possession of the Philippines "has put us in the very presence of the forces which must make the politics of the twentieth century radically unlike the politics of the nineteenth. They concern all nations, for they shall determine the future of the race." That declaration came, not in one of Roosevelt's vice-presidential campaign speeches, but in an article Wilson was writing for the *Atlantic Monthly*.[4]

The congruence in their political views should not be exaggerated. Roosevelt remained a defender of his social and economic group in the midst of the political arena. He leavened his views with perceptiveness and broad appreciation of the bases of popular discontent. Wilson was a detached observer. His views were based on an almost uncompromising intellectuality, but his original ambition and emotional sympathies kept him conversant with public affairs. Those differences had important effects later, but at the outset of the twentieth century the similarities between the two men were more important. Their agreement on an imperialist foreign policy was particularly significant. The United States, too, some spokesmen argued, was now an empire. At the beginning of the twentieth century, there was talk in various quarters about a new Augustan age, in which intellect and power would merge in ruling vast dominions. What better exemplars could have arisen for such an age than these two mutual admirers, advocates of a larger role in the world and men of letters who had become, respectively, chief executive of the United States and head of one of its most prestigious colleges?

· II ·
TWO
PRESIDENTS

In Europe, chiefly in France, after the seventeenth century down
to my personal adventures, an institution known as the *salon* played
a leading part. Its influence—political, intellectual, social—pervaded
the times . . . Distinguished civilized men and charming civilized
women came as a habit to the White House while Roosevelt was there.
For that once in our history, we had an American *salon*.

Owen Wister
Roosevelt: The Story
of a Friendship

When all is said and in spite of controversies and other difficulties,
Wilson *made* Princeton. There is not a Princeton man today, whether
friend or enemy, who will not admit this. When he started, Princeton
was an unprogressive college—of ancient and honorable traditions,
but unprogressive. When he went out, it was one of the strongest
universities in the country, with an able faculty and
with educational leadership.

Henry B. Fine, June 18, 1925

THE TWO PRESIDENCIES that Theodore Roosevelt and Woodrow Wilson occupied during the first decade of the twentieth century seemed to underline the contrast between the two men. Roosevelt enjoyed spectacular success as the first practitioner of the modern public side of the presidency of the United States. He exploited the new journalistic media to strengthen the office, and he began to build a power base apart from party organizations. He accomplished these feats not only through deliberate acts and utterances but also through an at least partly instinctive dramatization of himself, his family, and his social background. Substance matched show. Toward the end of his presidency Roosevelt listed his greatest accomplishments in this order: doubling the size of the United States Navy and sending the fleet on a round-the-world cruise; securing the route and starting construction of the Panama Canal; mediating the Russo-Japanese War and participating in the Algeciras Conference on the Moroccan crisis; instituting policies for conservation of natural resources; pursuing a strong and alert foreign policy; and making new moves toward the regulation of big business. After he left the White House in 1909, Roosevelt spent nearly a year on safari in Africa. Then he made a triumphal tour of Europe, where he visited kings and emperors and conferred with the most powerful and learned men of the Old World. His return to New York in June 1910 drew an unprecedented hero's welcome, with fireboats in the harbor and parades and throngs on shore. Theodore Roosevelt appeared to be on top of the world.[1]

At the same moment, having just suffered his second big defeat as president of Princeton University, Woodrow Wilson seemed at the end of his tether. Earlier he had taken the academic world by storm with his drive to complete the transformation of the old college into a leading university. In part he had followed the conventional path of erecting buildings, improving facilities, and attracting distinguished senior faculty. More important, he had made three bold departures. He had revamped the undergraduate curriculum; he had introduced a new form of instruction through a special group of younger teachers called "preceptors"; and he had proposed a novel plan for students to reside with their professors in "quadrangles." Wilson had also shown considerable talent for publicity. In frequent speeches and in newspaper and magazine articles, he had extolled Princeton as the vanguard of higher education. As a result, he had become the best-known college president in America. His career had faltered, however, in 1907, when alumni protests prompted the Princeton trustees to rescind their earlier approval of the quadrangle plan. That reversal slowed Wilson's momentum as an educational leader and dealt a blow from which his Princeton presidency never fully recovered. A second blow fell in May 1910 when, after a protracted struggle, he lost a fight over the location of a new facility for graduate students. The successive controversies divided Princeton so badly that Wilson would have had to leave sooner or later, even if political opportunity had not fallen his way in the summer of 1910. As matters stood, Wilson's university presidency appeared to end in failure.

Those differing appearances masked similarities between the two men. Roosevelt was not riding so high, nor was Wilson sinking so low as seemed to be the case at the middle of 1910. Despite the outward manifestations of triumph, such as picking his own successor, Roosevelt left the presidency with many objectives not achieved and with deep dissatisfactions. Revealingly, he placed his domestic actions, except for conservation, at the bottom of his list of accomplishments. During his last two years in office he had found himself stalemated by the leaders of his own party over issues relating to big business. The stalemate had begun in 1907, and Roosevelt had responded by becoming noticeably more receptive to measures to curb the power of large corporations. During those years Wilson had commenced a comparable political odyssey, abandoning a short-lived flirtation with conservative Democratic notions about state rights and limited government and emerging as a bright new face on the political scene. Both men were edging toward positions from which they could lead rising forces of discontent and reform. Despite his best intentions, Roosevelt was not about to forsake politics for retirement, and Wilson was about to leap from a university presidency into the political arena. The stage was set for the two men to emerge as equals and rivals.

· 6 ·

Public Performer

NO ONE COULD MISS THE SHOW that Roosevelt put on as president, yet the spectacular success of his performance raised questions about its significance and about the methods and purposes of the producer, director, and leading man. Undoubtedly many of Roosevelt's antics stemmed from unabashed delight in occupying the limelight. One of his sons supposedly remarked, "Father always wanted to be the bride at every wedding and the corpse at every funeral." The observation contained an element of truth. Roosevelt did have an unquenchable craving for attention and deference. Moreover, by the time he became president in 1901, he had lived for twenty years in the spotlight of publicity. His patrician background, which continued to be a principal source of public curiosity about him, also gave him ease and security in dealing with that curiosity. The Roosevelts brought refined taste and social glamour to the White House. With dignified simplicity, Edith Roosevelt redecorated the worn and dowdy dwelling, while her husband changed its official title from the Executive Mansion to the White House. The most glamorous family contribution came from his oldest child—the daughter of his first wife—pretty, high-spirited "Princess Alice." She dazzled the society pages with her doings among the upper crust, and her marriage to a well-born Harvard man, Representative Nicholas Longworth of Ohio, in a White House wedding in 1906, was the social highpoint of the decade.[1]

Conscious policy also lay behind the public image. Disputing Roosevelt's list of achievements at the end of his term, one journalist told him that his example to youth was his greatest accomplishment. "I am just an ordinary man," the president responded, "without any special ability in any direction." He had done only what "might have been accomplished by any average man who made up his mind to decide promptly and to act on his decisions." Then he added, "There *is* a lesson to youth in that, and I'm glad you thought of it that way." The creation of Roosevelt's legend began as soon as he emerged as a national figure in 1898, and as president he continued to nurture its growth. He also cultivated relations with the press by continuing and extending McKinley's practice of providing facilities and regular procedures for the reporters who covered the White House. Several of those reporters noted how sensitive he was to their deadlines and to their needs for stories. Roosevelt got excellent results from his handling of the press. As his journalist-biographer Henry Pringle observed, his invention of the "trial balloon" was "a stratagem that has been invaluable to politicians ever since." Roosevelt also tried to control the emphasis and content of his public exposure. For example, he welcomed coverage of hikes and hunting trips but forbade the press to take photographs of him playing or dressed for tennis. He advised his successor, William Howard Taft, likewise to suppress coverage of his golf, because both golf and tennis carried leisurely and effete connotations.[2]

The public side of Roosevelt's presidency represented more than a gloss on his performance in office or an agreeable way to enhance his power. In his approaches to domestic and foreign policy, consideration of his public impact formed a critical element. Popular awareness of major problems played a central role in the courses he adopted, and he viewed his conduct in both spheres as parts of a single political outlook. Writing at the end of 1902 about his moves to forestall German and British intervention in Venezuela, he asserted to the magazine editor Albert Shaw, "As with the trusts, my position has been consistent for a long time on the Monroe Doctrine." Roosevelt's list of accomplishments revealed the importance he gave to foreign affairs. He took stronger actions and, by his reckoning, accomplished more in the diplomatic sphere than in domestic affairs during his first four years in the White House. Between 1901 and 1905 he faced down apparent European threats of incursions in Latin America, established an American protectorate in Santo Domingo, at least tacitly abetted the Pana-

manian revolt against Colombia, which led to American acquisition
of the route for an isthmian canal, proclaimed the "Roosevelt Corollary" to the Monroe Doctrine, and brought Russia and Japan
together to end their war in the Far East. Those actions, together
with Roosevelt's motto "Speak softly and carry a big stick," seemed
to epitomize America's new-found role in world politics.[3]

In his first four years as president, Roosevelt revealed his
strengths and weaknesses as a diplomatist. For him, the Panama
Canal always stood near the top among his accomplishments. His
trip late in 1906 to inspect work on the mammoth engineering
project—the first presidential journey outside the United States—
was among the proudest moments of his life. But the circumstances
under which the United States acquired the route in 1903 raised
criticism that rankled Roosevelt. The Panamanian revolt had occurred, he claimed just after the event, because of Colombia's
"corrupt and evil purposes" and "complete governmental incompe-
tency," and the only opposition in the United States emanated from
"a small body of shrill eunuchs"—the mugwump crowd in the
Northeast. Although Roosevelt's superheated expressions betrayed
a trace of guilty conscience, he never doubted the righteousness of
his actions in Panama or of American domination of the Western
Hemisphere. His policies sowed a legacy of distrust in Latin America, especially through the Panamanian affair and the overbearing
pronouncement that came to be called the Roosevelt Corollary.
Actually, Roosevelt intervened less in Latin America than his successors Taft and Wilson, and his moves to establish the protectorate
in Santo Domingo in 1902 and to restore order in Cuba in 1906
showed considerable delicacy and regard for the opinions of other
Western Hemisphere countries. Not only was Roosevelt's bark
worse than his bite, but both bark and bite served larger purposes
that helped to explain, if not excuse them.[4]

His strategy for the Western Hemisphere stemmed in part
from his general view of the world. In his first annual message to
Congress in December 1901, Roosevelt called military intervention
among "barbarous and semi-barbarous peoples . . . a most regret-
table but necessary international police duty which must be performed for the sake of the welfare of mankind." The following year,
in his second annual message, he reiterated, "Wars with uncivilized
powers are largely mere matters of international police duty, essen-

tial to the welfare of the world." Roosevelt believed that because advanced nations must superintend the more backward peoples of the world, security interests and the Monroe Doctrine reserved such a role in the Western Hemisphere solely to the United States. He angered Latin Americans principally with his public enunciation of the so-called Roosevelt Corollary. In his December 1904 message to Congress he proclaimed, "Chronic wrong-doing, or an impotence which results in a general loosening of the ties of civilized society, may in America, as elsewhere, ultimately require intervention by some civilized nation, and in the western hemisphere the adherence of the United States to the Monroe Doctrine may force the United States, however reluctantly, in flagrant cases of such wrong-doing or impotence, to the exercise of an international police power." Since Roosevelt had already exercised such power, the statement seemed gratuitously offensive.[5]

Actually, proclamation of the Roosevelt Corollary was essential to his foreign policy. It came at the end of a long passage in his message to Congress in which he lectured Americans on their international duty. Roosevelt urged increased armament so that the United States could protect its interests and uphold justice in the world. Because "the same moral law" applied to nations as to individuals, "a great free people owes it to itself and to all mankind not to sink into helplessness before the powers of evil." Roosevelt preached that doctrine whenever he had a chance—in messages to Congress, in speeches, in press interviews. He hammered away at two points: the nation's need for strong arms and active involvement in the world, and the analogy between individual and national conduct. In May 1903, on his first visit to the West Coast, he gloried in American expansion, which he equated with the life of "the man who goes out to tread the rugged ways that lead to honor and success, the ways the treading of which means good work worthily done." True, all nations eventually passed away, but "the great expanding nations" of history left behind "indelibly their impress on the centuries . . . I ask that this people rise level to the greatness of its opportunities. I do not ask that it seek the easiest path."[6]

Roosevelt sought to arouse Americans to play a role in world affairs modeled after his personal ideal. Publicizing his actions and proclaiming the Roosevelt Corollary were means to lead Americans toward playing such a role. Sophisticated strategic thinking blended with emotional projections in his foreign policy. Because of his cosmopolitan, upper-class background, he had already been introduced to diplomats and leaders abroad, especially in Britain. When he entered the White House, his scholarship and his acquaintance with such intellectuals as Henry and Brooks Adams and the naval strategist Captain Alfred Thayer Mahan acquainted him with the latest thinking on America's international role. As a result he was much better prepared in foreign affairs than any of his predecessors since John Quincy Adams. His social position supplied a network of connections in the leading world capitals, which proved invaluable in his diplomatic dealings. Reading and reflection instilled in him a keen appreciation of the balance of power in international affairs and of his country's vital stake in certain aspects of that balance.

Roosevelt did not throw America's weight around in Panama and the Caribbean just for fun. He first became involved in 1902, after less than a year in office, when he deftly and secretly warned the Germans, by an implicit threat of war, to stay out of Venezuela. Roosevelt may have exaggerated European designs in the Western Hemisphere, but he did understand the propensities of weak Latin American regimes for running up and then defaulting on debts to foreign bankers. Those situations created standing temptations for outside intervention. Further, the European record of finding excuses to establish colonial beachheads in Africa and Asia offered scant reassurance. Roosevelt established the Dominican protectorate and proclaimed his corollary to the Monroe Doctrine to head off what he feared might be a similar imperial scramble in the Americas. Similarly, an isthmian canal controlled, maintained, and defended exclusively by the United States would play a critical part in achieving the naval strength needed to back up both his Latin American policy and a generally strong American posture in the world. In the passage preceding the Roosevelt Corollary, in his 1904 message to Congress, he avowed, "It is not merely unwise, it is contemptible, for a nation, as for an individual, to use high-sounding language to proclaim its purposes, or to take positions which are ridiculous if unsupported by potential force, and then to refuse to provide this force." A louder voice required a bigger stick.[7]

Important as they were, public posturing and statements constituted only one side of Roosevelt's foreign policy. The action that
received the greatest public acclaim at home and abroad was his
mediation of the Russo-Japanese War, which won him the Nobel
Prize for Peace, the first to go to an American. That prize seems
somewhat anomalous, inasmuch as it was awarded to an outspoken
advocate of armed force and a scourge of pacifism. Yet it was not
anomalous. The policies Roosevelt pursued in the Far East and
Europe were aimed at averting or containing conflicts among the
great powers and at promoting international stability. Behind both
the appearance and the reality of his public stances, the president
led an almost secret life as a sensitive, subtle diplomat. In the
friction with Germany over Venezuela in 1902, he spoke and acted
so softly and covered his tracks so well that it was half a century
before his diplomatic coup was recognized and appreciated. Similarly, in mediating the Russo-Japanese War in 1905, he did far more
than perform a disinterested act of international benevolence.[8]

Roosevelt's chief concern was to preserve the balance of power
in the Far East and Europe. Earlier, Russian aggrandizement in
Asia had troubled him so deeply that he had contemplated a move
of his own in response. He saw the Russo-Japanese War in part as
a possible unbalancing in the opposite direction by a victorious
Japan, which was a growing naval power in the Far East. He
worried still more about the war's wider ramifications, especially
for the maturing entente, which he supported, between Britain and
France against Germany. Since Britain was allied with Japan and
France was allied with Russia, a prolonged conflict might play into
the hands of Germany. Throughout 1905 Roosevelt engaged in
secret maneuvers through various channels, using his friends
Lodge, Taft, and Spring Rice as informal agents in London, Tokyo,
and Saint Petersburg. Through them he worked to bring the warring parties together and reach a settlement, which he facilitated
with the publicized negotiations at Portsmouth, New Hampshire.
He also evidently committed the United States to the side of Britain
and Japan. It was an extraordinary performance, which he repeated
on a smaller scale the next year in the Moroccan crisis. Sending an
American delegation to the Algeciras Conference of 1906 on the
flimsy pretext of a commercial treaty with Morocco, Roosevelt
backed Britain and France against German moves to embarrass and

drive them apart. Once more Roosevelt hid the evidence of his actions so well that it was years before historians began to uncover the extent of his involvement and the subtlety and adroitness of his accomplishments.[9]

Roosevelt's secretiveness did not reflect an uncharacteristic modesty. In 1909 he wrote a long private letter to Lodge in which he complained about Secretary of State John Hay, whom he had inherited from McKinley and who had served until his death in 1905. On important matters Roosevelt maintained that he had consulted Taft and Secretary of War Elihu Root, but "rarely did I consult Hay. The biggest matters however, such as the Portsmouth peace, the acquisition of Panama, and sending the fleet around the world, I managed without consultation with anyone; for when a matter is of capital importance, it is well to have it handled by one man only."[10]

Roosevelt's reticence about disclosing his diplomatic feats sprang from three sources. One was the obvious need for secrecy in conducting delicate diplomacy, which he fully appreciated. Another was the effect on Roosevelt of wielding power, particularly in dealing with other strong nations on a plane of equality; this lover of power usually found himself restrained by the exercise of power. In some instances, such as the Panamian affair and the Alaskan boundary dispute with Britain and Canada in 1902 and 1903, he did show adventuristic tendencies. But those events formed the exceptions, not the rule, in Roosevelt's foreign policy. The greater the authority and the stakes involved, the more the mature, reflective side of his personality came to the fore. Those circumstances hardly provided a model for statesmanship in a representative government. Roosevelt's lusty arrogance, at least on a verbal level, about his enjoyment of power has left lingering doubts about his ultimate stature as a leader. But the fact remains that in several situations of great potential danger for the United States and the world, he acted with restraint and self-effacement to preserve peace and order. That conduct, more than anything specific on his list of accomplishments, constituted his greatest achievement as president.[11]

The final factor that led Roosevelt to conceal his great-power diplomacy was American public opinion. He downplayed and masked his actions because his countrymen had so little awareness of or concern about international affairs. Moreover, traditional

American policies of isolation from affairs outside the Western Hemisphere, particularly in Europe, formed a barrier to openly avowed involvement in great-power politics. Nothing illustrated the dual drag of public ignorance and traditional isolation better than the Senate's amendments in 1906 to the Moroccan treaty negotiated at Algeciras and in 1908 to innocuous agreements from the international conferences at The Hague. The Senate amendments stated that these measures were "without purpose to depart from the traditional American foreign policy." In 1906 Senator Lodge, who knew better, defended Roosevelt's actions at Algeciras by insisting that "in entangling alliances, of course, no man wants to engage this country; we have no concern with the wars of Europe." Roosevelt frankly battled apathy and implicitly challenged the isolationist tradition in his utterances and publicized actions, but like any prudent politician, he recognized the limits of his situation. Besides concealing his own momentous breaks with the isolationist tradition, he never directly challenged it in public. Those limits hampered him later in his presidency and caused still greater troubles for Wilson during the next decade.[12]

In domestic affairs, public opinion confronted Roosevelt with nearly a contrary problem. Although McKinley had soundly beaten Bryan a second time in 1900, popular disquiet over the growth of big business had not disappeared. Most of the gigantic new corporate entities popularly called trusts had been formed during the years since McKinley's first election. Bryan and his followers had continued to denounce ties between their opponents and big business, and they had particularly charged that the Republicans' cherished protective tariff was the cause of the rising cost of living and the "mother of trusts." Meanwhile, new "reform" movements had arisen on the municipal level, particularly in such midwestern cities as Cleveland, Detroit, Toledo, and Chicago, with a common focus on alliances between business interests and political machines. Within the Republican party, dissident drives led by Robert M. La Follette in Wisconsin and Albert B. Cummins in Iowa had successfully challenged their dominant state organizations and were calling for novel measures to regulate business and to increase popular participation in politics, particularly through direct primaries. Such a situation seemed tailor-made for Roosevelt. In view of his earlier concerns about the trusts and his conflict with the New York Republican machine, he might have been expected to use his skill at dramatizing issues and arousing public concern in support of a nationwide crusade. A decade later he did do just that, but when he first became president he moved slowly and cautiously.

Regarding big business and most domestic concerns, Roosevelt's words and deeds were models of balance and restraint. In his first message to Congress in December 1901, he acknowledged that "tremendous and highly complex industrial development" had created "very serious social problems," which required new laws and new thinking. But he also warned, "The mechanism of modern business is so delicate that extreme care must be taken not to interfere with it in a spirit of rashness or ignorance." By the 1904 election, Roosevelt was advocating stronger measures of federal regulation over corporations, but in his December 1904 message to Congress he again cautioned against attempts "to deal with them in an intemperate, destructive, or demagogic spirit." His actions fitted his utterances. In 1902 the Justice Department breathed life into the Sherman Antitrust Act by successfully prosecuting James J. Hill's and J. P. Morgan's mammoth railroad combine, the Northern Securities Company. A string of well-publicized antitrust actions followed. Also in 1902 Roosevelt publicly intervened in the anthracite coal strike to secure a settlement in the face of the mine owners' intransigence. Most spectacularly, he championed the hitherto unheralded cause of conservation of natural resources, and he began sequestering millions of acres of public lands as forest preserves. Those actions—all of which he dramatized with customary flair—formed the basis of his 1904 campaign platform and slogan, "the Square Deal."[13]

The Square Deal contained more show than substance, but that fact had advantages as well as drawbacks for Roosevelt. Substantively he did not do much more than McKinley probably would have done if he had lived. Plans to prosecute the Northern Securities Company and to revive the Sherman Act were under way before Roosevelt's succession. In October 1901 he informed his brother-in-law, who was close to Morgan and other Wall Street magnates, "I happen to know that President McKinley was uneasy about this so-called trust question and was reflecting in his mind what he should do in the matter." The coal strike settlement duplicated a similar feat by Mark Hanna on McKinley's behalf in 1900, except that Roosevelt acted partly in public and received popular acclaim for his actions. Conservation was the one area in which his succession to the presidency made an indisputably substantive difference. Roosevelt's experiences as an outdoorsman, his scientific interests, and his friendship with Gifford Pinchot, a fellow patrician and one of the first professional foresters in the United States, combined to put him far in advance of public opinion on conservation issues. On those issues he became the agitator and arouser he declined to be on other domestic matters. Still, limited as his part was in addressing issues involving big business, Roosevelt's public stance was important. He lent respectability to concern over the trusts and kept both active and potential dissidents more reconciled to the Republican party.[14]

Even if Roosevelt had shared the views of such men as La Follette and Cummins, elementary prudence would have dictated caution when he first entered the White House. The progressive dissidents constituted a small minority within the Republican party. In firm control were the allies of big business, who enjoyed the backing of large electoral majorities in the Northeast and Midwest and feared little from the twice-defeated, divided Democrats. Roosevelt's own prospects did not look promising, either. Thus far, no vice-president who had succeeded a fallen president had gained election in his own right. Roosevelt faced an apparently formidable rival for the 1904 nomination in Senator Hanna of Ohio, who commanded great power among Republicans and held claims to the mantle of his friend McKinley. Yet, as John M. Blum has shown, Roosevelt disposed of Hanna and consolidated his position with little trouble. Now, in contrast to his earlier gubernatorial situation, he held greater power than any of the party bosses. Thanks in part to his training with Platt, he had learned how to exploit patronage and factional rivalries to eliminate any potential challenges to his nomination in 1904. Providentially, Hanna died suddenly early in that year, and Roosevelt enjoyed a free field within his party. The Democrats obliged him with an anti-Bryan reaction and the nomination of the colorless Alton B. Parker, who was buried in a Roosevelt landslide.[15]

It seems doubtful that anyone, even Hanna if he had lived, would have seriously tried to block Roosevelt's nomination in 1904. His popularity had mushroomed to such dimensions once he had become president that opposition to his candidacy would have been idiotic from the standpoint of party self-interest. In 1912 the party's bosses did deny him renomination, but at that point he had been out of the White House for three years and was challenging his own handpicked successor. The result then was a Republican disaster. Roosevelt's skill at intraparty intrigue undoubtedly smoothed his path in 1904, but he drew the greatest political strength from public exploitation of his personality and his office. Revealingly, he fretted constantly about his chances for nomination and election and persistently doubted his hold on the public fancy. The magnitude of his 1904 victory genuinely surprised Roosevelt and moved him so much that he immediately carried through a previously contemplated decision to announce that he would not run again in 1908. That decision turned out to be the biggest blunder of his political career. At the time, his reactions to seeking and winning the presidency showed he had not outgrown the need to prove himself.

Following the 1904 election, Roosevelt asserted his newly proven political prowess with a burst of activity that formed the high-water mark of his presidency. The message to Congress in which he expounded America's international duty and proclaimed the Roosevelt Corollary came less than a month after the election. During the next year and a half, through public and private diplomacy, he mediated the Russo-Japanese War and intervened in the Moroccan crisis. The same period witnessed his two main domestic legislative initiatives. In the field of railroad regulation, he steered through Congress the Hepburn Act, which gave the Interstate Commerce Commission its first real powers of investigation and ratemaking. In the field of consumer protection, he capitalized on public outcries against unsanitary processing, adulterated food, and false advertising to secure passage of the Pure Food and Drug Acts. In his pet field of conservation, he continued to publicize issues of waterpower development and land use through his own speeches and through White House conferences, even as he set aside large forest reserves. At a single stroke in March 1907 he snatched up sixteen million acres of public land for reserves just days before Congress abolished his authority to do so. That grab constituted Roosevelt's most arrogant single assertion of presidential power. For once, the Square Deal matched the big stick in substance and show.

Even at his peak of domestic activity, however, Roosevelt did not forsake caution and balance. The Hepburn Act emerged, as John Blum has demonstrated, from elaborate maneuverings around his party's barons on Capitol Hill. This performance offered an analogue at home to his behind-the-scenes efforts to preserve the balance of power abroad. Publicly, Roosevelt continued to advocate new governmental powers in dealing with business and to call for circumspection in exercising such powers. "We must not try to go too fast, under penalty of finding that we may be going in the wrong direction," he declared in August 1905. Nor did he warm to the reformers in his party and the journalists who were exposing political and business misdeeds. "La Follette impressed me as a shifty self-seeker," Roosevelt confided after the passage of the Pure Food and Drug Acts in 1906. In the midst of the fight for those laws, which was greatly aided by the description of the Chicago stockyards in Upton Sinclair's novel, *The Jungle,* Roosevelt decried those exposures. Invoking a character from John Bunyan's *Pilgrim's Progress*—"the man with the muck-rake"—he charged that although it was necessary to bring evils to light, "the man who never does anything else, who never thinks or speaks or writes, save of his feats with the muck-rake, speedily becomes, not a help to society, not an incitement to good, but one of the most potent forces for evil."[16]

Despite greater activity on the home front during his second term, Roosevelt never renounced his fundamentally conservative outlook. Prudence continued to dictate caution on issues related to business. Republican dissidents had gained strength in the Middle West and West since 1900, symbolized by La Follette's arrival in Washington in January 1906 as a senator from Wisconsin. Yet the party's Old Guard remained firmly in control in Congress and in the largest states. Roosevelt therefore cooperated with the leadership on grounds of party unity and effective action. Although he now held stronger cards, he believed he was playing the same game he had played with Platt in New York. The Hepburn Act disclosed, as Blum has incisively argued, Roosevelt's care in picking which issues to push and his adroitness in manipulating others' concerns. Public discontent over the tariff, on which Roosevelt confessed in 1906 he remained "rather an economic agnostic," left him unmoved except insofar as he could manipulate the Old Guardsmen's fears of revision. Railroad regulation appealed to him in part because he could propose clear steps of legislative action that promised concrete administrative results.[17]

Roosevelt also favored railroad regulation because popular sentiment on that issue appeared more manageable. "Now about the tariff," he had written early in his presidency: "There is no question that there is dynamite in it. It is the only matter now in view which has given me grave concern." Throughout his nearly eight years in office, Roosevelt played upon Old Guard nervousness about tariff revision, but he also kept the issue at arm's length, thereby leaving the dynamite to explode in his successor's face. Roosevelt's avoidance of the tariff, together with his excoriation of muckraking, revealed how little taste he had for public agitation while he was in the White House. Republican Senator Albert J. Beveridge of Indiana, who resembled Roosevelt in personal flamboyance and advocacy of foreign expansion, but who had a more volatile temperament, urged him in September 1906 to seize upon the rising discontent over the tariff. "I asked him to consider two facts," Roosevelt said he replied: "first, that we must under no circumstances promise what we do not intend to perform; and second, . . . [whether it would] be possible to have a revision without inviting disaster to the Presidential election." Years afterward Beveridge remarked that the Roosevelt's public reputation for impulsiveness was totally erroneous and was probably "due to his quick and emphatic manner of speaking, to his strenuous physical habit and actions." In fact, Beveridge recalled, when Roosevelt made decisions he wanted "clear, cold, practical thinking. A display of emotion usually made a bad impression upon him."[18]

The disparity that Beveridge noted between Roosevelt's public reputation and his private conduct as president was an inescapable price of his popularity. But the disparity went deeper than distortions created by his dynamic, highly dramatized personality. From the time he had first entered politics, Roosevelt had contrasted the roles of reformer and agitator on one side with the sober professional on the other. Despite his earlier fulminations against mugwumps and his praise for politicians, Roosevelt had based his career on an attempt to combine the two roles. His fascination and identification with Lincoln grew while he was in the White House. Lincoln had, he believed, achieved his overarching objectives of preserving the union and emancipating the slaves by combining eloquent utterances with shrewd, practical politics. Roosevelt similarly succeeded in combining the public and private sides of the presidency, particularly during the two years following the 1904 election. Yet tension persisted between his two roles, with one often having to be sacrificed to the other. The choice fell almost invariably on the side of manipulating the existing political situation at the expense of leading popular discontent. Roosevelt's preference for practical politics remained paramount almost as long as he was president.

The coincidence of his performance in domestic and in foreign affairs was revealing. In both arenas Roosevelt found himself restrained by being in power, and he profited by the restraints. This situation suited him better than any other. In 1904 the New York *Sun,* the journalistic voice of Wall Street, explained its endorsement of Roosevelt with the statement: "We prefer the impulsive candidate of the party of conservatism to the conservative candidate of the party which the business interests regard as permanently and dangerously impulsive." Although "impulsive" was a misleading word, that assessment caught the essence of Roosevelt's situation and advantage. He acted as the far-seeing, broadminded, dynamic leader of a conservative party. His primary task lay in making his party bend and adapt to change and discontent. His preference for the manipulative side of the presidency attested to his appreciation of the situation. His distaste for dissident politicians and muckrakers demonstrated his desire not to upset the domestic balance of power. Agitation might sometimes be useful, but only in measured doses, administered and controlled by himself. Later Roosevelt did try to play the converse role of the restraining leader of insurgent forces, and he did not do nearly so well. [19]

Much of his success sprang from his being president rather than in opposition, as he was later during his insurgent phase. Basically, however, Roosevelt succeeded because leading a conservative party was better suited to his views and personality. He acted with caution and restraint not only through political tactics but also through conviction and inclination. His distrust of such dissidents as La Follette rested on his sense of profound differences with them in outlook. He appreciated and to an extent shared the Old Guard

Republicans' suspicions that the dissidents held unsound views on issues relating to business and might be little better than the Bryanite Democrats. In his attitude toward the trusts, Roosevelt stood closer to the Old Guard than to the progressives. "I am in no sense hostile to corporations," he declared in his December 1905 message to Congress. "This is an age of combination, and any effort to prevent all combination will be not only useless, but in the end vicious." Roosevelt approved of large corporations as a manifestation of power, to which he was drawn in nearly all its forms, and as a contribution to the strength of the nation. He differed from the Old Guard in resenting the political influence of the trusts and in worrying about the popular resentment the trusts were creating.[20]

The antitrust prosecutions of the Roosevelt administration offered another example of greater show than substance. They were not all that numerous, nor were they part of a general assault on large corporations. Once more, however, the show served a purpose. When Roosevelt moved against the Northern Securities Company in 1902, J. P. Morgan came to the White House to tell him, "If we have done anything wrong, send your man to my man and they can fix it up." Roosevelt rejoined, "That can't be done." After the meeting the president remarked to the attorney general, "That is a most illuminating illustration of the Wall Street point of view. Mr. Morgan could not help regarding me as a big rival operator." That kind of thinking was what Roosevelt intended to squelch. Big business must learn its place, and tycoons like Morgan must stop posing as sovereign equals of the president of the United States. The supremacy of the government must be made clear to all. "I believe in corporations," Roosevelt affirmed in May 1905. "They are indispensable instruments of our modern civilization; but I believe that they should be so supervised and so regulated that they shall act for the interest of the community as a whole." Even more than the arrogance of big businessmen, what worried Roosevelt were the reactions that their wealth and lavish ways might spark among ordinary citizens. In his second annual message to Congress in December 1902, he warned, "Any kind of class animosity in the political world is, if possible, even more wicked, even more destructive to national welfare, than sectional, race, or religious animosity." By showing that the law applied equally to rich and poor, the well-publicized antitrust prosecutions were intended to blunt incipient class antagonisms.[21]

Roosevelt preached against class divisions at least as often as he expatiated on America's international role, and those arguments formed two of the three most fervent and often-repeated exhortations of his presidency. Over and over he urged that people be judged on their conduct and merit, not on their wealth. "No republic can permanently exist when it becomes a republic of classes," he asserted in 1904, "where the man feels not the interest of the whole people, but the interest of the particular class to which he belongs, or fancies he belongs, as being of prime importance." Nowhere did Roosevelt prove himself a finer spokesman for his conservative outlook than in his appeals to a deeper national loyalty and an organic view of society. Appropriately, in his December 1905 message to Congress he closed his plea for class harmony with a long quotation from Edmund Burke. This view of social and economic problems reflected his aristocratic background and his intellectual interests, but his expressions of that view were really ways of projecting his own personality on to the nation as a whole.[22]

Roosevelt's third major exhortation was a plea to rise above material concerns. Rejection of materialism lay at the heart of his approach to domestic and foreign affairs. On business issues he parted company with Republican dissidents and Old Guardsmen alike because he believed that both sides attached too much importance to material concerns. In his "muckrake" speech in April 1906, he decried "a mere crusade of appetite against appetite, . . . a contest between the brutal greed of the 'have-nots' and the brutal greed of the 'haves.' " Such conflicts bore "no significance for good, but only for evil." Radicals and reformers disturbed him most because of their manifest envy of the rich. "Envy is merely the meanest form of admiration," he asserted in 1903, "and a man who envies another admits thereby his own inferiority." Roosevelt preached an alternative ideal. In one of his first speeches as president, he praised the service of Civil War veterans: "You did it without one thought of the trivial monetary reward of the moment; you did it because your souls spurred you on." In 1905 he lauded the Civil War veterans again for having shown "the qualities which made you put material gain, material well-being, not merely below, but immeasurably below devotion to an ideal, when the crisis called for showing your manhood." That was the spirit Roosevelt sought to rekindle in meeting the challenges of the industrial era.[23]

The effort to arouse a self-sacrificing nationalism akin to the Civil War spirit shaped Roosevelt's approach to his party. "If the attitude of the New York *Sun* toward labor, as toward the trusts, becomes the attitude of the Republican party," he warned one Republican leader in 1904, "we shall some day go down before a radical and extreme democracy with a clash which will be disastrous to the Nation . . . It would be a dreadful calamity if we saw this country divided into two parties, one containing the bulk of the property owners and conservative people, the other the bulk of the wage-workers and the less prosperous people generally." Roosevelt believed that his policies and actions during his first term had forestalled such a division of the parties. "A well-defined opinion was growing up among the people at large," he told Cecil Spring Rice after the 1904 election, "that the Republican party had become unduly subservient to the so-called Wall Street men—to the men of mere wealth, the plutocracy; and of all possible oligarchies I think an oligarchy of colossal capitalists is the most narrow-minded and the meanest in its ideals. I thoroughly broke up this connection, so far as it existed."[24]

Roosevelt believed that he was saving his party from plutocracy and his country from divisive class politics, not by taking sides in current controversies but by summoning people to higher ideals. "I believe in material well-being," he avowed in May 1905; "I believe in those who built it up; but I believe also it is a curse if it is not accompanied by the lift toward higher things." Two months later he scorned envy and arrogance as springing "from a fantastically twisted and exaggerated idea of the importance of wealth as compared to other things." The nation rightly honored soldiers, statesmen, scientists, writers, and explorers more than businessmen because "money-making can never stand on the same plane with other and nobler forms of effort." Roosevelt's favorite example of noble effort remained the Civil War soldiers. On the eve of the 1904 campaign, he unilaterally increased pensions to Union veterans, a controversial action. Democrats denounced the move as "executive usurpation" and a payoff to a bloc of Republican voters. Yet, as William H. Harbaugh has argued, Roosevelt almost certainly had deeper motives. He was aiding the ordinary men who had fought and sacrificed because they could not afford to hire substitutes. Whether or not he felt lingering guilt about his father's part in the war, Roosevelt was clearly reminding his party of its heroic origins and his country of its finest hour. The 1904 outcome particularly gratified him, he told Owen Wister, "to have owed my election . . . above all to Abraham Lincoln's 'plain people.' "[25]

Roosevelt gave the ablest political performance of his life during the middle years of his presidency, when his best talents and the most important strains of his career converged. His apprenticeship in Republican politics had prepared him for the deft dealings through which he moved the party toward meeting domestic problems while preserving a modicum of unity. Significantly, Roosevelt reserved nearly all his opportunities as president for public persuasion—"a bully pulpit," he called the office—for appeals to transcendent national interests and higher standards of personal conduct, rather than redress or justice to particular people or groups. His advocacy of conservation exemplified such appeals. Roosevelt urged his countrymen to forgo immediate rewards and to rise above narrow self-interest in using natural resources, for the sake of future generations. Those arguments, like his other exhortations, were variations on the same theme—he was exhorting his country to undergo the kind of self-transformation on which he based his own life.

The excellence of Roosevelt's performance at the middle of his presidency extended beyond his political activities. His catholic interests and intellectual and aesthetic tastes led him to exploit the varied dimensions of his office to a degree that has never since been fully matched. His redecoration and renaming of the White House foreshadowed an interest in governmental promotion of the arts that had not existed since the 1820s. In 1904 and 1905 he directed the Treasury to redesign American coins, and he commissioned his friend, the leading sculptor Augustus Saint-Gaudens, to do the work. He thereby gave the country, he later boasted, "the most beautiful coinage since the decay of Hellenistic Greece." Roosevelt repeatedly badgered Congress to provide funds for scientific and cultural projects, particularly research and exploration by the Smithsonian Institution and the establishment of a national gallery of art in Washington. He also pioneered in using the presidency to set a public example of encouragement of art and learning. White House guest lists included leading writers, painters, sculptors, and scientists, and the president took pains to see that the press knew about and publicized those whom he entertained.[26]

More than public example prompted Roosevelt to gather culti-vated people around him. His circle of intimates brought such cultivated politicians as Lodge and Elihu Root, who succeeded Hay as secretary of state, together with sculptors such as Saint-Gaudens and painters such as Frederic Remington, such novelists as Wister, and such historians as Henry Adams and James Ford Rhodes. "Dis-tinguished civilized men and charming civilized women came as a habit to the White House while Roosevelt was there," recalled Wister. "For that once in our history, we had an American *salon.*" In presiding over his salon, Roosevelt fulfilled the long-standing ambition about which he had written from Dakota to his sister years before. He did not content himself with just setting a benign exam-ple. Rather, he actively promoted what he considered the best in American arts and letters. Saint-Gaudens ruefully discovered that his friend and patron had by no means given him an artistic free hand in designing coins, and Wister and Rhodes found their works subjected to Roosevelt's blue pencil when he read their manu-scripts. The best-publicized and somewhat comic episode in Roose-velt's efforts at cultural uplift came in 1906 and 1907, when he conducted an unavailing two-year campaign for simplified spelling. Such forms as "thoroly" and "thru" struck him as more logical and as proof of American cultural independence.[27]

Amusing though his many hobbies and projects often appeared, they reflected an aspect of his leadership that was serious, im-portant, and virtually unique among American presidents. Lewis Einstein later commented that Roosevelt seemed to him to rein-carnate the Italian Renaissance ideal of rounded and encompassing thought and action. Roosevelt embodied that ideal not just in his own life but in the way he tried to become a cultural arbiter after the manner of sixteenth-century Italian princes. His tastes often appeared to be old-fashioned and straitlaced, even though he de-fended Edgar Allan Poe's reputation and promoted the career of Edwin Arlington Robinson. Yet Roosevelt based his cultural views upon wide cultivation and genuine reflection. He cared deeply about the public impact of art and literature, and he believed that

the best works should promote civic virtue. Similarly, regarding
religion, he had no interest in theology, and he may have been a
skeptic about the existence of God and an afterlife. Yet he frequently called himself a preacher as president and constantly commended religious observances and activities for their social benefits. The Renaissance analogy extended further with Roosevelt·than
a similarity of roles. The historian Jacob Burckhardt described the
Renaissance political ideal in the phrase "the state as a work of art."
That was the ideal Roosevelt pursued during his presidency.[28]

Roosevelt's presidency acquired a special glow. As with a later
administration characterized by social glamour and cultural patronage, for many the glow burned brighter in nostalgia. No one
dubbed Roosevelt's administration Camelot, but Wister evoked his
leaving the White House with Tennyson's lines:

> But now the whole Round Table is dissolved
> Which was an image of the mighty world.

Actually, by the time he left the White House, the legendary
quality of his presidency had already grown frayed. The high point
came at the end of 1906, when everything was going splendidly.
The off-year elections registered only a slight erosion of Republican
congressional strength, and the dissidents gained a little more in
power within the party. In New York Charles Evans Hughes, a
clean-government Republican after the Roosevelt model, beat back
the gubernatorial challenge of the sensationalist newspaper publisher William Randolph Hearst, whom respectable people regarded as an unscrupulous demagogue. Right after the election the
president left for Panama, where he delighted in witnessing his
diplomacy bearing fruit in a massive feat of technonogy. After his
return he presided over the largest White House reception ever
held, when over 8,000 people flocked to shake his hand on New
Year's Day 1907. At the age of forty-eight, Theodore Roosevelt had
reached the apogee of his life.[29]

· 7 ·

Academic Reformer

THE HIGH POINT OF WILSON'S academic life occurred at the beginning of 1907 also. He had just celebrated his fiftieth birthday and had started to unveil the most ambitious departure in his presidency of Princeton. In a different and smaller sphere, Wilson had put on as remarkable a performance as Roosevelt between 1902 and 1907, and he had presented a comparable mixture of show and substance. Wilson did not pioneer in the growth of American universities to the same extent as such predecessors among university presidents as Daniel Coit Gilman of Johns Hopkins or Charles William Eliot of Harvard. Yet Wilson left his mark on the development of higher education, and he used his talents as a speaker and publicist to attract greater attention to the academic world than any other college or university president had done. Both because it was significant to the development of higher education and because it came immediately before his entry into politics, Wilson's term at Princeton has attracted more attention than any other university presidency in American history. Those reasons for this interest have contributed, however, to distorted views of his Princeton presidency. Most interpretations of its significance to higher education have cast that presidency in a misleading light and have overlooked its major thrust.

The two main interpreters of his presidency of Princeton have depicted Wilson as bent on combating both the German research ideal earlier championed by Gilman and the free elective studies for undergraduates introduced by Eliot. Laurence Veysey, in a study of Wilson's educational ideals and in his book *The Emergence of the American University* has placed Wilson in the camp of "liberal culture"—the movement that arose in the 1890s to revive the college's traditional humanistic function of cultural indoctrination of undergraduates. Henry W. Bragdon, in the fullest treatment of Wilson's academic career, has called him a "conservative reformer" because he defended older fields of study and sought to buttress Princeton's position as a small, isolated college that drew its students almost exclusively from wealthy, socially prominent families. Both interpretations have some validity. Wilson's graduate study at Johns Hopkins had made him disgusted with the German university model, while seventeen years of teaching had reinforced his preference for undergraduate instruction and his desire to prepare young men for public service. In "Princeton in the Nation's Service," his 1896 address to the sesquicentennial celebration, he had lauded "the old schooling in precedent and tradition," and he had castigated the sciences for having "too great a preponderance in method in every other branch of study."[1]

During his Princeton presidency Wilson laid the most stress on undergraduate education. Henry B. Fine, whom he appointed dean of the faculty in 1903 and who became his closest associate, maintained that Wilson's overriding aim was to "intellectualize the undergraduates." His largest reform at Princeton was the introduction of "preceptors" to guide the studies of small groups of juniors and seniors, somewhat like tutors as Oxford and Cambridge. The preceptorial system was an expensive innovation plainly intended to preserve Princeton's advantages as a small college. Wilson often depicted his work at Princeton as offering an alternative to Eliot's Harvard. He touted his institution as the vanguard of a new wave of system and discipline in college studies, in contrast to and in competition with the free-elective approach. At the outset of his presidency, Wilson took an outspokenly elitist attitude about the student body. In May 1903 he told a group of alumni, "I don't want any better description of the sort to send to Princeton than Cecil Rhodes gave in his provisions for Oxford scholarships." The following November he argued that education was of three kinds—for the masses, citizenship and vocational training, and a "third sort of education . . . intended to make those who take it fit to lead, to give them the general inclusive, instructed view of life . . . This higher sort of education is, by economic necessity only for the few." This was the education he meant to provide at Princeton.[2]

However, to picture Wilson as the leader of an educational counterreformation or defender of a privileged bastion is to cast his Princeton presidency in a false light. He did not have a grand scheme or program in mind when he was chosen for the office. "Fortunately, I never worked out the argument on liberal studies, which is the theme of my inaugural, before," he told his wife in July 1902, "never before having treated myself as a professional 'educator.' " Although Wilson exaggerated a bit, he was basically correct. During the protracted debates in the declining years of his predecessor's regime, the man who had taken the leading role not only as Patton's critic but also as exponent of "liberal culture" had been not Wilson but Andrew F. West.[3]

Rather than regarding his new office as an opportunity to implement a vision, Wilson employed a different model. "I feel like a new prime minister getting ready to address his constituents," he also told his wife in July 1902. "I trust I shall seem less like a philosophical dreamer than Mr. Balfour does"—a jibe at the newly chosen British prime minister. The Princeton presidency offered a foretaste of Wilson's political career by giving him a chance to test the model of leadership he had previously extolled—"expediency." He presided over the university and made his way as an educational reformer in response to concrete conditions. None of his three major departures arose solely from his own mind or as part of a larger scheme of "liberal culture." The first departure was an overhaul of the curriculum in a fresh way that combined requirements for broad study with elective specialization. Curricular reform was an idea whose time had come at Princeton; no subject had roiled the faculty more during Patton's last days. Wilson's contribution consisted mainly of removing Patton's restraining hand and letting the final product appear to emerge as a matter of consensus, while giving some deft guidance, which he let be felt as little as possible. That approach foreshadowed Wilson's light-handed collegial leadership on issues that others had exercised themselves over more than he had. It was an approach he later used as governor of New Jersey and as president of the United States.[4]

Wilson's second departure, the introduction of the preceptors, forecast another strong political characteristic—boldness. In place of a broad educational philosophy, he had a set of specific plans for his university. His brother-in-law Stockton Axson later claimed that in 1895 or 1896 Wilson had outlined the three departures of his Princeton presidency—the new curriculum; the tutorial scheme, which came to be called the preceptorial system; and the residential idea, later labeled the "quad plan." Although Axson's recollection sounds apocryphal, Wilson did submit a breathtaking analysis in his first report to the trustees in the fall of 1902. Two interrelated needs dominated his diagnosis of Princeton's condition. One was money: "the first thing that struck me when I came to look closely into its affairs was that it is insufficiently capitalized for its business." The other need was "a radical change of method" of undergraduate instruction in order "to make use, in a modified form, of the English tutorial system." Further, certain departments needed more distinguished faculty. These changes alone would require an endowment, Wilson estimated, of $6 million—more than $2 million above Princeton's resources at that time. In addition, such other desirable innovations as properly establishing the graduate school, on which West had been working for several years, founding a law school and a school of electrical engineering, and building a natural history museum would require another $6.6 million. Princeton's total endowment needs Wilson calculated at $12.5 million—then a staggering sum for any university.[5]

The new president insisted that nothing less could bring Princeton up to its true standard. "No institution can have freedom in its development which does not stand at the top in a place of real leadership," he avowed. "If Princeton should ever come to be generally thought of as standing below Harvard and Yale in academic development her opportunity for leadership and even for independent action within her own sphere would be gone." Princeton faced a simple choice. "Either we may withdraw from the university competition and devote ourselves to making what we have solid and distinguished, or we must find money enough to make Princeton in fact a great university." That statement set the keynote of Wilson's Princeton presidency. His subsequent successes and failures flowed from that perception of his office.[6]

Wilson lost no time in striving for leadership among universities. Fund-raising was essential. Even before his inauguration, Wilson privately approached rich alumni and other big potential donors. No task came harder to him; he regarded such efforts as a form of begging, and he achieved few spectacular successes in prying open the pocketbooks of the wealthy. Unfortunately, his comparative lack of success as a fund raiser played a critical role in his final struggle at Princeton. Speechmaking suited him much better. He soon established himself as probably the country's leading educational spokesman, as he traveled almost constantly to address Princeton alumni groups and religious, philanthropic, business, and social organizations.

Meanwhile, on campus Wilson instituted two long-overdue sets of reforms. First he finished McCosh's work of loosening Princeton's Presbyterian ties—a development that had suffered setbacks under Patton. Wilson broke the control of fundamentalist ministers and laymen over the board of trustees. As a result he was able to make faculty appointments without regard to church membership or religious views and to transform Princeton into an ecumenical, nonsectarian institution open to diverse viewpoints, particularly to modern scientific Biblical criticism. In 1905 Wilson appointed the first Jew to the Princeton faculty and in 1909 the first Catholic. At the same time he directed the first real departmental organization of the faculty and superintended a sharp raising of academic and disciplinary standards for students. His appointment of Fine as dean early in his presidency brought him an able lieutenant, whom he had known since their undergraduate days, and a man of equal and complementary intellectual ambition for Princeton. Fine was renowned as both a tough marker and disciplinarian of students and a brilliant spotter of scientific talent. In all, Wilson got his administration off to an impressive start.

The centerpiece of his presidency remained the new method of instruction. Wilson's institution of the preceptorial system offered an almost unsurpassed example of educational innovation. Although he had not raised the necessary endowment, he believed at the beginning of 1905 that he could garner short-term support to start on the project. Within six months he recruited fifty outstanding young instructors, who began teaching in the fall of 1905. The venture instantly met with success on all sides. Even though Wilson sprang the plan on the faculty without consultation, the older professors did not resent the newcomers because, as one recalled, "Every one liked the idea of a new assistant." Younger, more critical faculty members were delighted that the preceptors included so many highly trained outsiders. Of the thirty-seven who held doctorates, only three had received theirs from Princeton. "This infusion of new blood was the best thing that ever happened to Princeton," noted one preceptor who was also an alumnus. "The place was too inbred." The preceptorial system attracted widespread attention in newspapers and magazines, putting Princeton on the map educationally in a way that nothing else had done before and making Wilson something of an academic hero.[7]

The scheme, which offered benefits to everyone and apparently threatened no one, owed its success almost entirely to Wilson. Besides being bold in initiating the project and vigorous in pushing it through, he invested the effort with his own special inspiration. Wilson personally identified, contacted, and interviewed all the candidates, except those in mathematics and the sciences, where he delegated authority to Fine. Wilson could be even more winning with small groups and individuals than with large audiences. One skeptical candidate for a preceptorship recalled, "Before the talk was over, my loyalties were entirely committed to him. Had Woodrow Wilson asked me to go with him while he inaugurated a new university in Kamchatka or Senegambia I would have said 'yes' without further question." Wilson's persuasiveness in recruiting preceptors and in explaining the enterprise to faculty and alumni proved contagious. Students felt, one remembered, "a tang to the air," while a "dawning interest in studies" broke out even among the dilettantish clubmen. Forty years later one of the preceptors declared, after having taught in several universities, "Candor compels me to say that in my experience I have never known so great a college as that was and such a high degree of intellectual interest and vitality in any undergraduate body . . . That widespread mental elevation of an undergraduate body has been for me since those days an unrealized idea, an almost utopian dream."[8]

With the preceptors, Wilson did succeed for a time in "intellectualizing the undergraduates." Such success could not last, dependent as it was on one man's enthusiasm and a rousing send-off. The plan developed snags within two or three years. The preceptors did not receive regular faculty ranks with hope of advancement, and they had to teach an exhausting variety of courses, which left little time for scholarly work. True to some trustees' expectations, preceptorial instruction became a big drain on university resources, and the method was not suited to every discipline, particularly in the sciences. Fine used his allotments in mathematics and the sciences to hire promising researchers rather than teachers. Despite its flaws, however, the preceptorial plan showed Wilson's approach to education at its best. His main concern lay not in the content of undergraduate studies but in their method and spirit. He wished, as he said in his first public statement on the plan, to combine small-college intimacy with the "stimulating life" of a great university. "We want to make reading men of the undergraduates," he told a prospective preceptor, "and we wish to give them the best teachers we can possibly find to be their guides, philosophers, and friends in the process." True to his belief in expediency, Wilson put his faith in men, not systems. "It was these new men who revitalized Princeton rather than the machinery of the preceptorial system," maintained one preceptor. "It was not a 'system,' " argued another; "Wilson wanted it informal." In getting what he wanted, Wilson achieved one of the great successes in the history of American higher education. [9]

His greatest failure followed soon afterward, partly as a consequence of that feat. Wilson demonstrated boldness once more by proposing, almost immediately after the preceptorial system, a new residential plan. In November 1905 he suggested to an alumni group that the upperclassmen's eating clubs, which had proliferated in numbers and grown in social importance since the early 1890s, "might be made the nuclei of small educational communities," which would draw together the students' social and educational lives. Wilson's aim was twofold. One purpose of the plan he was evolving was further to intellectualize the undergraduates; the other was to supplant the growing influence of the eating clubs. Wilson's elitist views never included approval of the social exclusiveness and fashionable hedonism that prevailed in the clubs' luxurious new edifices. In February 1906 he made a note to himself asking, "What is the future of the Upper Class Clubs? More and more expense and only social aims or University aims? Danger that we will develop *socially* as Harvard did and as Yale is tending to do." Wilson wanted to avert what he saw as the polarization of the student bodies at those universities, between socially desirable dilettantes and serious students despised as "polers" or "grinds."

His favorite students were young men like Raymond B. Fosdick and Norman M. Thomas, of the class of 1905. Both were outstanding scholars who came from modest backgrounds and did not join clubs but who were also lively and attractive.[10]

Wilson's combined social and educational concerns led him in December 1906 to propose to the trustees the residential arrangements that came to be called the quad plan. He argued both that studies at Princeton required a more favorable "atmosphere" and that the rise of the clubs had caused a "decline of the old democratic spirit of the place and the growth and multiplication of social divisions." He recommended the creation of "colleges," again somewhat like those at Oxford and Cambridge, in which all classes of students would live and eat with resident faculty members. Wilson repeated those arguments privately to a handful of his closest friends on the faculty in April 1907, and he added a note of urgency by stating that the plan must be implemented before the clubs became too well entrenched. In a report to the trustees in June he downplayed the club aspect and stressed the educational need for the plan. "It is but part—an indispensable part," he contended in a speech to the trustees, "—of the purpose we have steadfastly set ourselves to accomplish, namely, the reorganization and revitalization of the University as an academic body, whose objects are not primarily social but intellectual." To Wilson's surprise, the trustees immediately approved the plan in principle and authorized him to proceed, with little discussion and only one dissenting vote. The announcement of the trustees' action drew more fanfare from the press. It looked as if Wilson had scored another triumph.[11]

Actually, he had committed the biggest blunder of his educational or political career. Students and alumni who were back for reunions greeted the announcement mostly with cool detachment, but throughout the summer of 1907 meetings and surveys of graduates exposed widespread opposition and protest, which were gleefully publicized by the anti-Wilson editor of the *Princeton Alumni Weekly*. The faculty backed the quad plan by wide margins in private communications with Wilson during the summer and in votes taken in the fall, but several influential members openly opposed the scheme, including Andrew F. West and John Grier Hibben, who made a painful personal break with Wilson. The trustees took alarm at the opposition, and their most influential member, M. Taylor Pyne, grew disillusioned with the president and engineered a vote to rescind the previous approval in October 1907. Wilson stood humiliated and almost resigned his presidency. Whereas the preceptorial system had provided a model of educational leadership, the quad plan offered a textbook demonstration of avoidable strategic errors. Why he faltered so badly so soon after succeeding so well offers an insight into Wilson's character that does have bearing on his political career.

His boldness had clearly led him astray. As Bragdon observes, Wilson paid the price of his unbroken success, which had reinforced his reliance on his own powers and judgment. Wilson often poked fun at Scotch-Irishmen for knowing they were right. "And I have not departed from the faith of my ancestors," he quipped in June 1907. As his most perceptive friends noted, Wilson's self-confidence formed the source of both his failures and successes, his weakness and strength. His most glaring failure with the quad plan lay in not consulting others and in not preparing for it. Except for the suggestion in November 1905, the plan had received no public exposure before it was announced as an accomplished fact in June 1907. The faculty and trustees also had heard little about the plan before Wilson broached it, which meant that important details had not been discussed and the president had not lined up support in advance. Most serious of all—and oddly in view of Wilson's analysis of Princeton's basic needs—he had given no consideration to finances. No single factor seems to have weighed more in the trustees' about-face in the fall of 1907 than threats of alumni withholding contributions and the fear that the university would be unable to pay for the quads. [12]

Other traits also entered into Wilson's failure with the quad plan. He showed obtuseness in not recognizing that the situation was different from the preceptorial system. He had discussed the preceptorial plan in advance broadly, though generally, and much smaller sums of money had been involved. Once the bulk of alumni opinion had apparently swung against the quad plan, Wilson seemed unable to trim sail or attempt compromise, and he neither anticipated nor grasped the significance of Pyne's defection. His behavior did not arise from the rigidity with which he has frequently been charged, but from his slowness to adapt to changing circumstances and his lack of taste and talent for intrigue. Those shortcomings hurt him again in his Princeton presidency and later in politics. Finally, for one who excelled at public speaking, Wilson allowed his explanations of the quad plan to suffer from a confusion of purposes. Although he dropped his own attack on the clubs in favor of stressing educational purposes, the social aspect remained uppermost to many, particularly to newspaper and magazine editors, who praised Wilson as a fighter against snobbery and privilege. Ironically, he could probably have gotten rid of the clubs, particularly if he had attacked them directly and invoked the precedent of McCosh's ban on fraternities in the 1870s. The attacks on the quad plan included surprisingly few defenses of the clubs. Even the plan's sharpest critics usually conceded that the clubs had a bad social influence. Moreover, since the clubs had not existed when the older and more influential alumni had gone to Princeton, few of them had club ties, and Wilson could almost surely have secured their abolition in exchange for abandoning or going slow on the quads.

Certain parallels with his later political career do seem applicable. Curiously, most interpreters have likened Wilson's effort as president in 1919 to gain American membership in the League of Nations with his last conflict at Princeton, over the graduate school, rather than with the quad plan. In fact, the conflict over the quad plan resembled the League fight much more closely. In both cases Wilson was pushing a scheme of his own choosing, and he may have failed to settle for half a loaf worth having. The strongest similarity in the two events lay in the role played by Wilson's health. In 1907, as in 1919, a stroke deeply affected his conduct. In May 1906 he suffered a serious stroke that left him partially blind in one eye and raised fears that he might not be able to continue as president of Princeton. A long summer vacation in England's Lake District apparently restored his health, although recurrent headaches and pain in his arms during the next year and a half indicated that he had not fully recovered.[13]

The chief effect of the stroke on Wilson's conduct in 1907 seems to have been in upsetting his judgment in presenting the quad plan. This was the only time in his educational or political career when he acted like a visionary unable to adjust to reality. While he convalesced in England in 1906, he wrote to his strongest trustee supporter, "The summer has brought to maturity plans for the

University which have for years been in the back of my head, but which never before got room enough to take their full growth." One of his faculty confidants recalled his saying in April 1907 that he had long "considered that it would take 25 years to work it [the quad plan] out. Now, however, it seemed to be immediately obtainable." It is hard to avoid concluding that the stroke lay at the root of Wilson's failure with the quad plan. That stroke and its probable effects on his emotional balance seem to have skewed his boldness badly. In the League fight in 1919 a much more severe stroke intervened at a different stage of the conflict and also affected his judgment, with different ramifications. In sum, the failure of the quad plan offered an instructive foretaste of how Wilson's personality traits and health could shape his performance in office—but so had his earlier successes with curricular reform and the preceptorial system. As his first experiences in a position of authority, those episodes could hardly have failed to illuminate his subsequent career, but they came nowhere near prophesying his remaining life, much less unmasking some determinative psychological pattern.[14]

In the shorter run, the failure of the quad plan marked the beginning of Wilson's descent from the pinnacle of his Princeton presidency. The surge of opposition by alumni and some faculty sprang from deeper sources than club loyalties. It revealed resentment toward Wilson's driving methods and the direction in which he was taking Princeton. Wilson's daughter Margaret later said that the break with "Jack" Hibben hurt him more than anything in his life except the later rejection of League membership. The break was symptomatic of the friction generated by his leadership. Wilson's pride contributed most to the estrangement, but Hibben was not blameless, either. His opposition to the quad plan had the quality of a worm turning. Hibben's timid, agreeable ways and intimacy with the president had earlier led him to be labeled "Wilson's check-off man." His domineering wife became one of Wilson's bitterest detractors in the parlor and dinner-table politics that so frequently split the academic community. Wilson's determination to make Princeton a leading university had prompted jokes about ruining a fine country club, although his goal was outwardly unassailable. Yet any change, no matter how attractive or unavoidable, can arouse resentment among those accustomed to old ways. Wilson had anticipated as much when he had asked rhetorically of some alumni early in his presidency, "Now, why do all of this? Why not be satisfied with the happy life at Princeton? Why not congratulate ourselves upon the comradeship of a scene like this, and say 'This is enough; what could the heart of man desire more?' " What indeed? was the answer implicit in much of the opposition to the quad plan. [15]

The defeat hurt most because of Wilson's drive, which he had declared at the outset of his presidency, to make Princeton America's top university. His three departures had been subordinate to that aim, and in his first five years he had succeeded in transforming Princeton from a prestigious but still somnolent college into a major university. In part Wilson followed the practices of those whom Thorstein Veblen dubbed "captains of erudition" by erecting buildings and raiding other institutions for big-name professors. During Wilson's presidency Princeton added to its plant a biological laboratory and museum, a gymnasium, a lecture hall, four dormitories, and a modern physics laboratory. The university also refurbished its historic original building, Nassau Hall, and acquired new tracts of land and an artificial lake for rowing. Professorial stars lured to Princeton included the mathematician James Jeans and the physicist Owen W. Richardson, both from Cambridge; the classicists Edward Capps and Frank Frost Abbott, both from Chicago, and the biologist Edwin Grant Conklin, from Pennsylvania. Despite his earlier distaste for the sciences, Wilson labored to build them up. He raised funds for laboratories, he gave Fine a free hand in appointments in the physical sciences, and he exercised his own inspirational talents in recruiting Conklin. Wilson's disciplined working habits did not make him an efficient administrator in all areas, but as his presidency wore on he increasingly delegated academic details to Fine and gladly availed himself of the trustees' proposal to appoint a business manager. [16]

In another way, by retaining Princeton's small size and primary focus on undergraduates, Wilson blazed a new trail among major universities. He did not expand the undergraduate body, although he supported efforts to attract larger numbers of graduate students. He rejected proposals to add professional schools, except for his unfulfilled desire to start a law school that would promote scholarly research in jurisprudence rather than train attorneys. The institution also suffered in some respects from not being located in a large city. Those choices and circumstances meant that the burden of pushing Princeton into the academic vanguard fell almost entirely on Wilson and his supporters. "It [Princeton] is not, in one sense, the one to take the leadership in the educational advancement," he observed in 1910. "The only reason that it did so in recent years was because the faculty knew what to do under the circumstances." He was excessively modest about his own part. Even though the institution had changed its name at the 1896 sesquicentennial and added a graduate school in 1900, "Princeton University" had remained a formal and mainly empty shell surrounding a college that was in the same league as Amherst, Dartmouth, and Williams until Woodrow Wilson filled it with an institution that could compete with Harvard, Columbia, and Chicago. Fine later summed it up best: "When all is said and in spite of controversies and other difficulties, Wilson *made* Princeton."[17]

Pushing Princeton to the forefront among American universities was the main thrust of his academic leadership. That thrust has been overlooked by those who have depicted him as an educational conservative and defender of privilege. Neither curricular views nor elitist sympathies concerned him most. Rather, Wilson was a "captain of erudition," not in Veblen's derisive sense but like other ambitious university heads who have striven to raise their institutions against better-advantaged rivals. Although he criticized both the German university model and Eliot's free-elective system, he based his criticisms on a shared commitment to their goals of research and writing by faculty and of intellectual liberation of the students. He would not have entered academic life himself except for the opportunity for research and writing; he could not have functioned as a college president without striving to raise students' intellectual horizons. Wilson strove for a practical combination of both objectives that would propel Princeton to the top spot among American universities.[18]

Wilson was competing in the immediate, expedient world of his educational peers. As he said at the outset of his presidency, he viewed Princeton in comparison with Harvard and Yale, especially Harvard. In June 1907, just after the trustees' initial approval of the quad plan, Wilson journeyed to Harvard to receive an honorary degree. Teasing his hosts gently about differences in heritage and curriculum, he declared, "Now we at Princeton are in the arena and you at Harvard are in the arena; and, though ideals in the field of the mind are not like ideals in the field of politics, while it is not necessary that one should go down and the other survive, I do believe that every ideal flourishes by reason of opposition made to it." It was not hard to guess which ideal he believed was winning in the university arena. The trustees' withdrawal of approval of the quad plan the following October fell as a particularly cruel blow because Wilson believed the torch of academic leadership lay within his grasp.[19]

Another blow soon followed with the eruption of the controversy over the graduate school. Unlike the quad plan fight, this controversy was not of Wilson's choosing, and it did not initially involve a question he regarded as critical to university development. The immediate issue was where to build the graduate college, a new residential facility for graduate students on which Dean West had been working for several years. At first he and Wilson had agreed that the college should be located on the campus, and Wilson had lauded the presence of industrious, serious-minded graduate students in their midst as a salutary influence on the undergraduates. But West meanwhile had developed divergent schemes. As a temporary measure from 1905 to 1910, a group of graduate students lived with a resident faculty master in an off-campus estate, and West became fascinated with the experiment in socially segregated, culturally refined living. At the same time the dean's admiration for Oxford and Cambridge, which exceeded and had a different basis from Wilson's admiration, led him to envision a sumptuous neo-Gothic establishment coexisting with but at a distance from the rest of the university. West also came to mistrust Wilson. He believed that when Wilson introduced the preceptorial plan and then proposed the quad plan, the president had broken promises to give priority to graduate school development. West waxed particularly vengeful over the quad plan, which he not only fought publicly but also used as an occasion to foment intrigue behind Wilson's back.

Some of West's enmity Wilson deserved for having neglected the dean and his plans, but he tried to avoid an open clash as long as possible by postponing consideration of where to locate the graduate college. The trustees did not decide the question until

April 1908, when they chose an on-campus location near the president's house—largely because a recent $250,000 bequest for a graduate residence stipulated construction on university "grounds." The question appeared settled until West reopened it in April 1909 by announcing a $500,000 gift from the soap magnate William C. Procter, who specified an off-campus site but on university property, thus satisfying the earlier bequest. After attempts at persuasion and compromise during the summer and fall of 1909, the controversy split Princeton into opposing camps. West, backed by Procter and Pyne, insisted upon the off-campus site; Wilson held out for a site on campus. Among the trustees, even bitterer arguments and more complicated maneuvers ensued than during the quad plan fight. First one side and then the other seemed to be winning. Wilson made his position public in the spring of 1910 when he took his case to the alumni in a well-publicized series of speeches. The controversy did not end until May 1910, when West secured a second gift, a bequest, rumored to be between $2 million and $10 million from the estate of a wealthy alumnus, and with West named as executor. "We have beaten the living," Wilson reportedly exclaimed with a laugh when he heard the news, "but we cannot fight the dead. The game is up."[20]

The game was also up for Wilson's presidency of Princeton. After this second major defeat, he would have had to leave sooner or later. He refrained from resigning immediately in deference to his supporters among the faculty and trustees. "I am not interested in simply administering a club," he told his brother-in-law. "Unless I can develop something I cannot get throughly interested." Questions remain about why Wilson fought and lost over the graduate college and what the controversy disclosed about his character and future political conduct. The issue of where to locate the graduate college differed from the quad plan not only in who raised it but also in being neither easy to understand nor readily apparent in importance. One trustee supposedly sniffed that he could not see why so much fuss was being raised over "where a boarding house should be located," while one of Wilson's faculty opponents called the controversy a teapot tempest. At times it seemed little more than a spat between West and Wilson, and neither man always showed himself to advantage. Here, too, Wilson may have missed an opportunity if his main objective was to get rid of West. Several times he declined to push for the dean's resignation because he wanted to avoid the appearance of a mere personality conflict. Ironically, just before the news broke of the big bequest in May 1910, some trustees were trying to put together a compromise that exchanged the off-campus location for West's resignation.[21]

The graduate college controversy did involve substantial stakes. Wilson believed that it required defending Princeton's hard-won standing among front-rank universities. He dug in his heels against West in part because the distinguished professors whom he had attracted to Princeton, particularly Capps and Conklin, charged that the dean's plan would repel the mature, dedicated graduate students whom the university needed to attract. Early in 1909 the mathematician Jeans resigned, citing as one of his reasons, "the failure of the Graduate Department to develop in the way in which we had hoped it would, and the utter absence (it seems to me) of hope for it in the future." At other points in the controversy, Capps and Conklin appeared in danger of leaving for the same reason. When Wilson took his case to the alumni in the spring of 1910, he stressed two points. One was the need for interaction between graduate students and undergraduates, for their mutual benefit. The other was that in taking on "university questions" Princeton had entered "the wide and general academic field where the right policy was a matter of action and reaction between ourselves and the other universities of the country and of the world. It became necessary for us to relate ourselves very carefully to the rest of the great world of universities, to square our methods with accepted methods of graduate study everywhere."[22]

Wilson did not lose the graduate college fight because West was a formidable antagonist. The dean had only two attributes the president lacked in the fight—skill as a fund raiser and good luck. Otherwise, he was a hapless, sometimes pathetic figure, out of his intellectual depth among the academic stars whom Wilson and Fine had attracted to Princeton. Wilson's true antagonist was Pyne, who seems to have been looking for ways to break the president's power ever since the quad plan episode. Pyne once more proved a resourceful intriguer. He conspired with Procter to use his gift to damage Wilson, who again showed himself slow in adjusting to tricky tactics and somewhat inept at parrying underhand thrusts.

But the outcome of the controversy did not depend upon Pyne's skulduggery. West's luck in receiving his bequest, which turned out to be much smaller than first reported, saved his position and his plan, but even if he had gone, the divisiveness of the fight would have ensured Wilson's eventual departure, too. Except possibly for deficiencies as an intriguer, Wilson's conduct in the controversy did him credit. He entered the fight only after trying to avoid a confrontation and at the behest of men whose judgment he valued. He showed no vindictiveness toward his opponents, and at a critical juncture he attempted a face-saving compromise and would most likely have gone along with the final formula for ending the controversy. His speeches to the alumni offered the best examples yet of his talent for public explication of complicated questions. Insofar as his performance in the graduate college episode prefigured his later career, it augured well.

Yet this controversy has occasioned a host of comparisons with his defeat in the League conflict of 1919. Starting with Edmund Wilson in 1927, a parade of writers has contended that the graduate college dispute revealed a psychological pattern that was repeated in the League fight, with nearly everyone casting West in the same role as Henry Cabot Lodge as Wilson's wily, successful adversary. Some parallels do exist. Wilson did lose in both conflicts, and in both he tried to break a deadlock by appealing over the heads of his opponents to their common constituency. But the differences are more striking. It was Pyne, not West, who was Wilson's foe in the graduate college fight, and Pyne had nowhere near the same significance that Lodge later did. Wilson remained reasonably healthy throughout this controversy, in contrast to both the quad plan and League fights. His behavior did not show the kind of effects that strokes induced in those other two conflicts, particularly not the unbalancing of judgment he showed in 1906 and 1907 and again in 1919. Wilson remained flexible in his positions throughout most of the dispute. When he got his fighting spirit up, he became a zestful, discerning warrior. Ironically, perhaps, the greatest similarity between Wilson's Princeton defeats and the League fight may have lain in his perception of their ultimate stakes. At both times he may have attempted the impossible—to make Princeton the nation's top university and to secure permanent peace through the League of Nations—but few would question the worthiness of the effort. In his final conflict at Princeton, Wilson fought skillfully and sensibly, and he lost gracefully when the odds tilted decisively against him.[23]

Part of his grace and balance undoubtedly derived from his having an alternative career in mind. His Princeton presidency had brought public visibility, which in turn had allowed him to dabble in politics. Starting after the 1904 election, Wilson emerged as a spokesman for conservative Democrats in opposition to both Bryan and Roosevelt. In 1906 he received a few votes in the New Jersey legislature as a minority Democratic nominee for United States senator, and there was talk of him as a dark-horse Democratic presidential or vice-presidential candidate in 1908. A more substantial possibility surfaced in 1909, when moves commenced toward making him the Democratic nominee for governor of New Jersey in 1910. Politics attracted Wilson in direct proportion to his academic frustrations. "I shall not willingly wait more than two years for the Princeton trustees to do what it is their bounden duty to do with regard to the reform of university life," he confided in November 1908. "At the end of that time I would be glad to lend my pen and voice and all my thought and energy to anyone who purposed a genuine rationalization and rehabilitation of the Democratic party lines of principle and statesmanship!" In February 1910 Ellen Wilson commented on one of the many compromise proposals in the graduate college fight, "There is one point in the plan which *does* appeal to me, viz. that it sets you free again to leave if you wish—that is to accept the nomination for governor and go into politics."[24]

If Wilson's defeats as president of Princeton made politics more attractive to him, they did even more than his academic accomplishments to make him attractive to broad segments of the public. Just as newspapers and magazines had portrayed him during the quad plan fight as a battler against snobbery, the press now cast him as an opponent of the influence of private wealth. Several interpreters have maintained that such publicity helped wean Wilson from conservatism by giving him a social-reform reputation to live up to. Those conflicts did affect Wilson's political and social views. Privately he started to make biting remarks about the idle rich. Publicly he stated that he wanted both to attract more high school students of slender means to Princeton and to make the sons of the wealthy as unlike their fathers as possible. For the most part, however, he avoided the social and economic implications of the Princeton controversies, despite clear temptations and the urging of some supporters to stress such matters. In the graduate college conflict, except in one speech that he immediately regretted, he stuck to the theme of university standards and the intellectual awakening of students, as he had done with the quad plan.[25]

Wilson kept his priorities straight. His highest aim at Princeton was intellectual, not social or political. In all his efforts he pursued a two-sided purpose. First, he wanted to make Princeton the nation's top university. Second, he sought to quash the pseudo rebellious student hedonism that already held sway in the clubs and was making headway in colleges across the country. His symbolic antagonist was a boy who did not enter Princeton until three years after Wilson left—F. Scott Fitzgerald. If Wilson had won his fights for the quad plan and the location of the graduate college, he would not have stemmed the tide of the "beautiful and damned" spirit among American youth any more than he would have knocked Harvard off the summit of the American university world. But Princeton would have become a different place, and Wilson's academic career would have had a much happier ending.[26]

Success in politics never completely took away the sting left from his Princeton presidency. While Wilson was campaigning for governor in October 1910, Pyne and his faction among the trustees forced his resignation in a summary fashion. Then they chose Hibben as his successor early in 1912, after long wrangling—moves that hurt still more. "Why will that not heal over in my stubborn heart?" Wilson asked as he watched Hibben's rise. "Why is it that I was blind and stupid enough to love the people who proved false to me, and cannot *love*, can only gratefully admire and cleave to, those who are my real friends?" Even after he became president, the Princeton conflicts haunted his waking thoughts and gave him nightmares. Although he decided not to return to live in Princeton after he left the White House, Wilson turned his attention to academic affairs in the last months of his life. Raymond Fosdick later recounted that in October 1923 Wilson told him "that his contribution to his generation—if he had made any—was in connection not so much with his political work as with his activities as a teacher and college administrator." He wanted to become president of a college at which he could take up where he had left off at Princeton, but nothing came of the idea. Wilson died less than four months later. Such academic fancies reflected the disappointments of a man broken in health and repudiated in politics, but they also showed how deep a mark his quarter century as a professor and university president had left on him. Part of Woodrow Wilson would always be an academic man.[27]

· 8 ·

Stalemate and Departure

THE YEAR 1907 ALSO BROUGHT a downturn in Theodore Roosevelt's fortunes. Except for choosing William Howard Taft as his successor and securing Taft's nomination and election in 1908, little went right for Roosevelt during his last two years in office. In October 1907 a financial panic hit Wall Street and burgeoned into a severe recession. Many financial spokesmen and Old Guard Republicans blamed the president, charging that he had undermined business confidence with his antitrust and regulatory policies. Ironically, Roosevelt's only real involvement with the economic slump came when he agreed to waive antitrust investigations so that United States Steel could acquire the Tennessee Coal and Iron Company; U.S. Steel claimed that it wanted to keep the firm from going under and worsening the panic. Bryan and his Democratic followers denounced the president's action as a sellout to big business.

Roosevelt's relations with the Republican leadership in 1907 and 1908 soured to the point of open hostility. Party chieftains on Capitol Hill not only stymied any further important domestic legislation, they also chipped away at the president's powers in such areas as conservation and indulged in acts of spite like refusing to publish reports by blue-ribbon commissions of inquiry he had appointed. Roosevelt usually maintained his dignity, although he bombarded Congress with a series of special messages calling for stronger measures to deal with business and labor problems. His one triumph, aside from assuring Taft's succession, came in 1907 when he deftly handled a dispute involving Japanese immigration and land ownership on the West Coast. While he appeased Japan with concessions in China, Roosevelt staged a show of force by dispatching America's battle fleet on its first round-the-world cruise—a move he regarded as his greatest single accomplishment.

Most of his trouble stemmed from his situation as a self-proclaimed lame duck. Roosevelt could have retained greater leverage over Congress and his party if he had either not renounced another term in 1908 or had hedged on the pledge and qualified it afterward. His manipulation of the tariff issue and his fencing with the Old Guard over railroad regulation had shown Roosevelt's capacity for playing cat-and-mouse games. By refusing to play the same way with the possibility of his running again, he forfeited a reservoir of political opportunity. Roosevelt had not acted impulsively when he made his pledge right after the 1904 election. He had calculated his action well in advance, and he had stuck to his pledge for two main reasons. First, he believed that no strong man should occupy the presidency for too long. "I believe in a strong executive," he told an English historian in 1908; "I believe in power, but I believe that responsibility should go with power, and that it is not well that the strong executive should be a perpetual executive." Second, Roosevelt recognized his public reputation as a power grabber and a disturber of constitutional niceties. What better way to counteract that reputation than to make the supreme political renunciation? He also told the English historian, "Most of all, I believe that whatever value my service may have comes even more from what I *am* than from what I *do*." Show required a sacrifice of substance.[1]

Personally as well as politically, his sacrifice was as unwise as it was noble. To renounce power was out of character for him. Roosevelt admitted to his military aide in 1908 that he was laying aside the "burdens" of the office "with a good deal of regret, for I have enjoyed every moment of this so-called arduous and exacting task." Roosevelt could hardly help missing the only job that ever satisfied him. Further, he would be leaving the presidency at fifty, younger than all but four other men have been on entering the office. "But my dear fellow," he confided to a friend two days before his term expired, "for Heaven's sake don't talk about my having a future. My future is in the past." Whatever dissatisfaction he later felt about his successor's performance, the root of his discontent lay in himself. Roosevelt was not going to be happy anywhere but in the White

House. He was sadly correct when he said that his best years lay
behind him. Just as exercising power had restrained and fulfilled
him, so relinquishing power unleashed and diminished him.[2]

Roosevelt's regret during his last two years as president ran
deeper than political frustration and personal disappointment. Part
of the sense of missed opportunity stemmed from his success in
keeping the nation at peace, the party intact, and the people reasonably contented. As his term drew to a close, Roosevelt recognized that he had presided over the United States in relatively
undemanding times, which had not required the highest exercise
of leadership. Like many other historians, he thought that great
events summoned forth great leaders. "If during the lifetime of a
generation no crisis occurs sufficient to call out in marked manner
the energies of the strongest leader," Roosevelt had observed in
1903, "then of course the world does not and cannot know of the
existence of such a leader; and in consequence there are long
periods in the history of every nation during which no man appears
who leaves an indelible mark in history." Roosevelt saw that as his
own fate. Inasmuch as Lincoln was his presidential ideal, he could
not escape contrasting the momentous days of the Civil War with
his own more prosaic times. The centenary of Lincoln's birth,
which fell less than a month before Roosevelt left office, served to
underscore the differences, as he made his next to last presidential
journey to speak at Lincoln's birthplace. To Roosevelt's credit, no
one has suggested that he, unlike at least one of his glamorous
successors, ever tried to foment crisis to enhance the significance
of his presidency.[3]

Lack of heroic challenge would have bothered him less if his
exhortations had succeeded in awakening Americans to play a
proper role in world affairs, to avoid class divisions, and to rise
above material concerns. The final two years of his presidency
brought disillusionment on all three counts. His skill in dealing
with the Japanese in 1907 did not overcome the domestic limitations under which he operated. In this case the limitations were
contradictory. Because of anti-Oriental prejudice in California,
Roosevelt had to deal for the first time with a diplomatic incident
that involved inflamed popular feelings at home. He admitted that
his policy started from the point "that this is a race question, and
that race questions stand by themselves. I did not clearly see this

at the outset." At the same time, the prevailing popular attitude of unawareness of international affairs remained impervious to the dangers created by such local feelings. Six years after he sent the fleet around the world, Roosevelt declared, "My prime purpose was to impress the American people; and this purpose was fully achieved." The cruise made a splendid impression on other nations. "But the impression made on our people was of far greater consequence."[4]

Roosevelt was deluding himself, and he knew it. In August 1907 he confessed to Taft his disquietude at the failure of Congress and the people to recognize international dangers and duties, particularly by not adequately defending the Philippines. He reluctantly concluded that "we shall have to be prepared for giving the islands independence of a more or less complete type much sooner than I think advisable from their own standpoint, or than I would think advisable if this country were prepared to look ahead fifty years and build the navy and erect the fortifications which in my judgment it should. The Philippines form our heel of Achilles. They are all that make the present situation with Japan dangerous." Such realism carried a bitter price, for Roosevelt believed, "To keep the islands without treating them generously and at the same time without adequately fortifying them and without building up a navy second only to that of Great Britain would be dangerous in the extreme." The United States had a momentous choice to make. "We cannot help playing a great part in the world," Roosevelt avowed in July 1908, "but we can very easily help playing that part well; and to be a great people and make a great failure is as unattractive a spectacle as history affords." He left the White House haunted by that spectacle.[5]

His failure to awaken Americans to their international role distressed Roosevelt not only as a bad thing in itself but also in relation to his other two exhortations. He differed from most of his countrymen in regarding foreign and domestic affairs as related parts of a single outlook rather than as separate concerns. Strength and duty abroad and order and justice at home were two sides of the same coin; national conduct remained the analogue of personal conduct. Roosevelt persisted in exhorting the nation to follow his own example of self-transformation and righteous behavior. In a speech in May 1907 he warned the "Nation to avoid . . . the lower promptings of our hearts, . . . [and not] to seek only a life of effortless ease, of mere material comfort." Material development signified "nothing to a nation as an end in itself." The end lay in pursuing ideals, and for his favorite example he once more pointed to the Civil War. "The qualities needed to make a good soldier, in this final analysis, are the qualities needed to make a good citizen; and the qualities needed alike by a soldier in time of war and by all citizens in time of peace are those which in their sum make up the characteristics that tell for a great and righteous people." Like other presidents after him, Roosevelt was trying to instill a wartime spirit of patriotic sacrifice and devotion in meeting peacetime challenges. Unfortunately, he came no closer to instilling such a spirit with his domestic exhortations than he did with his call to international duty.[6]

Nothing pained Roosevelt more keenly than his inability to bridge class divisions. Throughout his presidency he continued to exhort Americans to steer a middle course between what he called "the Scylla of mob rule and the Charybdis of subjection to a plutocracy," and he deliberately balanced denunciations of large corporations with equally fervent condemnations of socialism and violence-prone radicalism. He also continued to fear that class politics might undermine the American republic, just as such politics had wrecked the Roman Republic and successive governments in France between 1789 and 1871. Roosevelt repeatedly argued, as he did in October 1907, "that constructive change offers the best method of avoiding destructive change; that reform is the antidote to revolution; and that social reform is not the precursor but the preventive of Socialism." What disappointed him most was that those whom he intended to protect and benefit did not appreciate his purposes. Attacks by business spokesmen and the Republican Old Guard infuriated Roosevelt because he believed he was saving them from radicalism and destruction. The beginning of 1908 witnessed a sharp escalation in the frequency and fervor of his verbal assaults on "predatory wealth" and in his advocacy of governmental intervention in the economy. His tone and tactics often resembled those of a spurned lover intent on vengeance.[7]

The behavior of the Republican party in 1908 brought Roosevelt further distress. Aside from Taft's nomination—his only party success that year—the convention, platform, and vice-presidential nomination all revealed undiminished control by the Old Guard. Meanwhile the progressives grew increasingly restive as they became a stronger minority within the party. "My business was to take hold of the conservative party and turn it into what it had been under Lincoln," Roosevelt told a British journalist in November 1908, "that is, a party of *progressive* conservatism, or conservative radicalism." Plainly, he had come nowhere near doing that. Later Roosevelt scorned Taft for destroying his handiwork of a united party responsive to popular discontent over issues related to big business. Both at the time and afterward it seemed unfair for him to condemn his neophyte successor for failing at a task that would have taxed his own far greater political skill, resource, and experience, particularly in view of the dissidents' growing strength and restiveness. Roosevelt's unfairness cut even deeper; he blamed Taft for failing at a task at which he had already failed himself.[8]

Roosevelt's failure sprang from several sources. His divided concept of leadership hurt his performance. As long as he worked within the Republican party as a professional politician and behind-the-scenes manipulator, he had to cooperate to a large extent with the Old Guard and their business allies. When Roosevelt boasted, as he did after the 1904 election, that he had rescued his party from plutocracy, he did worse than delude himself. During the 1904 campaign, reports of the success of his Democratic opponent Parker in raising funds from wealthy contributors had rattled him, and he had authorized the Republican national chairman to put the bite on Wall Street for even bigger donations. Roosevelt could hardly break the grip of big businessmen on his party while he feasted at their table. His renunciation of another term in 1908 also hurt the party. Arranging the alliance between the Republican Old Guard and the dominant segments of the business community had taken a generation of effort by such men as Blaine, McKinley, and Hanna, and the union had been consummated under fire in the 1896 campaign. Roosevelt could not have undone or transformed that alliance in four or eight years as president. In 1912 he did come surprisingly close to wresting control of the party from the Old Guard–big business axis. If he had stayed in the White House after 1908 he might have come closer still.

But liberating the Republicans from Old Guard control would not have spelled success at Roosevelt's larger task of averting class division. His greatest failure as president lay in his attempt to get the people to avoid class politics and rise above material concerns. In those exhortations he faced a well-nigh insuperable difficulty. Political divisions in all modern democracies have tended to focus on material interests. Since the 1830s, economic interests had spawned the most salient issues in American politics, with the partial exception of the Civil War era. When Roosevelt held up an idealized conception of Civil War nationalism as his political standard, he was exalting an anomalous experience. Moreover, the 1896 election had reconfirmed the primacy of economic concerns. The followings of all the major factions during his presidency—Old Guard and dissident Republicans and state-rights and Bryanite Democrats—were clustered around the three economic concerns that had emerged as dominant issues in the 1890s: the tariff, currency, and corporate regulation. In decrying materialism, Roosevelt was swimming against the strongest tide in American politics.

Roosevelt's exhortation to a nationalism that transcended parochial interests formed his most significant political contribution and ensured his ultimate failure. His antimaterialist viewpoint placed him in a long tradition of western political thinkers who have regarded public good as higher than and separable from individual, private ends. Fittingly, Roosevelt's other political hero, after Lincoln, was Alexander Hamilton. He had long praised Hamilton for preaching a positive, expansive attitude toward national power; conversely, he had also long denigrated Jefferson for preaching the opposite attitude. Yet Roosevelt's affinity for Hamilton drew upon a deeper congruence. Cecilia Kenyon has argued that Hamilton and Jefferson differed fundamentally in their conceptions of the relations between private and public good. In Kenyon's view, Jefferson believed that people freely pursuing their interests would produce public good; Hamilton did not. Rather, Hamilton hatched plans for directing and harnessing people's private, selfish ends to a larger national interest. "It was Hamilton who was the greater idealist," observes Kenyon, "Jefferson the greater realist." Whether or not this view of Hamilton and Jefferson is correct, it comprehends the essence of Roosevelt's attraction to one and repulsion from the other. By these lights, Roosevelt preached Hamiltonian idealism as heroic and uplifting and scorned Jeffersonian realism as narrow and base.[9]

Idealistic nationalism furnished Roosevelt with the perspective from which he criticized the tendency of democratic politics to degenerate into a welter of special interests and short-sighted squabbles. He anticipated much of the debate that has recurred several times in the United States during the twentieth century over how to assure and sustain a sense of national purpose. Although Roosevelt started from an aristocratic viewpoint, he accepted broad popular participation in politics. "There have been aristocracies which have played a great and beneficent part at stages in the growth of mankind," he wrote in his autobiography; "but we had come to the stage where for our people what was needed was a real democracy; and of all forms of tyranny the least attractive and most vulgar is the tyranny of mere wealth, the tyranny of a plutocracy." The problem for Roosevelt was how to preserve the advantages of aristocracy—service, devotion, courage—while extending popular participation. He admitted in 1908 that "the aristocrat type . . . is hopelessly out of place in this country. But there is every reason why we should be gentlemen democrats."[10]

Roosevelt faced the same problem as Hamilton. He sought to pursue an overarching national purpose in a political environment that was inhospitable to aristocratic service. Hamilton's undoing, Roosevelt believed, had sprung from his attempt to promote the national purpose by harnessing it to the interests of a single class. Writing in 1906 to F. S. Oliver, an admiring biographer of Hamilton, Roosevelt criticized their mutual hero not only because he had distrusted the common people's ability to pursue higher goals but also because he was not a politician. Far from being a virtue, "among free peoples, . . . it is only in very exceptional circumstances that a statesman can be efficient, can be of use to the country unless he is also (not as a substitute, but in addition) a politician." Roosevelt believed that political skill and acceptance of popular participation had made Lincoln great. He followed the same course by trying to combine his twin roles of agitator and professional politician. On the one hand, he used his "bully pulpit" to exhort people to pursue such noble ends as social harmony and national greatness. Roosevelt acted like a preacher in the political realm by exhorting people to save themselves by rising above worldly interests. On the other hand, he worked with regular politicians who sought to serve selfish interests. He was fighting fire with fire, and the saint found that he enjoyed the heat as much as the sinners.[11]

In the end, however, Roosevelt's effort foundered on the same rock as he believed Hamilton's had. Means undid ends for him, too. His exhortations elevated the tone of political discourse, but they were as foredoomed as any evangelist's call for permanent renunciation of self-interest. Roosevelt suffered particularly from the absence of a major external threat or crisis—he lacked what Lincoln had had. Try as he might, Roosevelt could not make exhortation an adequate substitute for crisis. He fared little better on his tack as a professional politician. Although he had gained important specific victories, he won on terms other than his own. Instead of leading the nation away from the path of self-interest in his promotion of domestic reforms, Roosevelt abetted the clash of opposing interests. Republican dissidents warmed to him, not because they shared his larger nationalist vision, but because they thought he was championing their views. One of Roosevelt's main reasons for subsequently deciding to cast his lot with the dissidents was to restrain them from creating destructive class divisions and to redirect them toward serving what he saw as a higher national good. He succeeded even less in that endeavor than he had with the Old Guard.

Roosevelt did not have a tragic presidency. His earlier successes overshadowed and practically concealed his later failures. By less demanding political standards than his own, he succeeded admirably. He named his successor and saw him into office, and he left the presidency with his popularity intact. Clearly, he would be a potent political force in the future, no matter what he did. But Roosevelt's latter-day failures in the White House set the stage for still greater disappointments after he left. Several friends noted that when he returned from his long safari in Africa and tour of Europe in 1910, he seemed changed. He was more restless, more reckless, less patient with compromise. They attributed the change to his long solitude in the African bush, which had given him a chance to brood and reflect. In a way, Roosevelt was repeating his experience of twenty-five years before, when he had retreated to the ranch to assuage his sorrow and regain his political bearings. That earlier experience had hardened his commitment to professional politics. Now, however, as he dwelt on his renunciation of power and what he regarded as missed opportunities, he leaned the other way. "Of course a man has to take advantage of his opportunities," Roosevelt observed in a speech in England in May 1910; "but the opportunities have to come. If there is not the war, you don't get the great general; if there is not the great occasion, you don't get the great statesman; if Lincoln had lived in times of peace, no one would have known his name now."[12]

Some of his closest associates, including his son-in-law Nicholas Longworth, as well as Lodge and Taft, felt a sense of foreboding when Roosevelt returned to the United States in June 1910. He soon justified their uneasiness. The tumultuous public welcome when he landed in New York barely hid his silence about his party and his successor. He closed an oddly muted speech at the welcoming ceremonies by depicting himself as one who hoped "that the American people may never have cause to feel regret that once they placed him at their head." Theodore Roosevelt had come home in a troubled frame of mind. He was about to trade a year's safari in the physical wilderness of Africa for nine years of wandering in the political wilderness of America, wanderings that would consume the rest of his life.[13]

· 9 ·

Spokesman and Critic

IN 1910 WOODROW WILSON was also about to change his environment, from academic life to politics. Plans to gain him the Democratic nomination for governor of New Jersey started to come to fruition in June of that year. After meeting several times with the party's bosses, he issued a public statement in July acknowledging that if the Democrats wanted him to run, "I should deem it my duty, as well as an honor and a privilege, to do so." Privately, he explained to a Princeton trustee, "In view of what I have all my life taught in my classes of the duty of political service on the part of trained men, it would be very awkward to decline if the nomination should come to me unsought and unanimously in September." But Wilson did not go straight from the classroom to the campaign trail. His years as a university president had several profound effects on his thinking and actions. Without that public exposure, it seems doubtful that Wilson would have had either the inclination or the opportunity to enter politics. The Princeton presidency offered him a chance to exercise authority and test his aptitude for leadership and a platform from which to try the kind of parapolitical career he had envisioned when he had first chosen academic life.[1]

Wilson did not rush into commenting on current affairs or expressing personal commitments. During his first two years as president of Princeton, in his relatively infrequent remarks about then-current issues he stuck to mild expressions of sympathy for the farmers and stronger endorsements of colonial expansion and a larger world role. In the wake of the Panama affair he scoffed at "the anti-imperialist weepings and wailings that came out of Boston." In those views he remained close to his acquaintance in the White House. Wilson's politics took a dramatic new turn, however, immediately after the 1904 election. Speaking to a group of expatriate Virginians in New York in November, he urged them to help rejuvenate the Democratic party by repudiating "populists and radical theorists, contemptuous alike of principle and of experience" and by reasserting the "practices of the historic party," by which he meant reaffirming state rights and limited government. Wilson warned that the country, "as it moves forward in its great material progress, needs and will tolerate no party of discontent or radical experiment; but it does need a party of conservative reform acting in the spirit of law and of ancient institutions." The speech marked his debut as a political spokesman. A leading Democratic newspaper and some Bryanite stalwarts publicly scorned Wilson's arguments, thereby launching him as a recognized spokesman for the party's anti-Bryan wing.[2]

During the next three years Wilson capitalized on that role. He stepped up his noneducational speaking engagements and political comments. "We can't abolish the trusts," he declared in February 1905. "We must moralize them." A month later he praised Tammany Hall, the New York Democratic machine, for its effectiveness and good intentions. In 1906 Wilson made his first appearance at a party function, to deliver the Jefferson Day speech to a group of Tammany allies in New York. Instead of new laws, he called for "a new spirit in the enforcement of existing laws, an enlightened and purified intention." Americans must reject socialism and centralized government while preserving local and state powers, and law must not "take sides in the struggle between capital and labour." Later in 1906 Wilson took swipes at Roosevelt's antitrust prosecutions, and early in 1907 he denounced Republican tariff policies as a form of special privilege, though one that must be eliminated gradually and cautiously. In April 1907 he privately avowed, "Would that we could do something, at once dignified and effective, to knock Mr. Bryan once for all into a cocked hat!" The following August Wilson wrote for possible use by the New York *Sun*, "A Credo," in which he denounced Roosevelt's regulatory proposals for "attempting what government is not fitted to do" and for promoting "paternalism." Instead, Americans must cleave to the Constitution's guarantee of "that most precious of all the possessions of a free people, the right of freedom of contract."[3]

Wilson's espousal of the anti-Bryan Democrats' cause won him backing as well as attention. A number of Wall Street financiers and politicians who were unhappy with the ascendancy of Bryanites in the party began touting him as a presidential possibility. So did several editors, including Henry Watterson of the Louisville *Courier-Journal*, William M. Laffan of the New York *Sun*, and, most important, George B. M. Harvey of *Harper's Weekly*. Harvey had long harbored kingmaking ambitions in both his adopted state of New Jersey and the national Democratic party, and he had reportedly kept his eye on Wilson ever since his 1896 Princeton bicentennial address. After hearing another speech by Wilson early in 1906, Harvey started running at the top of the cover of each issue of *Harper's Weekly* the slogan "For President—Woodrow Wilson." Behind the scenes Harvey exerted himself in New Jersey for Wilson to receive the Democratic minority's nomination in the legislature for senator in 1906 and to be considered as a vice-presidential possibility at the 1908 Democratic convention. Harvey's biggest contribution came through his efforts to interest the New Jersey Democratic bosses in Wilson for governor in 1910. In January of that year Harvey evidently got the support of former Senator James Smith, Jr., the state party's leading figure, and by June arrangements for the nomination were virtually complete. By playing the anti-Bryan card, Wilson had come up with a winning hand.[4]

In other ways, however, his fling with Bryan's opponents served him badly. Wilson's gubernatorial campaign quickly showed how far he had strayed from the conservatives' views after 1907. His subsequent breaks with Smith after being elected governor and with Harvey and Watterson during his quest for the Democratic presidential nomination exposed him to repeated charges of ingratitude. Worse, his rapid conversion to advocacy of progressive measures of increased governmental intervention in the economy raised doubts about his political constancy and provided critics with grounds for questioning his sincerity. Interpretations of his political career have questioned when, how, and why he renounced his advocacy of state rights and limited government. These concerns have been well taken, since progressivism provided the vehicle for Wilson's political career. Yet the forms of the questions about his changing political stands have nearly always been misleading. Contrary to most accounts, Wilson was not a long-standing conservative who gradually converted to progressivism. Rather, he was a detached observer who, when he was nearly fifty, made his first foray into political engagement on behalf of conservative views. He dropped those views with almost unseemly haste during a single year and then set out boldly on the opposite tack.

For Wilson, the main attraction of conservative, limited-government views was their expediency. Three considerations made it expedient for him to join the anti-Bryan Democrats after 1904. First, as president of a socially prestigious private university that was dependent upon the generosity of wealthy businessmen, he may have been adapting to his environment. Appropriately, his engagement with the anti-Bryanites lasted only a short time after his halcyon days at Princeton, withering during the conflicts over the quad plan and the graduate college. The second attraction to conservative views lay in political opportunity. Having remained a Democrat, Wilson recognized that Parker's defeat left the conservative standard up for grabs in the face of a likely Bryanite resurgence. Whatever the long-run drawbacks, his championing of the opposition to Bryan showed he could calculate immediate political advantages and waste no time in seizing them. Finally, Wilson warmed to limited-government views because of his previous attitude of political detachment. Nothing in his permissiveness about allowable governmental activities required him to believe in the necessity or desirability of bold measures to attack private wealth or promote social welfare. In that approach, Wilson resembled Oliver Wendell Holmes, Jr., who likewise had no use for political absolutism but who opposed most forms of economic and social intervention by the government as either unworkable or illusory. Even at the height of his flirtation with the anti-Bryan Democrats, Wilson usually took care to separate himself from doctrinaire advocates of constitutional limitation and governmental non-intervention.[5]

But activism on the right wing of the Democratic party did not sit comfortably with Wilson, particularly because of the intellectual company he found himself in. His newfound cohorts made a fetish of obeisance to Thomas Jefferson as the prophet of supposedly immutable principles of state rights and minimal government. Never having liked Jefferson as a thinker, Wilson tried to avoid kneeling at his factional shrine. When he gave his Jefferson Day speech in 1906, he produced two different versions. In the written text Wilson noted that Jefferson's pronouncements on limited government belonged to "a time which was without railways and telegraph lines" and involved arrangements which "do not now concern us." When he delivered the speech, however, he repeatedly invoked "the spirit of Jefferson" to tell his listeners what they wanted to hear about resisting regulation and centralization. Wilson's difficulty went further than ambivalence about Jefferson. In March and April 1907, when he delivered the lectures that became *Constitutional Government,* he betrayed conflicting attitudes. On the one hand, he again scorned what he called the "Whig theory" of government—his label for old-fashioned thinking about constitutional absolutism and mechanistic separation of powers. He invoked Burke to declare, "Government is a part of life, and, with life, it must change, alike in its objects and its practices; only this principle must remain unaltered,—this principle of liberty, that there must be the freest right of opportunity and adjustment." On the other hand, he condemned new regulatory proposals and greater centralization, on the somewhat strained ground that they were not expedient.[6]

Wilson's personal and intellectual values also underlay his initial difficulty with the conservative Democrats. Because he lacked what his new party comrades regarded as Jeffersonian absolutism, as well as Holmes's extreme relativism, he had no basis for sustaining the kind of political stance required by allegiance to the anti-Bryan Democrats. Political advocacy confronted Wilson with the novel problem, for him, of reconciling his personal beliefs and ideals with intellectual analysis. A less committed intellectual might have felt tempted to forsake his detached, relativistic view of politics. Wilson seemed to do that once or twice, as in his 1907 "Credo." A more ardent believer might have sought a larger cause that would embrace both conviction and intellect. Roosevelt did that to an extent with his nationalism, and in their different ways Bryan and La Follette made their progressivism serve such a function. Instead, Wilson tried to blend his undogmatic, tolerant Christian faith with his unblinking political mind. As a result, his thinking became fuzzier and more complicated than before.

In a speech early in 1909 Wilson used a sailing analogy to explain his synthesis of principle and expediency. "Because, although you steer by the North Star, when you have lost the bearings of your compass," Wilson asserted, "you nevertheless steer a pathway on the sea—you are not bound for the North Star." Wilson's principles, derived from his religious faith, were his North Star, which pointed him in a general direction. Expediency, the actual sailing on the sea, required dealing with winds, tides, currents, obstacles, crew, and other vessels in following the course set by principle. In contrast to his earlier easygoing acceptance of expediency, however, he began after 1907 to praise those who stood up for principle against majority opinion and took lonely stands of conscience. He did not make such figures his political models, but he valued and admired them more.[7]

Wilson arrived at those perceptions and sympathies only after working his way through a conservative advocacy of limited government. The actual steps he took in forsaking his anti-Bryanite allegiance are not entirely clear. Social sympathies played a part. Wilson grew disenchanted with the rich during the Princeton conflicts, and in *Constitutional Government* he expressed a deep feeling for the farmers and small-town people of the South and West. Although he had been born and raised in the South, Wilson did not have the same grounding in the interests of the "plain people" of the hinterlands as Bryan or La Follette. But neither did he have the same allegiance to the northeastern financial and social upper crust as his wealthy patrons or, with a different thrust, Roosevelt. Although he could appreciate both sides, Wilson liked the outsiders more. Intellectual inclinations also played a part in weaning him from limited-government advocacy. The author of *Constitutional Government* could not help but recognize the disparity between scorn for the "Whig theory" of government and finickiness about new measures of economic intervention and regulation. In May 1908, two months after he revised the lectures for publication, his Princeton departmental colleagues held a debate on Roosevelt's policies. Although Wilson attacked the president, two-thirds of his colleagues, including nearly all the men he liked and respected most, took the other side. Moreover, in Wilson's words, "A young man named Corwin got up and wiped the floor with me." Corwin recalled "the evident pleasure that Mr. Wilson was taking in my performance." Actually, Wilson seldom enjoyed a challenge to something he really believed in. His speeches and writings in 1908 were about to show that he had begun to renounce conservative state-rights Democracy.[8]

Wilson may also have forsaken the anti-Bryanite viewpoint because it was unsuited to his temperament. He could not adapt his dynamic, assertive personality to the passive, negative political role exalted by the state-rights Democrats. In his approval of a more assertive foreign policy, Wilson had already shown an inclination toward governmental activism. In view of Wilson's previous political stances, he might logically have moved, as Roosevelt did, from assertive foreign policy to endorsement of domestic reform to serve larger national purposes. But more than chance intervened to divert Wilson temporarily down the byroad of state rights and limited government. His political thought, unlike Roosevelt's, had begun with an implicit acceptance of individual self-interest and had long included the assumption that governments produced public good by enhancing such interests.

The dalliance with limited-government views had an important lasting effect on Wilson's thought. In place of an earlier statist emphasis, his utterances now stressed the individual more. At the outset of *Constitutional Government* he asserted, "The individual is indisputably the original, the first fact of liberty. Nations are made up of individuals, and the dealings of government with individuals are the ultimate and perfect test of its constitutional character . . . Liberty belongs to the individual, or it does not exist." This new individualistic stress did not supplant Wilson's earlier affirmation of the value and scope of government, but it did create a tension in his thinking that pushed his views in different directions. Self-interest likewise appeared in a new light. His approval of private wealth and his advocacy of governmental neutrality toward capital and labor, though short-lived, introduced a novel emphasis on promoting social good through economic competition. "There is nothing evil in struggle itself," Wilson declared in his Jefferson Day speech of 1906. "The best service you can render me if I want something from you and you want something from me, is to lay your mind squarely alongside mine and let each one of us determine his muscle and his virtue in the contest." Wilson did not completely accept the proposition that the clash of competing interests in itself produced public good, and he continued to hold out visions of disinterested service. But he was moving in the direction of viewing conflicting interests as dynamic and potentially beneficient.[9]

The clearest proof of Wilson's incompatibility with limited-government views came in the ease and speed with which he dropped them. Because he did not immediately endorse specific measures, his switch to advocating governmental intervention in the economy struck some observers then and interpreters later as slow, even reluctant. His reluctance to get down to specifics masked his swift, total conversion to acceptance of governmental intervention and to suspicion of big-business influences. Early in 1908, while still condemning excessive regulation, Wilson arraigned the big financial manipulators for their "monopolistic purposes" and chicanery in securities dealings. At the end of September 1908, he carried the arraignment further by warning a bankers' convention, "There is a general feeling in this country that there is a difference between the general interest and the interests recognized by those who handle capital." If they wanted to avoid socialism, they could do so only "by proposing a better program. It is a case—in the vulgar—of 'put up or shut up.' " Nine days later Wilson asserted, "The present conflict in this country is not between capital and labor. It is a contest between those few men in whose hands the wealth of the land is concentrated, and the rest of us." Although he still warned against going too far, he affirmed, "I believe in governmental regulation."[10]

Wilson's general statements were more important than his specific caution. "You cannot make progress unless you know whither you are bound," he remarked in November 1909 on the relation between principle and expediency. "The question is not of pace. That is a matter of expediency, not of direction; that is not a matter of principle." By the latter part of 1908 he had reset his general course in the direction of increased governmental intervention and regulation. The particulars of which measures to espouse and when would follow in response to circumstances. The same considerations of principle, temperament, and social and intellectual sympathy that drove him away from limited-government views impelled him toward the opposite persuasion. In view of both the speed of his conversion and the relish with which he embraced his new viewpoint, temperament probably weighed most heavily. In addition, as Arthur Link has pointed out, calculations of personal advantage like those that had earlier attracted Wilson to the anti-Bryanite Democrats now impelled him toward the other camp. It had become clear by 1908 that the progressives were gaining strength in both parties, especially among the Democrats. "A politician, a man engaged in party contests, must be an opportunist," Wilson remarked in a speech in November 1907. ". . . If you want to win in party action, I take it for granted you want to lure the majority to your side. I never heard of any man in his senses who was fishing for a minority." By switching to the progressive side, he could follow his conscience and temperament as well as fish in majority waters.[11]

For the next two years, until his entry into active politics in 1910, Wilson managed to voice his new convictions without alienating his anti-Bryanite backers. How much deliberate thought he gave to retaining the support of such men as Harvey is not known, but he certainly seems to have shown shrewdness in retaining the editor's patronage. Throughout 1909 and the first half of 1910, Wilson steered clear of specific measures except for participation in the "short ballot" movement, a nonpartisan effort to reduce the number of elective offices in states and municipalities. The short ballot idea suited Wilson's old desire to increase political accountability by having voters choose fewer officials. It also offered a safe field for activity outside the main areas of party and factional conflict. Likewise, with Harvey's prompting, Wilson spoke out on the tariff, which was almost the only issue on which Bryanite Democrats and their party opponents still agreed. The Republicans also obligingly dramatized the tariff issue in the spring and summer of 1909 when Senator Nelson W. Aldrich of Rhode Island and his Old Guard cronies gutted President Taft's attempt at tariff revision. While writing an attack on the Republican tariff fiasco for one of Harvey's magazines, Wilson confessed, "I want to hit hard, and if I observe the rules of the game I hope I may be forgiven the zest and enjoyment with which I hit . . . This is what I was meant for, anyhow, this rough and tumble of the political arena."[12]

Wilson did not trim much in deference to his conservative sponsors. He continued to avoid genuflections toward Jeffersonian dogmas, and he based his criticism of the Republican tariff on approval of what he identified as true Hamiltonian protectionism, which was designed to benefit the entire nation, not special interests, as he charged Aldrich and the Republicans with doing. Wilson suggested that tariff reform be based upon the "old principle of Hamilton, in a new form and application," to be instituted through flexible, frequent revisions of the tariff in light of changing economic circumstances. That brush with ideological heresy disclosed the main thrust of Wilson's message to his fellow Democrats. Earlier, in December 1908, he had charged that the party's "old formula 'tariff for revenue only' has a barren sound in existing circumstances," because of its irrelevance to present reality. "What we want is not a set of issues which will sound like echoes of circumstances which no longer exist, but a set of issues arising out of and intended for the present." In 1909 and the first half of 1910 Wilson delivered the message repeatedly and with increasing sharpness— the Democrats and the country must discard old thinking and adapt to new conditions—and he invoked his organic conception of politics to justify that message. "We shall not live by recollection," he declared in February 1909, "we shall not live by trying to recall the strength of old tissue, but by producing new tissue." In March 1910 he urged New Jersey Democrats to cease to be "old men looking over our shoulders" and become "men of our own day, looking forward, looking about us, studying the needs and circumstances of the nation as a whole, and seeking an opportunity to make our counsels heard in the affairs of the country we love."[13]

If they paid much attention to his utterances, Wilson's anti-Bryanite backers probably found them diverting generalities but put little practical stock in them. They were mistaken, as they sooner or later discovered. Despite his lack of specifics on most issues, Wilson did not hide his belief that the Democrats' new thinking must move along lines favored by the Bryanites and dissident midwestern and western Republicans, who had now become party insurgents against the Old Guard and President Taft. Several times in 1909 he again lambasted the "Whig theory" of government and offered the organic metaphor as an alternative. Stating at one point that life was "a process of renewal," he asked, "and where does the new tissue of a nation come from? Does it come from above? Not at all. It comes from below. All the renewal of a nation comes out of the general mass of its people." In January 1910 he once more chided a gathering of bankers for their provinciality in neglecting the needs and initiative of the mass of people outside of the northeastern cities. In April 1910 he drafted a platform for the progressive faction of Pennsylvania Democrats in which he condemned the Republican tariff as "a means of patronage" and called for strengthening the antitrust laws and passing new conservation measures.[14]

On the eve of announcing his candidacy for governor, Wilson gave particularly strong indications of his latest views. Toward the end of May 1910 he confided to a former student that he shared "your views about the too narrow interpretation of the restrictions of the Constitution. I think that it is possible for the Democratic party really to disqualify itself from modern service by insisting too pedantically upon those restrictions." Two weeks earlier he had pointed the direction he wanted such "modern service" to take. "The future of this country does not rest with established successes," he informed another group of bankers, and he asked, "Are you seeing to it that the energy of this country is renewed from generation to generation—is refreshed with those bold individuals here and there who venture upon novel enterprises, who show courage and initiative in novel fields?" Those two themes—new governmental powers and renewal from the common ranks of society—formed the core of Wilson's new political position. With adaptations to changing situations, that viewpoint was the foundation of his career for the next ten years.[15]

Wilson's entry into politics involved more than a controversial college president getting a shot at the governorship of a middling state. The gubernatorial nomination, he told a Princeton friend after one of his meetings with Harvey and the New Jersey bosses in June 1910, "is the mere preliminary of a plan to nominate me in 1912 for the presidency." All his backers were predicting such an easy, overwhelming victory in New Jersey "that my chances for the presidential nomination would in such circumstances be better than those of any other man." That talk contained a lot of daydreaming. Many things could happen on the road to the governor's office and the White House. But the thinking behind those predictions was well founded. Everyone involved knew that a career of national significance was being launched. Woodrow Wilson was embarking on an adventure that would consume the rest of his life and have a major impact on the United States and the world.[16]

· 10 ·

Adversaries

ROOSEVELT AND WILSON continued to admire each other through Roosevelt's first term in office. The president commended one of Wilson's published speeches in 1902 as a "really notable address . . . As a decent American I want to thank you for it." The Princeton president not only upheld their common allegiance to an assertive foreign policy, he also praised Roosevelt again for making himself too big for the politicians to ignore. "The politicians said to themselves," Wilson declared in 1903, "the only way we can quiet this man is by putting him in one of the highest offices and seeing what he can do." Bad luck dogged their efforts to get together. A carriage accident kept Roosevelt from attending Wilson's inauguration at Princeton, and family illnesses prevented Wilson from accepting invitations to the White House. Finally, in December 1905, when the Army-Navy football game was played at Princeton, the Wilsons entertained the presidential party at lunch, and the two men attended the game together. At halftime they walked across the field, one faculty member recalled, "Roosevelt exuberant, smiling, delighted, waving his hat, acknowledging the plaudits of the multitude and tugging along the dignified University president who followed 'with conscious step of purity and pride,' if not reluctant, at least not equally ebullient." Unfortunately, no photograph of the event has survived. It was the second and last time that the two men appeared together in public. It was also the climax of their mutual admiration.[1]

Wilson moved first in ending the good feelings between them. In his new role as an anti-Bryan Democratic spokesman after 1904, he attacked Roosevelt and the Republican dissidents as well as the Bryanites of his own party. Publicly, Wilson muted his criticism of the president for a while. In March 1906 he asserted, "We hurry and rush and live a strenuous life, and at the end of it we see many things done, but nothing finished." An acquaintance remembered Wilson saying privately during the summer of 1906 "with a smile that he found it difficult to admire the politician as much as the man." As he got more involved in politics, his attacks sharpened. In August 1907, in his "Credo," Wilson told the president to stay in his constitutional place and let the courts and Congress exercise their powers "without suspicion of undue or covert executive influence." In a newspaper interview the following November, Wilson commented, "I have not seen much of Mr. Roosevelt since he became President, but I am told he no sooner thinks than he talks, which is a miracle not wholly in accord with an educational theory of forming an opinion." He also described a British cartoon he had seen about Roosevelt's crusade to reform spelling, showing the president using a small hatchet to nick a huge tree representing the English language, while Uncle Sam sighed, "Ah well, boys will be boys!" Wilson added, "It hit the nail on the head."[2]

Never one to duck a fight, Roosevelt responded in kind to Wilson's criticisms. Presidential dignity and his attacker's still-slight political stature precluded public replies. Privately, however, he lashed out at Wilson. In December 1907 Roosevelt praised his friend Wister for a speech in which he had condemned the teaching in most American colleges. Lumping Wilson with William Graham Sumner, the noted economist and Yale professor, he asserted, "I do not feel that Sumner and Wilson have any real place in the study of economics and government." In August 1908 Roosevelt thanked the magazine editor Lyman Abbott for sending him a passage from Wilson's *Constitutional Government*. "That is a great quotation from Woodrow Wilson," Roosevelt commented. "I had not read the book because I have felt rather impatient with his recent attitude on certain matters, notably the effort to control corporations; but this is a really first-class paragraph." Shortly afterward, in November or December 1908, Cleveland H. Dodge, who was Wilson's closest friend and strongest supporter among the Princeton trustees and an old friend of Roosevelt's, had lunch at the White House with the president. "Theodore told us how much he

admired you, your writings your ability &c," Dodge recounted to
Wilson. " '*But* I cannot say that I like his political utterances.' "
Those mixed views in 1908 conveyed the last even partially favorable judgment that Roosevelt uttered about Wilson, and it was
fitting that he ended on a note of political opposition. By the time
he left the White House in 1909, politics had opened a permanent
breach between the two men.[3]

Their mutual estrangement contained a mixture of accuracy and
irony. In his criticisms in 1906 and 1907, Wilson showed less perception about Roosevelt than when he had lauded him earlier as a
public force apart from the professional political organizations. His
dismissal of the president's juvenility and impulsiveness related
more to appearance than reality. Appropriately, as he abandoned
his advocacy of limited government, Wilson started to praise
Roosevelt again, usually obliquely, but with his old insight. On two
occasions in March 1909, he complimented the ex-president publicly. At first Wilson praised Roosevelt backhandedly for having
kept "us all at white heat" and for having taken Americans through
a "process of awakening," which must now give way to constructive
work "without any more fuss, and without any more rhetoric." A
few days later, however, he lauded Roosevelt unreservedly for
having understood "the foreign relations of the country as few
others do." In January 1910 he called Roosevelt "the most formidable president we have recently had" because he had conducted
so much important political business publicly. Writing another
article for one of Harvey's magazines in March 1910, Wilson recalled "how seasoned politicians shivered when he [Roosevelt]
spoke in public" because of what he might divulge. "He may have
chosen and chosen very astutely which confidences to keep, which
to break," Wilson surmised, but Roosevelt had basked in popular
favor because he had grasped the widespread distrust "of the managing politicians."[4]

It was a shame that Roosevelt was out of the country and most
likely never learned about Wilson's changed attitude toward him.
But even if he had, he might not have changed his opinion of his
erstwhile critic. The readiness and vehemence with which Roosevelt dismissed Wilson suggested that his regard for his one-time
professorial admirer had been fragile and had depended upon unbroken praise from him. His linking of Wilson with Sumner was

revealing. It betokened not only the ready damnation Roosevelt visited upon academic critics as impractical mugwumps but also the depth of his convictions about his own approach to politics. Roosevelt had once privately characterized William Graham Sumner as "a college professor, a cold-blooded creature of a good deal of intellect, but lacking the fighting virtues and all wide patriotism." Such men had the worst of both worlds, being nearly "as wrong on public questions as any Tammany alderman" and "quite unable even to understand the lofty ambition which, for instance, makes you desire to treat the tariff as something neither good nor bad in itself." That characterization stemmed from Roosevelt's rejection of materialism and self-interest, on which he based his whole approach to politics. By lumping Wilson with Sumner, Roosevelt cast him into the outer darkness of unheroic thinkers who were totally wrong and pernicious in their influence.[5]

Roosevelt differed from Wilson in having an ability to combine incisiveness with unfairness. During the next ten years, as their rivalry grew and their ambitions clashed over an ever-widening field, Roosevelt frequently showed wisdom in his malice toward his adversary, as in his comparison of Wilson with Sumner. That judgment also opened the line of criticism that was leveled against Wilson long after both men died. The insight in the comparison lay in Roosevelt's perception that Sumner and Wilson shared a detachment and an appreciation of material interests. Although the Yale professor advocated the least possible governmental intervention in social and economic life, he based his arguments on a grim reckoning of human nature that resembled Holmes's viewpoint. Further, Sumner appeared to uphold the pursuit of material self-interest to the virtual exclusion of all other social and political aims. He differed from Wilson mainly in being more consistent in these views and pushing them to logical extremes. Roosevelt was right to detect the underlying resemblance and thereby to suspect that Wilson was not his kind of idealist.

Ironically, however, the thrust of that criticism led to the most common charge against Wilson—that he was an "idealist" in the pejorative sense of an impractical dreamer who could not adjust to reality. Although Roosevelt originated the allegation of impracticality and leveled it ceaselessly in later years, nothing infuriated him more than hearing Wilson called an idealist. There was poetic justice in his discomfort, because he showed his greatest unfairness in attempting to fix the impractical, mugwump stereotype on Wilson. In so doing, Roosevelt willfully refused to recognize the areas of agreement and similarity between them.

Both men were not only political intellectuals but also variations on the same type of intellectual. Both men were artists of power. The difference between them as political intellectuals resembled the Apollonian and Dionysian syntheses of emotional and rational elements in art. Roosevelt, the Dionysian artist, favored the primacy of emotion. Wilson was the Apollonian, favoring the primacy of reason. It was an important difference, but essentially one of emphasis within a common framework.

Their divergence over ideals and self-interest in politics did not make them opposites, either. Roosevelt recognized that people usually follow their interests, and he repeatedly acknowledged that men must provide for their families' material welfare before they can pursue higher aims. For his part, Wilson did not stress material interests to the exclusion of ideals. "This is the one country which has founded its polity upon dreams," he declared in November 1907 in a speech extolling disinterestedness. In answer to Thomas Carlyle's renowned crack about how to make an honest nation out of a multitude of rogues, he asserted that the way to do it "is by making the most of the rogues not interested in the particular transaction that made the others dishonest." Class politics and clashing interests also troubled Wilson. "For the things that perplex us at this moment," he stated in February 1909, "are the things which mark, I will not say a warfare, but a division among classes; and when a nation begins to be divided into rival and contestant interests by the score, the time is much more dangerous than when it is divided into only two perfectly distinguished interests which you can discriminate and deal with."[6]

On other matters the two men continued to see nearly eye to eye. Lyman Abbott's letter has not survived to disclose which passage in *Constitutional Government* delighted Roosevelt, but he would have relished much of the book, particularly its treatment of the presidency. As early as 1899 Wilson had disavowed the assessment in *Congressional Government* of the primacy of Congress, and he had argued that the new importance of foreign affairs was shifting the balance of power in favor of the president. "He has become the leader of his party and the guide of the nation in political purpose, and therefore in legal action," Wilson asserted in *Constitutional Government.* In line with both his concern over the diffusion of power and his organic perspective, Wilson depicted the presidency "as the unifying force of our complex system," in constructive defiance of "a very mechanical theory of its meaning and intentions." He also exalted the president's party leadership. "There is no national party choice except that of President," he wrote. "No one else represents the people as a whole, exercising a national choice"; but his leadership sprang less from the party's organization than from his "vital link of connection with the thinking nation. He can dominate his party by being the spokesman for the real sentiment and purposes of the country, by giving direction to opinion." As many interpreters have observed, that analysis offered a forecast of Wilson's presidency. It also implicitly conveyed the finest praise of Roosevelt's presidency. Wilson paid Roosevelt the high compliment of understanding him; he later paid him the still higher one of imitating him.[7]

Wilson's shift to a more interventionist view of government after 1908 brought him back into agreement with Roosevelt on most issues. Although Wilson endorsed few specific measures, the general stand he was taking allowed him to espouse most of what Roosevelt was proposing. Their similarities also included a continuing common admiration for Hamilton. Both men responded enthusiastically to F. S. Oliver's biography, published in 1906. It was in a letter to Oliver that Roosevelt condemned Sumner. In April 1910 Wilson stated in a speech, "One of the most interesting books of recent years is Mr. Oliver's biography of Hamilton; and one of the most interesting passages in that biography is where he points out that no opposition could really defeat Alexander Hamilton, whether he was in office or not, because he alone had a constructive program." That estimate echoed Wilson's praise for Roosevelt; it was too bad the ex-president did not hear it.[8]

By 1910 the pieces were falling into place for conflict between the two men, a conflict defined largely by party circumstances and other people's perceptions of them. In April 1910 Lyman Abbott complimented Wilson on his progressive stance but added, "I am too much of a Hamiltonian to adopt it." Abbott asked whether Wilson had read Herbert Croly's new book, *The Promise of Amer-*

ican Life, which he called "an interesting & valuable application & extension of Hamiltonian principles. I would like to see a new alignment of parties in this new adjustment of the old question between individualism & organization." That remark foreshadowed the terms and some of the supporting cast in the conflict between Roosevelt and Wilson. Abbott was editor of *The Outlook*, the magazine Roosevelt had joined and later used as his journalistic platform. Croly took much of the inspiration for his "Hamiltonian" critique of American politics from Roosevelt, and he also became one of the ex-president's ablest journalistic supporters. It was ironic, in view of Wilson's admiration for Hamilton and his coolness toward Jefferson, that he was being thrown into contrast with Roosevelt and Croly. But, as both sides sensed, differences of substance did separate Roosevelt from Wilson, and the differences were accentuated by the two men's respective partisan situations. Theodore Roosevelt and Woodrow Wilson were entering the field for a duel over the course of national politics.[9]

Illustrations

THE DUDE

Theodore Roosevelt in 1884, a studio photograph taken in New York to promote one of his books.

THE PROFESSOR

Woodrow Wilson, circa 1885, a photograph taken while he was a professor at Bryn Mawr College, his first academic post.

TWO PRESIDENTS

John Singer Sargent painted portraits of Roosevelt and Wilson while each was in the White House. The Roosevelt portrait was painted in 1905, the Wilson one in 1917.

THE LEARNED POLITICIAN

(*Right*) Roosevelt at his favorite pastime of reading, in the doorway of a ranch house in Colorado, April 1905.

(*Below, left*) Roosevelt after receiving one of his many honorary degrees, at the University of Washington, April 1911.

(*Below, right*) Roosevelt addressing a crowd in Nahant, Massachusetts, August 1905. Seated at Roosevelt's right, with his hand to his head, is Henry Cabot Lodge.

THE SCHOLAR IN POLITICS

(*Right*) Wilson in June 1910, while he was still president of Princeton University and shortly before he became a candidate for governor of New Jersey.

(*Below, left*) Wilson receiving the news of his nomination for president, at Sea Girt, New Jersey, July 1912. With him is his secretary, Joseph P. Tumulty.

(*Below, right*) Wilson speaking from the rear platform of his campaign train, Bradford, Ohio, September 1912.

THE COLONEL JUMPED TO HIS FEET. SPEAKING DIRECTLY AT WILSON, HE
RUNNING THE GOVERNMENT. V

A DEBATE THAT NEVER HAPPENED

A doctored photograph, circa June 1911, showing
Roosevelt and Wilson supposedly sharing the same

ED! ABSOLUTELY BULLY! MY DEAR WOODROW, WHILE I AM IN WASHINGTON
AROUND THE COUNTRY RAISING CAIN!"

platform. The two men never engaged in a face-to-face
debate, and no authentic photograph of them together
survives.

TWO CARTOONISTS' VIEWS OF WILSON

"Professor Wilson Visits Congress," by Max Beerbohm, 1914, captures
the apparent contrast between Wilson's academic background and the
less elevated atmosphere of professional politics.

Rollin Kirby of the *New York World* deeply admired Wilson. This 1915
cartoon depicts Wilson's middle course toward World War I, between
William Jennings Bryan's pacifism and Roosevelt's belligerency.

HELPING THE PRESIDENT.

A CARTOONIST'S VIEW OF ROOSEVELT, 1916

Jay Norwood "Ding" Darling of the *Des Moines Register* fervently admired Roosevelt. The cartoon above stresses his dynamism.

This "Ding" cartoon depicts Roosevelt's apparently self-sacrificing aid to the Republicans and their bearded nominee, Charles Evans Hughes.

THE MODEST VIOLET.

ANOTHER POINT OF VIEW

Kirby of the *World* criticized Roosevelt frequently and stingingly. The cartoon above refers to his famed "heroic mood" statement.

HELPING HUGHES.

Here Kirby portrays Roosevelt's self-dramatization on the campaign trail for Hughes.

PEACEMAKING, 1919

Wilson talking with French premier Georges Clemenceau in a Paris courtyard during the peace conference. Standing behind Wilson is Arthur James Balfour, the British foreign secretary; between Wilson and Clemenceau is Admiral Cary T. Grayson, the president's physician; to Clemenceau's left in the straw hat is Ray Stannard Baker, press secretary to the American delegation and later Wilson's official biographer.

· III ·

THE GREAT CAMPAIGN

But I am a radical who most earnestly desires to see the radical programme carried out by conservatives: I wish to see industrial and social reforms of a far-reaching nature accomplished in this country, and I wish to see them accomplished, not under the leadership of those who will materially profit by them . . . I want to see that movement take place under sober responsible men, not under demagogues.

Theodore Roosevelt, December 13, 1910

I tell you, gentleman, that the so-called radicalism of our time is nothing else than an effort to release the energies of our time. This great people is not bent upon any form of destruction. This great people is not in love with any kind of injustice. This great people is in love with the realization of what is equitable, pure, just, and of good repute, and it is bound by the clogs and impediments of our political machinery . . . Our forefathers were not uttering mere words when they spoke of the realization of happiness.

Woodrow Wilson, February 21, 1911

AT ONE POINT WHEN THEY WERE RUNNING against each other for president in 1912, Woodrow Wilson called Theodore Roosevelt "a very, very erratic comet now sweeping across our horizon." The description was apt. Roosevelt's return to the United States in June 1910 had coincided with the appearance of Halley's comet, and the ex-president's political conduct soon fulfilled many people's forebodings. During the summer and fall of 1910 he hit the campaign trail to boost insurgent Republicans, and he staked out bold positions on domestic issues, particularly on the touchy question of the review of legislation by the courts. Although he did not openly criticize his successor, Roosevelt could not conceal the breach between them. President Taft had earlier opposed many of the insurgents whom Roosevelt now supported, and Taft took conflicting stands on such matters as judicial review. After another year of chafing at Taft's weakness and at the widening Republican split, Roosevelt seized command of the insurgents in February 1912 and challenged the president's renomination. He won most of the primaries, but his candidacy fell short at the convention. Presidential control of the party, which he had earlier perfected to nominate himself and Taft, now defeated him. Roosevelt charged a "steal" and urged his delegates to walk out. At the end of June 1912 he suggested that they form a new party based upon reform and morality, and he had already admonished them, "We stand at Armageddon, and we battle for the Lord."[1]

Roosevelt's was not the only fast-moving star on the political horizon. Since leaving the Princeton presidency in 1910, Wilson had enjoyed a meteoric rise from neophyte candidate for governor of New Jersey to frontrunner for the Democratic nomination for president. Although he got the gubernatorial nomination through the backing of party bosses, Wilson quickly detached himself from them to run successfully as his own man. Once in office he fought his erstwhile patrons and pushed through a state reform program that included laws governing public utilities, primaries, and corrupt campaign practices. Wilson drew comment as a presidential possibility as soon as he entered politics, and the publicity he gained in 1911 with his gubernatorial accomplishments and out-of-state speaking tours made him the early favorite for the nomination. At the beginning of 1912, however, his candidacy faltered in the face of unreconstructed southern loyalties and opposition by party bosses. Wilson prevailed at the convention only after a threatened deadlock. A combination of the Democrats' antiquated two-thirds rule and sharp dealing by his managers on the scene finally enabled him to win. Wilson took the news of his nomination on July 2, 1912, calmly and told his nephew, "For myself, I feel very solemn about the whole thing."[2]

The race that followed constituted one of the great campaigns in American history. A three-way contest with a major party split, it recalled the 1860 election, when the fate of the nation had hung on the outcome. No such momentous stakes rode on the 1912 election, despite Roosevelt's insistent comparison of his new Progressive party with Lincoln's Republicans. Yet the campaign crackled with excitement. The most colorful politician since the Civil War squared off against the most articulate politician since the early days of the Republic.

Everyone recognized that the race was between Roosevelt and Wilson. Taft remained a candidate solely to spoil Roosevelt's chances. Thanks to the main contenders' gifts as campaigners, the major issues received extensive, though not always totally clarifying, exposure. By September 1912 the contest had turned into an ideological duel between Roosevelt and Wilson, chiefly over the issue of how to control large corporations, or trusts. Doubts have persisted about whether the two men really differed much in substance over the trusts, but the debate did present differing attitudes toward the purposes of governmental intervention in the economy, the proper distribution of power in society, and the ends of politics itself. For the only time except perhaps for Jefferson's first election in 1800, a presidential campaign aired questions that verged on political philosophy. It was a remarkable moment.

· 11 ·

Insurgent

THEODORE ROOSEVELT'S BREAK with William Howard Taft has often been compared to a classical tragedy. The conflict with his successor did appear to have an inevitability that defied the ex-president's efforts to avoid a clash. Although he felt unhappy at leaving office and had misgivings about Taft's appointments, Roosevelt tried not to interfere. "I went out of the country and gave him the fullest possible chance to work out his own salvation," Roosevelt complained to Lodge on the eve of his return home in 1910. Yet news of Taft's troubles confirmed doubts Roosevelt had already entertained. Reports of the Republicans' discontent with Taft and of the fight over conservation between Gifford Pinchot and Secretary of the Interior Richard Ballinger left Roosevelt "horribly puzzled." When Taft fired Pinchot as head of the Forest Service in January 1910, Roosevelt urged Pinchot to come to Europe and tell his side of the story. The two men met in Italy in April 1910 and conferred for several hours. "One of the best and most satisfactory talks with T.R. I ever had," Pinchot noted in his diary.[1]

The same day he saw Pinchot, Roosevelt opened his mind in a long, anguished letter to Lodge. "Very possibly if Taft had tried to work in my spirit, and along my lines," Roosevelt conceded, "he would have failed"; but he blamed his successor for joining the Old Guard, toward whom he felt unassuaged bitterness. "I don't think that under the Taft-Aldrich . . . regime there has been a real appreciation of the needs of the country." Roosevelt recoiled from the situation that awaited him at home. To refrain from attacks would scarcely help, because he could not "avoid saying things which, no matter how impersonal and general I keep them, shall seem to stand in contrast with what has been done in the past year." Nor would Roosevelt let himself "be put into the attitude of failing to stand for the great principles which I regard as essential. I may add that it looks to me as if the people were bound to have certain policies carried out, and that if they do not get the right type of aggressive leadership—leadership which a Cabinet of lawyers, or an Administration which is primarily a lawyers' Administration, is totally unfit to give—they will turn to the wrong kind of leadership. I might be able to *guide* this movement, but I should be wholly unable to *stop* it, even if I were to try."[2]

Roosevelt was prophesying the part he would play during the next two and a half years. The four concerns he mentioned to Lodge remained uppermost. First, as he observed, his personality and reputation made him the strongest presence in American politics, whatever he did or said. Second, Roosevelt continued to believe that the highest political values were at stake in the current political controversies. In July and August 1910 he told British friends that he deplored past American tendencies toward "a divorce between the national and the democratic ideas" and that he wanted "what you would call an 'imperialist democracy.' " Third, Roosevelt still believed that the Republican party had to be rescued from a split between unseeing standpatters and unsound radicals. Now, however, he favored trying to restrain the radicals rather than enlightening the standpatters. In August 1910 he warned Pinchot against "over-Radicalism. Remember that the extreme men on the Insurgent side are really working for defeat just as much as are the Cannon-Aldrich leaders." Finally, when he sneered at "a lawyers' Administration," Roosevelt skirted the most controversial issue he would later raise—criticism of the courts. That issue did more than anything else to harden Old Guard opposition to him and rouse Taft to join the fight.[3]

All four concerns immediately impinged on Roosevelt when he entered the midterm political campaign at the end of August 1910. On a two-week foray westward in support of insurgent Republicans, he again demonstrated his undiminished drawing power with the public and the press. Although he said little that was novel or exciting, he attracted big, enthusiastic crowds and extensive newspaper and magazine coverage. Roosevelt also stirred insurgent ardor and Old Guard consternation. As before, his style and manner gave his speeches a public impact that was greater than their content or delivery might have merited and was often different from what he intended or desired. Roosevelt's speeches on his western tour and later in the 1910 campaign made up the most extended, reflective exposition of his domestic political thought that he ever gave. Those speeches, which were soon published in a book titled *The New Nationalism,* constituted his best political testament.[4]

Aside from a somewhat greater specificity about regulatory legislation, nothing in *The New Nationalism* was new to Roosevelt except the title phrase. He had taken the phrase from Herbert Croly's *The Promise of American Life,* a work he admired and publicly praised. He used the term in his longest and most important speech, at Osawatomie, Kansas, on August 31, 1910. America needed a "New Nationalism," Roosevelt avowed, in order "to deal with new problems. The New Nationalism puts the national need before sectional or personal advantage." Despite the new term, Roosevelt was delivering his familiar exhortation to pursue higher ideals. Because he was speaking at the site of John Brown's antislavery raid in 1856, he could scarcely avoid reference to the Civil War. He called the war a "heroic struggle," and he urged that "civil life be carried on according to the spirit in which the [Union] army was carried on." Of Roosevelt's three main preachments, the call to international duty received little attention in that speech and in the campaign. He did admonish his audience at Osawatomie "continually to remember Uncle Sam's interests abroad," and he did devote another speech soon afterward to a call for a bigger navy and for fortification of the Panama Canal.[5]

At Osawatomie Roosevelt again repeated Lincoln's dictum that the rights of labor were superior to the rights of property. He also advocated stronger railroad regulation, workmen's compensation laws, prohibition of child labor, and graduated income and inheritance taxes. But he hastened to warn, "If I could ask but one thing of my fellow countrymen, my request would be that, whenever they go in for reform, they remember the two sides, and that they always exact justice from one side as much as from the other." The preachment against class conflict formed the most prominent theme in Roosevelt's 1910 speeches. In September at Freeport, Illinois, he declared, "We cannot afford to do wrong to any rich man and to the head of any corporation . . . Woe to us if, under the guise of uplifting popular rights, we do wrong to some one else." In Columbus, Ohio, he coupled praise for labor unions with denunciation of violence in strikes and labor disputes: "After law and order has been obtained,—not before, after—then comes the question of seeing that absolute justice is done."[6]

Roosevelt in 1910 particularly stressed avoidance of class conflict because of this third concern—restraint and redirection of Republican insurgency. In nearly every speech he cautioned insurgents again moving too fast, expecting too much, and following irresponsible leaders. "Distrust the demagogue and the mere visionary as you distrust that hidebound conservative," he urged in his first appearance on the western tour, an address to the Colorado legislature in Denver. ". . . Remember that if you fall into the Scylla of demagoguism, on the one hand, it will not help you that you have avoided the Charybdis of corruption and conservatism on the other." As earlier, Roosevelt advocated limited, sensible reform measures to forestall class polarization, which might result in revolution. At Osawatomie he acknowledged, "One of my chief fears in connection with progress comes because I do not want to see our people, for lack of proper leadership, compelled to follow men whose intentions are excellent, but whose eyes are a little too wild to make it really safe to trust them." But could anyone provide "proper leadership" except Roosevelt himself?[7]

His admonitions about responsible leadership also sprang from his vision of political ideals that transcended material interests. In his 1910 speeches, except for brief endorsements of specific reform measures, Roosevelt spoke almost entirely in broad general terms. At Denver he maintained that the federal government must be strengthened in order to regulate big business. "All we wish to do on behalf of the people," he affirmed, "is to meet the nationalization of big business by nationalized government control." At Osawatomie he extolled his doctrine of New Nationalism as "impatient of the utter confusion" of states attempting to handle national issues and scornful of "the impotence which springs from the overdivision of governmental powers." Most of all, Roosevelt once more summoned people to rise above narrow, material interests. At Osawatomie he called for "a genuine and permanent moral awakening." A week afterward in North Dakota he asserted that material wealth "must not be allowed to commercialize our minds." Later in September at Syracuse, New York, he argued, "Material well-being is a great good, but it is a great good chiefly as a means for the upbuilding upon it of a high and fine type of character, private and public. Upon our national well-being as a foundation we must upbuild the structure of a lofty national life, raised in accordance with the doctrine that 'righteousness exalteth a nation.' "[8]

The speeches collected in *The New Nationalism* expressed Roosevelt's basic political viewpoint so well mainly because they came at a particularly fitting point in his career. As he observed at Syracuse, he was repeating "what I again and again said" as president, and he had only "very slightly developed the doctrines contained in these presidential addresses in order to meet the development of new conditions." Despite his appropriation of the term New Nationalism from Croly's book, Roosevelt owed little to that writer. Rather, as John M. Blum and others have pointed out, the influence ran in the other direction—Roosevelt had provided a model and inspiration for Croly. Conversely, the attraction of Croly's work for Roosevelt lay in seeing himself praised and in having his own ideas and approach reinforced and refined. What was different in *The New Nationalism* from Roosevelt's earlier utterances was his release from the confinements of the presidency.[9]

The 1910 campaign furnished the first opportunity since his vice-presidential candidacy in 1900 to make an openly political speaking tour. Moreover, no longer having to cooperate with the Old Guard leadership permitted him to bring his preachments closer to the current political scene. But Roosevelt was not a candidate himself yet. In 1912 the exigencies of office-seeking once more forced him to focus on certain salient issues—on bossism in the contest with Taft for the nomination and, later, on the trust question in the race against Wilson. As a result, in 1912 Roosevelt was not able to develop his basic positions nearly as well as he did in *New Nationalism*. In 1910 Roosevelt momentarily fused his political roles of responsible leader and reform agitator in a fashion that enabled him to give the best single account of his approach to politics.

The association with Croly was fitting for two reasons: It summed up Roosevelt's previous political stance, and it pointed toward the part Roosevelt would play in 1912 and for a time afterward. The writer and the ex-president saw eye to eye in their deepest beliefs. Each rejected what he regarded as the Jeffersonian legacies of limited government and unfettered individualism, which Croly dismissed as "at bottom the old fatal policy of drift." Each correspondingly venerated what he considered the Hamiltonian heritage of powerful government and elite leadership, which Croly praised as "one of energetic and intelligent assertion of the national good," Each called for a union of democratic and nationalistic values, such as Lincoln had forged during the Civil War. Both men also welcomed larger-scale business enterprise and disliked old-fashioned, small-scale economic competition. Croly went further in *The Promise of American Life* than Roosevelt did in *The New Nationalism* in lauding huge corporations as "an important step in the direction of the better organization of industry and commerce" and in urging the abandonment of trust busting in favor of government regulation of the trusts. But Roosevelt's call in his Denver speech for "nationalized government control" of large corporations and his previously expressed doubts about the antitrust policy betokened his agreement with Croly. In 1912, to the chagrin of many of his supporters, Roosevelt would espouse trust regulation and thereby broach the most heated and lengthily debated issue of his third-party presidential campaign.[10]

Above all, Roosevelt elicited and welcomed Croly's admiration because of their common idealism. Both men based their political thought on the belief that people must be made to rise above selfish, material interests in the pursuit of a higher national purpose. "The only fruitful promise of which the life of any individual or any nation can be possessed," Croly announced at the outset of his book, "is a promise determined by an ideal." The ideal that beckoned America, he maintained, was democracy, by which he meant the fullest and freest participation of all citizens in determining their lives. Greater democracy was America's promise, "and if its Promise is to be fulfilled, it must be prepared to follow whithersoever that ideal may lead." But the nation's democratic promise could be fulfilled, he contended, only "through a certain measure of discipline; not merely by the abundant satisfaction of individual desires, but by a large measure of individual subordination and self-denial." Throughout *The Promise of American Life*, as he expounded his ideas about uniting nationalism and democracy, Croly harped on the "necessity of subordinating individual desires to fulfillment of a national purpose," and he closed with a discussion of education and secular evangelism as means "by which human nature can be raised to a higher level." Roosevelt could not have expressed his basic idealism better himself.[11]

The last sentence of the book disclosed Croly's deepest, but curiously, least noticed, affinity with Roosevelt. "The common citizen can become something of a hero and something of a saint," he wrote, "not by growing to heroic proportions in his own person, but by the sincere and enthusiastic imitation of heroes and saints, and whether or not he will ever come to such imitation will depend upon the ability of his exceptional fellow-countrymen to offer him acceptable examples of heroism and saintliness." Croly shared Roosevelt's convictions about the utility of religious devotion and observances in promoting the nobler sort of politics that they wished to see prevail. Through Croly's protégé, Walter Lippmann, their brand of political idealism and their interest in fostering something like a civil religion would extend far into the twentieth century, especially in Lippmann's most ambitious books, *The Good Society* (1937) and *Essays in the Public Philosophy* (1955). That legacy of Roosevelt's transcendent idealism at once underscored his aristocratic conservative assumptions and pointed to the appeal he would have for certain American intellectuals. Beyond his attraction to youth through his well-publicized zest and glamor, Roosevelt, through his thought, enlisted the devotion of some of the brightest political minds of his era.[12]

The public enthusiasm he aroused in 1910 naturally gratified Roosevelt. Yet aspects of his reception disquieted him. As he ruefully confided to his oldest son, he thought he was alienating both Republican factions—"the Western radicals" by his mildness and the eastern Old Guardsmen by appearing "well-nigh an anarchist." Roosevelt misread his problem with the insurgents. Some did want him to go further in advocating regulatory measures and attacking the Old Guard, while others, especially La Follette, distrusted him. But most of the Republican insurgents supported Roosevelt more fervently than ever, which created a problem. Although Roosevelt was delivering messages of moderation, he was stirring up the insurgents even more than before. This disparity between intent and effect was a corollary of his vivid, dynamic personality.

It was one of the prices he paid for the popularity that formed the basis of his political power.[13]

Not all of his public impact in 1910 was unwitting. Roosevelt did not misread the hostility he was fomenting among the Old Guard. Some of their antipathy sprang from the same personality impact that gained him insurgent support, but most of their revulsion reflected the issue that Roosevelt emphasized at the outset of the 1910 campaign—criticism of the courts. In his first speech of that campaign, to the Colorado legislature, Roosevelt charged that judicial interpretation by the Supreme Court had "lagged behind" new industrial conditions and spawned a series of "negative decisions to create a sphere in which neither nation nor state has effective control." Two decisions he specifically condemned. One was *United States* v. *E. C. Knight Company* in 1895, in which the Court had drastically narrowed the scope of the Sherman Anti-Trust Act; the other was *Lochner* v. *New York* in 1905, a sweeping antiregulatory decision that had struck down a state maximum-hours law for bakery workers. Roosevelt cited those cases as examples of the Court's actions "against popular rights."[14]

Newspaper accounts of his remarks stirred impassioned protests by conservatives, partly because of a mishap with the press. Reporters on the train to Denver badgered Roosevelt into giving them an incomplete outline of the speech, on which most of them based their stories about an attack on the Supreme Court. The protests against the speech annoyed Roosevelt. As president, he had already criticized the courts and, as he pointed out to Lodge, he based his statements at Denver on suggestions made by a member of the Court, his friend and appointee, Justice William H. Moody. Yet Roosevelt was too canny a politician not to realize that he was waving a red flag at the Old Guard. Whereas he had tucked earlier criticisms of the Court in to lengthy presidential messages, he was now jabbing Republican Old Guardsmen in their most sensitive spot—concern for the sanctity of the law and defense of property rights. His criticisms of the courts then and later in 1911 and 1912 destroyed whatever basis might have remained for accommodation with the party bosses. Their implacable opposition raised a formidable barrier to Roosevelt's chances for another Republican presidential nomination.[15]

By itself, Old Guard opposition made his path within the party difficult but not impossible. If Taft had not decided to run again, the Old Guard almost certainly could not have blocked Roosevelt's nomination in 1912. The most important effect of his criticism of the courts was that it aroused Taft to gird for battle against his predecessor. Just as Taft's handling of Pinchot and the insurgent Republicans had confirmed Roosevelt's doubts about him, so Roosevelt's aspersions on the Supreme Court did the same thing for Taft. In May 1910, before the ex-president's return from abroad, Taft had commented privately, "Roosevelt had a good deal of contempt for the judiciary." He also believed that Roosevelt's "impatience with the delay of the law" made him "not unlike Napoleon." Taft claimed to his brother that the Denver speech "came like a bolt out of a clear sky," but he immediately became convinced that Roosevelt was "going quite beyond anything that he advocated while he was in the White House, and has proposed a program which it is absolutely impossible to carry out except by a revision of the federal Constitution."[16]

The break between Roosevelt and Taft had tragic elements, because each man's greatest virtue impelled him to fight the other. The two did not differ that much in their political viewpoints. Taft also pictured himself as a responsible conservative pursuing reform to stave off threats of revolution. In August 1910 he confided to his military aide that he saw a movement arising for "absolute socialism." In contrast to Roosevelt's temptation "to try to guide it," Taft said that "he felt the way to meet it was by direct challenge and by fighting it out at the ballot box." Yet more than tactics separated the two men. Taft offended Roosevelt's political calling because he fumbled both as a party professional operating within the Republican factional situation and as a popular leader attempting to channel discontent in constructive directions. Roosevelt affronted Taft's judicial sense of rectitude both because he trifled with respect for law and the Constitution and because he consorted with elements that each of them considered dangerously radical. With those traits on the line, they could not avoid the battle that would wreck both their political careers.[17]

The battle was not yet at hand. After his western tour Roosevelt stopped criticizing the courts and toned down his endorsement of specific reforms. He made appeasing gestures to the Old Guard, such as praising the recent tariff and campaigning in Massachusetts for Lodge and in Ohio for the Republican gubernatorial nominee, Warren G. Harding. Roosevelt attempted to repair relations with Taft through a joint appearance in Connecticut, which turned out badly. He also spoke more explicitly about his desire to temper Republican insurgency. When he addressed the chamber of commerce in New Haven, Connecticut, in December 1910, Roosevelt characterized himself as "a radical who most earnestly desires to see the radical programme carried out by conservatives." Such men as his listeners, "who ought to be the leaders in the community," must lead the rising reform movement "for the very reason that you have no selfish interest in it." Temporarily at least, Roosevelt was again trying to loosen up the conservatives as well as rein in the radicals. Taft was not disposed to attack, either. To his brother, he resolved "that the only course for me to pursue is to sit tight and let him [Roosevelt] talk."[18]

Such mutual forbearance allowed the truce between Roosevelt and Taft to last through 1911. But constant strains ruled out any durable peace or real cooperation. For Roosevelt, concern over larger values meshed with gloom at the Republican split to produce a mood of rarely relieved worry and frustration. The 1910 election results bore out his worst fears. A Democratic sweep cut down Old Guard and moderate Republicans alike. Roosevelt's personal favorite, Henry L. Stimson, lost a gubernatorial bid in New York, while his closest ideological comrade, Albert J. Beveridge of Indiana, was defeated for reelection to the Senate. The Democrats gained control of the House of Representatives and elected enough senators to form an anti-Taft majority with the Republican insurgents. They likewise captured or retained governorships in New York, Ohio, Indiana, Massachusetts, Connecticut, and New Jersey, where Wilson emerged as the party's brightest new presidential prospect. Except for Lodge's reelection to the Senate from Massachusetts, the few Republican victories in 1910 brought no comfort to Roosevelt. Radical insurgents won in California, Iowa, and particularly Wisconsin, where La Follette, whom Roosevelt had pointedly refrained from supporting, was reelected to the Senate and carried in his whole state ticket. In December 1910 the insurgents formed the Progressive Republican League, through which they pledged to pursue an ambitious reform program to curb big business and promote popular government and to launch a campaign to contest Taft's renomination.

The organized intraparty opposition to Taft put Roosevelt in a quandary. Caution, along with loyalty to such close friends as Lodge and Elihu Root, who were Old Guard loyalists, and Stimson, who joined the Taft cabinet in 1911, dictated keeping his distance from the Progressive Republican League. Moreover, Roosevelt knew that if he did not oppose his successor's renomination and let him lose the 1912 election, as more and more observers expected Taft to do, then he, Roosevelt, would become the Republicans' inescapable choice in 1916. The nomination could even fall to him in 1912, if Taft withdrew or, as Root and others thought might happen, if nervous party leaders tried to draft Roosevelt to save them from defeat. All he had to do was wait, and sooner or later the presidency would be his again. But waiting no longer satisfied Roosevelt. His restlessness, as well as his assessment of the issues and personalities involved in the insurgents' revolt, kept him from spurning them entirely. "I am particularly anxious," he told one of their leaders in January 1911, "that in the progressive movement we shall not find ourselves landed where so many other movements have landed when they have allowed enthusiasm to conquer reason."[19]

Roosevelt justified his off-again, on-again attitude toward the insurgents by repeatedly invoking the example of Lincoln's middle way between the abolitionists and the defenders of slavery. But the analogy did not resolve his quandary. If the concerns behind current reform agitation were as significant and as imperiled by false prophets as Roosevelt believed, then the path of duty might lie in joining the insurgents in order to lead and restrain them. That assessment weighed more and more heavily on him during 1911. Such men as Pinchot argued that he was indispensable, and he watched the Progressive Republican League line up behind La Follette, whom he disliked and distrusted as much as ever, for the 1912 presidential nomination. On the issues Roosevelt swung back toward the insurgents, first by again endorsing most of their specific reform measures in one of his *Outlook* columns in January 1911 and then by resuming his attack on judicial obstructionism in a series of columns in February and March. In a speech in October he sharpened his attack on the courts by endorsing the principle of popular reversal of decisions, although he did not yet say what form such reversal should take. Throughout 1911 Roosevelt also continued in speeches and in his *Outlook* columns to preach against class conflict and materialism, to invoke Lincoln as a symbol of inspired moderation, and to urge restraint upon the progressives.[20]

What finally impelled Roosevelt to break with Taft and run for the Republican nomination was a combination of deeper values and personal feelings. His first open attack came, not over the domestic concerns that agitated the insurgents, but over foreign affairs in an incident in which Roosevelt aligned himself with his erstwhile Old Guard cohorts Lodge and Root. In an *Outlook* column in September 1911, Roosevelt assailed the arbitration treaty the Taft administration had negotiated with Britain as a "sham." He dismissed the treaty for settlement of disputes as a piece of devious diplomacy which, because it included questions of national honor and vital interest, was both unworkable and potentially dangerous to American security. Renewing his preachment on international duty, Roosevelt implored his countrymen to pursue "righteousness first." They must recall their glorious history of fighting for just causes and, rather than heed "the timid and short-sighted apostles of ease and of slothful avoidance of duty," they should dare to play "the part of the just man armed." Roosevelt's criticisms, together with the efforts of Lodge and Root in the Senate, helped scuttle the treaty, which Taft finally withdrew rather than ratify with stringent reservations. On his side the president felt not only hurt by the charges but also confirmed in his suspicions of his predecessor. "The truth is," Taft wrote a friend, "he [Roosevelt] believes in war and wishes to be a Napoleon and to die on the battle field. He has the spirit of the old berserkers."[21]

Roosevelt's opposition to the arbitration treaty struck many as excessive and, in view of his own peace initiatives as president, as inconsistent or hypocritical. From Roosevelt's standpoint it was neither. He was venting a long-held contempt for advocates of peace. During his travels abroad he had privately deplored the influence of "mugwumps, ultrapeace-advocates and maudlin, hysterical sentimentalists, plus Bryanites" on American foreign policy. In May 1910, in his address of acceptance of the Nobel Peace Prize, Roosevelt had tempered his endorsement of "an international police power" with a reminder that nations must look out for themselves until such a police power could be established. His visit to Europe had also revived his fears about dangers to the balance of power and had reinforced his convictions about the need for strong American armed forces. Roosevelt had discussed the navy once on the campaign trail in 1910 and, speaking at Harvard in December, he had condemned disarmament proposals for trying "to turn it[the United States] into an Occidental China," defenseless and contemptible. When he first learned the terms of Taft's arbitration treaty, Roosevelt denounced it to Lodge as "an act of maudlin folly" and urged him to oppose it, despite outcries from "mushy philanthropists, and shortsighted and greedy creatures on Boards of Trade."[22]

Roosevelt's reaction to the arbitration treaties revealed his state of mind as he approached the break with Taft. By the fall of 1911 he had convinced himself that his deepest values were at stake in the current political controversies. As always when he expounded on those values, international duty formed a trinity with anti-materialism and rejection of class conflict. Likewise, projections of his own character, especially with regard to physical strength and courage, underlay his preachments about the right course for the United States and the world. Further, his scorn for mugwumps, sentimentalists, and reformers as a type remained fresh, even as he contemplated leading a movement that included large complements of such folk. Standing on the brink of his plunge into reform leadership, Roosevelt was forsaking neither his original conservative outlook nor his attempt to combine the roles of responsible leader and agitator. He was preparing less to join the progressives than, in a later generation's term, to co-opt them.

Although Roosevelt's values were a critical factor in his decision, it seems unlikely that he would have run for the nomination or that Taft would have fought back if each man had not felt personally wounded and affronted by the other. The historians who have studied the break most closely, George E. Mowry and William H. Harbaugh, have concluded that the final, precipitating event came at the end of October 1911, when the Taft administration brought an antitrust suit against the United States Steel Corporation. Included in the bill of particulars against the steel company was its acquisition of the Tennessee Coal and Iron Company in 1907, which Roosevelt had approved. The ex-president felt not only incensed at the implication that he had been duped but also betrayed by Taft, who had, he claimed, seconded his action at the time. In January 1912 Roosevelt's sister Corinne told a close friend of both men, "If it had not been for that Steel suit! I was talking with Theodore only last week, and he said that he could never forgive." With Taft, too, the personal dimension loomed large. At the end of December 1911 he told Archie Butt, his military aide, "I could not subordinate my administration to him and retain my self-respect, but it is hard, very hard, Archie, to see a devoted friendship going to pieces like a rope of sand."[23]

Roosevelt evidently decided to seek the nomination in January 1912. He orchestrated plans for a group of Republican governors to ask him publicly to announce his availability. La Follette's candidacy and the Progressive Republican League's previous commitment to him presented an obstacle, but the Wisconsin senator's apparent physical collapse during a speech on February 2 furnished a ready excuse for most of the insurgents to abandon him. On February 21, at Columbus, Ohio, just before giving a speech in which he endorsed popular recall of judicial decisions and called for regulating rather than breaking up big business, Roosevelt told reporters, "My hat is in the ring." Three days later he replied formally to the governors' request. Bowing to their entreaty, he stated that the voters should choose the Republican nominee for president through direct primaries. Privately, he told friends that not to run "would be cowardice, a case of 'il gran rifiuto' "—a reference to Dante's tale in the *Divine Comedy,* of the monk's refusal of the papacy and his retreat to his cell. He hoped by his candidacy "to draw into one dominant stream all the intelligent and patriotic elements, in order to prepare against the social upheaval which will otherwise overwhelm us."[24]

The intraparty campaign that followed added little to the debate over governmental regulation. It came to focus almost exclusively on the question of popular choice versus boss rule. In March Roosevelt retreated a bit from advocating recall of judicial decisions. He did not mean for such procedures to apply to the Supreme Court or the Constitution, he explained, but he also continued to condemn the trustbusting approach. Increasingly, however, he concentrated on denouncing his opponents for thwarting the will of the people and on declaring that momentous consequences were at stake in his bid for the Republican nomination. Speaking in New York in March, he compared present conditions in the United States to those in prerevolutionary France, and he urged Americans to reject the French example of "splitting into the two camps of unreasonable conservatism and unreasonable radicalism." At Louisville in April he avowed, "The Republican party is now facing a great crisis. It is to decide whether it will be as in the days of Lincoln, the party of the plain people, . . . or whether it will be the party of privilege and of special interest, the heir to those who were Lincoln's most bitter opponents." At last Roosevelt believed he had found the event that could summon forth the full measure of his leadership.[25]

Because he believed that he had met his moment in history, Roosevelt gave less and less heed to past friendship and party loyalty. By May 1912 the campaign had degenerated into name-calling. Roosevelt dubbed Taft a "puzzlewit" and a "fathead," while Taft accused him of being an "egotist" and a "demagogue." The president was also acting from a combination of deeper values and personal feelings. "I believe I represent a safe and saner view of our government and its Constitution than does Theodore Roosevelt," Taft told a friend in January, "and whether beaten or not I mean to labor in the vineyard for those principles." Roosevelt's candidacy and public criticisms stung Taft and stiffened his resolve. "I shall not withdraw under any condition," he vowed to his brother in April. "I represent a cause that would make it cowardly for me to withdraw now." Even though he thought he would lose the election, Taft was determined "to secure the nomination if I can, under the rules that the Republican party convention has established, in spite of all the threats to bolt or to establish a third party."[26]

Taft's reference to convention machinery and a threatened bolt disclosed the positions the two sides had taken. Although the Republican convention at Chicago in June 1912 featured fireworks and dramatic confrontation, its outcome was virtually foreordained. The opposing factions had determined their probable conduct months in advance. On the campaign trail in the spring of 1912, Roosevelt proved once more that he was the most popular politician alive. He drew his customary huge crowds and whipped them up to a pitch of enthusiasm, usually despite the mundane content and graceless delivery of his speeches. More important, he translated public enthusiasm into votes. Roosevelt won all but two of the Republican primaries he entered, and he particularly savored the thumping he gave the president in Taft's home state of Ohio. The primaries did not select anywhere near a majority of convention delegates, but Roosevelt also did well in some states where delegates were chosen by state and local conventions through the Republican organizations. Most of those convention victories came, not as a result of insurgent sentiment, but through the efforts of party leaders who, as Root had predicted, feared defeat with Taft and backed Roosevelt as the best bet to win in November.[27]

Yet such calculations of party interest swayed few leading Republicans in 1912. All the big state bosses and the most prominent national figures, including Root and Stimson, stuck with Taft despite the likelihood that he would lose the election. Lodge resolved his conflict between personal and party loyalties by neither supporting nor opposing Roosevelt. It might seem odd that the hardened professionals who dominated the Republican party would pick a probable loser over a proven winner, but their choice sprang logically from ideology and an assessment of political allegiances in the electorate. In their rejection of Roosevelt, no single element weighed more than his criticism of the courts. That criticism had convinced conservatives that he held dangerous views on fundamental questions involving the defense of private property and unfettered business enterprise. Moreover, the prospect of defeat in 1912 did not dishearten the Republican bosses. They felt sure their party's sojourn in opposition would be brief, reasoning that the Democrats' unsoundness on economic issues and their tinkering with the tariff would frighten business, cause a depression, and restore the Republicans to power in 1916. In short, the bosses were betting that Roosevelt was wrong. They believed that material self-interest could not be overcome and that the issues raised by the insurgents would prove ephemeral in the face of an enduring majority built by the Republicans in 1896 mainly on economic concerns.[28]

Roosevelt's primary successes, Taft's determination to stay in the race, and the bosses' assessments—all these coalesced in a strategy of exploiting presidential and Old Guard control of the convention machinery to assure Taft's renomination. At the outset of the convention neither candidate commanded an undisputed majority, so the nomination depended on the awarding of 254 contested delegate votes. The Republican National Committee gave 235 to Taft and only 19 to Roosevelt. The challenger almost certainly deserved more, although probably he could not have been given enough to gain a convention majority. As it was, the commit-tee's high-handedness and the imperiousness with which Root, the convention chairman, stifled protests on the floor allowed Roose-velt to cry foul and provided his delegates with a perfect excuse to walk out. The president and the party leaders felt justified in their actions, because their overriding objective was to maintain party control against the day when sound politics and economics would be restored. Defeat in the coming election mattered little, Taft confided, "if we can retain the regular Republican party as a nu-cleus for future conservative action."[29]

After thirty years as a professional politician and after having twice run the party steamroller that crushed his forces at the 1912 convention, Roosevelt had anticipated his opponents' moves. As early as March he had complained, "Taft is using every species of dishonest pressure through patronage." Starting in April he had threatened to bolt "if the political thugs in our own party handle enough votes," as they were doing. Contesting Taft's renomination did not require Roosevelt to cross a political Rubicon. He had the valid excuse of trying to save the party from defeat. Merely by swallowing the result of the convention and perfunctorily endorsing Taft, he would have remained the favorite for the nomination in 1916. Yet Roosevelt believed that he had cast his die when he broke with Taft. As he viewed the situation, no course remained open to him except a party bolt if he did not win the nomination. Both personal and ideological considerations would have required him to continue his fight even if the Old Guard had moved with greater finesse and had not provided a dramatic pretext for his third-party plunge.[30]

On the personal side, the restlessness and recklessness his friends had noticed after his return in 1910 played a large part in his decision. Since leaving the White House, Roosevelt had brooded on the absence of great events in his presidency, which had pre-vented it from assuming heroic stature. His persistent comparisons to Lincoln had shown that he was grasping for ways to magnify current politics and his role in them. His insistence upon criticizing the courts betrayed his growing distaste for the kind of compromises and factional diplomacy he had previously practiced and had held up as a model of leadership. It is hard to escape the conclusion that Roosevelt was daring the Republican Old Guard to oppose him and warning them that any future presidency of his must be largely, if not completely, on his terms. In 1916, under different circumstances and with a different issue uppermost, Roosevelt declared that "it would be a mistake to nominate me unless the country has in its mood something of the heroic." Four years earlier he served the same notice on his party.[31]

Ironically, Roosevelt's conservative motives in taking command of the Republican insurgents also left him little choice other than a party bolt. Several times in 1911 insurgent colleagues and his eldest son had suggested that the Democrats might present reform-minded people with an acceptable alternative in 1912, particularly if Wilson were their nominee. Roosevelt had spurned those suggestions, dismissing the Democrats the same way the Old Guard did. In October 1911 he had said that he could not find "any ground for permanent hope in the Democratic party," because of its large contingent of "bourbon reactionaries," its radicals, who were "for the most part foolish," and its attachment to "States' rights as against National duties." Wilson he had scorned in December 1911 as "pretty thin material for a President," in view of his short political career and recent espousal of reform measures. Roosevelt had admitted, however, that the New Jersey governor was "still the strongest man the Democrats could nominate." Yet for the same reasons that the Old Guard anticipated a Democratic victory over Taft with equanimity, Roosevelt viewed the prospect with alarm. Inasmuch as he and his opponents both regarded the Republican party as the only acceptable vehicle for a politically sound approach to current issues, whichever side lost could hardly have avoided committing some act of party apostasy.[32]

Whether Roosevelt believed he could be elected president at the head of a third-party ticket in 1912 is not clear. He constantly sought parallels between his position and the situation during the sectional conflict of the 1850, when the Republican party was founded. He hoped that the two parties might be on the verge of breaking up over the issues of progressivism, as the Whigs and Democrats had broken up over slavery. Nearly everything hinged on what the Democrats did in their convention at the end of June. When Wilson's candidacy faltered badly early in 1912, it seemed increasingly likely that the speaker of the House, Champ Clark of Missouri, would be the Democratic nominee. Although he was not a state-rights man, Clark had no reputation as a reformer, seemed to be a colorless hack, and enjoyed the covert backing of such machines as Tammany Hall. One friend of Roosevelt's noted that Bryan, who was attending the Republican convention as an observer, had talks with Roosevelt and his supporters. No promises were made, but there was a strong impression that Bryan might support Roosevelt's new party if the Democrats nominated Clark or some state-rights advocate. During the Democratic convention one of Roosevelt's sons was privately reported as saying, "Pop is praying for the nomination of Champ Clark."[33]

Yet if Roosevelt hoped for victory in the election, he hardly counted on it. On June 17, the day the Republican National Committee awarded the disputed delegates to Taft, Roosevelt addressed a separate meeting of his supporters at Chicago and delivered what was generally conceded to be the finest speech of his career. Declaring that the contest over the nomination "has become much more than an ordinary party fight," Roosevelt denounced the Taft forces for "a crime which represents treason to the people, and the usurpation of the sovereignty of the people by irresponsible political bosses, inspired by sinister influences of moneyed privilege." He arraigned the whole system of "the corrupt alliance between crooked business and crooked politics," which was stealing the nomination from him and control of the Republican party from his supporters. "The parting of the ways has come," Roosevelt announced. The Republican party must stand "for the rights of humanity, or else it must stand for special privilege." In a ringing close, Roosevelt vowed, "Assuredly the fight will go on whether we win or lose"; it would be far better "to fail honorably" in their cause than "to win by foul methods . . . We fight in honorable fashion for the good of mankind; fearless of the future; unheeding of our individual fates; with unflinching hearts and undimmed eyes; we stand at Armageddon, and we battle for the Lord."[34]

For perhaps the only time in his life, Roosevelt's oratory matched his magnetic personality. He approached the heights of eloquence that Bryan had achieved in 1896 with his Cross of Gold speech and which Wilson later reached in some of his presidential addresses. In part, Roosevelt's eloquence reflected the drama of the moment. It was fitting that the Armageddon speech resembled Bryan's, which had likewise come at a juncture on which a great political career had hinged. But the source of Roosevelt's unwonted eloquence ran deeper than the occasion. One close observer later commented that his insistence on balance and qualification had usually prevented him from being a real orator. The primacy Roosevelt had given to working as a professional within the political organization had made him downplay public advocacy on current issues and deliver his major preachments in highly generalized terms. Since 1910, however, he had often given freer rein to advocacy, and now he was at least temporarily casting off the bonds of professionalism unabashedly to champion a cause.[35]

The sheer joy of Roosevelt's martial language indicated how much his long effort to combine political roles had cost him in repressing his attraction to idealistic reform. But his newfound freedom also carried a stiff price. In Roosevelt's depiction of himself and his followers as soldiers in a holy cause, the embrace of self-sacrifice bordered on foolhardiness. It resembled the suicidal cavalry charge that had prompted the celebrated comment that it was magnificent but it was not war. Roosevelt's stand at Armageddon was noble, but by his own previous lights, it was not politics. This one speech did not signify that he had forsaken practical, professional politics for reform agitation. His desire to restrain the progressives required him to continue to combine his two political roles. Yet his decision to make a fight that was carrying him beyond the confines of his party and his previous political methods, culminating in this speech, showed that Roosevelt had abandoned the balance between those roles that had provided him with his greatest strength and success.

If a few events had turned out differently in 1912, especially if the Democrats had obliged Roosevelt with a weak or conservative candidate, then his new Progressive party might have followed in the footsteps of the pre–Civil War Republicans. Even without winning in 1912, they might have established a strong second party, as the Republicans had done in 1856. Thereby they would have changed the face of American politics and put Roosevelt in line for the kind of heroic, historically momentous presidency he craved. It was a noble dream, but it was also a bad mistake. Too many imponderables blocked the fulfillment of his vision. The outcome of the 1912 election as well as later political developments would show that the Republican bosses had correctly appreciated the importance to the voters of mundane, material concerns. As governor and president, Roosevelt had shared their realism, however much he had regretted it, and he had never seriously contemplated such a daring but doubtful leap as the one he was now taking. As Blum has observed, being out of power deprived Roosevelt of the wisdom and restraint that had made him a successful statesman. Adventure and eloquence would offer meager recompense for the exile from power to which he now consigned himself for the remaining years of his life.[36]

· 12 ·

Frontrunner

WOODROW WILSON'S CONFLICT with Theodore Roosevelt did not have the same apparent inevitability as the ex-president's break with his successor. If Wilson's and Roosevelt's presidential candidacies had not collided in 1912, they would almost certainly not have become major rivals. Several bad turns of fortune for Wilson in 1910 and 1912 almost did prevent him from running against Roosevelt. Yet the similarities in the backgrounds, circumstances, positions, and appeals of the two men made a confrontation between them a fitting climax to both their careers. Despite Wilson's lack of previous political involvement, his emergence on the national scene by winning the New Jersey governorship paralleled Roosevelt's rise through the New York governorship twelve years before. The gubernatorial chair of a northeastern state furnished each man with a springboard to the White House, and each secured that springboard through a combination of opposites—his own popular, extraparty appeal and the patronage of a boss-led political machine.

The parallel was not perfect. Wilson was not a war hero nor a long-publicized, sometime clean-government advocate, rancher, and police commissioner. He therefore enjoyed nothing approaching Roosevelt's ready public recognition and spontaneous adulation. Unlike the New York Republicans a decade earlier, the New Jersey Democrats in 1910 had languished in opposition for fifteen years. Their boss, "Jim" Smith of Newark, a former United States senator, did not run a tightly organized, efficient machine like Platt's. Rather, he operated as the senior member of a group of largely independent and more or less equal local leaders. Nor did

Wilson start with outside backing from his state's antimachine reformers, as Roosevelt had. Nearly all the opposition to Wilson's
nomination for governor came from the small band of dissident
Democrats who year in and year out had battled Smith and his
cohorts. Smith had to struggle around the clock at the state convention at Trenton in September 1910 not only to squelch the
dissidents but also to persuade wary regulars to pick this unknown
quantity to head the ticket. "It was the busiest night of Smith's
political life," observed a veteran journalist. The boss's labors succeeded, and on September 15, 1910, Woodrow Wilson came to
address the delegates, probably only a handful of whom had seen
or heard him before, as their nominee for governor.[1]

His speech electrified the convention, thereby underscoring
the parallel with Roosevelt. It was Wilson's personal magnetism
and gifts as a speaker, as much as his earlier state rights advocacy,
that had moved George Harvey to boost his political career and to
secure Smith's endorsement for the gubernatorial nomination. Wilson now demonstrated his talents and appeal for the first time in a
political campaign and on his own behalf. He assured the delegates
that he had made "absolutely no pledge of any kind," and he
promised "a new and more ideal era in our politics," which would
witness "a renaissance of public spirit, a reawakening of sober
public opinion, a revival of the power of the people." When Wilson
offered to stop and let his listeners go home after their long session,
cries arose, "Go on!" and "You're all right!" Wilson called for a
public service commission to regulate utilities, modeled after the
one established in Wisconsin by La Follette's followers, and he
advocated stricter control of businesses. "We must reconstruct, by
thoughtful processes, economic society in this country," declared
Wilson, "and by doing so will reconstruct political organization.
This reconstruction will be bigger than anything in American history." Wilson stirred the delegates, who mobbed him and tried to
carry him on their shoulders, and his performance also attracted
favorable comment from newspapers and magazines around the
country, particularly in New York and the South. The press welcomed him as a distinguished addition to the front rank of American
politicians and predicted a bright future for him.[2]

Wilson's appearance before the state convention set the tone of
his gubernatorial campaign. Although Smith and the Democratic

bosses had been indispensable to his getting the nomination, they presented the greatest obstacle to his winning the election. In the campaign Wilson sought to downplay their backing, as he had done at the convention. He constantly declared his independence and called for more idealistic politics, and he struck a strongly reformist note on state issues. His convention speech, particularly the advocacy of a public service commission modeled on Wisconsin's, instantly converted most of the dissident Democrats to his cause. Joseph P. Tumulty, a leading party insurgent, exulted to a friend, "If Wilson stands for legislation of that calibre, Jim Smith will find that he has a 'lemon.' " In view of New Jersey's unbroken Republican voting habits since 1894, Wilson needed to do more than unite his own party. Before 1910 antimachine and business-regulatory sentiments in the state had flourished mainly in the Republican party, particularly among a group of insurgents and municipal reformers who called themselves "New Idea" Republicans. The New Idea men fared no better in their party than the Democratic dissidents had, but they exerted influence over independent voters and disgruntled Republicans, particularly Roosevelt's admirers. The key to victory, Wilson's shrewder advisers repeatedly told him, lay in shedding the stigma of Smith's sponsorship in order to appeal to independents and Republican insurgents.[3]

Wilson lost little time following their advice. As a fledgling politician, he had a few lessons to learn about his new calling. Wilson at first informed party leaders that he would avoid the whirlwind campaign style associated with Roosevelt. Within less than a month, however, he was making a frenetic series of appearances before enthusiastic crowds. Wilson initially believed that his campaign expenses would not, he told a friend, "run above a few hundred dollars," which he planned to pay "out of my own pocket." The campaign eventually cost over $100,000, nearly all of which came from a few big contributors, principally Smith himself, Harvey's Wall Street friends, and wealthy Princetonians.[4]

According to some reports, Wilson's early speeches seemed a bit formal, and his arguments sometimes went over the heads of less-educated listeners. If that was the case, he soon corrected the flaw. Wilson became a pungent campaigner who hammered away at his opponent's weaknesses. He frequently reminded voters that the Republican candidate, Vivian Lewis, had been chosen by the

Republican machine and that the New Idea group's spokesman, George L. Record, had been booed and shouted down at the state Republican convention. When Lewis pledged that he would be a "constitutional governor" who would not try to influence the legislature, Wilson shot back that he would be "an unconstitutional governor" who would use every legitimate means of persuasion to fight for his programs. Wilson rejected patronage pressure as "immoral," but he vowed to use unceasing public pressure: "I give notice now that I am going to take every important subject of debate in the Legislature out on the stump and discuss it with the people."[5]

Wilson had more trouble finding the substance than the form of his appeal to independents and New Idea Republicans. At the beginning of the campaign in September 1910, he struck several cautionary notes about regulatory measures and attacks on corporations. Those initial arguments sounded much like the counsels of restraint Roosevelt was giving at the same time to Republican insurgents on his western tour. "We shall not act either justly or wisely," Wilson admonished the state convention delegates, "if we attack established interests as public enemies." He condemned Republican antitrust policies for "too much talk and too few practicable suggestions," and he declared, "Government is not a warfare of interests." In his first newspaper interview after receiving the nomination, Wilson expressed doubts about two widely approved reform measures—direct primaries and popular election of senators. In one of his first campaign speeches he defended the courts, making a veiled slap at Roosevelt's criticisms and asserting, "The characteristic of all great governing peoples has been poise, patience and ability to make for progress by these virtues."[6]

Those statements, together with Wilson's earlier limited-government advocacy and Smith's patronage, repelled many New Idea Republicans. George Record immediately attacked him as a tool of the bosses and challenged him to debate specific issues. Wilson responded to the challenge by agreeing to answer publicly any questions put to him in writing. On October 17 Record published an open letter in which he asked thirteen questions about whether Wilson favored such measures as a public service commission, corporate regulation, primaries, and corrupt campaign practice laws. Record also demanded to know whether Wilson opposed "the boss-system," which, he asserted, existed in all states and both parties. Wilson answered Record with his own public letter in which he repeated the questions about favoring specific measures and answered simply "yes." As for the boss system, Wilson asserted that he would break it up through political reforms, by electing independent men to office, "and by pitiless publicity." He also reaffirmed his own independence, declaring, "I regard myself as pledged to the regeneration of the Democratic party which I have forecast above." Wilson's reply to Record caused a sensation. It removed doubts about his reform sentiments and won over independents and New Idea Republicans. "That letter will elect Wilson governor," Record reportedly said when he read the reply.[7]

The election returns on November 8, 1910, bore out Record's prediction. Wilson won with 54 percent of the total vote and a margin of nearly 50,000 over Lewis—the second largest plurality in New Jersey history. He ran ahead of his ticket, although Democrats generally did well, gaining four congressional seats and a big majority in the lower house of the legislature. The result left no doubt about Wilson's personal appeal and the insurgents' contribution. "It was no Democratic victory," Wilson told Harvey a week after the election. "It was a victory of the 'progressives' of both parties who are determined to live no longer under the political organizations that have controlled the two parties of the State." The magnitude and the character of Wilson's victory prompted comparisons with Roosevelt. Newspapers and magazines across the country again hailed him as a major new leader and forecast his presidential candidacy in 1912. Some who wrote to Wilson hoped for a sounder approach to reform, while others wanted him to take up reform advocacy like Roosevelt. Wilson agreed with all the comparisons. "If the independent Republicans who in this State voted for me are not to be attracted to us," he warned Harvey, "they will assuredly turn again, in desperation, to Mr. Roosevelt, and the chance of a generation will be lost to the Democracy: the chance to draw all the liberal elements of the country to it, through new leaders, the chance that Mr. Roosevelt missed in his folly, and [the chance] to constitute the ruling party of the country for the next generation."[8]

Wilson's assessment was as premature as the press plaudits. Yet the comparison with Roosevelt went to the heart of his political promise. Although Wilson did not enjoy the same wide popular recognition as Roosevelt had earlier, he had gained considerable visibility among better-educated people and well-informed journalists through his writing and speaking and particularly through his Princeton presidency. Wilson's Princeton background lent intellectual and social distinction to his new political career and gave him appeal outside regular party channels. Those characteristics, in which he resembled Roosevelt, accounted for the extraordinary attention his gubernatorial nomination and election received from newspapers and magazines throughout the country. Such attention from the press at the moment of his entry into politics offered still another parallel with Roosevelt. Like the dude of the 1880s in state politics, the professor-become-governor in the 1910s suffered no hour of obscurity as he made his way onto the national scene.

Although Wilson's more restrained and polished speaking style contrasted with Roosevelt's, he quickly showed a comparable ability to attract and stir crowds. In making his public impact he often struck the same chords as the ex-president. Wilson repeatedly appealed in the gubernatorial campaign for disinterested service and a new birth of idealism. Americans were on the threshold, he declared in a speech in October, "of the age in which politics is a great altruistic undertaking, in which men's veins will throb all those unselfish purposes which after all underlie all the great accomplishments of the human race, for the standard of statesmen is the common interest, and the common interest cannot be thought out interest by interest." Wilson did not depict such service and idealism only in high-flown terms. Partly to offset the unworldly connotations of his academic background, he frequently remarked on how much he liked to talk to ordinary working people, because they were in intimate, daily contact with the realities of life. Wilson likewise exulted in the combative side of politics. In his last speech of the campaign, he urged men to join "the fight against special privilege, but you know that men are not put into this world to go the path of ease; they are put into this world to go the path of pain and struggle." Wilson, too, believed in the strenuous life.[9]

Beyond the easily recognized similarities in their circumstances and styles, Wilson and Roosevelt were linked by a common approach to the rising of insurgency. In particular, two aspects of their approach bore a strong resemblance—partisanship and detachment. Just as Roosevelt strove from 1910 until the 1912 convention to capture antimachine, anticorporate sentiment for the Republicans, Wilson strove to make the Democrats the vehicle of such sentiment. Starting early in the gubernatorial campaign, Wilson stressed the Democrats' commitment to greater popular participation in politics and to regulation of big business. His party offered the only hope for reform, he stated in a newspaper interview at the beginning of October 1910, because the "Republican party has been guilty of forming an unholy alliance with the vast moneyed interests of the country." Wilson softened his partisanship when he praised the New Idea Republicans in New Jersey and insurgents elsewhere, and he admitted that being out of power had saved the Democrats from too close ties to big business. Wilson also continued to stray from party orthodoxy on the tariff and state rights. Once more he condemned protectionism in Republican practice but not in principle. "I am not a preponderant state rights man," Wilson conceded in September 1910: "I desire the energetic cooperation of the several law-making powers by our system in the common undertaking of reform." Above all Wilson called again for new party positions, dismissing earlier platforms as "documents taken out of a forgotten age." Even if they had agreed on everything else, Wilson and Roosevelt would have clashed in their desire to make their respective parties the main beneficiary of the rising progressive sentiment.[10]

The two men likewise shared a detached stance toward their reform followings. The strongest progressive elements in both parties consisted of spokesmen for the interests of farmers and small-town people, who harbored suspicions and resentments not only about big business and political machines but also about larger cities in general and the metropolitan areas of the Northeast in particular. Among the Democrats, Bryan and his followers in the South and West had championed programs for regulating corporations since 1896. Among the Republicans, party insurgency and advocacy of comparable state regulatory programs had found greatest support in the Middle West, with state reform movements like La Follette's in Wisconsin and Cummins's in Iowa, and in the West, where similar antimachine, anticorporate insurgent movements were about to sweep into power in California and Washington. Yet the two men who aspired to lead these elements were urbane denizens of northeastern states and Ivy League college graduates—and both had once enjoyed social and political ties to prominent businessmen among their party allies.[11]

Like Roosevelt, Wilson differed from his party's progressives in more than circumstances. At the beginning of his gubernatorial campaign, when he expressed caution about the trusts and skepticism about primaries and popular election of senators, he disclosed his divergence from most Bryanites and insurgent Republicans on those issues. Record and the New Idea Republicans were right to doubt whether Wilson was at one with them in his heart, just as La Follette and a few other insurgents correctly suspected Roosevelt's underlying commitment to their views. But their detachment sprang from different sources. Wilson was detached from the progressives principally because of his intellectual convictions, while Roosevelt's detachment resulted from his social background and projection of his personality into politics. This basic difference between them pointed to the divergence that would grow with their competing presidential candidacies and contribute to shaping the rest of their careers.[12]

Contrary to what Record and his friends thought, Wilson's initial caution and skepticism about their favored issues did not reflect debts to or sympathies with Smith and the New Jersey Democratic machine. Rather, those attitudes derived from Wilson's intellectual approach to politics. Two weeks before he received the gubernatorial nomination, he restated his organic, evolutionary viewpoint in an address to the American Bar Association. "We do not fight to establish theses," he asserted. "We do not pour our blood out to vindicate philosophies of politics." Wilson drew a sharp distinction between the "two great empires of human feeling"—religion and politics. Whereas religion embodied spirit and thought, politics found expression "in institutions . . . not in our own souls merely, but in the world of action outside of us as well," and it required order, adjustment, and adaptation. Wilson's separation of religion and politics differed fundamentally from Roosevelt's effort to inject what he considered a quasi-religious spirit of idealism and sacrifice into politics. Despite a shared idealism in style and to some extent in content, Wilson did not adopt Roosevelt's brand of political evangelism.[13]

The different sources of their detachment created correspondingly different political identities. Wilson's restrained manner and belief in self-control combined to make him circumspect about specific issues and programs. His anti-ideological viewpoint, drawn from Burke, made him oppose socialism and all of what he considered theoretical schemes for remaking society. Within those inclinations and commitments, however, lay the dynamic, relativistic view of politics that had already led Wilson to espouse the general proposition of more interventionist government. In his speech to the bar association Wilson also welcomed "a great reconstruction" of economic and political systems, which demanded "creative statesmanship as no age has done since the great age in which we set up the government under which we live . . . I do not fear revolution. I do not fear it even if it comes. I have unshaken faith in the power of America to keep its self-possession."[14]

Wilson's problem was the opposite of Roosevelt's, whose dramatic manner and nervous temperament made him seem bolder than he was. Wilson's self-possession made him seem more restrained than he was. That disparity between manner and substance accounted for some of the distrust felt by Record and the New Idea group. Other insurgents similarly distrusted Wilson as he rose to national prominence in 1911 and 1912. Another reason for such distrust was that he reversed the politician's usual procedure of moving from the particular to the general; in his thinking about politics he moved from the general to the particular. Having set his overall direction when he rejected limited government in 1907 and 1908, Wilson espoused specific measures gradually, as he faced concrete situations. This was the practical application of his long-held regard for expediency as the one true way to practice politics. "If any tissue of my body stopped growing it would die," he asserted in the opening speech of the gubernatorial campaign. "If any part of the body politic were to lose its impulse for progress, it would die. The only thing that is conservative is growth." The Burkean thinker reinforced the progressive politician within Wilson.[15]

Wilson's and Roosevelt's approaches to politics dictated two critical differences in their stands between 1910 and 1912. Those differences were difficult to discern at first, but they foreshadowed the major separation between them during the coming decade. The first arose with the model of leadership that Wilson proposed. Curiously, the New Jersey Republicans did not disparage his academic background as various opponents, including Roosevelt, did

later in the national arena. Before his nomination some friends had
questioned Wilson's fitness for the rough-and-tumble of politics.
His old friend Robert Bridges had asked him how he would deal
with a hostile legislature. Eyes snapping, Wilson responded,
"Well, I can *talk*, can't I?" Starting with his rejoinder to Lewis
about how he planned to be an "unconstitutional governor," Wilson
emphasized the value of speaking out on issues to form public
opinion. Although his prescriptions sometimes sounded like Roosevelt's allusions to the "bully pulpit," he had a different conception
in mind.[16]

At a moment of personal trial during the gubernatorial
campaign—the day Pyne and his opponents among the Princeton
trustees forced his resignation from the university presidency—
Wilson outlined his basic concept of political leadership. "You cannot make opinion overnight," he stated, harking back to his earliest
political writings. Forming opinion required debate and public
exposure because it "must be based, built together; it must be
made up of the ideas of united men having a united purpose."
Parties were indispensable instruments in forming opinion because
important issues required "long tedious processes of discussion."
Wilson reaffirmed his opposition to "the secret power of the political machine," but he maintained that the cure did not lie in breaking up parties. Instead, "We want to save and moralize parties—
save them by a sense of responsibility and teach them that right
conduct is service of the community and what is right." Again
implicitly criticizing Roosevelt, Wilson told a fable of the wind and
the sun vying to get a man to take off his cloak. When the wind
howled, the man only wrapped the cloak more tightly around him,
but when the sun warmed him, he gladly removed it. "Parties
respond to other things than the whip," Wilson declared. "I have
never known anything useful done under the whip, but I have
known very many useful things done under the kindly warmth of a
great principle."[17]

Wilson was applying to politics the gentle, collegial concept of
leadership he had employed at the beginning of his Princeton
presidency. Whether he would hold to that concept as governor or
president any more than he had done earlier remained to be seen.
But Wilson's invocation of the concept showed that he entered
politics subscribing to a different set of methods from Roosevelt's

and that he shared the widespread misgivings about the ex-
president's supposed dictatorial tendencies. Together with their
respective partisan ambitions, Roosevelt's and Wilson's differing
conceptions of leadership formed the basis for significant conflict
between them.

Those conceptions of leadership also pointed to their second
critical difference—the philosophical divergence that had been evident in their earlier utterances. Wilson did not espouse heroic
leadership after the Roosevelt model because he did not believe it
was necessary or wise. Instead of exhorting people to rise above
their ordinary interests to promote public good, he urged pursuit
of such interests unfettered by special privilege as the way to
achieve the good society. Not until fairly late in the 1912 presidential race did Wilson pin a label on his position—"the New Freedom"—comparable to Roosevelt's New Nationalism, but their
clash of philosophies was already implicit in the fall of 1910, when
Roosevelt coined his phrase and Wilson made his first campaign.

This second critical difference between them was easy to miss
in 1910. In appealing for idealism and criticizing narrow self-
interest, Wilson did sound like Roosevelt, and he persisted in
refusing, except rarely and perfunctorily, to bow to Jefferson as a
symbol of Democratic legitimacy. Yet the divergence from Roosevelt did underlie Wilson's gubernatorial campaign. From the outset
he emphasized economic concerns. When he upheld "the common
interest," he observed, "Each class must also think of the interest
of the rest; they must try to come to a common understanding, in
a common sympathy, with a common thought and purpose, and
then if we can get a spoke[s]man, an honest man, to lead them, we
will recover the prestige and hope and accomplishment of American politics." In his next to last campaign speech in November
1910, Wilson hit upon what would become his main theme in
1912—restoration of freedom to Americans, particularly economic
freedom—and his major thrust against Roosevelt—the charge of
paternalism. Once more identifying the Democrats with the common people, Wilson asked, "Do you want big business beneficently
to take care of you, or do you want to take care of yourselves? Are
you wards or are you men? Do you want the court to appoint
guardians for you or are you old enough to take care of yourselves?"

Wilson's position needed further development, but he was moving toward the debate with Roosevelt in 1912.[18]

The path to that contest looked deceptively easy at first. Wilson gained further national attention and comment on his presidential prospects immediately after the 1910 election, when a dramatic opportunity arose to display bold leadership. At the time of his nomination, rumors had circulated that Jim Smith had wanted a glamorous candidate who would swell the Democratic vote sufficiently to elect a majority in the legislature and thereby enable him to be elected once more to the Senate. Smith had never publicly denied the stories, but George Harvey and others had assured Wilson that the rumors were without foundation. Moreover, Smith had not entered the state's nonbinding primary for the senatorial nomination. The primary had been won in September by James E. Martine, a follower of Bryan and a perennial Democratic office seeker. Once the Democrats had won their majority in the legislature, however, reports reappeared about Smith's plans to return to the Senate and about his and the other bosses' schemes to ignore the primary results and to ditch Martine when the legislature met in January 1911. Three days after the election in November, Wilson evidently tried to get Smith to bow out and to suggest someone other than Martine, who had a reputation for fecklessness, as a compromise candidate. The boss coyly declined to disclose his intentions.[19]

Smith's refusal to stand aside presented Wilson with a nearly foolproof opportunity to reap political advantage. Losing no time, he privately warned Harvey of his determination to oppose Smith and back Martine for the Senate seat, and he began lining up support among legislators and party leaders. A visit to Smith's home early in December, to make a personal plea not to run, failed to dissuade the boss. Wilson then made public his stand against Smith and for Martine. He spent the rest of the month and the first three weeks of January 1911 meeting with legislators and speaking to public meetings. When the legislature voted, a week after Wilson's inauguration as governor, Martine won on the second ballot. Smith, who had received only ten votes on the first ballot from his home county, had withdrawn before the final vote in bitterness and disgrace. Wilson savored his triumph and the nationwide publicity the fight had generated, but he also admitted privately, "I am getting more credit than I deserve." Wilson recognized that he had faced a foolish, discredited boss and a weak, disorganized machine whose opposition had been an undisguised boon. "Smith is a fool— an old fool," snorted the irascible editor Henry Watterson, "—and deserved what he has got. The case was as clear as a chunk of sunshine and he should have seen it."[20]

Smith and the New Jersey bosses may have been pushovers, but their rout got Wilson's governorship off to a spectacular start. The 1911 session of the legislature, which lasted from January through April, furnished his first test in power. He swiftly translated his earlier writings and academic experience into governmental practice. Besides his wonted boldness, which he had already shown in answering Record and taking on Smith, Wilson drew upon his prime ministerial model, as Arthur Link has pointed out, by preparing a legislative program in advance and then by working through his party caucus to enforce discipline and enact his measures. Further, Wilson fulfilled his promise to be an "unconstitutional governor" by taking such unheard-of steps as attending Democratic caucus meetings and going out on the hustings to advocate his program and denounce opponents, particularly Smith's minions. Wilson's reform agenda comprised four measures—a primary law, a corrupt practices statute for elections, a workmen's compensation law, and an act creating a public service commission to regulate transportation and public utility companies. "I got absolutely everything I strove for," he exulted at the end of the session, "and more besides," including educational and municipal reform measures. "I came into office in the fulness of time," Wilson acknowledged, "when opinion was ripe on all these matters . . . and by never losing sight of the business for an hour, but by keeping up all sorts of (legitimate) pressure *all the time*, kept the mighty forces from being diverted at any point."[21]

Wilson's performance deserved all the attention and accolades it received, but it hardly made him an ideal governor. Even in the 1911 legislative session, occasional failures marred his record. The Republican-controlled state senate, for example, rejected his recommended ratification of the constitutional amendment to allow an income tax. As an administrator, Wilson did reasonably well. He put in long hours at his desk and attended to his duties efficiently.

According to at least one close observer, however, he showed little liking for such chores as making appointments and dealing on a day-to-day basis with fellow office holders. Reporters never tired of asking Wilson about how he made the switch from a supposedly cloistered academic life to the political arena. Wilson usually answered with a variation on a quip about how much tamer and more civilized "real" politicians were, compared to academic politicians. "Let me tell you," he reportedly informed one journalist, "that Jim Smith and the bunch of New Jersey politicians I have been battling at Trenton are neophytes in the arts of intrigue compared with some of these Princeton politicians." Wilson's success against Smith and with his program seemed to bear out that estimate, but the 1911 legislative session marked the high point of his governorship.[22]

Wilson's shortcomings as governor did not stem from any finickiness or impracticality that might be ascribed to his academic background. He had quickly shed his initial shyness about taking the stump, and drawing upon his natural combativeness, he had grown to relish the campaign trail so much that he really never left it while governor. In addition to his presidential campaigning in 1911 and 1912, Wilson made extended speaking tours in New Jersey to advocate his programs during the legislative session, to endorse municipal reforms during the summer of 1911, to support progressives and oppose machine Democrats in the primaries the following September, and to back sympathetic Democrats in the November legislative elections. His greater difficulty in adjusting to politics, and one of his two shortcomings as governor, lay in his distaste for dealing with fellow politicians on a personal basis. That came from the same solitary tendencies he had shown as a university president. When he exerted himself, Wilson got on well with other leaders, as he did in opposing Smith and enacting his program. He sometimes showed a frolicsome, playful streak—singing, telling jokes, and even dancing with legislators at informal parties. But those efforts never came naturally to him. After describing some high jinks with state senators at Atlantic City, he confided, "Such are the processes of high politics! This is what it costs to be a leader!"[23]

Wilson's second shortcoming as governor resulted from his presidential candidacy. During the 1912 New Jersey legislative

session, he failed to repeat his previous legislative success. The
Republicans had gained control of both houses of the legislature
and were determined to make him look bad in an effort to damage
his presidential prospects. Moreover, Wilson was paying the price
of instant national prominence. At no time during his governorship
did he operate outside the national political limelight. Such attention undoubtedly enhanced his performance at the beginning of his
governorship. As his term wore on, however, and the national
campaign intensified, his presidential prospects proved highly distracting and prevented him from pushing his legislative programs
as vigorously as he had earlier.[24]

By the time of his gubernatorial inauguration in January 1911,
three separate drives were under way to nominate Wilson for the
presidency. One included Harvey and the Wall Street–connected
Democrats who had sponsored his entry into politics. Although
Harvey remained active on Wilson's behalf early in 1911, the governor's antimachine and regulatory actions soon cooled the editor
toward his one-time protégé. Wilson likewise felt increasingly uncomfortable about Harvey's patronage. In December 1910 he
warned an organizer of the second presidential drive, "It would not
be wise to have Colonel Harvey as a public sponsor." The second
drive started among a collection of Protestant clergymen and journalists, teachers' and professors' groups, Princeton alumni, and college students—all of whom saw in Wilson someone of their own
kind who was doing good deeds in politics. These groups, which did
not form tight organizations, began to spring up in December 1910,
when a former student of Wilson's made plans to form clubs in
colleges around the country. Often linked to campus YMCA chapters, the college clubs attested Wilson's special attraction to religious and social-service-minded youth. By June 1912 they had
formed over a hundred organizations with 10,000 members. Teachers supplied corps of campaign workers in primaries and the election, particularly in rural areas of various states.[25]

The third Wilson presidential movement proved the most con-
sequential. In February 1911 the new governor noted that a few
amateur New Jersey politicians and some "Southern friends of mine
in New York" were putting together "some kind of organized movement to advocate my claims for the nomination for the Presidency."
Wilson did not discourage this movement, but he did not turn it

over to Harvey. Instead, he asked another New York magazine editor, who had known him for many years and who had also previously touted him as a presidential possibility, to guide the movement. He was Walter Hines Page, who shared Wilson's southern background and newfound reformist leanings. Together with another expatriate southerner and former Princeton student of Wilson's, William F. McCombs, Page kicked off an organized presidential drive. They raised money, hired a full-time publicity agent, and helped arrange an out-of-state political tour by Wilson in May and June 1911. McCombs soon displaced Page at the center of the organization, and joined by yet another southern expatriate, William Gibbs McAdoo, he became the effective, if often neurotic, manager of the presidential campaign.[26]

The diverse character of his support shaped Wilson's pursuit of the Democratic nomination. His own convictions, the desires of his newer and more numerous backers, and main chance all combined to make opposition to political machines, big business, and special privilege his overriding themes. From the outset of his presidential campaign, Wilson sought to portray the Democrats as the truly progressive party and himself as the boldest, most advanced progressive they could nominate. Speaking to a group of reform Democrats in Philadelphia in February 1911, he set the tone of his appeal by sounding once more like Roosevelt. Proclaiming himself a "radical," Wilson lauded the people's "unending struggle for things which they have not yet obtained," and he warned reformers not to be deceived "by the literary theory of American institutions," which stressed constitutional absolutism and limited government. He praised the western insurgents' experiments with the referendum and direct legislation for "trying not to destroy, but to restore representative government." Soon afterward, on the speaking tour that took him to the Middle West and West in May and June 1911, Wilson endorsed the initiative, referendum, and recall, and he frequently repeated his self-designation as a "radical." Further, in the Philadelphia speech, although he criticized Hamilton, he still called him "one of the greatest statesmen that this country has ever had."[27]

From the beginning Wilson also developed his implicit differences from Roosevelt in his approach to the progressives' concerns. He closed the Philadelphia speech in February 1911 with the avowal "that the so-called radicalism of our time is nothing else than an effort to release the energies of our time." Wanting only justice and purity, the American people were "bound by the clogs and impediments of our political machinery. What we are trying to do is to release its generous forces. They are not forces of envy." Releasing popular energy to renew society became Wilson's major argument in pursuing the presidency. In April 1911 he spelled out his position further and coined a memorable phrase when he scorned the Republicans for their exaltation of big business, as "a body of trustees, who shall administer the affairs of the nation for the benefit of those who haven't sense enough to conduct it themselves." Republican thinking was not only fallacious but also perverse, because big businessmen had the least understanding of people's needs. "The men who understand the life of the country are the men who are on the make, and not the men who are already made." In May 1911 Wilson added, "The nation does not consist of its leading men. It consists of the whole body of the people. You never heard of a tree deriving its energy from its buds or its flowers, but from its roots."[28]

New notes crept into Wilson's utterances as he developed his argument. On his western tour in May 1911, he said kinder words than before about Jefferson, and he identified himself as a "Jeffersonian." At the end of that tour Wilson lashed out at the concentration of economic power by trusts in the Northeast, which had "shut and double bolted" the doors of opportunity to new enterprises in other parts of the country. He particularly denounced and called for destruction of the "money monopoly." These new stands represented not just sharpening convictions but shrewd politics as well. For Wilson, the key to the Democratic presidential nomination lay in staking out an unmistakably progressive position opposed to bosses and big businessmen, which would have appeal outside and inside his party. The Democrats' national standing in 1911 mirrored their previous condition in New Jersey—prolonged exile from power and confirmed minority status. A winning candidate would therefore have to draw votes from independents and dissident Republicans. The progressives' issues seemed to offer the best, perhaps the only, chance for a Democrat to do that in 1912. Both his newness to politics and his resemblance to Roosevelt made Wilson obviously the candidate with the greatest extraparty appeal, which in turn made him the apparent frontrunner for the nomination in 1911.[29]

A progressive-leaning Democrat also had to win over an internal constituency. Ever since his nomination in 1896, William Jennings Bryan had advocated most of the economic regulatory measures favored by progressives in both parties, and he maintained a large, devoted following, mainly among southern and western Democrats. The personal and ideological leadership of the "Great Commoner" had made him the single most powerful figure in the party. As a result, as Wilson observed in April 1911, "no Democrat can win whom Mr. Bryan does *not* approve." As the governor of a northeastern state and as a man with an anti-Bryanite past, Wilson started with two strikes against him in Bryan's book. "The fact that you were against us in 1896 raised a question in my mind in regard to your views on public questions," Bryan told Wilson in January 1911, "but your attitude in the Senatorial race has tended to reassure me." Their first meeting occurred when Bryan gave a religious talk at Princeton in March, and it proved friendly. Wilson believed he acquitted himself well as both a progressive and a fellow orator when they shared a speakers' platform for the first time the following month. Wilson's arguments for the release of popular energy, his compliments to Jefferson, and his attacks on the trusts all served to make him more acceptable in the eyes of the Great Commoner and his following.[30]

As a party outsider and political newcomer, Wilson had no choice but to play reformist, antimachine, anticorporation cards. Those cards alone, however, could not win him the presidential nomination. Even when Wilson's nomination seemed a sure thing in 1911, signs of trouble appeared. Wilson's original anti-Bryanite support waned in direct proportion to his more explicit endorsements of political and economic reform. Finally, in December 1911, Harvey cornered Wilson and extracted an admission that the editor's support was hurting him in some quarters. Harvey thereupon dropped his magazine's endorsement and tried unsuccessfully to embarrass Wilson with insinuations of ingratitude. Although the falling away of Harvey and other anti-Bryanites did not hurt, it did highlight the one-sidedness and fragility of Wilson's support. Among Wilson's managers, McCombs came closest to being a party professional, and throughout 1911 he worried constantly about the candidate's appearing too radical, which might hurt him in the South, and his relatively slight backing among recognized Democratic leaders. Those two areas—the South and the party organization—proved to be Wilson's weakest spots and nearly prevented him from getting the nomination.[31]

It was ironic that there was opposition from the South, inasmuch as that section also provided early and continuing support. Wilson identified himself as a radical in the spring of 1911 in part because, he explained privately, "I wanted a chance to tell my friends in the South what I thought, just what my programme is, before they went further and committed themselves to me as a 'favorite son.' " His endorsement of the initiative and referendum evidently did raise doubts among some southerners, who feared any new voting arrangements as potential means to enfranchise blacks. In the fall of 1911, in response to pleas from McCombs and other southern supporters, Wilson retreated from his advocacy of those measures and stated that local conditions should determine their adoption. Actually, his radical reputation and his endorsement of the initiative and referendum were symptoms rather than the cause of Wilson's problem in the South. The cause lay in the same place as his support—his southern birth and background. As soon as Wilson had entered politics, a number of southern editors and political spokesmen had hailed him as a native son who might end the section's exclusion from national power. Yet Wilson enjoyed that opportunity because he no longer lived in the South and had risen to prominence in the North. Appropriately, the core of his most important presidential drive consisted of men like himself, expatriate southerners.[32]

The division between Wilson's supporters and opponents below the Potomac boiled down to a contest between reconstructed and unreconstructed southerners. The bulk of the opposition came from old-style bosses, or "bourbons," who distrusted him mainly as a party outsider. Yet resistance also came from such farmer radicals as James K. Vardaman of Mississippi and Tom Watson of Georgia, who were suspicious of his anti-Bryanite past. The common ground for this alliance of southern opposites was the suspicion that Wilson had adapted himself too well to one form or another of northern culture. Starting in February 1912 his southern opponents joined forces behind the candidacy of Oscar W. Underwood of Alabama, the majority leader in the House of Representatives, and Underwood won most of the southern primaries and conventions that were contested against Wilson. Not all was lost. Wilson retained strong backing, particularly in North Carolina, South Carolina, and Texas. He remained the second choice, often the private first choice, of many Underwood delegates. But he fell far short of a majority among the delegates from his native section, much less in the convention as a whole.[33]

Southern opposition overlapped with the second and more serious weakness of Wilson's candidacy—scanty support among Democratic professionals. As Taft's reelection prospects dimmed, Wilson's main attraction, his appeal outside party ranks, carried less weight with Democratic leaders. Further, Wilson did not hold an exclusive claim to the progressive mantle, as Bryan showed by not endorsing but merely not opposing him. Unfortunately for Wilson's nomination chances, the party's highest-ranking office holder, Speaker of the House Champ Clark, commanded both the organizational loyalties and, as a long-time follower of Bryan, the progressive credentials within the party. Clark's dour demeanor and vapid oratory gave him a reputation as a party hack that made him easy to underestimate. After he entered the presidential race in January 1912, he outpolled Wilson in most of the primaries and conventions outside the South. With support from William Randolph Hearst's newspapers and local machines, both of which alleged that Wilson was anti-immigrant, Clark inflicted particularly damaging defeats in Illinois, Massachusetts, and California during April and May. No candidate entered the Democratic convention in June 1912 with a majority or anywhere near the two-thirds required for the nomination, but Clark led Wilson by more than a hundred votes on the first ballot. Trapped between Clark and Underwood, Wilson looked lost.[34]

His faltering candidacy underscored the differences between him and Roosevelt and between Democrats and Republicans. Wilson had attained neither the popular appeal nor the proven winner status that brought Roosevelt so close to seizing his party's nomination despite opposition from organization leaders. His candidacy fell further short of Roosevelt's because Democratic machines in various states successfully withstood his challenges and because he ran afoul of inflammatory attacks by such demagogues as Tom Wat-

son and Hearst. On the other hand, few if any of Wilson's opponents were as implacable as Roosevelt's Republican adversaries.
He therefore retained some chance for the nomination as long as he
stayed in the field. Wilson fought back hard. Strenuous campaigning in Illinois and Georgia kept him away from the New Jersey
legislative session in April. In May he had to fend off an attack by
Smith's forces in the New Jersey primary. Usually cheerful and
fatalistic, he did confess to an old friend at a low point, "It begins
to look as if I must merely sit on the sidelines and talk, as a mere
critic of the game I understand so intimately—throw all my training
away and *do* nothing."[35]

On the eve of the presidential race, defeat and retirement from
politics struck Wilson as a particularly malign fate because he had
so clearly articulated the position from which he wanted to run. In
his campaign during the first five months of 1912, he continually
advocated the release of popular energies to renew society. "I am
interested in nothing so much as releasing the energy of the country," he avowed in February. "That, to my mind, is the whole task
of politics, to release the honest energy of the country." Wilson still
often echoed Roosevelt. In March he compared the issues of 1912
with those of the 1850s, likewise invoking the aegis of Lincoln, and
he declared that he had "not the least feeling of piety on the
question of [tariff] protection. The whole question is one of expediency pure and simple." But those statements pointed in a different
direction from Roosevelt's utterances. Wilson grew steadily more
insistent on the necessity of renewal from below. In April he used
Lincoln's example to assert, "The governing forces of this country
are not going to come from the well known families. They are not
going to come from men whose names we know." He also stressed
the primacy of economic concerns. In May he noted that it was no
accident that the petitions in the Lord's Prayer began with a plea
for bread: "The foundation of our lives, of our spiritual lives included, is economic." The task of government was therefore "to
make those adjustments which will put every man in a position to
claim his normal rights as a living human being."[36]

In the spring of 1912 Wilson began to articulate an approach to
reform that was acceptable to Bryan and to rural Democrats, differentiated from Roosevelt's, and based upon his own fundamental
view of politics. Wilson now stated his "ever renewed admiration"
for Jefferson and hailed the coming restoration of the South to

national leadership, with its "great unexhausted reserves of unused thought, of unemployed power." Moreover, in applying Jefferson's thought to current problems, he raised three issues that would dominate his New Freedom program—"a tariff fitted to actual conditions," "a currency system elastic indeed," and destruction of "the process of monopoly." Wilson justified his stands with repeated expressions of an anti-ideological political philosophy. In April he declared himself "a disciple of Edmund Burke, who was opposed to all ambitious programmes on the principle that no man, no group of men can take a piece of paper and reconstruct society. I believe that politics, wise statesmanship, consist in dealing with one problem at a time and the circumstances of each particular case." On that philosophical foundation Wilson based his approach to progressive concerns. Also in April 1912 he affirmed, "Progressiveism [*sic*] is the adaptation of the business of each day to the circumstances of that day as they differ from the circumstances of the day before." It would have been a shame if Wilson had not had a chance to test his approach in combat with such a worthy foe as Roosevelt. [37]

The final irony in Wilson's quest for the nomination came in the way he eventually prevailed. The Republican debacle at Chicago and Roosevelt's bolt earlier in June made it seem more likely still that the Democrats could win with any candidate. At the convention in Baltimore Clark gained a majority when Tammany delivered New York's votes to him on the tenth ballot. The nomination seemed about to fall into his hands. Since 1844 every candidate who had gotten a majority had gone on to be nominated. After the tenth ballot Clark prepared a victory statement, and Wilson telegraphed McCombs, his co-manager with McAdoo at Baltimore, to release his delegates. But McAdoo declined to use the telegram and instead telephoned Wilson and got the instructions rescinded. Thereafter, Wilson's forces held firm and maintained a pact with the Underwood camp not to withdraw in Clark's favor. After another twenty ballots and interminable behind-the-scenes argument and dealing, Wilson's votes overtook Clark's. After another thirteen ballots, when Illinois abandoned Clark, Wilson gained a majority. At last, on July 2, after four days of voting, the Underwood forces capitulated on the forty-sixth ballot and put Wilson over the top. [38]

The obvious irony of the 1912 convention was that the Democrats' most attractive progressive candidate owed his nomination to the party's most antiquated device, the two-thirds rule. Like most antimachine Democrats, Wilson opposed the rule, but without it he would have lost. The irony extended further. Of the three main factors that contributed to Wilson's victory, only the two less important ones owed something to his broader appeal. The first and ultimately most potent factor was, as Link has shown, old-fashioned horse trading at the convention. Particularly critical were McAdoo's skill and persistence in holding Underwood's managers to their bargain and in getting Illinois's boss-led delegation to forsake Clark. The second factor was southern loyalty, which furnished the basis for the pact with the Underwood forces. Wilson remained their second choice because most of them preferred a progressive expatriate southerner to a border state man with northern machine backing. The third factor was the vociferous, frequently meddlesome influence of Bryan. The Great Commoner belatedly backed Wilson at the convention because Wilson forthrightly repudiated potential support from Tammany and Wall Street, while Clark equivocated. But Bryan's antics at the convention sprang almost as much from the urban versus rural, ethnic versus "native" conflict that was to nearly wreck the Democrats in the 1920s. The prolonged balloting at Baltimore offered a foretaste of what would happen again in San Francisco in 1920 and, most disastrously, at Madison Square Garden in 1924.[39]

For the present, however, few read grim portents. After such a protracted, often apparently forlorn struggle, Wilson greeted the news of his nomination in an understandably subdued mood. He told reporters that he appreciated the honor but that at the moment "I feel the tremendous responsibility it involves even more than I feel the honor." Wilson soon recovered his aplomb, but he remained grave. "My nomination was a sort of political miracle," he told one friend. ". . . It is awesome to be so believed in and trusted." Despite the candidate's mood, the lines of the next battle were forming. A Democratic senator informed Wilson that La Follette believed "the real fight would be between you and Roosevelt in November . . . a view very generally shared by the shrewdest of the Washington correspondents and many well-informed members of Congress." The insiders were right. Wilson's nomination was about to pit the most promising contender against the mightiest former champion in an awesome political title bout.[40]

· 13 ·

On the Hustings

THE RACE BETWEEN ROOSEVELT AND WILSON got off to a slow start. Neither man showed much taste at first for attacking the other. Aside from his private dismissals of Wilson during 1911, Roosevelt had said next to nothing about the New Jersey governor. Wilson had implicitly criticized Roosevelt's attacks on the courts and his overbearing leadership, and privately he had scorned the ex-president's opposition to Taft's renomination as an "insane distemper of egotism!" Yet Wilson had also continued to laud Roosevelt for awakening people to the need for reform, and in his gubernatorial campaign he had praised the New Nationalism. By the end of 1911 Wilson was relishing the prospect of running against Roosevelt. "*That* would make the campaign worth while," he had confided to a friend. The two men's paths crossed on May 27, 1912, when Roosevelt campaigned in Princeton during the New Jersey primary. Wilson stood silently at the back of the crowd, while an exhausted Roosevelt dealt in generalities and delivered what one observer called "the worst speech I ever heard from him." In his own speech about an hour later, Wilson referred to the rivals for the Republican nomination as "two very militant gentlemen" whose personal quarrel was distracting attention from such serious concerns as the trusts, banking, and labor conditions. That was the closest Roosevelt and Wilson came to a face-to-face debate at any time in their careers.[1]

Their nominations for the presidency did not immediately plunge Roosevelt and Wilson into personal combat, but contrasts in their followings, styles, and ideologies did appear from the outset.

By coincidence, their campaigns officially began on the same day in August 1912. The Progressive party convention, which gathered on August 5 in Chicago, represented a novel departure in American politics. The Progressives had, as participant-journalist William Allen White noted, a prim, upbeat, middle-class tone, which was alien both to the seamy style of professional politics and to the embittered accents of earlier protest movements. Singing "Onward Christian Soldiers," "The Battle Hymn of the Republic," and the Doxology, the delegates gave the convention the air of a religious camp meeting. Such prominent reformers as the social worker Jane Addams and former senator Beveridge graced the speakers' platform. The delegates typified the economically secure, college-educated younger men and women, previously uninvolved in politics, whom the Progressive party attracted in all parts of the country.[2]

The Progressive following attested to the undiminished appeal of Roosevelt's vivid, well-dramatized personality, social standing, and reform advocacy. As always, he held a special attraction for youth, particularly college students and aspiring professionals, and he cut across Wilson's appeal to the same groups. No precise tally has been or probably can be taken, but the fervor and later prominence of many of Roosevelt's youthful backers in 1912—including Alfred M. Landon, Henry A. Wallace, Felix Frankfurter, Walter Lippmann, and Dean Acheson—suggest that outside the South and apart from the YMCA, teachers, and some religious groups, he exerted greater appeal than Wilson among the nation's future leaders. Likewise, Roosevelt's endorsement of minimum wage and workmen's compensation laws, abolition of child labor, and woman suffrage drew the backing of social justice reformers and prominent feminists, while his trust regulation stance attracted some businessmen. His ideas and his heroic approach to leadership enlisted ardent support from such journalists and intellectuals as White, Croly, and Lippmann. Between its members and its quasi-religious overtones, Roosevelt's Progressive party constituted a crusade that was at once hopeful and circumspect, iconoclastic and respectable, righteous and glamorous.[3]

The Progressives' attractiveness as a crusade did not make up for their deficiencies as a political party. Veteran politicians were scarce at the Chicago convention. Of the leading insurgents against

Taft, only Beveridge and Senator Joseph M. Dixon of Montana joined the new party. Others, such as Cummins, William E. Borah, and George W. Norris, either supported Roosevelt personally but retained their Republican allegiance or stayed neutral. Among younger Republican progressive politicians, only the movement in California led by Hiram W. Johnson, and to a lesser extent the one in Washington, moved over into the Progressive camp. In Wisconsin La Follette remained unforgiving toward Roosevelt, and he backed Wilson in a way that avoided open endorsement but was clear to his followers. From a professional's point of view, the Progressives were, as Blum has characterized them, "a politician's Gothic horror," long on fervor and noise but short on organization and staying power.[4]

No one recognized the frailty of his political creation better than Roosevelt. In August 1912, both before and after the Progressive convention, he admitted privately that Wilson would probably win and that his new party had missed its chance when the Democrats had failed to nominate a conservative or a nonentity. Roosevelt's doubts showed when he addressed the convention on August 6, 1912. As 15,000 people cheered him for almost an hour, waved red bandannas, and sang hymns, one reporter noted that Roosevelt looked bewildered. "They were crusaders," the reporter commented; "he was not." But Roosevelt knew he had to play the hand circumstances had dealt him. He justified his candidacy with a long "Confession of Faith," in which he again enunciated his basic ideas and tried to stake out a position in contrast to both the Republicans and the Democrats.[5]

Roosevelt dwelt at length on the evils of "class government." He charged both of the old parties with practicing class government "in the interests of the rich few," but he also warned anew against pitting "the needy many" against big business and the wealthy. Roosevelt rejected equally those who exalted material prosperity regardless of its consequences—the Republican Old Guard—and those who would end the maldistribution of wealth at any price—the Bryanite Democrats. "The task of the wise radical must be to refuse to be misled by either set of false advisers" and to pursue the national interest. Privately, Roosevelt affirmed after the convention that he was leading the Progressives, despite the near certain prospect of defeat, because "we may be able to give the right trend to our democracy, a trend which will take it away from mere greedy shortsighted materialism."[6]

The path away from materialism lay, he told the Progressives, through a combination of more stringent economic and political reforms on one side and a different approach to the trusts on the other. In his "Confession of Faith," Roosevelt took the boldest domestic stands of his career. He called for the establishment of national party primaries and steps to ensure popular accountability by the courts. He also endorsed stricter regulation of manufacturing, minimum wage and maximum hours laws, abolition of child labor, employers' liability provisions, and government-backed pensions and insurance. At the same time Roosevelt expounded his trust regulation position more fully than before. The trust issue had already agitated the Progressives behind the scenes at Chicago. The platform committee had originally inserted a plank advocating stronger antitrust laws and restoration of competition, yet when Beveridge and George W. Perkins, Roosevelt's principal businessman backer, had alerted him to this, Roosevelt had twice vetoed the plank. As a result the Progressive platform contained no mention of antitrust laws.[7]

In his speech to the convention Roosevelt denounced the present antitrust statutes and their application as signs "not of progress, but of Toryism and reaction." He advocated an approach to regulation of the trusts modeled on the Interstate Commerce Commission and attuned to actual economic conditions. "We are in favor of honest business, big or little," Roosevelt avowed. "We propose to penalize conduct and not size." His trust regulation argument formed the longest segment of his speech to the convention, and it broached what soon became the hottest issue of the campaign against Wilson. Roosevelt did not speak lightly or unwittingly. Earlier his trust position had raised denunciations from Democrats and doubts from Republican insurgents. The fight over the Progressive antitrust plank revealed how few shared his views, even among those who had followed him into the new party. In spelling out his position on the trust issue so fully, Roosevelt was serving the same notice on the Progressives as he had earlier on the Republicans with the court issue—they had better be in a "heroic mood" to follow him and accept his convictions.[8]

Roosevelt also gave his followers plenty of what they wanted to hear. In addition to flaying Old Guardsmen and advocating reforms, he devoted much of his speech to denouncing the Democrats. Their 1912 platform, charged Roosevelt, betrayed "an archaic construction of the States'-rights doctrine" and purveyed economic quackery reminiscent of free silver in 1896. Withal, Roosevelt accused the Democrats of espousing "Toryism not Progressivism." His main rival he mentioned just twice in passing as "Professor Wilson." Privately, Roosevelt had earlier conceded that Wilson was "an able man" unlikely to prolong "Taft's muddleheaded inability." He also regarded the Democratic nominee as a man of few firm convictions—an opportunistic Johnny-come-lately to progressivism and "not a Nationalist." The next evening, August 7, Roosevelt seemed a bit shaken when he received the Progressive nomination. He made no acceptance speech but simply thanked the delegates.[9]

A few hours before Roosevelt accepted the Progressive nomination, Wilson accepted the Democratic nomination in a contrasting scene and manner. In accord with hoary custom in both of the older parties, Wilson did not attend or address the convention, either before or after his nomination. He awaited the arrival of an official party delegation to inform him of his selection and then responded with an acceptance speech. The ceremony took place on August 7, at the summer residence of New Jersey governors in the resort town of Sea Girt. Standing in the sweltering afternoon sun, Wilson waited through the notification speeches before delivering a lengthy reply; contrary to his preferred practice, he read from a prepared text. The formality and conventionality of the occasion underscored Wilson's ironic position as the Democratic nominee. His original presidential prospects had been good because he was attractive to Republicans and independents as well as Democrats, and his nomination had spiked Roosevelt's chances in the election. Now, however, thanks to Roosevelt's bolt, Wilson found himself largely dependent upon his own party. Aside from scattered Republican bolters, some independents, and La Follette in his covert way, Wilson drew virtually all his support from Democrats. It was their undivided backing that made him the likely winner in November.[10]

Despite the inauspiciousness of the situation, Wilson struck as
fervent and independent a note as Roosevelt had in his acceptance
speech. "We stand in the presence of an awakened nation, impatient of partisan make-believe," Wilson asserted at the outset.
He again echoed Roosevelt when he declared that the country was
susceptible "to unselfish appeals" and when he avowed, "The nation has been unnecessarily, unreasonably at war within itself."
Wilson refrained from attacking rival candidates and parties
openly. He once more said kind words for tariff protection as a
principle and pledged gradual reductions in rates "in such a way as
will least interfere with the normal and healthful course of commerce and manufacture." Wilson sounded most like his Progressive
opponent when he identified himself on the trust issue as "not one
of those who think that competition can be established by law
against the drift of a world-wide economic tendency . . . I dare say
we shall never return to the old order of individual competition,
and that organization of business upon a great scale of cooperation
is, up to a certain point, itself normal and inevitable." Some in his
partisan audience might have wondered whether their nominee
was a Republican in Democrat's clothing.[11]

Yet those similarities only partially obscured the ideological
difference between Wilson and Roosevelt. In his acceptance
speech on August 7 Wilson again painted a vision of renewal from
below and spelled out measures through which he wanted to implement that vision. He implicitly scorned both the Republicans and
Roosevelt for paternalistic attitudes toward popular interests, and
he declared, "No group of directors, economic or political, can
speak for a people. They have neither the point of view nor the
knowledge." Truly representative government must be restored,
Wilson argued, through "an effort to give voice to this great body
through spokesmen chosen out of every grade and class." He specified a number of measures as essential to such a restoration, including a tariff freed from favoritism and privilege, "the regulation of
trusts and the prevention of monopoly," banking and financial
reform, labor laws to make working conditions better and safer,
national presidential primaries and popular election of senators,
conservation, and government promotion of agricultural training.
Wilson lacked Roosevelt's inflammatory style, but it was hard to
find significant differences in their specific reform endorsements.[12]

Their divergence lay deeper, concerning the role of individual economic self-interest in promoting public good. Once more, rather than preaching renunciation of such interests, Wilson held that they must be harmonized. "As servants of all," he avowed, "we are bound to undertake the great duty of accommodation and adjustment." Despite what Roosevelt soon charged, Wilson did not cast government in the passive role of umpire in those processes. In two areas he advocated active government intervention on the side of less-advantaged interests. Legislation to promote the health, safety, and prosperity of industrial workers, whom Wilson called "the backbone of the nation," could not be regarded as class legislation or as anything but "a measure taken in the interest of the whole people, whose partnership and right action we are trying to establish and make real and practical." Similarly with business, although competition could not be established by laws, "it can in large measure be revived by changing the laws and forbidding the practices that killed it, and by exacting laws that will give it heart and occasion again. We can arrest and prevent monopoly." Wilson was on his way to joining the debate with Roosevelt. He had broached the issue that would elicit their sharpest clash, and he had bared their deeper divergence over the methods and ends of political life.[13]

The two main contenders soon started attacking each other. Wilson did not share the sanguine estimates by others of his chances in the election. Later in August he confided that as he and Roosevelt faced the voters, "he appeals to their imagination; I do not. He is a real, vivid person, whom they have seen and shouted themselves hoarse over and voted for, millions strong; I am a vague, conjectural personality, more made up of opinions and academic prepossessions than of human traits and red corpuscles. We shall see what will happen!" Wilson regretted that he was popularly misunderstood, but he had no intention of trying to match Roosevelt's personal appeal. "Are people interested in personalities rather than principles?" his daughter recalled him asking during the campaign. "If that is true they will not vote for me." Instead, Wilson decided to hit Roosevelt on his most vulnerable issues, and a fortuitous meeting helped him draw up his plan of attack.[14]

On August 28, 1912, Louis D. Brandeis, the renowned and controversial Boston "people's attorney" and economic reformer, met Wilson for the first time at Sea Girt. For three hours they talked, principally about the trust issue. "I drew him out for my own benefit," Wilson told reporters at the end of the meeting. Brandeis explained that he had condemned Roosevelt's trust approach as "regulated monopoly," which meant enshrining economic "absolutism" and thereby "trying to make evil good, and that is a thing that cannot be done." Brandeis asserted that government must seek "to regulate competition instead of monopoly, for our industrial and our civil freedom go hand in hand." Those arguments supplied Wilson with the cutting edge of his New Freedom.[15]

One should not make too much of Brandeis's contribution. As Croly and Roosevelt had done, Brandeis influenced Wilson by refining thoughts he had previously entertained and by clarifying a direction in which Wilson was already moving. Brandeis did not originate Wilson's concern with the trusts, which dated back at least to 1906, nor did Wilson fully embrace Brandeis's economic and political views. On the trust question, Wilson's campaign speeches soon made it clear that he did not share Brandeis's belief that bigness was in itself an economic evil. Some years later Brandeis recalled, "Wilson did not realize the importance of bigness." No record indicates that the two men then or later discussed Brandeis's preference for decentralized government and state and local initiatives. Although Roosevelt presently accused Wilson of favoring limited government, Wilson had never at any time, except during his brief anti-Bryanite fling, believed in any kind of government but a strong, centralized one. Yet Brandeis's contribution to the 1912 campaign was critical. By furnishing a tactical opening and live ammunition, he got Wilson off to a lively start and precipitated the debate with Roosevelt. Wilson was correct when he told Brandeis in November, "You were yourself a great part of the victory."[16]

Wilson launched his first strike against Roosevelt in a Labor Day speech at Buffalo. He professed hearty agreement with the goals of the Progressive party's platform, particularly aid to labor and the disadvantaged. "But there is a central method," Wilson added, "a central purpose, in that platform, from which I very seriously dissent." Rather than try to disentangle government from special interests, he charged, Roosevelt's party proposed "a consummation of the partnership between monopoly and government, because when once the government regulates the monopoly, then monopoly will see to it that it regulates the government." The Democrats, in contrast, meant to regulate competition to prevent the trusts from unfairly crushing competitors. "In other words," Wilson observed, "ours is a program of liberty, and theirs is a program of regulation." That observation brought Wilson to his most devastating accusation against Roosevelt—that he was a paternalist. The Progressive platform, argued Wilson, envisioned "acting as a Providence for you . . . I don't believe there is any other man that is big enough to play Providence. I have never known any body of men, any small body of men, that understood the United States. And the only way the United States is ever going to be taken care of is by having the voices of all the men in it constantly clamorous for recognition of what is justice as they see the light."[17]

Those remarks conveyed the main message of Wilson's New Freedom, although he did not coin that phrase for another month. Brandeis's influence was apparent in the attack on Roosevelt's approach to trust regulation as both a sellout to big business and a denial of freedom. But Wilson made those ideas his own by incorporating them into his depiction of society undergoing constant renewal from below. It was in that context that he made a celebrated remark that many later reformers would hold against him. First he drew an extended contrast between the alleged paternalism of the Progressives and his own model of listening to and speaking for public opinion. In the process he countered sneers by Roosevelt and others about his unfitness for the presidency because he was a "schoolteacher." Then he declared, "What I fear, therefore, is a government of experts." Wilson deplored the Progressives' alleged imputation that only a small number of highly trained people understood the job of governing. If the people themselves did not "understand the job, then we are not a free people. We ought to resign our free institutions and go to school to somebody and find out what it is we are about." In short, democratic government must remain self-government, no matter how complex the economic and social problems became. That was the point Brandeis had helped Wilson to grasp and with which he flayed Roosevelt for much of the 1912 campaign.[18]

Roosevelt wasted no time in hitting back. Four days after Wilson spoke, he replied to the criticisms of his trust regulation approach by observing that all previous attempts to break up the trusts had failed. He added, "You recall Mr. Pierpont Morgan said 'You can't unscramble the eggs in an omelet.' " First Taft and now Wilson had proposed to unscramble the eggs through lawsuits, but all such efforts were futile. Wilson's denunciation of a "government of experts" Roosevelt dubbed "the exact attitude always taken by the respectable ultra-conservative in matters of this nature." It was not the Progressives' trust regulation approach, but "the Taft-Wilson programme" that sought to legalize monopoly "under the guise of a make-believe assault on monopoly." Only the Progressives offered something different from both the Republicans' and the Democrats' "vague, puzzled, and hopeless purpose feebly to continue the present policy." Only the Progressives offered a "definite and concrete" program that promised results "by punishing his [the businessman's] conduct and not merely his size; and we will effectively, and not merely nominally, curb and control the big trusts which are actually or potentially guilty of anti-social action." With this hard-hitting reply, the debate was joined.[19]

Roosevelt soon continued his counterattack. If the trust issue was his Achilles' heel, Wilson's was his past advocacy of limited government and his recent conversion to progressive measures. Roosevelt's only, admittedly slim chance to win lay in attracting Bryanite and other Democratic votes by depicting Wilson as a sham progressive. Roosevelt had charged Wilson with insincerity over the trust issue, but he needed an opening to make his larger argument more effective. A mishap of Wilson's with the press, like his own over the court issue on the way to Denver in 1910, supplied Roosevelt with just the opportunity he needed. In a speech in New York on September 9, Wilson stated, "The history of liberty is a history of the limitation of governmental power, not the increase of it." In context, that sentence formed part of an elaboration of Wilson's plea to keep government in touch with citizens. Quoted out of context, however, as it was in newspaper reports carried across the country, the sentence smacked of the state-rights, limited-government viewpoint that Wilson had once, briefly, championed.[20]

Roosevelt pounced on his opponent's apparent misstep. Speaking at San Francisco on September 14, Roosevelt quoted the offending sentence, which he called "the key to Mr. Wilson's position," and dismissed it as "a bit of outworn academic doctrine

which was kept in the schoolroom and the professorial study for a
generation after it had been abandoned by all who had experience
of actual life. It is simply the *laissez-faire* doctrine of English political economists three-quarters of a century ago." Roosevelt ridi-
culed all notions of applying that doctrine to American industrial
conditions. "In the present day," he declared, "the limitation of
governmental power, of governmental action, means the en-
slavement of the people by the great corporations who can only be
held in check through the extension of governmental power."
Roosevelt claimed "to take flat issue" with Wilson. His Progressives
proposed "to use government as the most efficient instrument for
the uplift of our people as a whole," and they proposed "to use the
whole power of government to protect all those who, under Mr.
Wilson's *laissez-faire* system, are trodden down in the ferocious,
scrambling rush of an unregulated and purely individualistic indus-
trialism." Unfair though they were, those charges drew blood.[21]

By mid-September 1912 the Roosevelt forces felt pleased with
the way the campaign was going. Their candidate had not only held
his own against a more fluent speaker, but he had also evidently
seized the initiative. Whether Roosevelt had dented Wilson's
Democratic support remained to be seen, but he certainly seemed
to have arrested any erosion of independent and insurgent Republican support and put Wilson on the defensive. When Roosevelt
made a second campaign swing westward at the end of September,
his staff arranged to keep him informed of what Wilson was saying,
and he was relishing the debate with his opponent. Roosevelt had
already resorted to answering Wilson's generalities on the trust
issue with facts and specifics. He toned down his normally slashing
style to attack Wilson with ridicule and with solemn declarations of
Progressive principles. "It was Wilson, Wilson, Wilson, all the time
in the private car," recalled Roosevelt's press aide, "and nothing
but Wilson and his record in the Colonel's talks. We believed we
were on the way to drive Wilson into one of his characteristic
explosions, with result [*sic*] that could only be detrimental to his
campaign."[22]

The optimism of Roosevelt's backers was justified, but only up
to a point. Since this was the fourth national campaign in which
their candidate had either run or played a commanding role, their
forces enjoyed an edge in experience. Wilson, as a novice presiden-

tial candidate, took time to find his stride. Roosevelt's reply on the trust issue and his attack on Wilson's governmental views compelled Wilson to answer. Waffling a bit on the trust issue, Wilson reiterated in the middle of September that he, too, objected to businesses' conduct, not their size. Further, he tried to differentiate trusts from big businesses. "A trust is an arrangement to get rid of competition," Wilson argued in a speech in Iowa, "and a big business is a business that has survived competition by conquering in the field of intelligence and economy. I am for big business, I am against the trusts." Wilson soon asked Brandeis for further advice, and the two held another conference in Boston on September 27. In a speech delivered a few hours after their meeting, Wilson condemned the "point of bigness . . . where you pass the point of efficiency and get to the point of clumsiness and unwieldiness." Wilson never resolved the inconsistency in his thinking about business size, but during the remainder of the campaign he followed Brandeis's suggestions about stressing ways to restore competition.[23]

Inasmuch as politics was his subject far more than economics, Wilson rebutted Roosevelt's attack on his governmental views more cogently and forcefully. Speaking in Pennsylvania on September 23, Wilson stated that "there is one principle of Jefferson's which no longer can obtain in the practical politics of America." That was the dictum "that the best government is that which does as little governing as possible, which exercises its power as little as possible." Wilson did not fear "the utmost exercise of the powers of the government of Pennsylvania, or of the Union, provided they are exercised with patriotism and intelligence and really in the interest of the people who are living under them. But when it is proposed to set up guardians over those people and to take care of them by a process of tutelage and supervision, in which they play no active part, I utter my absolute objection." As John Wells Davidson has suggested, Roosevelt had done Wilson a favor by attacking his governmental views, because Wilson sharpened those views and reaffirmed his progressivism in response. In fact, he turned the ex-president's attack back on him and drew blood in return.[24]

It is doubtful whether much danger existed of Roosevelt goading Wilson into a self-destructive act. Why Roosevelt and his aides believed they could manage such a feat is not clear, for Wilson did not have a record of "characteristic explosions." Roosevelt evidently did succeed to some degree in getting Wilson's goat. Late in September and during the first half of October, Wilson grew increasingly pointed in his criticisms. He hinted again at Roosevelt's alleged dictatorial tendencies. He called him "a very, very erratic comet" and charged him with having forfeited the people's trust by failing to carry out his reform programs while he had been president. Those attacks apparently did reflect some jealousy of Roosevelt's personal popularity. "A great many people in the United States have regarded me as a very remote and academic person," Wilson observed in a speech in October. "They don't know how much human nature there has been in me to give me trouble all my life." Wilson stopped attacking Roosevelt, however, when an insane bartender shot and wounded the ex-president in Milwaukee on October 14. Wilson immediately lauded Roosevelt as "that gallant gentleman" who had done "a vast deal to wake the country to the problems that now have to be settled," and he uttered no more personal criticisms before the election.[25]

Wilson had not been about to make a false move. Though hard-hitting, his attacks on his opponent were by no means intemperate, and they were no more unfair than Roosevelt's charges about his governmental views. By the latter part of September Wilson had regained the upper hand in the campaign and thereafter he never lost it. He began to hit his full stride while he was jousting with Roosevelt over the trusts and repulsing the attack on his governmental views. Wilson never really went on the defensive. Instead he hammered away at government by "a smug lot of experts," and he summed up the trust question by asking, "Are you going to have fresh brains injected into the business of this country, and the best man win, or are you going to make the present combinations permanent?" In addition to rebutting the charge that he believed in limited government, Wilson struck blows of his own by referring to Roosevelt's party as "the third party" and "the irregular Republicans, the variegated Republicans," but almost never as the Progressives. Most important, he repeatedly stressed his own themes of release of popular energy, social renewal from below, and representative government through public opinion.[26]

Wilson's western tour during the first half of October constituted an almost unqualified triumph. In the first speech, at Indianapolis, he restated his positions, renewed his attacks on Roosevelt, and coined his campaign slogan by urging Democrats "to organize the forces of liberty in our time in order to make conquest of a new freedom for America." Wilson frequently returned to the advocacy of freedom as he contrasted his program with Roosevelt's. "America is never going to choose thralldom instead of freedom," he declared in Nebraska. The Democrats offered a "program of freedom, . . . a program of general advantage." Wilson worked both sides of the partisan street on his western tour. He appeared with Bryan in the Great Commoner's hometown of Lincoln, Nebraska, which Wilson called "the Mecca of progressive Democracy." In Kansas and Illinois he stole Roosevelt's thunder by linking his own progressivism to his listeners' antislavery and Civil War Republican heritage. Wilson also cast aspersions on Roosevelt's reform credentials by reminding people that "such genuine progressives as Robert La Follette," whom he repeatedly praised, did not support the "third party." The only sour note on the tour emanated, literally, from his own voice. During a second speech in Indianapolis, Wilson severely strained his voice and had to rest it as he traveled homeward the day before Roosevelt was shot.[27]

Roosevelt also strained his voice, more seriously than Wilson, but his troubles ran deeper than that. By the second week in October Roosevelt realized that his attacks on Wilson had fallen short and that he had himself gone on the defensive. In a cracking voice in Chicago on October 12, Roosevelt protested, "I'm not for monopoly when we can help it. We intend to restore competition; we intend to do away with the conditions that make for monopoly. But there are certain monopolies you can't prevent." Breaking up the steel trust would not lower prices to the consumer or improve conditions for workers. Roosevelt charged his opponents with "losing sight of the main thing—men and women. We're for men. Free competition and monopoly—they're all the same thing unless you improve the condition of the workers." Roosevelt declared that he did "not care a rap" about how large a share of an industry the capitalists might own. "What I am interested in is getting the hand of government put on all of them—this is what I want."[28]

Apart from the weakness of his party, Roosevelt's biggest problem in the campaign lay in his failure to get much of his message across to the public. His speeches in September and the first part of October conveyed much less of his thinking about avoidance of class conflict, progressive self-restraint, and rising above materialism than either his New Nationalism speeches of 1910 or his "Confession of Faith" to the Progressive convention. Whereas Wilson varied the exposition of his views while engaging in their debate, Roosevelt usually stuck doggedly and narrowly to trust regulation and governmental power. He seems to have fallen into his own trap in trying to discredit Wilson's progressive credentials. At all events, the assassination attempt on October 14 presented a heaven-sent opportunity for Roosevelt to escape from his predicament. Hospitalization gave him a chance to rest his voice, and the incident itself supplied an unmatched dramatic occasion for him to hark back to his broader viewpoint.

Wounded in the chest on the way to a speech in Milwaukee, Roosevelt insisted on going on with the appearance. "I have altogether too important things to think of," he declared, "to feel any concern over my own death; and now I cannot speak to you insincerely within five minutes of being shot." Roosevelt compared his present campaign to leading his regiment in war, and he pointed to the attempt on his life as an illustration of the need "to prevent the coming of the day when we shall see in this country two recognized creeds fighting one another, when we shall see the creed of the 'Havenots' arrainged [sic] against the creed of the 'Haves.' When that day comes then such incidents as this to-night will be commonplace in our history." Because the Progressives were struggling to forestall that day, Roosevelt avowed, "I never in my life was in any movement in which I was able to serve with such whole-hearted devotion as in this; in which I was able to feel as I do in this that common weal. I have fought for the good of our common country."[29]

That was a perfect closing line. Roosevelt should have stopped there, as the audience was begging him to do. Instead he rambled on, feeling the effects of shock, finally stopping after he had made another attack on Wilson for adhering "to the old flint-lock, muzzle-loaded doctrine of States' rights." That last blast detracted only slightly from his condemnation of class conflict and his appeal to a warlike spirit of sacrifice and common purpose. From his hospital bed two days later, Roosevelt sent a telegram to the Progressives: "Tell the people not to worry about me, for if I go down another will take my place. For always, the army is true." The incident in

Milwaukee allowed Roosevelt to put on the kind of show at which he excelled. His speech would have made a superb dying declaration, and one cannot help suspecting he was disappointed that the cup of martyrdom passed him by. As it was, he spent the rest of October convalescing and made only one more major speech before the election.[30]

That speech, to a mass rally in New York on October 30, represented Roosevelt's finest performance on the campaign trail. Although a realistic appraisal of his prospects had tempered his crusading fervor, he struck a few sparks, as in the Armageddon speech. For the most part, however, he presented another thoughtful exposition of his basic views, as he had done earlier in the New Nationalism speeches. Possibly honoring Wilson's renewed personal truce, Roosevelt refrained from mentioning either of his opponents. He also avoided any reference to the trust issue, in part because he had retreated from his earlier forthright rejection of the antitrust approach. On October 19, from his hospital bed, Roosevelt had issued a statement in which he advocated strengthening the Sherman Act along lines that, though he did not know it, had been proposed by Brandeis. As Harbaugh has observed, that statement virtually duplicated the Progressive antitrust platform plank Roosevelt had earlier vetoed.[31]

In his last major speech Roosevelt admonished his followers not to "permit the brutal selfishness of arrogance and the brutal selfishness of envy, each to run unchecked its evil course. If we do so, then some day smouldering hatred will suddenly kindle into a consuming flame, and either we or our children will be called on to face a crisis as grim as any which this Republic has ever seen." Rather than "let an unchecked and utterly selfish individualistic materialism riot to its appointed end," Roosevelt urged Progressives "to be just to all, to feel sympathy for all, and to strive for an understanding of the needs of all." Although he admitted that his party's principles were as old as the Ten Commandments and the Golden Rule, Roosevelt also proposed to cast out "dead dogmas of a vanished past. We propose to lift the burdens from the lowly and weary, from the poor and oppressed." He ended with an evocation of the Civil War. Eschewing sectionalism and seeking southern support, Roosevelt declared, "We appeal to the sons of the men who followed Lee no less than to the sons of the men who followed Grant; for the memory of the great deeds of both is now the common heritage of honor which belongs to all our people, wherever they dwell." With that appeal, Roosevelt rested his case for the Progressives. [32]

Wilson had the final weeks of the 1912 campaign largely to himself, and he made the most of them. When Roosevelt was shot, Wilson immediately announced, over the objections of his campaign managers, that he would suspend speaking until his opponent recovered. Although it was a generous gesture, the respite also allowed Wilson to rest his strained voice for several days before resuming a limited schedule of appearances. Not until Roosevelt left the hospital and announced plans for his last speech did Wilson go back to barnstorming. In his last speeches he again dwelt mainly on the restoration of competition, release of energies, and social renewal. Although these speeches included some of his best efforts in the campaign, he did not perform as well as he might have. As Davidson has observed, Wilson did not note or take advantage of Roosevelt's retreat on the trust question. He also failed to emphasize the New Freedom, which he had previously stressed on the western tour. [33]

Wilson did become more specific about how and why he wanted to restore competition. On October 18 he resurrected his earlier phrase when he declared, "What this country needs above all else is a body of laws which will look after the men who are on the make rather than the men who are already made." Only from them, the people with "the average enterprise, the average initiative," could the nation gain renewal and growth. Wilson elaborated on that point ten days later to draw a critical distinction between his position and Roosevelt's. Whereas the ex-president increasingly emphasized aid to the lower orders of society, Wilson announced his belief that the "great middle class" constituted "the originative part of America, the part of America that makes new enterprises, the part into which the ambitious and gifted workingman makes his way up, the class that saves, that plans, that organizes." Wilson depicted middle-class people crushed between the trusts above and the workers controlled by the trusts below, and he asserted that the government must come to their rescue because "every country is renewed out of the middle stratum." [34]

His emphasis on a thrifty, enterprising middle class, recalling William Graham Sumner's "forgotten man," made Wilson seem more conservative to later critics than he really was. That stress

came as part of his continuing, though now implicit, attack on
Roosevelt's alleged paternalism. In one speech in October Wilson
coined another phrase: "We do not want big-brother government
. . . I do not want a government that will take care of me. I want
a government that will make other men take their hands off so I can
take care of myself." Further, Wilson defined the middle class so
broadly that it included practically everybody. At one of his last
appearances before the election, he again held up Lincoln as the
best example of renewal from below. America had no class "so high
that men haven't climbed into it from the bottom, if there is any
bottom." That was America's pride, "and if out of the average men
we can't get our great men, then we have destroyed the very
springs of renewal in this America which we have built in order to
show that every man born of every class had the right and the
privilege to make the most of himself." With that vision of democratic renewal, Wilson closed his campaign.[35]

The results of the election on November 5, 1912, contained
almost no surprises. They provided both consolation and disappointment for each of the three major candidates. As predicted,
Wilson won by a comfortable popular margin, with 6,293,019 votes,
and carried forty states to sweep the Electoral College. But his
popular vote represented only 43 percent of the total and came
almost entirely from the normal Democratic constituency. Outside
the South Wilson gained a majority only in the new state of Arizona;
his overall showing fell 100,000 votes below Bryan's 1908 total.
Roosevelt finished a respectable, though not a close, second with
4,119,507 votes and winning pluralities in six states. That was an
impressive achievement, particularly because he polled over
600,000 votes more than Taft, who carried only Utah and Vermont.
But Roosevelt's vote represented a personal endorsement, not a
party showing. Progressive state and congressional candidates
trailed him badly nearly everywhere, and in most cases they ran
behind both Democratic and Republican contenders. The
Progressives did well only on the West Coast, where in California
and to a lesser degree in Washington they had supplanted the
regular Republican organizations. Despite his humiliating defeat Taft took comfort in having helped keep Roosevelt out of the
White House and in the Republicans remaining under conservative control.[36]

The only surprises in the results came in two areas. One was the vote polled by the veteran Socialist candidate Eugene V. Debs. His vote of 901,873 was more than double his 1908 showing and was the largest share of a popular total won by a Socialist candidate before or since. The other surprise came in the Rockies, where Roosevelt did worse than expected. In four of the seven mountain states he came in third, and he did particularly poorly in certain agricultural and mining areas. Roosevelt also showed weakness in the Northeast, even placing third in his home state of New York. In a larger sense the biggest surprise of 1912 was that there were no other surprises. Aside from Debs's showing, the result practically duplicated the 1908 pattern. The total vote increased by just over 150,000, all of which could be accounted for by the increased Socialist vote. Just as Wilson had captured only the normal Democratic vote and had fallen 100,000 votes short of Bryan's showing four years before, Roosevelt and Taft had done the same thing with the normal Republican vote; their combined total fell more than 70,000 votes below Taft's 1908 showing. No realignments or large, perceptible voter shifts had occurred.[37]

Some of the outcome might be attributed to Wilson's virtually foreordained victory, since increased voter turnout usually occurs only when the election is expected to be close. But the results remain puzzling. One of the most exciting campaigns in American history, fought between the two most attractive available candidates and over important, hotly debated issues, failed to change many votes. The biggest winner in 1912 was politics as usual. The question remains, why?

· 14 ·

The New Nationalism versus the New Freedom

FEW PEOPLE AT THE TIME or later asked why such an extraordinary election had produced such an ordinary result. None of the three principal candidates faced the question squarely. Fittingly for a victor, Wilson looked to the future. "The result fills me with hope that the thoughtful Progressive forces of the Nation may now at last unite," he announced the day after the election. "It is delightful to see the forces of the Democratic party united," Wilson told Bryan more realistically, "and their union should now bring fruit of the richest sort." Taft regretted that he had drawn only "the irreducible minimum of the Republican party," but he still hoped that "the incapacity of the Democratic party and their leader will make itself known in a way unmistakable." Roosevelt's crusading fervor cooled again as the returns came in, and he assessed the results with the greatest penetration. "The strength of the old party ties is shown by the fact that, although we carried the primaries two to one against Taft at the polls, about as many Republicans voted for him as for me," he told Pinchot. He also lamented the lack of difference that voters had evidently apprehended between himself and Wilson on critical issues, particularly the trusts.[1]

Roosevelt had touched upon the two major factors that shaped the 1912 results and the main considerations in assessing the significance of his race against Taft and Wilson. The best feeling for how events would go had come from the Republican bosses when they had decided to block Roosevelt even at the cost of likely party defeat. They had bet that the agitation in their own party, in Roosevelt's new party, and among the Democrats would not shake the basic alignment of the electorate in their favor. The results bore out their hopes in three areas: first, the distribution of the votes in a pattern that nearly duplicated the 1908 result; second, the decline of Roosevelt's and other Republican insurgents' support after the convention; and third, the gap between the vote for Roosevelt and for the other Progressives. Further, without a doubt, the Old Guard completely controlled the Republican party.[2]

In the longer view, the Old Guard's reckoning of the most important issues also came close to the mark. Economic concerns related to the tariff, currency, and trusts retained the greatest potency with the bulk of the voters. Roosevelt's troubles with the trust issue, first within his new party and then in the campaign against Wilson, had partially revealed his failure to alter people's overriding material concerns. "We have keyed our note very high," he admitted after the election, "probably too high for the people thoroughly to catch it, at least at first." Yet the outcome of the election augured little better for Wilson. He had done no more than hold on to the minority Democratic constituency that Bryan had built and maintained since 1896, mainly on the three main economic issues. Wilson probably could have won in a two-man race against Taft, but he almost certainly would have lost against Roosevelt alone. He owed his victory to the Republican split. As in the nomination, he won the election because of the peculiar conditions and his opponents' liabilities, not his own strengths. Whether Wilson could change that situation would determine both the success and duration of his presidency and the future prospects of his party.[3]

The other factor that shaped the outcome in 1912, as well as its larger significance, was the electorate's perception of the differences between Roosevelt and Wilson. Most observers have believed that the voters saw little to choose between the two men on major issues. The persistence of the basic party alignments does suggest that in the absence of either a close contest or public perception of clear-cut differences on issues, the voters stuck with their habitual allegiances. Moreover, the increased Socialist vote may have reflected not so much growing radicalism as an undercurrent of dissatisfaction with the two leading candidates. The unevenness of the debate in 1912 probably also diminished public recognition of the differences between Roosevelt and Wilson. In presenting their respective campaign themes, they were like a ukulele and a violin. Roosevelt thumped away forcefully and repetitiously at a few chords, mainly trust regulation and stronger government. Wilson played deftly on a wide range of arguments, from representative government to economic competition to social renewal, with many specific adaptations and variations. Which approach was more effective never received a fair test, since they did not run a two-man race and since Roosevelt's campaign was cut short after he was shot. Under those circumstances many voters may have had understandable difficulty in perceiving differences between the two contenders.[4]

A more important consideration is whether the voters' perceptions were correct. According to the great majority of analysts at the time and later, Roosevelt and Wilson did not differ greatly on the major issues. A classic statement of that view came a few years afterward when William Allen White wrote, "Between the New Nationalism and the New Freedom was that fantastic imaginary gulf that always has existed between tweedle-dum and tweedle-dee." Much evidence supports that view. Both Roosevelt and Wilson strained to accentuate their differences and thereby, albeit often unwittingly, misrepresented each other.[5]

In his attempts to depict Wilson as a bogus progressive, Roosevelt wielded the charges of "toryism" and state rights, both to woo reform Democrats and to stave off insurgent Republican defections. The ease with which Wilson refuted the charges exposed their unfairness. Similarly, aspersions on "Professor Wilson" and his "academic theories" relegated Wilson to the mugwump stereotype Roosevelt had been using for nearly thirty years. Along with fulminations against false "idealism" and dishonest articulateness, such imputations of impracticality and of finickiness bordering on cowardice constituted the arrows most frequently flung against Wilson for the rest of Roosevelt's life. In 1912 Wilson neatly turned the "schoolteacher" charge to his own advantage as he contrasted his view of representative government with Roosevelt's supposedly overbearing ways.[6]

Wilson in turn did Roosevelt and his views three disservices that were somewhat less serious. First, in his criticisms of Roosevelt's trust regulation approach, Wilson perhaps unintentionally reinforced suspicions that his opponent sought to serve big business. The prominence in Progressive councils of such tycoons as George W. Perkins and Frank Munsey lent apparent credence to those suspicions, and many Progressives distrusted those men's influence and motives. Moreover, the fears of Brandeis and others that the regulatory agencies would be subverted by big business did prove to be well founded under the Republican regimes of the 1920s. But to insinuate that Roosevelt believed in anything but the supremacy of government and subordination of business distorted his deepest values. Wilson's second disservice lay in helping to perpetuate notions about Roosevelt's alleged dictatorial tendencies. The ex-president's restraint when he was in power and his renunciation of office had abundantly proven the falsity of those notions. Finally, Wilson cast aspersions on the sincerity of Roosevelt's reform convictions. When he declined to call the Progressives by their chosen name and harped on their lack of support from La Follette and other Republican insurgents, Wilson was also playing the game of trying to steal Roosevelt's supporters. Minimizing the differences between Roosevelt and the Republican Old Guard was as unfair as Roosevelt's tarring him with the state-rights brush.

The distortions by both candidates arose from the heat of the campaign but also in part from the two men's agreement on many specific issues. Roosevelt and Wilson had to play up their differences because on matters of immediate concern, their real differences were few. Their outward differences in style, following, and party spirit lacked substance, even at the outset of the campaign. As the editors of *The Letters of Theodore Roosevelt* have pointed out, despite Roosevelt's denunciations of the Democratic platform, the only differences between it and the Progressive platform were in the Progressives' endorsement of tariff protection and woman suffrage, silence on the trusts, and slightly stronger advocacy of aid to labor, as contrasted with the Democrats' friendlier posture toward farmers. In the course of the campaign Wilson endorsed virtually every specific reform measure Roosevelt favored, with the principal exception of woman suffrage, and he frequently reasserted his partial sympathy for tariff protection. During his first term as president, as Link has observed, Wilson enacted most of the 1912 Progressive platform, including abolition of child labor and legislation favoring organized labor, and he switched to support of woman suffrage in 1915 and 1916.[7]

Their unanimity on current issues extended to their limited concern about two important matters. One was the question on which they parted company in 1912—woman suffrage. In fact, neither man felt strongly about the issue, regarding it as entirely a matter of expediency. Roosevelt probably held more traditional views of women's roles and sex difference, but because he needed the support of such women reformers as Jane Addams, he endorsed nationwide woman suffrage in 1912. Wilson, who had taught in a woman's college and had two suffragette daughters, declined either to support or to oppose the proposition as a federal question, mainly out of deference to antisuffrage Democratic elements in the South and Northeast.[8]

The other issue on which they shared a limited concern was race. Roosevelt qualified as the more self-conscious white racist of the two. He incorporated racial categories into his basic views, and he believed that blacks were decidedly inferior to whites. As president he had made such gestures as inviting Booker T. Washington to dinner at the White House in 1901 and appointing a well-qualified black man, Dr. William D. Crum, to head the Charleston customhouse in 1903. But Roosevelt had also meted out harsh and hasty punishment to the regiment of black troops accused of starting a riot in Brownsville, Texas, in 1906, and he had tried to woo southern whites to the Republicans by loosening party ties to blacks. His search for southern support culminated in 1912 with the Progressives' open renunciation of federal involvement in race relations. As a result, the Progressives' southern efforts gained some ground with Roosevelt placing second in eight of the eleven former Confederate states.[9]

For a white man born and raised in the nineteenth-century South, Wilson held surprisingly mild racial views. As a young man he had defended efforts to educate blacks, and he had spread disquiet among his southern relatives by inviting Booker T. Washington to his inauguration as president of Princeton in 1902. Although he had rarely written or talked much about racial matters, Wilson believed that blacks were not innately inferior to whites and would eventually, probably in two or three centuries, achieve a measure of economic and political, if not social, equality in America. Such views had hardly impelled him to challenge discrimination against or neglect of blacks, however. At Princeton Wilson had maintained the university's long-standing ban on admitting blacks. During the 1912 campaign he did give mild encouragement to a black movement in support of his candidacy led by Bishop Alexander Walters and W. E. B. DuBois, but he maintained his distance from them. As president, Wilson sanctioned attempts by several of his southern Cabinet members to introduce segregation into federal departments. His administration also witnessed a decline in the percentage of government jobs held by blacks, although the numbers of black jobholders increased somewhat.[10]

The similarities and agreements between Roosevelt's and Wilson's positions did not mean, however, that no important differences separated them. The view expressed in White's "tweedle-dum and tweedle-dee" simile was wrong. During the presidential campaign, clear signs of their ideological divergences surfaced. Further, when one juxtaposes the New Nationalism with the New Freedom, as White did, the differences between them become unmistakable. The 1912 campaign grew so heated not only because of the main contenders' clashing ambitions and ingrained combativeness but also because of their recognition of the ideological gulf between them. Mutual distortions and the requirements of their political situations prevented the two men from exposing the split as clearly as they could have done, but the outlines of their divergence showed up on the two issues they discussed most in 1912—the trusts and leadership.

The trust issue might appear to be another area of agreement masked by each man's misrepresentations of the other's position. Wilson's inconsistency about bigness and Roosevelt's retreat to reaffirmation of the antitrust laws did make it difficult to perceive any great difference between them. Further, Roosevelt never went so far as Croly earlier and Lippmann later in equating bigness in business with efficiency or in portraying big businessmen as quasi-statesmen who were coming to be less and less motivated by profits and more and more by altruism. Similarly, Wilson never consistently adhered to either Brandeis's equation of bigness with inefficiency or his convictions that the overriding concern of businessmen with profits was ineradicable. The Wilson administration later did mount a vigorous antitrust drive, but it was hardly an all-out assault on large corporations. After the United States entered World War I, Wilson presided over the kind of government-business partnership in managing the economy that had earlier been envisioned by apostles of the New Nationalism.[11]

Roosevelt and Wilson were not always consistent when they debated the economic implications of bigness in 1912, yet their arguments reflected economic considerations that pointed to their own deeper concerns. They disagreed over bigness less in the abstract value they put on it than in their interpretations of facts about it. In his strictures against "toryism" and "flint-lock" thinking, Roosevelt implicitly accepted three propositions: that the biggest corporations had for the most part achieved their stature through efficient competition, that large corporations were here to stay, and that present economic conditions represented progress. But for him those were not the most important concerns. When he expounded on such matters as "conduct not size," how businesses treated workers and consumers, and putting "the hand of government" on them, he was voicing his true concern. He believed that the main economic task of government lay in protecting the victims and clients of large-scale enterprise through greatly strengthened regulation and supervision. Some might hold that he was anticipating John Kenneth Galbraith's concept of "countervailing power" between big business and big government. Actually, Roosevelt wanted an overwhelming governmental supremacy that did, in a nonpejorative sense, deserve the designation "paternalism." His vision of public supervision and protection forecast much of the twentieth-century welfare state from a standpoint that resembled approaches taken by his contemporaries among British Liberals, and after World War I by British Conservatives and by various European spokesmen of the center and right, particularly in Italy and Germany. This approach accepted corporate roles and responsibilities in the economy and sought governmental economic management, not so much out of compassion for or identification with the individuals affected, as in the interest of social harmony and national strength. To turn Roosevelt's own epithet nonpejoratively back on himself, this was a "tory" approach to the welfare state. It has remained rare in the United States.[12]

Wilson disagreed on all points. In his distinction between big business and the trusts and in his insistence on restoring competition, he implicitly accepted three opposite economic propositions: that comparatively few of the biggest corporations had

achieved their stature through efficient competition, that those
corporations were not necessarily here to stay, and that present
conditions did not always represent progress over the past. Wilson
advanced his side of the argument less clearly than Roosevelt did
on those matters. For him, too, the most important concerns lay
elsewhere. In his discussion of the trusts Wilson emphasized two
considerations. One was governmental regulation of competition.
Far from believing in laissez-faire, Wilson maintained that government must intervene actively and continuously in the economy
because "unregulated competition" had resulted in the growth of
the trusts and the stifling of competition. The other consideration
he stressed was the entry of new competitors into the market.
Contrary to their public images, Wilson held much more dynamic
economic views than Roosevelt. He believed that the main task of
reform was to revitalize the economy through governmental actions
to open the market to fresh entrants. Wilson also forecast a central
element in the twentieth-century welfare state—public action to
promote the economic interests of the less advantaged. This was, in
later usage, a "liberal" approach, and it has been at the heart of the
major American sources of support for the welfare state.[13]

Roosevelt's and Wilson's concerns behind the trust issue
pointed to the basic divergence in their approach to politics—the
place of self-interest in the pursuit of social good. This appeared
most clearly during the 1912 campaign in their conceptions of
leadership. It was fitting that their differences should emerge most
sharply there, for at heart each man cared much more about politics
than economics. Roosevelt's repeated, sometimes almost savage
attacks on Wilson's governmental views indicated that he once
more sensed the "unheroic" underpinnings of Wilson's politics.
Because he believed so fervently in the need for transcendent national ideals, Roosevelt probably sincerely mistook Wilson's position for a state-rights, limited-government viewpoint. Innocently
or not, however, he misrepresented the issue between them. It was
not then and never would be the strength or activism of government. Rather, it was the proper method of leadership and, thereby,
the true purpose of government.

Wilson grasped and articulated the essential political issue between them much better than Roosevelt. The leadership issue
boiled down to inspiration versus education. With his prophetic,

evangelical approach Roosevelt sought, in the root sense of the word, to inspire. He wanted to breathe into people a resolve to be better than they were, to instill in them devotion to larger goals and greater effort. With his "schoolmaster" approach to leadership, Wilson similarly sought, in the root sense, to educate. He wished to draw out of people recognition of their own best interests, to let them enlighten their ordinary pursuits. The issue between them over the purposes of government came down to one of paternalism versus representation. Roosevelt believed that in the right kind of government, leaders inspired by visions of unifying, uplifting national ideals would guide the people. For Wilson, popular interests would be genuinely represented by leaders who listened to the people. Wilson repeatedly urged audiences in the 1912 campaign not to vote for him unless he was expressing their aspirations and beliefs. "I do not wish to be your master," he avowed at one point. "I wish to be your spokesman."[14]

Those arguments infuriated Roosevelt. Besides seeming to suggest that Roosevelt had dictatorial tendencies, Wilson's contentions sounded suspiciously like excuses for governmental inaction. Often labeled laissez-faire, commendations of individual initiative and self-reliance and condemnations of governmental intervention had formed staple political arguments in the United States and Britain for nearly a century. Roosevelt understandably seized upon Wilson's arguments for self-reliance to scorn him as a false progressive. Though plausible, Roosevelt's reasoning was fallacious. Wilson's concern for self-reliance sprang not from any attachment to limited-government views, but from his anticipation of the most telling criticism of the modern welfare state. Both friends and foes of that view have deplored the proposition that governmental promotion of social welfare tends to convert recipients of aid into wards of the state. Wilson perceptively condemned the paternalistic implications in Roosevelt's position.[15]

Wilson's criticisms also exposed a central element in Roosevelt's political approach—his aristocratic assumptions. Although Roosevelt sincerely believed in broad popular participation in politics, he never thought that that offered a cure-all for the problems of a modern industrial society, as many Bryanites, insurgent Republicans, and Progressives did. Roosevelt wanted to preserve the heroic virtues of disinterested service and nonmaterial goals. He continued to seek ways to promote such virtues among citizens whose main concerns were economic. Roosevelt made a noble effort with the Progressives in 1912, but he fell short, as he had before, largely because he lacked the catalyst of a crisis in which to rouse people to higher duties. "Unfortunately, it is not with us," he told a fellow Progressive just after the election, "as it was with the Republicans in [18]56 after their defeat. We have not the clear-cut issues as to which we take one side and our opponents the other side, and as to which the conscience of the people is deeply stirred." From 1910 through 1912 Roosevelt had once more tried and failed to instill a sense of unifying national purpose analogous to the Civil War spirit.[16]

Roosevelt similarly exposed two weaknesses in Wilson's political approach. One was his lack of realism on the trust issue. Roosevelt raised a valid objection when he doubted whether Wilson could succeed with trustbusting any better than Taft or, although he did not say so, himself. When he argued that the size of firms was a less important concern than their social and economic role, particularly as gauged by their treatment of workers and consumers, Roosevelt made an incisive point, although Wilson agreed with him to an extent. Yet Wilson, like Brandeis, did betray an old-fashioned faith that people acting freely in the marketplace would serve the larger good of society. Roosevelt showed greater originality when he questioned the social and economic efficacy of marketplace behavior. His criticisms did not mean that he had a better solution to the trust problem, but he did come closer to recognizing the overriding need to make large-scale private economic power accountable to society through its governmental representatives.[17]

Roosevelt's and Wilson's differences over the trust issue had profounder economic implications than either man probably realized. In common with a few other analysts and some union leaders, such as Samuel Gompers of the American Federation of Labor, Roosevelt appeared willing to cast aside traditional values of individual ownership and management for the sake of higher wages, better working conditions, fairer prices, and more wholesome products. Roosevelt sometimes used the word "collectivism" to describe his arguments. He evidently did accept at least in part the idea of abandoning individual autonomy to collective bodies, not only for corporations but also for unions and government agencies, for the sake of better results from the economic process. Wilson, like Brandeis, though less consistently so, adhered to the older ideal of freedom through individual ownership and management and the argument that individual entrepreneurship remained essential to ensure the inventiveness and initiative that were essential to economic growth and improvement. Wilson's conception of the economy was, therefore, at once more traditional and more dynamic than Roosevelt's.

The second weakness in Wilson's politics that Roosevelt uncovered was his belief in meritocracy. Despite his emphasis on social renewal from below, Wilson admitted that he cared most about upward mobility for the most able people, particularly those from the middle classes. Roosevelt correctly questioned whether such mobility was the most important consideration in a modern industrial society, particularly as opposed to higher wages and safer working conditions for industrial workers and lower prices and better-quality products for consumers. Although Wilson defined the middle classes broadly and favored aid to industrial workers and consumer groups, he did talk in the 1912 campaign as if restored competition and greater upward mobility offered social and economic panaceas. Wilson's comparative lack of economic realism and his meritocratic sympathies sprang from narrowness in apprehending some contemporary problems. Between 1910 and the 1912 election Wilson had shown himself to be a deeper, more insightful political thinker than Roosevelt, but he had not yet matched the ex-president in perceptiveness about current economic and social conditions.

Roosevelt's and Wilson's respective political weaknesses reflected both their personal projections and their social and economic backgrounds. When he continued to uphold heroic virtues, Roosevelt was once more exhorting Americans to emulate him by rising above limitations, renouncing crass commercial goals, and exalting public service. He remained an aristocratic conservative in his views, which accounted for much of the friction with his Progressive followers. Roosevelt had originally fashioned his political viewpoint as part of an effort to preserve a dominant Republican party representing the nation's economically and socially advantaged groups and regions. He had first joined the insurgent Republicans and then bolted with the Progressives in large part because the would-be beneficiaries of his policies had spurned him. Roosevelt often talked about seeking democratic Jeffersonian ends through nationalistic Hamiltonian means. With the Progressives, however, he was pursuing what he regarded as Hamiltonian goals of transcendent nationalism and disinterested leadership through a Jeffersonian following bent on promoting its own interests. The combination spelled trouble for leader and party alike.

Wilson's meritocratic sympathies made a better fit with his partisan and social situation. Despite long residence in the Northeast and his association with Princeton, Wilson had never ceased to identify himself with hard-working, upwardly striving people from the South and West. He was one of them, and when he exalted such people as the indispensable agents of social renewal, he too was urging Americans to emulate him. Wilson fell quickly and easily in step with the Bryanite wing of the Democrats because he could sincerely tell them what they wanted to hear. Despite a lingering aroma of farmer radicalism, those Democrats were mainly people like Wilson; they were aspiring middle-class southerners and westerners, who resented the economic and cultural domination of the Northeast and wanted the same things he wanted. With the Democratic progressives, Wilson had a Jeffersonian following seeking its own interests. Whether he knew it or not, he was also a leader out of the mold of Jefferson, a man who was intellectually and socially detached from his followers but spiritually in tune with them and their aspirations.[18]

To an extent, Roosevelt and Wilson stood as twentieth-century analogues to Hamilton and Jefferson. The passage of time and the changed face of the United States had introduced differences between them and their mentors. Unlike Hamilton and Jefferson, they did not differ over governmental power and centralization, despite Roosevelt's assertions to the contrary. Nor did they laud either manufacturing or agriculture as morally or socially superior to the other. Roosevelt, with his ranching and hunting background, was more of a devotee of rural life, but he also held the more approving view of large-scale industry. Roosevelt likewise departed from Hamilton in despising plutocracy and in wanting to curb and channel the influence of wealth instead of seeking to work through it. But Roosevelt and Wilson did differ fundamentally over the same matters—their conceptions of human nature and the role of self-interest in society—that they believed had separated Hamilton and Jefferson. Roosevelt's New Nationalism and Wilson's New Freedom presented distinct views of how to promote social good, based upon what each man to a degree regarded as Hamiltonian and Jeffersonian conceptions of people's nature and interests.

Roosevelt remained, by his lights, self-consciously Hamiltonian and anti-Jeffersonian in his views. For all his bouoyancy and his spirits, Roosevelt was not an optimistic man, and his politics were not based upon an optimistic view of people. He regarded individuals' selfish, private interests as not only barriers to the attainment of public good but also sources of antisocial passion and potential civil conflict. Yet he did not rely mainly on repression and authority, except occasionally during such periods of heightened tension as the mid-1890s and, later, World War I. Rather, he exhorted people to pursue higher national ideals. But at no time did Roosevelt believe that simply letting people have what they wanted or making them happy was a means to social betterment. For him, those ways led to materialist degeneracy, a widening gulf between greedy plutocrats and the envious masses, social revolution, and national doom. As with himself, Roosevelt never fully trusted what he perceived to be other people's basic instincts. He could never relax in the pursuit of self-overcoming virtues, for others as well as himself.[19]

Roosevelt's failure to convert a majority or even a substantial minority of his countrymen to pursuit of higher goals was foreordained. Even if he had gotten the breaks he needed in 1912, he would ultimately have failed to get his insurgent Republican or Progressive followers to renounce their own interests in favor of national ideals, just as he had failed earlier with the Old Guard. Despite his pessimism about people, Roosevelt indulged in fantastic naiveté in believing that many could be persuaded voluntarily to renounce their interests more than briefly. Further, he never seemed to recognize either that the dominant groups in society would continue to fare better than others under his programs or that it was unjust to ask the disadvantaged to forgo their interests. Despite his frequent preachments about realism and practicality, Roosevelt often was an "idealist" in two pejorative senses of the term—as an impractical visionary and as someone who did not recognize the selfishness in his views.

Roosevelt's misfortune lay in not having a war in which he could act upon his beliefs. His worst time began later, after the outbreak of World War I, which he viewed as a perfect historical occasion for his kind of heroic leadership. He knew he required a great national crisis, like Lincoln's with the Civil War, to practice his politics to the fullest. Only in such a situation could he have succeeded in rousing people and parties to self-sacrificing service and heroic action. Whether or not he could have wrought permanent political changes, Roosevelt would almost certainly have altered the subsequent history of the Republican party. With his heroic virtues and renunciation of materialism, he represented a road not taken for American conservatism.

During the 1912 campaign Wilson came closer than at any other time in his political career to becoming an exponent of what he saw as Jeffersonian views. Although his religious background helped make him cheerfully fatalistic about himself, Wilsons' politics were based upon an optimistic view of people. He regarded individuals' selfish interests as not only inescapable facts of life but as instruments that must be used to improve society. Wilson differed from many fellow Democrats in his intellectual detachment, his continuing admiration for Hamilton, and—despite his self-proclaimed scorn for experts—his recognition of the need for trained personnel and specialized knowledge in governing a modern industrial nation. But he agreed with his Bryanite party brethren in seeking to satisfy the desires of a majority of the people. Wilson stressed freedom as the essential means to pursue social betterment because he believed that the continual rising of talent from below would ensure energy, growth, and renewal in society. In the sharpest contrast to Roosevelt, Wilson professed not to fear social conflict, and his nonchalance about the prospects of revolution recalled Jefferson's quip about watering "the tree of liberty . . . with the blood of tyrants."[20]

But Wilson did not offer a total contrast to Roosevelt. If he had been consistent, he would have embraced self-interested competition as the best means to improve society. Wilson continued to eschew class politics and to appeal to elevated national ideals, with the result that he often sounded like Roosevelt. Their apparent similarity was deceptive. Rather than accepting or rejecting self-interested competition, Wilson maintained that people could pursue their own interests and a unifying national purpose at the same time. In a speech in October 1912 Wilson asserted, "We must not settle the war of classes by enabling one class to overcome another, even though it be the bigger class of the two, but we must overcome class prejudice and class warfare by making classes understand one another and that there is a common interest which transcends every particular interest in the United States." Roosevelt would have put it differently, but he pursued the same goal.[21]

Wilson was more realistic than Roosevelt in recognizing that a better society could come only by serving the interests of a majority. He did not entirely renounce service to particular interest groups. He claimed that aid to industrial workers and farmers would help such large and vital segments of society that everyone's interests would be served. Wilson did not yet embrace the proposition that government should foster the interests of less-advantaged groups or regions, but he had gone a long way toward the "broker state," which became the central political concept in support of governmental aid to social welfare and regulation of private economic activity in twentieth-century America. Recurrent debates over the national purpose and outcries against special interests have shown that the greatest weakness of the broker state concept is the point that Roosevelt attacked—the degeneration of interest-group politics into narrow conflicts that strain national cohesion and debase politics into a scramble for favors. Wilson had no answer to Roosevelt's questions about how to promote national unity, except to work through coalitions of interests. His performance at that task played a big part in shaping not only his presidency and the fortunes of his party but also the main course of twentieth-century domestic American politics.

The confrontation between Roosevelt and Wilson did not end with the 1912 election. The two men had taken each other's measure and tested their differences. In a chastened mood following his defeat, Roosevelt temporarily reverted to a milder attitude toward his opponent. Once more he privately called Wilson the Democrats' "strongest man" and a good prospect for presidential success. That mood quickly passed. By late November Roosevelt confided,

"I think him a very adroit man; I do not think he has any fixity of conviction." Wilson said little about Roosevelt even in private, but his actions as president soon showed that his predecessor and rival occupied a prominent spot in his mind.[22]

Thus far, foreign affairs, which had been an important element in Roosevelt's break with Taft, had not entered his confrontation with Wilson. Except for two passing allusions by Roosevelt and one by Wilson, neither man mentioned foreign affairs during the 1912 campaign. Shortly before his inauguration, Wilson told a friend in Princeton, "It would be an irony of fate if my administration had to deal with foreign problems, for all my preparation has been in domestic matters." The irony of fate overtook Wilson as soon as he took office, and foreign affairs swiftly furnished a new field of conflict between him and Roosevelt. Once World War I broke out in August 1914, their confrontation rose to a pitch of fury that not only shaped the rest of both men's lives but also affected critical events for the United States and the world.[23]

· IV ·

THE WARRIOR
AND THE PRIEST

In some respects, Roosevelt comes into sharpest focus when he is placed opposite Wilson, for there was something elemental in his antipathy for that good gentlemen. One is reminded of Nietzsche's distinction between the Warrior and the Priest. The Warrior with all his natural strength and virility exults in the free and unabashed exercise of the will-to-power. He is the man of true nobility, the man of honor transcending self-interest . . . For the Priest he reserves a special loathing, since he sees that the Priest is also driven by the will-to-power, but in a perverted way that is forever confounding the Warrior, frustrating his manly passion, and denying him his rightful status in society. For the will of the Priest is not the frank, straightforward will of the Warrior but rather the devious influence of a crafty intellect, which compensates the Priest for his physical weakness by investing cowardice with the semblance of morality, by embellishing weakness with the holy glow of enlightenment, self-denial, and the gentle Christian virtues.

Robert Endicott Osgood
*Ideals and Self-Interest in
America's Foreign Relations*

THE CONFLICT between Theodore Roosevelt and Woodrow Wilson continued for seven years after the 1912 election. It consumed the rest of Roosevelt's life and nearly all of Wilson's presidency. This final conflict began slowly, and both men often failed to engage the other's main arguments. Wilson's accession to power gave him primacy for the first time in his relations with Roosevelt. Further, when Wilson succeeded during his first term in enacting reform legislation and welding the Democrats into a disciplined, progressive party, Roosevelt found himself marooned in a disintegrating third party. Partly as a consequence of Wilson's accomplishments at home, the domestic side of his ideological rift with Roosevelt received less exposure than their 1912 debates had seemed to promise. Discerning observers sometimes grasped their differences, and at various times Roosevelt bared the basis of their divergence over social and economic reform. But domestic political issues constituted a diminishing facet of the conflict between them.

Two other matters dominated their strife. One was personal performance in the presidential office. Inasmuch as he succeeded at the very tasks that had stymied Roosevelt—enactment of a sweeping reform program and transformation of his party into a vehicle for progressivism—Wilson unavoidably earned his predecessor's envy. He heightened that envy by adopting a bolder strategy and a milder manner. Just a month into his first term, on April 8, 1913, Wilson broke the custom, initiated by Jefferson, of presidents not addressing Congress in person—it was a move Roosevelt had earlier feared to make. Thereafter Wilson spoke on Capitol Hill more often than any president before or since. He also bent the Democrats to his will and policies in ways that Roosevelt had never been able to do with the Republicans. All in all, Wilson gave the impression of mastery through restrained, dignified persuasion. His performance occasioned frequent contrasts with Roosevelt's allegedly overbearing manner and reputedly egotistical self-dramatization. Such contrasts understandably rankled Roosevelt.

The other matter that dominated their conflict, and the area that took the longest to develop, was foreign affairs. Their disagreement did not fully emerge until after the outbreak of World War I in August 1914, but once foreign affairs surfaced as an area of contention, it furnished the most heatedly and persistently contested set of issues between Wilson and Roosevelt. Foreign affairs became the principal vehicle for expressing their personal and ideological differences. Even before the war, Roosevelt's ire at Wilson's diplomacy in Latin America, particularly in Mexico, and his resentment at the treaty of indemnity with Colombia over the Panamanian revolution portended a full-scale clash. But the World War lent special edge and moment to their conflict.

Irony abounded in this conflict. The earlier foreign policy views of the two men, particularly their imperialist ardor, had been even more similar than their domestic reform stands. Wilson began to renounce imperialism before World War I, and he based much of his conception of a postwar settlement on national "self-determination." Roosevelt remained a steadfast, though chastened, believer in great-power hegemony. Yet in practice they retained areas of agreement, and their discussions of intervention in the war and the assurance of lasting peace afterward included overlapping arguments. When the United States entered the war in April 1917, a chance for cooperation between them arose when Roosevelt asked to be allowed to raise a division to fight on the western front. Wilson's refusal rekindled Roosevelt's fury, but by the end of 1918 he was apparently tempering his attacks in anticipation of being the next Republican presidential nominee. Roosevelt's death on January 6, 1919, robbed him of his chance to lead the nation once more.

Death did not end Roosevelt's conflict with Wilson. The final act took place during 1919, with the struggle over the peace settlement and American membership in the League of Nations. The

Republican opposition was led by Senator Henry Cabot Lodge, who filled the role of Roosevelt's ideological heir and surrogate. The struggle ended with Wilson's political ruin. In October of that year Wilson suffered a massive stroke that left him partially paralyzed and unable to function fully as president. League membership failed as the Senate deadlocked over accepting Wilson's or Lodge's terms of joining. The Republicans won the 1920 elections in a landslide swelled by popular revulsion against Wilson's policies at home and abroad. Yet his defeat did not close the conflict, either. The debate he and Roosevelt had started over the purposes of domestic politics continued for another sixty years, particularly among liberals and reformers. The two men's foreign policy arguments persisted even more strikingly, as their attitudes dominated the long-running conflict over American world leadership. The ideological legacies left by Wilson and Roosevelt have yet to be exhausted in twentieth-century American politics.

· 15 ·

Party Leader

WOODROW WILSON BECAME ONE of the two or three most controversial presidents in American history. Although much of the conflict surrounding him at the time and afterward involved World
War I, his controversiality did not result originally or primarily
from the war or other events abroad. It sprang instead from his
indisputable success as a domestic president. During his first term
Wilson compiled a spectacular, possibly unmatched, record of legislative and party leadership. In the twentieth century only Franklin D. Roosevelt's New Deal from 1933 to 1936 and Lyndon B.
Johnson's Great Society in 1964 and 1965 rival Wilson's accomplishments with the New Freedom between 1913 and 1916. Because Wilson lacked the national emergency and the peculiarly
favorable political conditions that aided those two later presidents,
his feats were all the more remarkable. Yet it was from Wilson's
success at home that his deep and lasting controversiality sprang.

He has shared his controversial status among presidents with
Andrew Jackson and, to a lesser extent, Thomas Jefferson, for much
the same reasons. Like Jefferson, Wilson functioned first and foremost as a party leader. Like both Jefferson and Jackson, he headed
a coalition that advanced the interests of particular sections and
occupational groups in opposition to the interests of others, with
overtones of class conflict. That circumstance introduced an inescapable core of divisiveness into Wilson's presidency. It also guar-
anteed the repeated rises and falls in his historical reputation.

Wilson followed and resembled Theodore Roosevelt in championing "the people" against "special interests." But the task he

faced in his presidency was essentially different, and gained a different outcome. Previous efforts by Roosevelt, and by Taft after him, to move the Republican Old Guard toward stricter regulation of big business and broader popular participation in politics had produced meager practical results. Yet their reform conservatism had produced a rhetorical and ideological compensation. They had been able to promote inclusiveness and reconciliation rather than division and conflict. In fact, Roosevelt had been a no less partisan president than Wilson became. He had also sought, albeit sometimes unknowingly, to promote particular economic and sectional interests. But his ideological position had allowed him to appeal to national unity, pursuit of transcendent ideals, and renunciation of self-interest. As a result, Roosevelt had enjoyed advantages in reputation and in aspects of leadership that eluded Wilson.

With the Democrats Wilson faced a task similar to Roosevelt's as leader of the Progressive party. He, too, sought to temper, guide, and restrain an excited following of reformers. After sixteen years of Bryan's leadership and tutelage, the majority of Democrats required no prodding to support measures to curb the power of big business. Conservative northern Democrats either stood discredited, like George Harvey and Jim Smith, or they lay low in local satrapies, after the manner of New York's Tammany Hall and other city machines. The southern bourbons, in contrast, eagerly supported the Wilson administration. They were hungry for patronage after sixteen years in opposition and proud to have in the White House a native son of their own section. Wilson filled half his cabinet with resident or expatriate southerners. Leading congressional Democrats pledged their cooperation, even though most of them had opposed Wilson's nomination and many still distrusted his ideological bent. Wilson further confirmed that bent and at the same time bowed to what his confidant, Colonel Edward M. House, dubbed "a purely political necessity," when he conferred the first and most prestigious cabinet appointment, the secretaryship of state, on Bryan. In all, when he took office in March 1913, the new president's prospects for enacting a reform program were enviable.[1]

Two factors—Wilson's own studies as a political scientist and the opportunity afforded him by the Democrats—combined to make party leadership the cornerstone of his presidency. Ameri-

cans expected their president, Wilson wrote in a public statement
a month before his inauguration, "to be the leader of his party as
well as the chief executive officer of the government, and the
country will take no excuses from him. He must play the part and
play it successfully, or lose the country's confidence. He must be
the prime minister, as much concerned with the guidance of legislation as with the just and orderly execution of law." Party leadership alone did not make Wilson's presidential course completely
clear or simple. Partly in response to Roosevelt's indictments of
both the older parties in 1912, Wilson had repeatedly pledged to
forge the Democrats into a progressive party. In January 1913 he
announced that he would "pick out progressives, and only
progressives" under his administration. Two months later he privately told a cabinet member that the federal courts needed "a very
different sort of men," who were free from ties and biases "in favor
of the Big Interests rather than the superior rights of all the
public."[2]

Wilson tried to keep those promises. According to the recollection of his postmaster general, Albert Sidney Burleson, Wilson
informed him soon after the inauguration "that my administration
is going to be a progressive administration. I am not going to advise
with reactionary or standpat Senators and Representatives in making these appointments. I am going to appoint forward-looking men
and I am going to satisfy myself that they are honest and capable."
Burleson, a former representative from Texas, regarded himself "in
some degree as an intermediary between Wilson and Congress."
He replied to the president with a lecture about the importance to
the men on Capitol Hill of appointments, particularly local ones,
and about the need to use patronage to enact a legislative program.
Burleson's arguments and a few frustrating stabs at overseeing
lesser appointments soon brought Wilson around. A year later,
after scoring several legislative triumphs, he reportedly confessed
to Burleson, "What you told me about the old standpatters is true.
They will at least stand by the party and the administration. I can
rely on them better than I can on some of my own crowd."[3]

Burleson's tale of the president stooping from idealistic heights
to conquer through mundane politics almost certainly contained
apocryphal embellishments. Wilson had always blended reformist
convictions with practicality. The appointments of Bryan and of

Burleson himself betokened fidelity to partisan requirements. Wilson's other cabinet choices and higher appointments embodied mixed concerns for progressive views, administrative competence, or both those qualities combined with political influence. Wilson's willingness to cooperate with conservative and machine Democrats varied with the time and place. In the North during its first two years, the administration battled Tammany, the remnants of the New Jersey machine, and, to a lesser extent, the Illinois bosses— all with scant success. In the South, in contrast, the president soon abandoned his insurgent prenomination backers and traded White House neutrality for bourbon support in Congress. Either way, Wilson's choices between reform inclinations and party regularity reflected the priority he had set before his inauguration on "the guidance of legislation."[4]

By making legislation his top priority, the new president brought his best skills into play. Wilson relied on a mixture of boldness, persistence, flexibility, and collegiality to push through his great trio of New Freedom measures—the Underwood-Semmons tariff, the Federal Reserve Act, and the combination of the Clayton Anti-Trust Act and the Federal Trade Commission Act. In addition, he secured congressional repeal of the exemption of American coastal shipping from tolls on the soon-to-be-completed Panama Canal, a move to ease a diplomatic controversy with Great Britain. All of these measures went from proposal to enactment within the eighteen months between April 1913 and October 1914.

Wilson showed his wonted boldness at once. He plunged ahead with the first two measures, tariff revision and banking reform, and he appeared in person at the opening of Congress in April 1913 to advocate a lower tariff. Because the tariff remained the one issue on which nearly all Democrats agreed, its revision went quickly in the House; Underwood's bill was passed by a two-to-one majority on May 8. Twice before, however, under Grover Cleveland in 1894 and Taft in 1909, lobbying by protectionist interests and skulduggery in the Senate had scuttled tariff revision bills passed by the House. The pattern appeared about to recur in 1913, inasmuch as the Democrats held only a thin senatorial majority, which was riddled with potential protectionist defectors. Wilson again moved boldly. He issued a public statement on May 26 denouncing "so insidious a lobby" for spending so much money "to create an artificial opinion and to overcome the interests of the public for their private profit." The denunciation sparked a senatorial investigation that exposed lobbying activities and holdings affected by the tariff. Opposition to the bill was thereby dampened, and when the tariff passed the Senate in September 1913, many rates were further revised downward. To offset revenue losses, the first graduated income tax accompanied the tariff. This initial legislative victory was all the sweeter because it proved that Wilson could succeed where his predecessors had failed.[5]

Successful pursuit of banking reform required greater persistence and flexibility. "It is not like the tariff," Wilson told a friend in June 1913, "about which opinion has been definitely forming long years through. There are almost as many judgments as there are men. To form a single plan and a single intention about it seems at times a task so various and so elusive that it is hard to keep one's heart from failing." The chief problem lay in reconciling two cross-cutting issues: whether to establish a centralized or a decentralized reserve system, and how much governmental control or supervision to require in such a system. In December 1912 Wilson began conferring with Representative Carter Glass of Virginia, the chairman of the House Banking Committee, who wanted a decentralized, privately controlled system. Wilson insisted upon "some body of central *supervisory* control," but he encouraged Glass to proceed. By early June the House committee was ready to present a bill to establish a decentralized private system. Meanwhile, advocates of government-controlled reserves, principally Bryan and several Democratic senators, had presented alternative ideas and plans. Both sides threatened to hold out for their respective schemes, and the president had to resolve the impasse.[6]

Wilson listened and kept a genuinely open mind. "I have never been a banker," he told reporters. "I have never had large transactions at banks, so that the technique of it is something I would rather leave in other hands." Also, on June 11, he conferred at the White House with Brandeis, who strongly favored public control and probably reinforced Wilson's own inclination in that direction. A week later Wilson instructed Glass to revise the House committee's bill. Wilson made his second appearance before Congress on June 22 to urge passage of a banking bill under which control "must be public, not private, must be vested in the Government itself, so that the banks may be the instruments, not the masters of business, and of individual enterprise and initiative." That presidential intervention ultimately proved decisive, although approval by the House in September came only after further wrangling, in which Wilson had to enlist Bryan's aid to pass the administration-backed bill. The Senate threw up more obstacles, as conservatives dragged their feet and Wall Street spokesmen belatedly proposed a European-style central bank. Wilson maintained a patient front and engaged in some political dealing to win Senate approval, which finally came in December 1913. The Federal Reserve Act, combining government control with private participation and central authority with regional banks, was Wilson's greatest single legislative monument.[7]

Antitrust legislation posed another problem of reconciling conflicting approaches. Late in 1913, as the Federal Reserve Act neared final passage, Wilson began studying the two main antitrust proposals, designed to spell out in law prohibited business activities or to establish a regulatory agency to oversee trade practices. At first Wilson apparently favored the statutory approach. In January 1914 he made another speech to Congress, in which he called for a measure that "will bring new men, new energies, a new spirit of initiative, new blood, into the managment of our great business enterprises." The House Judiciary Committee, under the chairmanship of Henry D. Clayton of Alabama, drafted a new antitrust law, which the House passed early in June 1914. The main debate in both houses over the Clayton bill concerned exempting labor unions from the antitrust laws—an objective Samuel Gompers and the American Federation of Labor had been seeking for nearly twenty years. Even though he felt personal sympathies for labor, Wilson believed that exempting the unions raised legal problems, and he held out against far-reaching relief from the antitrust laws. Nevertheless, labor spokesmen hailed the Clayton bill's limited exemptions as their "Magna Charta." Gompers thanked Wilson effusively for giving him the pen used to sign the bill into law in October 1914.[8]

By the time the Clayton bill passed the House in June 1914, the main controversy over antitrust policy had shifted elsewhere. As with banking reform, an alternative scheme had emerged. A group of independent progressives headed by Brandeis was arguing that administrative regulation, by staying abreast of changing trade conditions, offered the best antitrust approach. Wilson swung over to their ideas late in the spring of 1914. The advocates of an independent trade commission had found, he told a Senate supporter, "a better way of dealing with the only really debatable part of the Clayton bill." Wilson appears to have endorsed their approach for two reasons. First, as usual, he valued Brandeis's advice; second, Roosevelt was once more denouncing Democratic antitrust policies in preparation for the 1914 congressional elections. Democrats could not, Wilson told the senator, "afford to show the least hesitation or lack of courage on this point which is going to be the point of attack during the campaign, as Mr. Roosevelt has kindly apprised us." Wilson pushed the Federal Trade Commission bill through the Senate and House in August and September 1914. He had to fend off charges by Democratic and Republican progressives, echoing his own earlier accusations against Roosevelt, that he was selling out to big business. In the end, Wilson had things both ways on the antitrust issue. The Clayton Act and the Federal Trade Commission became complementary pieces in governmental regulation of business.[9]

The antitrust measures completed Wilson's original New Freedom program. By keeping Congress in continuous session for a year and a half—a practice heretofore unheard of, even during the Civil War—and by sticking to his policy goals, Wilson had fashioned a legislative achievement of unprecedented scope and significance. Clearly, the previous agitation of the issues by Bryan, Roosevelt, and other reformers had helped to pave the way, but Wilson's accomplishments owed most to his party leadership. On one other measure, repeal of the Panama Canal tolls exemption, he even bested his former rivals for the 1912 Democratic nomination, who now made up the House leadership. Speaker Clark and Majority Leader Underwood opposed the repeal because it broke a 1912 Democratic platform pledge. Wilson resorted to personal persuasion and patronage pressure through Burleson, and he won House passage with surprising ease in March 1914. In the Senate he again exercised patience to wear down his opponents, and in June 1914 he finally prevailed. With the repeal of the canal tolls exemption, Wilson not only settled a bothersome dispute with Britain, he also demonstrated near total mastery of the Democrats. The only unanswered question about his party leadership was what might happen if he and Bryan should ever clash. In view of their cordial working relationship and Bryan's frequent aid in the legislative victories, any conflict between them seemed highly unlikely in the summer and fall of 1914.[10]

The most remarkable feature of Wilson's legislative triumph—especially when compared with the later feats of Franklin Roosevelt and Lyndon Johnson—was that he eschewed a driving, cajoling personal assertiveness. The collegiality he practiced derived from the concept of leadership he had enunciated in the 1912 campaign. America could not move forward, he declared in January 1913, "by anything except concert of purpose and of judgment. You cannot whip a nation into line. You cannot drive your leaders before you." During the banking reform struggle in September 1913 he confided to a friend that press reports of "bending Congress to my indomitable individual will" were nonsense. The men on Capitol Hill were following him "because they see that I am attempting only to mediate their own thoughts and purposes. I do not know how to wield a big stick, but I do know how to put my mind at the service of others for the accomplishment of a common purpose. They are using me; I am not driving them." Six weeks later Wilson told reporters, "I haven't had a tariff program. I haven't had a currency program. I have conferred with these men who handle these things and have asked the questions, and then have gotten back what they sent to me—the best of our common counsel."[11]

Wilson's likening himself to the lead horse of a team rather than a coach driver was accurate and revealing. Much of his success with the tariff, banking, and antitrust legislation derived from his willingness to take advice and change his mind. Not having technical knowledge or settled preferences about customs duties, banking procedures, and business regulation helped him maintain flexibility. More important, however, to his supple handling of those matters were his long-standing convictions about being adaptable and expedient in pursuing broad goals. In his last message as governor of New Jersey, he had reiterated, "The rapidly changing circumstances of the time, . . . both in the political and in the industrial world, render it necessary that a constant process of adjustment should go on." If any previous experience had provided a model for Wilson's legislative leadership as president, it was his first years as president of Princeton when he had practiced comparable collegiality, allowing ideas and programs to develop with light-handed guidance. As governor he had exerted more driving force. There the issues had been more clearly defined, and he had dealt with generally less able leaders.[12]

Wilson's presidential collegiality resulted not only from his outward beliefs in representation and spokesmanship but also from his inward relation to his office. "Everything is persistently *impersonal*," he told a friend two weeks after the inauguration. "I am administering a great office—no doubt the greatest in the world—but I do not seem to be identified with it: it is not me, and I am not it." Experience and success did not change that attitude. A year later Wilson stated in a speech, "In between things I have to do as a public officer, I never think of myself as President of the United States, because I never have had any sense of being identified with that office." Rather, he felt "just as much outside of it at this moment as I did before I was elected to it." Wilson admitted that he frequently had "to look grave enough and self-possessed enough" to suit the office, but he could "hardly refrain every now and again from tipping the public a wink, as much to say, 'It is only "me" that is inside this thing.' " Those statements betrayed more than a becoming modesty. Wilson's sense of separation from the presidency furnished an antidote to the egotism that has afflicted many presidents and that could have spelled trouble for someone so self-reliant and self-confident.[13]

Wilson's presidential modesty and sense of separation also had a specific target. His crack about "a big stick" and his "wink" conveyed a pointed contrast with Roosevelt. During Wilson's first year in office, his predecessor and recent opponent seldom strayed from his thoughts. In February 1913, not long before the inauguration, Colonel House recorded Wilson saying that "if a man 'on horseback' should attempt to override the desires of the people, it would meet with failure. He thought that if Roosevelt should attempt it, the attempt would be a fiasco and look like overa [sic] bouffe." In April 1913, at a White House lunch on the day Wilson first addressed Congress, someone remarked that the small Progressive contingent had looked glum. Wilson's cousin noted that the president laughed and said "that probably they were mad because that was one thing their Teddy had *not* thought of doing!"

Surveying Wilson's legislative accomplishments at the end of 1913, House reinforced the president's belief that collegiality was the secret of his success. Wilson treated senators and representatives like gentlemen, House told him, "without making they [sic] feel he was President . . . Cleveland and Roosevelt always made them feel they were in the presence of the Chief Executive, and they resented it."[14]

The press and the public likewise contrasted Wilson with Roosevelt. Most commentators stressed the apparent differences to Wilson's advantage. The most extended such comparison came in an unpublished essay by the young radical journalist John Reed. "I never met a man who gave such an impression of quietness inside," Reed wrote after interviewing Wilson in May 1914. The president possessed a quiet inner core, "a principle, a religion, a something, upon which his whole life rests. Roosevelt never had it, nor Taft. Wilson's power emanates from it. Roosevelt's sprang from an abounding vitality." Outwardly, Reed observed, Wilson's quiet, orderly ways contrasted with "that violent slamming of doors, clamor of voice, secretaries rushing to and fro, and the sense of vast national issues being settled in the antechamber that characterized Roosevelt's term in the White House." Wilson's office gave the impression "of powerful organization, as if no moment were wasted—as if an immense amount of work were being done. Somehow I never could feel that in Roosevelt's office." Two years later the veteran reporter Ray Stannard Baker, who subsequently became Wilson's biographer, made a similar observation after a conversation with the president. "I talked with both Roosevelt and Taft when they were in the White House, especially the former, and often," Baker recorded in his diary in May 1916, "but neither could deliver himself so completely, reasons and all, as Wilson. Wilson applies the scientific method to his own mental processes . . . I never have talked with any public man who has such a complete control of his whole intellectual equipment as he."[15]

Such comparisons dwelt unfairly on Roosevelt's superficial bustle and self-centeredness, but they did point to genuine differences between the two men. In matters of legislative accomplishment and party mastery, Wilson went further faster than Roosevelt had done. Much of his greater success did derive from stricter concentration on party leadership and domestic reform. Wilson's involvement in foreign affairs did not account for the difference in their domestic accomplishments. Even before the outbreak of World War I, Wilson found himself more embroiled in serious diplomatic problems, particularly those arising from the Mexican revolution, than Roosevelt had ever been. Yet too ready a comparison of their partisan and legislative records is misleading because they faced such different tasks in the White House. Roosevelt had followed the delicate, daunting course of awakening and unbending a solidly conservative party. Wilson led an aroused, reasonably united reform-minded party. As Arthur Link has pointed out, Wilson's biggest troubles with the Democrats in 1913 and 1914 came from farmer and labor radicals who wanted him to go further in attacking big business and in extending government aid to their constituencies. If Roosevelt had won in 1912 and had carried Progressive congressional majorities in with him, he might have wrought comparable legislative feats.[16]

Implied and stated contrasts between the two men's collegiality were similarly misleading. Roosevelt had not been able to deal so easily and frankly with his party's congressional leaders because he had differed from them in his attitudes toward big business and his responses to party insurgency and reform agitation. With his cabinet and party confidants, however, Roosevelt had dealt as easily and cordially as Wilson did, and in one respect he had done better.

Wilson's cabinet relations and general administrative competence later became areas in which his historical reputation largely reversed the favorable contemporary comparisons with Roosevelt. Wilson subsequently came to be widely viewed as an aloof, imperious figure who neither consulted nor dealt closely with his top lieutenants. His judgment of men and his performance in all areas except legislative leadership and party dominance have also frequently received low marks from historians, political scientists, and other writers. Nearly all of those denigrations of Wilson have contained a converse exaltation of Roosevelt, most often implicit, sometimes briefly argued. Although many of those judgments have drawn upon Wilson's performance during and after World War I, they did not originate primarily in foreign affairs. Rather, they resulted from the two men's personalities as expressed in their presidencies. Roosevelt's extroverted manner and his ability to attract talented subordinates and colleagues were held up in contrast to Wilson's supposed withdrawal and aloofness.[17]

Later aspersions on Wilson's cabinet relations were wrong. Throughout most of his two terms in office, he encouraged free-wheeling discussions of the most important domestic and foreign policy issues. Secretary of the Navy Josephus Daniels described him at cabinet meetings as "the moderator," who elicited, "what he was fond of calling 'common counsel.'" Far from dominating meetings, Daniels recalled, Wilson pursued "a course, as he often said, more like a Quaker meeting, in which after full discussion the President would say, 'It seems to me that the sense of the meeting is so and so.'" No one in Wilson's cabinet, with the partial exception of Bryan, attained the premiership status that Elihu Root had held under Roosevelt. Nor did Wilson groom any member as his successor, as Roosevelt had done with Taft, although McAdoo used his record as secretary of the treasury to seek the Democratic presidential nomination in the 1920s. In administrative and political talent, however, Wilson's cabinet stacked up well against Roosevelt's or any other. It included such able men as McAdoo, Daniels, Newton D. Baker, who became secretary of war in 1916, and Thomas W. Gregory, who served as attorney general from 1914 to 1919. Wilson allowed his cabinet members free rein in running their departments, and he almost always backed their decisions, even when they caused political embarrassment.[18]

Much of the later downgrading of his cabinet relations relied on complaints by certain cabinet members about not being consulted on important matters. The first such complaint came in August 1913, when Colonel House recorded in his diary, "McAdoo complained that the President took no one into his confidence," that the cabinet seldom met, and that he, McAdoo, was not privy to instructions given to special diplomatic agents in Mexico. The following October Wilson denied the rumors, probably inspired by McAdoo, that he was relying less on the cabinet. "Nothing is more useful to me, speaking for myself," he told reporters, "than the cabinet meetings and the interchange of views that we take up there, and the routine information that is exchanged, making it a sort of clearinghouse." It was revealing that the first complaint came from McAdoo. The treasury secretary's transparent ambitions encompassed notions of a cabinet premiership and the presidency itself. It was also fitting that McAdoo's dissatisfaction involved not being consulted about matters outside his department. It was even more revealing that his complaint and nearly all the subsequent ones by cabinet members were made to House. The colonel's carefully masked ambitions included stage managing and setting grand policy designs for the administration.[19]

Even at a discount for sources and biases, however, the complaints about Wilson's cabinet relations did have a point. Unlike Roosevelt, Wilson did not establish intimate personal relations with the members of his cabinet, and he did not create an inner circle of privileged advisers whose competence spanned the whole or much of the range of administration policies. Of his immediate predecessors, Wilson most resembled Taft in his orderly, businesslike ways. As a result his administration had a quieter tone than Roosevelt's, but it also lacked the aura of glamor and the spirit of adventure that had brightened the Roosevelt years, both because of Wilson's social background and because of his personality. Despite his long association with Princeton, he remained a plain-living, middle-class man who valued privacy. He and his family did little entertaining in the White House, and they did not become pacesetters for society, as the Roosevelts had done. Nor did Wilson follow Roosevelt's example of intellectual and cultural patronage. Within his administration Wilson's social ways never permitted the top echelon to assume the aspects of an exciting, exclusive upper-class club, which had made membership in Roosevelt's inner circle so gratifying.[20]

Lack of intimacy with cabinet members and other politicians also reflected Wilson's solitary personality. Within his family circle and with old friends, he was warm, fun-loving, and relaxed. He could be highly effective and persuasive in face-to-face contacts with senators, ambassadors, editors, and others with whom he dealt. But, as in the past, he did not enjoy those contacts. No matter how successful he was at personal persuasion, he always found it hard work. As president, Wilson retained the working habits he had formed as a professor and college president. He spent long hours alone reading and thinking in his study; he drafted statements, memoranda, diplomatic dispatches, and major speeches in his shorthand; and he wrote those, along with a stream of letters to family members, close friends, and Colonel House, on his own typewriter. Fortunately, Wilson's self-discipline and ability to relax saved him from overwork, except at times of crisis, and he enjoyed relatively good health during most of his first term.[21]

His solitariness—so unusual among politicians, much less presidents—often elicited concern from colleagues and drew fire from opponents. "It is really a defect in his usefulness as an Executive," wrote House in his diary, "for the reason that he does not get many side lights on questions. He seldom reads the newspapers and gains his knowledge of public affairs largely from the matters brought to his attention, and his general information is gotten from a cursory glance at the Weekly Press." Those habits of Wilson's later formed the basis for further unfavorable comparisons with Roosevelt. A number of writers have argued that introversion and insufficient give-and-take in personal relations formed Wilson's deepest flaws as a statesman. Those criticisms, though plausible, applied much less to Wilson's accomplishments than to his public image. Except during the struggle over membership in the League of Nations in 1919, when his deteriorating health particularly affected him, Wilson's solitariness and self-reliance rarely caused him to make mistakes or suffer political damage at home. Foreign affairs were another matter, but even there the harm done by those traits was not decisive.[22]

In one respect Wilson's solitude in the White House was no defect at all; in other respects he overcame it fairly satisfactorily. As both practitioners and students of politics have pointed out, politicians seldom get the detachment they need to gain perspective on the ceaseless, constantly changing, frequently contradictory demands made upon them. Wilson turned his solitary habits to advantage by taking time to plan, ponder, and reflect. He often relied upon solitude to maintain his calm and reason in provocative, emotionally charged situations. Reflection and self-control played a big part in his successes in domestic and foreign affairs. Moreover, both House and Wilson himself exaggerated how little he read in the press, although his difficulty in reading did rule out his scanning large numbers of newspapers and magazines, as Roosevelt had done.[23]

Joe Tumulty, Wilson's secretary, partially filled the information breach by clipping noteworthy items and furnishing summaries of press opinion and coverage. Tumulty also compensated for the president's distaste for day-to-day contacts with politicians and reporters. Although he had been a long-time insurgent Democrat in New Jersey, Tumulty had grown up in the world of urban machine politics, and he dealt comfortably with the details of relations with senators, representatives, and state party leaders. He lubricated the administration's political workings and frequently mitigated frictions caused by his chief's distant manner.[24]

Colonel House, who performed similar functions at a higher level, played four distinct roles in the Wilson circle. The first role, from which the others derived, was personal friendship with Wilson. Because he was a wealthy man of leisure who had renounced office holding, House offered Wilson the kind of availability and apparently unselfish loyalty that several presidents have found valuable. "We then fell to talking of friends who uncovered their desires from time to time," House wrote in his diary four days before Wilson's inauguration, "and he said he had become almost skeptical of friendship because there were so few who were disinterested." Besides seemingly wanting nothing for himself, House had a soft, ingratiating manner and a well-developed talent for intimacy with men. These traits allowed him to become virtually the only person outside the Wilson family with whom the president unwound and shed the burdens of office on a regular basis. "He said he enjoyed talking with me," House recorded in December 1913, "because he did not have to think about what he was saying."[25]

Their friendship also assuaged a psychological yearning in Wilson. House partially filled the painful void left by his broken intimacy with Jack Hibben. Wilson unconsciously regarded House, as he had Hibben, as something of a stooge. In August 1915 he appraised House for Edith Bolling Galt, who was soon to become his second wife. Wilson praised House's ability to win "the confidence of all sorts of men," yet he conceded, "But you are right in thinking that intellectually he is not a great man. His mind is not of the first class. He is a counsellor, not a statesman. His very devotion to me, his ardent desire that I should play the part in international politics that he has desired and foreseen for me, makes him take sometimes the short and personal view when he ought to take the big and impersonal one." Moreover, just as Hibben had grown closest to Wilson during a time of trial following his

1906 stroke, House reached his peak of intimacy and influence during the months of grief and loneliness following Ellen Wilson's death in August 1914. This intimate friendship also ended in a bitter break during the Paris peace conference in 1919, over what Wilson once again perceived as disloyalty. By then, however, House had long since ceased to be Wilson's closest confidant.[26]

House's status depended not only on providing comfortable companionship but also on acting as a high-level domestic political intermediary. This was in fact his initial role in the Wilson circle. After their first meeting in October 1911, House made himself useful to Wilson by supplying additional connections in his home state of Texas and with Bryan, whom he had known for many years. He cemented his intimacy with Wilson by offering campaign advice, providing a private meeting place at his New York apartment, and furnishing information and opinions after the election about prospective appointees. House wanted to make foreign affairs his special province. Through confidential contacts with European statesmen during 1913 and 1914, he began to promote schemes for American leadership among the great powers, his third role with Wilson. But those diplomatic activities did not assume major importance until after the outbreak of the World War. During the first two years of the Wilson administration, House concerned himself mainly with patronage, Democratic factional squabbles, and to a lesser extent, domestic policies. In all, he functioned in much the same way as Tumulty did, to compensate for the president's solitariness.

House's unassuming manner and his grasp of domestic and foreign policy could have made him a uniquely valuable lieutenant, perhaps even the Wilson administration's informal premier. Unfortunately, as his literary proclivities revealed, he aspired to play an additional, covert role. In September 1912, when Wilson's victory in the election became well-nigh certain, House started to keep a diary in which he disclosed his ambition to shape the course of world history by manipulating his high-placed acquaintance. In 1911, before meeting Wilson, House had written an anonymous novel entitled *Philip Dru, Administrator*. The novel told the story of a benevolent dictator who reformed the United States, expanded its territory, and formed a concert of great powers under American leadership to rule the world. During the first two years of Wilson's presidency, House repeatedly drew parallels between Wilson and his fictional hero. In September 1914 he noted in his diary about the schemes in the novel, "I have a feeling that we largely agree, although when I wrote Philip Dru I had never met the President nor read any of his books. As far as I can see, his thoughts and mine have run parallel for a long while, almost from youth."[27]

What made the colonel's covert role so insidious was not just the concealment of his ambition, although that led him to mislead and lie to Wilson and others. Rather, because he sincerely believed that he was self-effacing, House felt few constraints other than the risk of losing his influence. From the first days of the administration he sought to undermine certain leading figures, most notably Bryan and Daniels, and he also worked to promote his favorites, particularly Secretary of Agriculture David F. Houston. By lending a sympathetic ear to cabinet members' complaints about the president and by abetting the discontent of such climbers as McAdoo, House gained still greater influence. Those underhanded dealings assumed their most devious and alarming aspects in foreign affairs during the World War. Worst of all, in his near mystical identification of Wilson with Philip Dru, House spun fantasies that loosened his grip on reality. Often he did not realize how badly he misrepresented situations or how desperately he was seeking to embody his dreams through Wilson and others. The colonel's temptation to become the author of events, as of his novel, made him a dangerous man to have close to any president, especially Wilson, for whom he filled emotional and political needs.[28]

The most immediately striking contrast between Wilson's solitariness and Roosevelt's gregariousness lay in their respective relations with the press and, partly as a consequence, in their popular images. As governor and on the campaign trail, Wilson had gotten along well with reporters, and he made a fine start in the White House by instituting the first regularly scheduled press conferences. Twice a week at the outset, then weekly, Wilson met with reporters for off-the-record but often indirectly attributable question-and-answer sessions, and he established easygoing, bantering relations with them. Wilson occasionally showed annoyance, and he sometimes fielded questions rather than answering them, but he rarely dodged sharp inquiries, nearly always maintained good humor, and showed frequent flashes of wit. As in his dealings with politicians, however, Wilson never learned to enjoy these encounters. In July 1915 he used the pressure of war-related diplomacy as an excuse for discontinuing the press conferences. He bowed briefly to Tumulty's entreaties to resume the meetings at the end of 1916, but the events leading to American entry into the war quickly ended them for good.[29]

The contrast between Wilson's chariness and Roosevelt's ease with the press reflected their social backgrounds and previous experiences as much as their personalities. As a member of the upper class and a politician whose entire career had profited from public attention, Roosevelt had long since reconciled himself to intrusions by reporters. Nothing illustrated the contrast between him and Wilson better than their opposite attitudes toward publicity about their families and personal lives. Roosevelt had accepted and usually, though not always, welcomed such publicity. In contrast, Wilson remained a relentlessly private person who discouraged attention to himself, his wife, and his daughters. Conversely, the generally greater affection that reporters felt for Roosevelt resulted largely from his accessibility, his appreciation of their professional needs, and, above all, the steady supply of colorful copy.[30]

Wilson paid a price for his privacy in the public impressions he created through the press. Although he inspired respect for his accomplishments, many people thought of him as a totally rational, controlled being intent only on his work. That reputation bothered Wilson. In March 1914, in the same speech in which he tipped a "wink," he also decried "the variety and falseness in the impressions I make." Wilson particularly deplored notions that he was "a cold and removed person who has a thinking machine inside . . . On the contrary, if I were to interpret myself, I would say that my constant embarrassment is to restrain the emotions that are inside of me. You may not believe it, but I sometimes feel like a fire from a far from extinct volcano, and if the lava does not seem to spill over it is because you are not high enough to see into the basin and see the caldron boil." A few months later Woodrow Wilson publicly complained about his alliteratively august name. "It is always a good sign if a man's comrades abbreviate his first name," he stated in a speech in November 1914. "There is almost the touch of the hand in the mere familiarity of the designation . . . I have always been sorry that I did not myself bear a first name that yielded to the process." Cultivating publicity about his talent for mimicry, fondness for limericks, and knowledge of baseball might have enabled "Tommy" Wilson to vie more successfully with "Teddy" Roosevelt for public affection.[31]

Popular impressions of Wilson changed after the outbreak of World War I. His steadiness in the face of provocation and his determination to stay at peace earned him warm gratitude as well as sober respect. War-related issues and his reelection campaign in 1916 allowed him to leave Washington on extended speaking tours and to renew contact with the public. Yet Wilson never did gain the same hold on the popular imagination as Roosevelt had earlier. His popularity continued to depend chiefly on his successes and later, with failure, faded quickly. Roosevelt endured defeat and took unpopular stands during the World War and was still able to make a comeback that by the time of his death would bring the presidency almost within his grasp.[32]

·16·

Crossroads of Politics

MUCH OF THEODORE ROOSEVELT'S political resilience sprang from the ideological advantage that was inherent in his approach to social conflict. Wilson appeared to sweep all before him in 1913 and 1914, but the situation really mirrored his and Roosevelt's respective positions seven years earlier. Once more a successful president was not riding so high nor had his beleaguered rival sunk so low as seemed to be the case. This time each man was playing the opposite part. Roosevelt did feel beleaguered during the four years that followed his 1912 defeat. Wilson's legislative and partisan feats bore out Roosevelt's fears about the Progressives. "If the Democratic party acts on whole wisely and sanely," he had privately predicted at the end of 1912, "it may be that the Progressive Party will be eliminated." As the Progressives suffered repeated setbacks during the next two years, his foreboding came to pass. Finally, the state and congressional elections of November 1914 left them with only scattered pockets of strength, mostly in the West, with California the only state under Progressive control.[1]

Roosevelt fought hard for his party. In 1913, before he left on his South American trip, he involved himself in organizational matters, and after he returned he mounted a barnstorming campaign for Progressive candidates during the summer and fall of 1914. But Roosevelt's heart was no longer in the fight, and his major concerns were shifting. The string of defeats and the outbreak of the World War contributed to Roosevelt's flagging interest in his party's fortunes and in domestic reform, but those events accelerated a change in him that was already well advanced. Early in 1913 Roosevelt confided to Lodge, with whom he was resuming his close friendship, "The various admirable movements in which I have been engaged, have always developed among their members a large lunatic fringe; and I have had plenty of opportunity of seeing individuals who in their revolt against sordid baseness go into utterly wild folly." During 1913 and 1914 Roosevelt spent much of his time in nonpolitical pursuits. He wrote his autobiography and then stayed for seven months in South America, where he made an expedition into the Brazilian jungles that nearly cost him his life. "As soon as I got back here I was plunged into politics," he told a British friend on his return, "—and really under very disheartening conditions; for the confusion passes belief and the malignance of the Republican leaders, together with the wild-eyed folly of a number of my own people, combined to make my course anything but easy."[2]

Those forlorn struggles of 1913 and 1914 afforded few opportunities for Roosevelt to advance his political thinking beyond the positions he had taken in 1912. He repeatedly flayed both of the older parties as boss-ridden and reactionary, and he heaped further scorn on the Democrats for their alleged devotion to state rights. He still upheld the Progressives as a vehicle for "sane radicalism." Roosevelt also continued to advocate regulating big businesses in a way that would, he declared in July 1913, "abandon the utter folly of discriminating against them on the ground of size instead of on the ground of conduct." But different emphases did intrude into his public and private statements. Explaining his regulatory approach in July 1913, Roosevelt declared, "This is merely part of the doctrine of administrative control of big corporations. The control should not be hostile to the corporation . . . Our purpose is to see that there is a proper division of prosperity. But there can be no division unless the prosperity is there to divide." Privately, Roosevelt expressed growing distaste for the more radical Progressives, whom he persisted in labeling the "lunatic fringe." He also grew increasingly reluctant to take sides in disputes between labor and capital or to favor bold government ownership schemes. "It is a mere matter of expediency," he informed William Allen White in July 1914, "whether a given thing should be run by private individuals or by the Government."[3]

The election results in November 1914 accelerated Roosevelt's drift away from reform. The Progressives had gone "way ahead of the country as a whole in morality," he told his daughter, "and the country will need too long a time to catch up with them." The smashing comeback of the Republican Old Guard buttressed his renewed preference for practical politics. "The fundamental trouble was that the country was sick and tired of reform," Roosevelt declared to White. Even more than stolid two-party voting habits or any feeling of revulsion from radicalism, a business recession beginning in the autumn of 1913 was what hurt reformers with the people. "They felt the pinch of poverty; they were suffering from hard times; they wanted prosperity and compared with this they did not care a rap for social justice or industrial justice or clean politics or decency in public life." Although he probably did not know it, Roosevelt was adopting the reasoning of the Old Guard in 1912; by agreeing with them, he was reverting to his earlier preference for their approach to politics. By the end of 1914 Roosevelt cared far more about the World War and military preparedness than about anything else, but even without those new concerns he would still have forsaken his reform crusade.[4]

Wilson drew a different conclusion from the 1914 results. The Democrats, whose House majority fell from seventy three to twenty five, suffered their biggest losses in the Northeast and Middle West. In the West, however, they retained most of their House seats, picked up two new governorships, and added a senator. Nearly all these gains came from votes captured from the faltering Progressives. The sectional disparity led Wilson and others to conclude that his reelection in 1916 and the Democrats' chance to retain power lay in attracting Progressives. "What I get solid satisfaction out of is the support the West gave us, the real heart of America," Wilson observed to a friend. ". . . That gives me vital comfort and a very lively hope. We have had a change of venue. A different part of America now decides, not the part of America which has usually arrogated to itself a selfish leadership and patronage of the rest." When reporters asked him to comment on the elections, the president replied, "My comment will, I hope, be the action of the next two years. I am very much more interested in doing things than talking about them."[5]

He did a lot. After the new Congress convened in December 1915, Wilson gave a further display of his legislative and party leadership. In some ways he even surpassed his earlier triumph. The next nine months witnessed the passage of seven major pieces of domestic legislation. These included the creation of the Tariff Commission, though with only advisory powers; establishment of the Shipping Board to regulate and aid the merchant marine; rural credits measures, which extended long-term governmental loans to farmers; prohibition of child labor in interstate commerce; workmen's compensation for work done under government contract; an eight-hour day for interstate railroad workers; and sharply increased income and inheritance taxes for the wealthy. In addition, Wilson nominated and gained Senate confirmation for Brandeis to the Supreme Court, pushed through an increased military and naval preparedness program over opposition from his own party, and beat back a revolt by congressional Democrats against his foreign policy. All the while, he was dealing with diplomatic controversies arising from the World War. The most critical issues involved Germany's submarine warfare, but Wilson also had to contend with Mexico's unending tribulations, which led to Mexican raids on United States territory and then American military intervention.

This second display of Wilsonian leadership should not be overestimated. The 1916 measures included no legislative monuments comparable to the Federal Reserve and antitrust acts, nor did most of them require as much presidential planning, perseverance, and mediation as the earlier measures had done. In some cases, particularly aid to agriculture, Wilson simply gave freer rein to the Democrats in Congress, and the new taxes emerged with no help or action by him. Of the new measures, the eight-hour day for railroad workers quickly became the most controversial. It came in response to a threatened nationwide strike and had to be hustled through Congress, Wilson admitted, "by circumstances we had hoped never to see." Other matters, however, engaged even more of his gifts for leadership than the earlier program. With Brandeis's confirmation and the child labor law, Wilson again exercised both collegial persuasion and probably patronage pressure on balky senators and representatives. When he promoted military preparedness, he took his case to the public in January and February 1916, making his first speaking tour since he had entered the White House. He then secured its passage through deft negotiation with his critics on Capitol Hill. On foreign policy issues he staged showdown votes in both houses over support for his submarine negotiations with Germany, leaving his party opponents humbled in March 1916.[6]

The preparedness and submarine controversies answered the last remaining question about Wilson's mastery of the Democratic party. In June 1915 Bryan resigned as secretary of state in public protest over Wilson's response to the Germans' submarine warfare. Although detractors heaped calumny on him, the Great Commoner retained a devoted following, particularly among southern and western Democrats. Moreover, for the last twenty years he had served as the party's foremost spokesman on military and foreign policy, nearly always in pacific directions. Those circumstances made it politically perilous for Wilson to choose to increase military preparedness and to engage in repeated confrontations with Germany. When Wilson went on his speaking tour for preparedness at the beginning of 1916, Bryan dropped hints about opposing the president's renomination. Bryan also made several trips to Washington to rally Democratic congressional opposition to the preparedness and submarine policies.

Wilson won decisively on both issues. In February 1916 he compromised on the most controversial section of the military program—the army reserve force. Thereafter the preparedness program encountered no further trouble in Congress. On March 2 Wilson sent Burleson and McAdoo to the Capitol with a handwritten note to the Democrats, in which he urged them "to clear up the existing situation and relieve the present embarrassment of the Administration in dealing with the foreign relations of the country." The next day the Senate tabled a resolution critical of his submarine policy by a vote of 68 to 14. On March 7 the House tabled a similar resolution, 276 to 142. Only two Democratic senators and thirty-three Democratic representatives opposed the president. No question remained about who led the party.[7]

Nor did any question remain about where Wilson was leading the party. As the 1916 Democratic platform boasted, the Wilson administration had enacted the most important planks of the 1912

Progressive platform, and the party had adopted "the spirit of Progressive Democracy." Many questioned the sincerity of these attempts to steal the Progressives' thunder. To Roosevelt the move merely offered more proof of Wilson's lack of convictions. "As for politics here," Roosevelt told a British friend in June 1916, "Wilson is, I think, as insincere and cold-blooded an opportunist as we have ever had in the Presidency." Many of Roosevelt's followers disagreed. The ex-president scuttled the Progressive party that same month in order to support the Republican nominee, Charles Evans Hughes, but a number of prominent Progressives backed Wilson. The Wilson supporters included a majority of the 1912 Progressive platform committee and several of the party's most brilliant intellectuals, such as Herbert Croly and Walter Lippmann. Party direction and control counted most with Lippmann, who announced in October 1916 that he was supporting "the Wilson who is temporarily at least creating, out of the reactionary, parochial fragments of the Democracy, the only party which at this moment is national in scope, liberal in purpose, and effective in action."[8]

Yet doubts have persisted about Wilson's motives and convictions. Several historians later argued, along Roosevelt's lines, that Wilson made a belated, opportunistic conversion from the limited reform posture of the New Freedom to the bolder, more statist approach of the New Nationalism. That interpretation is correct only in that it recognizes the practical calculations underlying Wilson's 1916 strategy, and emphasizes his willingness to push reforms that were more far-reaching than earlier. In other respects that interpretation is wrong, especially in alleging that he made an ideological leap from his previous commitments. Wilson had declined to push agricultural relief and child labor measures in 1913 and 1914. But he had held back mainly because he was worried about how much more he could get out of Congress, whether the proposed measures were practicable or constitutional, and how much they were supported by public opinion. It was not Wilson's convictions—which embraced government ownership of telephone and telegraph systems and support for striking miners in Colorado and West Virginia—that made him go slower at one time and faster at another. Rather, it was his openly avowed regard for expediency. "I am sorry for any President of the United States who does not recognize every great movement in the Nation," he declared in

July 1916. "The minute he stops recognizing it, he has become a back number."[9]

Wilson readily admitted that he had changed his mind on specific matters, including woman suffrage, but at no time did he indicate that his basic thinking had changed since 1912. New issues, particularly those involving the World War and Mexico, were brought up in many of his speeches in 1916, and control of big business received less attention. But Wilson still stressed the same themes of releasing popular energies and renewing society from below. He talked the same idealistic language that he and Roosevelt had talked in 1912, and he continued to display ambivalence about clashes of self-interest. "There is only one thing in this world, gentlemen, that binds men together," Wilson stated in a speech in July 1916. "That is unselfishness. Selfishness separates them. Selfishness divides them into camps." Soon after the election in November, Wilson asserted, "What I have tried to do is to get rid of any class division in this country, not only, but of any class consciousness and feeling. The worst thing that could happen to America would be that she should be divided into groups and camps in which there were men and women who thought that they were at odds with one another."[10]

In one fundamental respect Wilson had changed by 1916. He was not moving closer to Roosevelt's New Nationalism, but he was going through and beyond the political approach that many insurgent Republicans and Progressives had sought when they had marched behind that banner. Wilson's actions on rural credits, the eight-hour day, and child labor showed his willingness to use government to aid and protect less-advantaged groups. His approval of the tax measures condoned using governmental power to take wealth away from more favored groups and sections. Nor, despite his disavowals of selfishness and class divisions, did those actions represent simply practical exceptions to his views. In July 1916 Wilson explained his preference for labor over capital by asserting, "Labor is in immediate contact with the task itself—with the work, with the conditions of the work, with the tools with which it is done, and the circumstances under which they are used; whereas, capital, in too many instances, is at a great remove." During the presidential campaign he upheld measures to aid agriculture as a means for "doing absolute and full justice to the farmer" by supplying the instrumentalities "which were necessary to put the farmer upon the same footing as the other industrial workers of the country."[11]

Wilson stopped short of openly approving competition of interests or frankly celebrating governmental favor to the less fortunate, but he came close to those positions. In one 1916 campaign speech he used his organic, evolutionary political philosophy to maintain that "the whole nature of our political questions has been altered. They have ceased to be legal questions; they have more and more become social questions, questions with regard to the relations of human beings one to another." Government now dealt "with the substance of life itself." Mechanical, legalistic processes no longer sufficed. "The whole art and practice of government consists, not in moving individuals, but in moving masses. It is all very well to run ahead and beckon, but, after all, you have got to wait for the body to follow." Ironically, Wilson advanced that argument to justify his former lukewarmness toward woman suffrage. He was enunciating the basic tenets of the broker state and welfare state views that later held sway among Democrats and in reformist circles. Wilson was forecasting the most significant development of the next half century of American politics.[12]

By embracing the idea of using government to advance the interests of less-advantaged groups and regions, Wilson also earned immediate political reward. His reelection in 1916, while retaining bare Democratic majorities in Congress, vindicated the strategy of appealing to Progressive support. He aligned a solid interest-group coalition behind his party. "It was 'The winning of the West' by Woodrow Wilson this time," chortled Colonel House, in a pun on the title of Roosevelt's history. West of the Mississippi, Wilson carried all but four states. In the Rocky Mountain area, as David Sarasohn has observed, he improved on Bryan's earlier showings and forged pro-Democratic alignments that would last for a generation. Although issues involving the World War and Mexico played a part, the outcome in the West turned most clearly on attracting erstwhile Progressives and enlisting farmer and labor groups. Support by farm organizations, particularly the newly founded Non-Partisan League, accounted for much of Wilson's winning margin in the Plains states. Miners flocked to the Democrats in the Rockies, and transferred Socialist votes proved indispensable to victory in Washington and California. Throughout the West, as far as can be determined, majorities of the men and women who had voted for Roosevelt in 1912 turned to Wilson in 1916.[13]

But it took more than the West to win. By attracting Progressives and a farmer-labor following there, Wilson repeated Bryan's 1896 feat of putting together the "Great Crescent" of the South and West. Like Bryan, Wilson would have lost if he had not also captured Ohio, the only large state in the Northeast or Middle West that the Democrats won in 1916. Without Ohio Wilson's western sweep would have proven unavailing against the Republicans' renewed hold on the heavily populated states of the Northeast and Middle West. Several factors were critical in Ohio, including a vigorous state Democratic party and the prohibition issue, which hurt the Republicans. But above all else, labor support helped swing the state to Wilson. His administration's pro-labor sympathies, particularly the eight-hour law, gained him ardent union backing. By carrying Ohio, Wilson became the first Democrat in twenty-four years to crack the Republican heartland in a two-party contest. In enlisting the support of labor to manage that feat, he attracted an essential element of the coalition that later made the Democrats the majority party for half of the twentieth century.[14]

The time for building such a majority was not yet at hand. Wilson paid a price for forging a coalition of disaffected sections and interests. The most striking aspect of the 1916 election was not that Wilson won but that Hughes almost did. All the advantages of incumbency, spectacular legislative accomplishment, successful diplomacy, and flawless campaigning brought Wilson reelection by only a narrow margin. In spite of the unhealed split of 1912, a lackluster campaign performance, and a faltering organization, Hughes and the Republicans came within an eyelash of victory. The 1916 results reconfirmed the electoral alignment that had been wrought in the McKinley-Bryan contest twenty years before. Those results also vindicated the reasoning of Taft and the Republican Old Guard in 1912 that retaining party control would soon restore them to power. The return of Roosevelt and other leading Progressive bolters, such as Beveridge and Hiram Johnson, and Hughes's background as a reform governor of New York did not prevent the Republican campaign from taking an unmistakably conservative turn. Denunciations of the eight-hour law as "class legislation" became the Republicans' favorite battle cry in 1916. As Link has pointed out, the two parties had not been so sharply divided since 1896, and the Republicans revealed only slightly diminished strength.[15]

One clear consequence of Wilson's success with reform legislation and his attraction of Progressive support in getting reelected was to destroy the informal bipartisanship that had sustained "progressivism" before 1912. In 1913 and 1914 Republican insurgents and Progressives had betrayed a growing tension between their reform views and their need to differentiate themselves from the Democrats. By 1916—with the glaring exception of La Follette and the less blatant one of George W. Norris—one-time insurgent Republican senators and representatives were voting more and more with their Old Guard colleagues, against such measures as Brandeis's confirmation and the child labor and eight-hour laws. The erstwhile insurgents often resorted to tortured arguments to justify their conduct, but as Laurence James Holt has pointed out, when they were forced to choose between reformist convictions and party loyalty, they nearly always chose party. After Roosevelt publicly abandoned his party, most of the Progressives who had earlier been Republican office holders made their way back to their original partisan home. In the 1916 campaign erstwhile insurgents and former Progressives joined in denouncing the Democrats' "class legislation." The Republican party had been made safe for conservatism.

Wilson's partisan success ensured his lasting reputation for divisiveness. In the short run he undermined the anti–big business and pro–social welfare forces by identifying them with the weaker of the two major parties. The ideological advantage that Roosevelt enjoyed again eluded Wilson. During the 1916 campaign, as earlier, Roosevelt largely declined to spell out his alternative approach to domestic reform, but he did not neglect it completely. Twice while campaigning for Hughes, Roosevelt attacked Wilson on the eight-hour issue in ways that bared their continuing ideological divergence. At the end of September he admonished, "For justice in dealing between capital and labor he [Wilson] has substituted the policy of craven surrender to whichever side has the superiority of brute force." Two weeks later Roosevelt alleged that Wilson had not "stood by the honor and interests of the United States in this matter." To take the right action "needed courage. It needed disinterestedness. It was necessary that the man taking it should put duty to the nation first and political and personal considerations last."[16]

In Roosevelt's eyes Wilson was still forsaking transcendent national ideals for his own and others' selfish, parochial interests. Their basic ideological divergence received its clearest exposure in Roosevelt's last speech of the 1916 campaign. After denouncing Wilson's foreign policy for showing insincere idealism, he scorned the president's domestic policies for "frank cynicism of belief in, and appeal to, what is basest in the human heart. In a recent speech at Long Branch he said to our people, as reported in the daily press, that 'You cannot worship God on an empty stomach, and you cannot be a patriot when you are starving.' No more sordid untruth was ever uttered." How could Wilson claim not to "know that never yet was there a creed worth having, the professors of which did not fervently worship God whether their stomachs were full or empty?" How could Wilson uphold a nation "which did not develop among her sons something at least of that nobility of soul which makes men not only serve their country when they are starving, but when death has set its doom upon their faces?" For Roosevelt the fundamental task of politics remained that of inspiring people to rise above the self-interest that Wilson sought to serve.[17]

In the two years of life that remained to him after the 1916 election Roosevelt did not discuss domestic issues any more than he had earlier. American entry into the World War in 1917 made military and foreign policies still more pressing concerns for him. But unlike other Republicans and former Progressives, Roosevelt did not go back on his reform commitment. "I am a very radical democrat, and I grow more, rather than less, radical, as I grow older," he stated privately in November 1917; "but I am equally radical in the insistence on orderly liberty." As always, Roosevelt drew domestic inspiration from soldiers' sacrifices. "Most certainly the nation can be redeemed from mere gross, self-indulgent materialism," he asserted publicly also in November 1917, "and from the silly, sham-sentimentality which so often goes hand in hand with materialism." The Bolshevik revolution in Russia reinforced both Roosevelt's abhorrence of what he considered dangerous radicalism and his insistence upon soundly conceived reform to prevent violent upheaval. He privately likened La Follette and several of his own former Progressive followers to the Bolsheviks, and in public he repeatedly condemned radical groups and doctrines. "Class hatred is a mighty poor substitute for American brotherhood," Roosevelt declared in June 1918. "If we are wise we will proceed by evolution and not revolution. But Bourbon refusal to move forward at all merely invites revolution."[18]

When Roosevelt offered those counsels of reform conservatism, his political star was rapidly rising. By early 1918 many of his once implacable Republican foes, including Taft, Root, and Penrose, were turning to him for counsel and leadership. As the year wore on, Old Guardsmen, insurgents, and ex-Progressives alike touted his presidential candidacy in 1920, and he looked like the odds-on favorite for the Republican nomination. Roosevelt greeted his refurbished fortunes with defiant declarations of his convictions. "I would not lift a finger to get the nomination," he confided to a friend in the fall of 1918. If the Republicans wanted him, "they will take me without a single reservation or modification of the things I have always stood for!" Publicly, Roosevelt demanded in October 1918 that Republicans must espouse "sane radicalism," and in November he outlined a far-reaching government program of public works, hydroelectric power development, aid to agriculture, old age pensions, and health and unemployment insurance. In December 1918, in one of his last public statements, Roosevelt warned, "The soldiers who in this war have battled at the front against autocracy will not submit to the enthronement of privilege at home." When he went to his grave a month later, his reform banner was flying high.[19]

Death robbed Roosevelt not only of another term in the White House but also of his opportunity for the heroic presidency on his own terms that he had craved for the last decade. Whether he could have weaned the Republicans from their pro-business materialism was doubtful. Their responses to Wilson's domestic programs had shown their steady rightward drift. Their fond embrace of Warren Harding and Calvin Coolidge in 1920 would attest their wish to renounce all kinds of reform at home and abroad. Harding's slogan of "not heroics, but healing; not nostrums, but normalcy" represented a repudiation of Theodore Roosevelt as much as of Woodrow Wilson. Moreover, most of Roosevelt's popularity with Republicans in 1918 stemmed from his foreign policies, which intervention in the war seemed to vindicate, and from fear that the Democrats could not be beaten in 1920 without a strong candidate. No one could foresee that Wilson's collapse and the postwar souring of the political atmosphere would diminish the party's need for someone like Roosevelt.[20]

Yet the intriguing possibility remains that he might have chastened the Republicans' love affair with business and material prosperity. Roosevelt's renewed popularity also rested on the acceptability of his domestic reform views despite rightward Republican inclinations. Wilson's commitment of the Democrats to advancing the interests of the disadvantaged highlighted Roosevelt's fundamental conservatism. In 1917 and 1918 he emphasized that conservatism by denouncing radicals, reiterating his trust regulation approach, and rejecting socialism. "Government ownership should be avoided wherever possible," Roosevelt asserted in July 1918; "our purpose should be to steer between the anarchy of unregulated individualism and the deadening formalism and inefficiency of widespread State ownership." By the time of his death, Roosevelt and the Republicans had found mutually acceptable grounds for reconciliation. If he had lived, the unexpected turn of events in 1919 and 1920 would hardly have prevented him from winning the nomination and the presidency. As president in the 1920s, he could at least have dampened the rampant materialism of the decade and leavened his party's pro-business ardor with a different brand of conservatism and made them champions of governmental action after the manner of the Tory party in Britain during the next three generations. Roosevelt's death in January 1919 depleted the Republican party's ideological estate and altered much of the subsequent course of American politics.[21]

During his second term as president, Wilson resembled Roosevelt in giving less emphasis to domestic issues and in using the idealistic language of disinterestedness and sacrifice. His attempt to end the World War at the beginning of 1917, intervention that same year, the full-scale war effort in 1917 and 1918, and his struggle to make peace and gain American membership in the League of Nations in 1919, which ended with his physical collapse—all served to make reform and social justice at home comparatively minor concerns during the rest of his political career. Most of Wilson's later statements on domestic matters reflected his overriding concern for international affairs. The war, Wilson declared in March 1918, "is certain to change the mind of Europe as well as the mind of America. Men everywhere are searching democratic principles to their hearts in order to determine their soundness, their sincerity, their adaptability to the real needs of life." Henceforth "every program must be shot through and through with utter disinterestedness," and no party "must try to serve itself, but every party must try to serve humanity."[22]

Yet as his statement indicated, Wilson, like Roosevelt, retained his commitments to reform and viewed the war as an opportunity to advance his domestic views. The Wilson administration instituted a far-reaching program of governmental economic planning and controls, which included partial direction of industrial and agricultural production and complete takeover of the railroads and telephone and telegraph lines. Those wartime measures introduced unprecedented governmental centralization and power and promoted cooperation among big businesses; they therefore struck observers at the time as a fulfillment of Roosevelt's New Nationalism. Some writers later maintained that the wartime economic measures offered further evidence of Wilson's conversion from more limited, less statist views. The administration's promotion of cooperation among large industrial units and its enlistment of leading businessmen to help run the economic war effort also drew denunciations as sellouts of Wilson's earlier crusades. Subsequent commentators correctly noted that those practices provided the model for Republican policies in the 1920s of fostering a partnership between government and business. Appropriately, the chief architect of those later Republican policies, Herbert Hoover, received his first official position and enhanced his political prospects when Wilson appointed him food administrator in 1917.[23]

Wilson's wartime actions did not betoken shifts in his thinking or abandonment of his reform and party aims. Strong, centralized government had nearly always met with his approval. His wartime economic policies represented a further adaptation to changing circumstances, in pursuit of what he believed were the most important popular interests. Besides, the administration not only relied on business cooperation but also enlisted labor support, principally through Gompers and the A.F.L. In return for no-strike pledges and moderated wage demands, the unions received governmental aid in organizing drives. As a result, their membership grew by more than half to over four and a half million by the war's end. At the same time Wilson pushed income, inheritance, and corporate taxes drafted by McAdoo, with the avowed purpose of making big business and the wealthy pay a large share of the financial cost of the war.[24]

But the administration did not tilt consistently leftward. The specter of revolution raised by the Bolsheviks alarmed Wilson as much as Roosevelt. Wilson's last published writing, in August 1923, six months before his death, was a short magazine article entitled "The Road away from Revolution," in which he maintained, "The sum of the whole matter is this, that our civilization cannot survive materially unless it be revived spiritually." Earlier, in his December 1919 message to Congress, Wilson had argued, "The seed of revolution is repression. The remedy for these things must not be negative in character. It must be constructive."[25]

Yet the Wilson administration conducted and condoned repeated crackdowns on radical organizations, as well as on dissenting individuals and publications. Even before the Bolshevik revolution, Wilson secured passage of the Espionage Act, under which the radical union, the Industrial Workers of the World, was smashed and Socialist leader Eugene Debs was convicted and imprisoned. Starting in the fall of 1919 newly appointed Attorney General A. Mitchell Palmer mounted the lengthy campaign of raids, arrests, and deportations that became known by the label "Red Scare." Wilson neither approved nor knew anything about Palmer's actions, but the administration's repressions of free speech and dissent severely damaged his support and later reputation among reformers and civil libertarians.[26]

The wartime antiradical drives marked the beginning of Wilson's political downfall by alienating many of the former Progressives and independent reformers whom he had earlier attracted. But their alienation hurt more in the postwar controversy over foreign policy. More immediate damage came from other activities. "Politics is adjourned," Wilson declared in May 1918. Despite repeated charges by Roosevelt and leading Republicans to the contrary, he did run a nonpartisan war effort. Departing from previous American practices, Wilson did not confer top military and civilian posts on members of his own party with an eye to advancing their political careers. But the war effort was not bipartisan either. Wilson angered the opposition by refusing to give a command to Roosevelt and by sidelining Leonard Wood, the general who was closest to Roosevelt and the top Republicans. He also made almost no effort to give the other party a sense of participation or a stake in the conduct of the war. Unassuaged frustrations left the Republicans resentful and ready to take partisan revenge.[27]

In October 1918 Wilson compounded his failure in bipartisanship with what has usually been regarded as one of his biggest blunders. As the 1918 congressional elections approached, he issued a public appeal to elect Democratic majorities in the House and Senate as proof that Americans "wish me to continue to be your unembarrassed spokesman in affairs at home and abroad." Roosevelt and other leading Republicans promptly denounced the statement, and when they won slim majorities in both houses they crowed that the people had repudiated the administration. Actually, Wilson's appeal only aggravated already inflamed partisan feelings. It may have helped reduce Democratic losses, which stemmed mainly from normal midterm attrition and stresses within the sectional and interest-group coalition he had put together in 1916. On the Great Plains the wheat farmers deserted the Democrats out of resentment at alleged administration favoritism to cotton planters under wartime price controls. In the Northeast and Middle West, Republicans made headway, as they had in 1916, by attacking the tax measures as assaults by southern and western radicals on those wealthier regions.[28]

The appeal for a Democratic Congress provided a fitting climax to Wilson's domestic political career. Earlier in 1918 he had taken practical steps toward implementing his long-held ideas about party responsibility. During the spring and summer he worked through administration loyalists to defeat a number of antiwar Democratic representatives and senators in the primaries, principally in the South. Not only did Wilson succeed where Taft had failed in 1910, he also carried out the only successful party purge by a twentieth-century president. In January 1920, after his stroke and in the face of senatorial opposition to membership in the League of Nations, Wilson urged his party "to give the next election the form of a great and solemn referendum" on the peace treaty. Despite premonitions of electoral disaster and waning concern over foreign affairs, the Democrats remained committed to Wilson's record and programs, and they went down to defeat in 1920 in a massive popular repudiation of him and his works. The party's fortunes and the president's reputation would rise again, but Wilson had sealed his reputation for divisiveness by making himself first and last the leader of a party that represented a sharply defined coalition of interests and opinions.[29]

Wilson's overriding concern with world peace and the League of Nations became an obsession during his last two years as president. But that concern did not dampen his ardor for reform or alter his basic conception of leadership. International considerations made him more radical in his view of capital and labor. "It seems certain," he confided to his brother-in-law during the summer of 1919, "that some commodities will have to become the property of the state, the coal, the water powers and probably the railroads. Some people would call me a socialist for saying this." Wilson insisted he was not a socialist, but he did believe that American leaders must "think internationally as our labor masses are thinking. We can meet Bolshevism only with bold liberalism." Publicly, Wilson had cabled Congress from the peace conference in May 1919, "The question which stands at the front of all others amidst the present great awakening is the question of labor . . . how are the men and women who do the daily labor of the world to obtain progressive improvement in the condition of their labor, to be made happier, and to be served better by the communities and the industries which their labor sustains and advances?"[30]

After the Democrats' stunning defeat in the 1920 elections and the failure of the United States to join the League, family and friends remarked on how well Wilson bore those failures. Sympathetic observers attributed his resilience to his religious faith and strength of character. Others questioned whether his stroke and physical deterioration might have impaired his grasp of reality. In fact, much of Wilson's equanimity stemmed from his conception of leadership. During the last months of his life he told his brother-in-law that he thought it was good he had lost the League fight. "If we had gone into the League of Nations when I got back [from the peace conference]," he explained, "it would have been a personal victory for me. Now if we go in, it will be the deliberate and considered action of the American people." About a year earlier

Wilson had mentioned to a friend that he had been rereading and meditating about Burke, whom he again called "the Apostle of Expediency." Wilson added, "I have been endeavoring to sum up in a phrase the philosophy of expediency." The phrase he chose was "Expediency is the wisdom of circumstances." Like Roosevelt, Wilson went to his grave with his political banner proudly unfurled.[31]

·17·

Designs of Diplomacy

THE CONFLICT between Theodore Roosevelt and Woodrow Wilson over foreign affairs was deep, intense, and probably inescapable. Yet it contained "an irony of fate" in at least three aspects. One irony lay in the resemblance between Wilson's initial diplomatic behavior in 1913 and 1914 and Roosevelt's more than a decade earlier. Contrary to his own view of himself and to most later interpretations by students of his diplomacy, Wilson was neither ill-prepared nor reluctant to deal with foreign affairs. Since 1900 he had written and spoken little about diplomatic concerns and events abroad, but he had retained a strong interest in those areas. Between the 1912 election and his inauguration in March 1913, Wilson initiated a review of Philippine policy, decided to appease the British on the Panama Canal tolls issue, reportedly approved House's ideas about great-power cooperation, and vowed to fill ambassadorships with qualified men, not "the merely rich who were clamoring for them." In depth of concern and breadth of acquaintance with foreign affairs when he entered the White House, Wilson did not match Roosevelt, but he did recall Roosevelt in the confidence and relish with which he seized the reins of diplomatic leadership.[1]

As a diplomatist, Wilson continued to recall Roosevelt in style and working methods during his first year in office. Eight days after his inauguration he echoed the Roosevelt Corollary in a public pronouncement on Latin American policy: "Cooperation is possible only when supported at every turn by the orderly processes of just government based upon law, not upon arbitrary or irregular force."

Deeds followed words, particularly in Latin America. The Wilson administration pursued and advanced Roosevelt's and Taft's interventionism in the Caribbean and also launched a bold, though often clumsy, attempt to guide the Mexican revolution in paths of democracy and social justice. In the Far East the United States became the first power to recognize the new republican government in China. Wilson and Bryan also abruptly canceled the Taft administration's project for participation by American bankers in an international loan to China because they considered it compromising to Chinese independence. With Japan the new administration faced a recurrence of the diplomatic tensions that had plagued Roosevelt because of anti-Oriental discrimination in California. Wilson and Bryan handled those problems with about the same vigor and ultimate lack of success as Roosevelt had done.[2]

Wilson's personal diplomatic methods resembled Roosevelt's in blending dominance with partnership and informality. With his first secretary of state, Bryan, he formed a harmonious, productive relationship based upon almost daily meetings and consultation and mutual respect. A division of labor developed between them. Bryan managed most Latin American matters, except Mexico, and he promoted schemes for peace and arbitration. Wilson handled the canal tolls issue, and he kept Colonel House's projects, such as they were, strictly to himself. Both men participated equally in the Mexican and Japanese controversies, but with Wilson always in command. To a somewhat greater degree than Roosevelt, Wilson departed from formal diplomatic channels, particularly when he sent the journalist William Bayard Hale and former Minnesota governor John Lind as special emissaries to Mexico. But he also relied heavily on such ambassadors as Walter Hines Page, in London, who epitomized the higher-toned, nonwealthy appointee whom he preferred, and Paul S. Reinsch in Peking, who had been the leading American academic expert on the Far East. Similarly, among foreign envoys in Washington, Wilson established good relations with Roosevelt's old friend Sir Cecil Spring Rice, who arrived in 1913 as British ambassador, and his predecessor's former cohort Jules J. Jusserand, who was still French ambassador.[3]

The second ironic aspect of Wilson's and Roosevelt's conflict over foreign affairs lay in the similarity of their initial views. At the outset of his presidency, Wilson stood closer to Roosevelt than

almost any other Democrat. He was also closer to Roosevelt than
such Republicans as Taft and many insurgents and, as future events
would show, most Progressives. Although Wilson's imperialist ardor had dissipated since 1900, his basic outlook still reflected that
former enthusiasm. In February 1913 House recorded him as stating that "he did not share the views of many of our present day
statesmen that war was the [*sic*] so much to be deprecated. He
considered it, as an economic proposition ruinous, but he thought
there was no more glorious way to die than in battle." Wilson's
early actions toward Mexico bore out those sentiments. He adopted
a peremptory tone with the Mexican leader, General Victoriano
Huerta, and resorted to various maneuvers to depose him. In April
1914 Wilson inflated a minor incident into a pretext for sending
American troops to occupy Veracruz. As several writers have observed, the Veracruz affair was an incident that was looking for an
excuse to happen.[4]

The Veracruz affair, which turned into a fiasco, marked a major
turning point in the development of Wilson's foreign policy. American intervention lent apparent legitimacy to Huerta as a Mexican
patriot, and it turned his opponents, whom Wilson had sought to
aid, against the United States. Wilson learned quickly from his
mistake. Except briefly and in a limited way in the spring of 1916,
he resisted pressures to intervene in Mexico throughout his presidency, despite furious denunciations from critics, including Roosevelt. The reactions of Huerta's opponents taught Wilson lessons of
patience and forbearance, which he later applied not only in trying
to aid the liberal forces in Mexico but also in responding to later
revolutions, especially the Bolshevik triumph in Russia in 1917.
Regarding Mexico, he told the secretary of war in August 1914,
"there are in my judgment no conceivable circumstances which
would make it right for us to direct by force or threat of force the
internal processes of what is a profound revolution, a revolution as
profound as that which occurred in France. All the world has been
shocked ever since the time of the revolution in France that Europe
should have undertaken to nullify what was done there, no matter
what the excesses then committed." Wilson was on the road to
"self-determination" and his response to the upheavals sparked by
World War I.[5]

The Veracruz affair had a still deeper impact on Wilson's approach to foreign policy. The fighting that accompanied the occupation killed nineteen American servicemen and wounded seventy-one. Several observers noted that reports of those casualties shook Wilson. Three weeks later, on May 11, 1914, at a memorial service for the fallen, the president called war "only a sort of dramatic representation, a dramatic symbol, of a thousand forms of duty . . . I fancy that there are some things just as hard to do as to go under fire. I fancy that it is just as hard to do your duty when men are sneering at you as when they are shooting at you." Wilson honored most "men who are brave enough, steadfast enough, steady in their principles enough to go about their duty with regard to their fellow men, no matter whether there are hisses or cheers." Almost exactly a year afterward, on May 10, 1915, in his first public statement after a German submarine sank the liner *Lusitania*, killing 1,198 people, including 128 Americans, Wilson declared, "There is such a thing as a man being too proud to fight. There is such a thing as a nation being so right that it does not need to convince others by force that it is right." Veracruz had started teaching him about "being too proud to fight."[6]

The Veracruz incident served as a catalyst in deepening and redirecting Wilson's approach to foreign affairs. From his first foreign policy utterances as president, he had voiced high-flown, sentimental, quasi-religious expressions about America's mission and example to the world. To some degree such utterances were inescapable rhetorical flourishes in an age of fulsome oratory and lip service to "idealism" in all endeavors. Ringing declarations about promoting peace, freedom, and justice abroad were also well-nigh unavoidable among Democrats. Since 1900 their major and really only prominent spokesman for foreign policy had been Bryan. Fittingly, the Wilson administration's purest and simplest notes of idealism flowed from the secretary of state. The president, striking similar chords, was getting in tune with his party.

Yet major differences persisted between Wilson on one side and Bryan, his fellow Democrats, and later many insurgent Republicans and Progressives on the other. In his idealistic utterances Wilson drew upon a more intellectual and relativistic religious background than did Bryan and many of the others. Unlike Bryan, he never regarded peace itself as a goal to be pursued under nearly all circumstances. Unlike many progressives of various persuasions, Wilson did not recoil from international politics in horror at the threat of involvement in World War I. In those respects he remained closer to Roosevelt than to his own political followers and allies. But Wilson was not a Rooseveltian wolf in Bryanite sheep's clothing. Rather, he was revising his foreign policy views to accord with his personal moral values and political circumstances, as he had done earlier with his domestic views. During his first year and a half as president, but particularly in the aftermath of the Veracruz incident, Wilson sought to reconcile his earlier fondness for war and involvement in power politics with the pacific biases of his party and the diplomatic implications of his own domestic reform views.

The key to reconciling those conflicting elements in his foreign policy Wilson found in the same place as in his domestic policy— anti-ideological acceptance of the pursuit of interests. Even in his belligerent musings to House in February 1913, he had regarded war "as an economic proposition ruinous." A few days later he had reacted to the early troubles in Mexico by confiding to his family, "There's no chance of progress and reform in an administration in which war plays the principal part." From the outset of his presidency, Wilson's diplomatic outlook had reflected such reservations about foreign involvements. Many of the administration's miscalculations in Mexico stemmed from his and Bryan's suspicions of the influence of American business interests and their ready sympathies with the anti-Huerta forces. In his major address on Latin American policy at Mobile, Alabama, in October 1913, Wilson warned, "It is a very perilous thing to determine the foreign policy of a nation in the terms of material interests." That sentence sounded like one of Roosevelt's denunciations of materialism, but by "material interests" Wilson meant the influence of big business. "We have seen material interests threaten constitutional freedom in the United States," he declared, and he intended to stand against those interests in the rest of the Western Hemisphere.[7]

Actually, Wilson made material considerations one of the bases of his evolving foreign policy. In the Mobile speech he waxed lyrical about "the tides of commerce" and trading opportunities to be opened by the Panama Canal. As a means to foster healthier, more competitive American business, foreign trade was a vital part of his New Freedom program of social and economic renewal. Much of Wilson's distaste for military intervention, formed after Veracruz and maintained during World War I, rested on his repugnance toward war's wastefulness and his concern about being distracted from reform at home. He also eschewed notions of international do-goodism. "There is a great deal of cant talked nowadays about service," he asserted in May 1914. "Service is not merely getting out and being busy and butting into other people's affairs, and giving gratuitious advice. Service also and chiefly consists in comprehension." To serve anyone required that "I have got at least to put myself, imaginatively, in his place and see the world as he sees it." As Wilson moved toward "being too proud to fight," he did not forget self-interest and practicality.[8]

Those matters of worldly concern, particularly of material interests, formed the basis for his foreign policy conflict with Roosevelt. Many writers later depicted their conflict as a clash of "idealism" and "realism." Wilson supposedly spun grand but impossible visions of peace, while Roosevelt championed less attractive but vital concerns for security and survival. In fact, Wilson's and Roosevelt's conflict went much deeper and was far more complicated. As more perceptive students of their diplomacy have observed, each man was both an idealist and a realist, albeit of different stripes. It was Roosevelt's idealism, not his realism, that was at the heart of his conflict with Wilson.[9]

The final ironic aspect of their conflict was that it took so long to start. Its belated beginning resulted in part from the same circumstances that muted Roosevelt's attacks on Wilson's domestic policies in 1913 and the first half of 1914—the long expedition to South America and disenchantment with the Progressives. Roosevelt restrained himself also because, in comparing Wilson with Taft, he conceded privately that Wilson had greater political ability than the president who had come between them. He and Lodge implicitly agreed that foreign relations were no worse at least than under the previous administration. But behind Roosevelt's public truce lay a growing irritation with Wilson's and Bryan's foreign policies. He privately criticized their handling of the Japanese and Mexican controversies, and in September 1913 he told Lodge that he found Bryan "the most contemptible figure we have ever had as

Secretary of State, and of course Wilson must accept full responsibility for him."[10]

As in his earlier break with Taft, an incident Roosevelt took as
a personal affront spurred him to mount his first public attack. The
alleged affront occurred early in 1914 when the Wilson administration negotiated a treaty with Colombia, under which the United
States was to pay an indemnity of $25 million and express regret
over the revolt and secession of Panama in 1903. Wilson and Bryan
believed they were making a friendly gesture that would improve
Latin American relations. They were also inadvertently hitting one
of Roosevelt's most sensitive spots. The ex-president reacted with
predictable fury. In July 1914 he sent a public letter to the Senate
Foreign Relations Committee in which he blasted the treaty as "a
crime against the United States, an attack upon the honor of the
United States," and nothing less than "the payment of blackmail."
Every action he had taken in the Panama affair, Roosevelt affirmed,
"was not only open but was absolutely straight . . . Every action we
took was in accordance with the highest principles of public and
private morality." When the World War broke out a month later,
a full-fledged foreign policy confrontation between Roosevelt and
Wilson was another conflict looking for an excuse to happen.[11]

Nothing else could have arrayed the two men against each other
so totally as World War I. Almost from its outbreak the "Great
War" engaged Wilson and Roosevelt across the entire range of their
thought and emotions. The inescapably momentous character of
the war magnified the significance of both men's views and actions
in the history of the nation and the world. Consequently, and this
was almost equally important to them, the war drew forth their
most deeply ingrained attitudes about their own identities and their
most strongly held values of personal conduct. If it was inescapable
for them to clash over foreign policy, the World War ensured that
their conflict would be an epic one.

Like just about everyone else in the world in August 1914,
Wilson and Roosevelt were stunned by the suddenness of the outbreak of fighting. Unlike most of their contemporaries, however,
neither man was unprepared for the war in Europe or its probable
impact on the United States, including the possibility of intervention. Wilson had recently received reports from Colonel House
about belligerent sentiment in European capitals. He implemented

the routine, traditional procedures of proclaiming American neutrality and tendering good offices to the belligerent countries, but he also spoke out at once to urge calm. "I want to have the pride of feeling that America, if nobody else," Wilson declared on August 3, "has her self-possession and stands ready with calmness of thought and steadiness of purpose to help the rest of the world." Two weeks later Wilson issued his renowned public appeal: "The United States must be neutral in fact as well as in name during these days that are to try men's souls." Americans must remain "impartial in thought as well as in action" and must demonstrate "the fine poise of undisturbed judgment, the dignity of self-control," in order "to do what is necessary and disinterested and truly serviceable to the peace of the world."[12]

Certain immediate concerns had prompted Wilson's appeal for impartiality. He was particularly worried about sympathies for the belligerents among ethnic groups from opposing European countries and dissident subject nationalities. But deeper considerations also underlay his admonitions. Wilson's public messages remained the same throughout the first several months of the war. In December 1914 he squelched the agitation for increased military preparedness initiated by Representative Augustus Peabody Gardner of Massachusetts, who was Lodge's son-in-law, and soon joined by Lodge and Roosevelt. The president declared in his state-of-the-union speech to Congress that anything more than his administration's limited defense program "would mean merely that we had lost our self-possession, that we had been thrown off our balance by a war with which we have nothing to do, whose causes cannot touch us, whose very existence affords us opportunities for friendship and disinterested service which should make us ashamed of any thought of hostility or fearful preparation for trouble." In calling for calm, self-control, and service, Wilson was applying his own prescriptions for personal conduct to the American people. He was casting himself in the role of the United States on the world stage.[13]

Wilson warned against excessive, uncontrolled emotion for two reasons. First, he deplored the effects of such emotions in his own life; and second, he believed that the World War would arouse these feelings among his countrymen. In November 1914 Wilson received a stinging reminder of his own and others' need for self-control when a delegation of black spokesmen led by William Monroe Trotter visited the White House to protest against segregation policies under his administration. Angered by Trotter's spirited assertion of black rights, the president snapped back, "You are an American citizen, as fully an American citizen as I am, but you are the only American citizen that has ever come into this office who has talked to me with a background of passion that was evident." The meeting ended stormily, and newspaper reports of the exchange with Trotter added to the public furor over official racial discrimination. Wilson later regretted his conduct. "When the negro delegate threatened me, I was damn fool enough to lose my temper and to point them to the door," he told Josephus Daniels. Instead of noncommittally hearing them out, "I lost my temper and played the fool." By projecting onto the United States his own need to overcome "a background of passion," Wilson sought to avoid comparable flareups on the international scene.[14]

He believed that the war would provide many occasions for arousing Americans' passions. Besides emotions stirred up by sympathies for the belligerents, Wilson particularly feared irritations caused by interference with overseas trade and shipping. In September 1914, as he began to deal with Britain's blockade of Germany, Wilson reportedly read Colonel House a passage from his *History of the American People* about Madison's troubles leading to the War of 1812. "Madison and I are the only two Princeton men that have become President," House recorded him as saying. "The circumstances of the War of 1812 and now run parallel. I sincerely hope they will not go further." It was those fears and concerns—not indifference or feelings of remoteness from the war—that led Wilson to squelch the preparedness agitation. In his eagerness to rebut Gardner, Lodge, and Roosevelt, Wilson misrepresented his own view of the World War. It was a war with which he believed Americans had a great deal to do and whose ramifications, if not causes, he knew could touch the United States.[15]

World War I introduced two new elements into Wilson's thinking about foreign affairs. One was a heightened sense of the significance of his actions, a sense he shared with Roosevelt. "It is perfectly obvious that this war will vitally change the relationships of nations," his brother-in-law recalled Wilson telling him in August 1914. Four departures must occur, he believed, to reestablish peace at the end of the war. There must be no more conquests;

there must be equal rights for all nations, great and small; there must be no more private manufacture of munitions; and "there must be an association of the nations, all bound together for the protection of the integrity of each, so that any one nation breaking from this bond will bring upon herself war; that is to say, punishment, automatically." Four months later Wilson confided to a journalist that he hoped "for a deadlock in Europe." The opportunity, he believed, "of a just and equitable peace, and of the only possible peace that will be lasting, will be happiest if no nation gets the decision by arms; and the danger of an unjust peace, one that will invite further calamities, will be if some one nation or group of nations succeeds in enforcing its will upon the others." Further, inasmuch as Wilson thought Germany was probably "not alone responsible for the war, . . . it might be well if there were no exemplary triumph and punishment."[16]

The need for reform of international relations, especially for machinery to maintain peace, the desirability of a compromise peace, and the relativity of blame for the war—those views at the beginning of World War I formed the core of the foreign policies Wilson pursued during the rest of his presidency. In them lay the germs of his three greatest diplomatic efforts—his championship of a league of nations, starting in May 1916; his pursuit of what in January 1917 he called "a peace without victory"; and his advocacy of the principles he outlined in January 1918 as the Fourteen Points. Those views, together with his concern about American intervention, made clear that from the war's outbreak he regarded his diplomacy as fraught with peril and opportunity.

Yet Wilson's heightened sense of the significance of foreign affairs did not displace other considerations. His urgings of national self-control reflected his own calm assessment of the war. Among his advisers Colonel House, much like Roosevelt, gave the war overweening importance and favored the Allies. "I find the President singularly lacking in appreciation of the importance of this European crisis," he complained in his diary in September 1914. "He seems more interested in domestic affairs, and I find it difficult to get his attention centered upon the one big question." Even at a discount for House's self-centeredness, his observation was correct. Wilson did not lavish attention on the war to the exclusion of everything else; for him, the biggest political events of the fall of

1914 were the state and congressional elections. Considering his underlying concerns about the war, Wilson viewed it with remarkable equanimity.[17]

Wilson probably would not have found the last part of 1914 and first part of 1915 unusually trying or unhappy except for the circumstance that the outbreak of World War I coincided with the death of his wife, Ellen Axson Wilson, on August 6, 1914. Grief devastated Wilson. As Roosevelt had done thirty years before, he buried himself in work and tried to forget himself in devotion to duty. But Wilson found such conduct harder than had Roosevelt. He valued his personal happiness more and was less attracted to self-sacrifice after stoic and heroic models. Overcoming the pain of loss and numbing depression nearly daunted Wilson, as he repeatedly confessed to his family, House, and intimate women friends. "After all, the hardest enterprise in the world is to rule one's own spirit!" he confided to one of them in November 1914. "After that to rule a city were a pastime!" Private torment added depth and intensity to his public admonitions of national self-control.[18]

The impact of Wilson's personal tribulations should not be exaggerated. The strain sometimes affected his official conduct, as in his confrontation with Trotter and the black spokesmen in November. Not until the end of the war, however, when ill health undermined his emotional balance, did Wilson's performance in office again suffer from such lapses. His grief affected his policies chiefly by increasing House's influence for a time. By offering solace, the colonel gained still greater intimacy and trust with the president, thereby laying the groundwork for the critical diplomatic role he arrogated to himself at the beginning of 1916. At bottom, however, Wilson's trials only reinforced his analogy between personal and national self-control. Wilson had first grasped that analogy in the wake of Veracruz, before any premonitions of his wife's death; he drew it again in "being too proud to fight," after he had gained a new chance for love and happiness. Wilson was holding to the course he meant to steer in the wake of both personal tragedy and global conflict.

Roosevelt, in contrast, had some difficulty at first in finding the course he preferred for himself and the United States. The outbreak of World War I did not entirely surprise him, nor did he hesitate to draw his customary lessons from the fighting, particularly from Germany's violation of Belgian neutrality. Those events demonstrated, he said privately, "the utter folly of the present administration and its pacificist supporters" in promoting arbitration schemes instead of increasing military preparedness and asserting the Monroe Doctrine. Yet Roosevelt took a surprisingly detached attitude toward the European belligerents. Unlike the British and many Americans, he did not at once condemn Germany's actions in Belgium. Instead, he declared in his first public statement about the war, "I am not taking sides one way or the other . . . When giants are engaged in a death wrestle, as they reel to and fro they are certain to trample on whoever gets in the way of the huge, straining combatants, *unless it is dangerous to do so.*" Apart from the inescapable need for military preparedness, Roosevelt argued, Belgium's plight mainly demonstrated the weakness of international law in lacking both judges and police to enforce obligations.[19]

Those reactions revealed the conflicting strains of thought and emotion that Roosevelt had to reconcile. His initial relativism regarding the two sides reflected his long-standing conviction that international affairs required countries to be willing and able to resort to armed force. From that standpoint Roosevelt unhesitatingly renewed his previous calls for greater military preparedness. After November 1914 he gladly joined in denouncing the Wilson administration's alleged neglect of the nation's defenses. At the outbreak of the war Roosevelt also privately scorned the administration's "little arbitration treaties which promise impossibilities" and which were negotiated by Bryan, "a professional yodeler, a human trombone," and Wilson, "a college president with an astute and shifty mind, a hypocritical ability to deceive plain people." Roosevelt's first public statement about the war may have appeared to support the president, but his initial detachment was based on far different considerations, including a thoroughgoing distrust of Wilson.[20]

The other main root of his initial detachment lay in strategic calculations. Inasmuch as he himself had struggled to preserve the balance of power in Europe and the Far East during his presidency, Roosevelt at first disliked the prospect of victory by either side. Although he soon began to favor the Allies, he thought Germany unlikely to win. Even if Germany did win, he told a British friend, "she will not be able to reduce Russia to impotence, she will not materially have harmed England, but will have turned it into a great military power, and in probability will have excited in the United States a feeling of active hostility." Conversely, the presence of Russia and Japan among the Allies worried Roosevelt. "If Germany is smashed," he added, "it is perfectly possible that later she will have to be supported as a bulwark against the Slav by the nations of Western Europe," while the United States had to fear "always the chance of hostility between us and Japan, or Oriental Asia under the lead of Japan." Strategic realism initially inclined Roosevelt also to favor something like "a peace without victory."[21]

Cool calculations of national interest did not, however, constitute all or even the greater part of Roosevelt's attitude toward the war. From the beginning, Germany's conduct in Belgium struck him as dastardly. Britain's entry into the war, ostensibly to honor treaty obligations to Belgium, earned his private admiration and praise. Those attitudes arising from the Belgian case quickly eroded Roosevelt's initial relativism toward the belligerents. "Germany is absolutely wrong," he reportedly confided to some Progressive supporters early in September 1914. At the same time he regretfully told a British friend that in the United States "there is no opportunity for the display of heroic qualities." In his second public pronouncement on the war, Roosevelt criticized Wilson for proclaiming "a neutrality so strict as to forbid our even whispering a protest against wrong-doing, lest such whispers might cause disturbance of our ease and well-being." Within a month of the outbreak of the World War, Roosevelt was starting to call for heroic assertion of the nation's ideals.[22]

Two circumstances made him move more circumspectly toward asserting his ideals than he might otherwise have done. One was his leadership of the Progressives. Roosevelt concentrated on domestic issues during the 1914 campaign, and he deferred to the foreign policy views of his followers, many of whom had lauded Wilson's nonintervention in Mexico and favored government manufacture of munitions. "I told my own friends that as I was doing what I could for them this fall," Roosevelt informed Lodge, "I should not make an attack which they thought would hurt them but that after [the] election I should smite the administration with a heavy hand." The other circumstance restraining Roosevelt was his internal conflict about the war. Subsequently, he rationalized his initial relativism toward the belligerents by ignoring it, and he deleted the reference to death-wrestling giants from the collection of his foreign policy articles published in January 1915 as the book *America and the World War*. But Roosevelt still had to reconcile his observations on the inescapable need for military preparedness with his mounting desire for the United States to play a part in uplifting international morality.[23]

Roosevelt profited from those restraints as he addressed the larger issues raised by the war. In his September 1914 *Outlook* article, "The Belgian Tragedy," Roosevelt argued that to avoid a similar fate the United States must not only strengthen itself militarily but must also "create international conditions which shall neither require nor permit such action [as Germany's] in the future." The time had come for steps to put "effective force behind arbitration and neutrality treaties." Once more Roosevelt scorned "the worthlessness when strain is put upon them of most treaties," and he decried disarmament talk as "on an intellectual par with recommendations to establish 'peace' in New York City by doing away with the police." But he offered a positive alternative when he concluded, "surely the time ought to be ripe for the nations to consider a great world agreement among all the civilized military powers to *back righteousness by force*. Such an agreement would establish an efficient world league for the peace of righteousness."[24]

That declaration made Roosevelt the first important spokesman in the United States to endorse the idea of a league of nations during World War I and the first to advocate American participation in such a league. Wilson did not disclose his support for those positions until the middle of 1916. Others, such as Taft, who became head of the League to Enforce Peace, the organization that promoted those positions, and Lodge, did not make similar endorsements until the spring of 1915. Between September and December 1914 Roosevelt discussed the World War, an international league, and America's strategic and moral stakes regarding both in a series of articles for Sunday editions of the *New York Times*. These articles, collected with the two earlier *Outlook* pieces as the book *America and the World War*, did for Roosevelt's foreign policy what the 1910 speeches collected in *The New Nationalism* had done for his domestic policies. They also came at a particular time and under special conditions that allowed him to give the best exposition of his views on world affairs.

As with his domestic views in 1910, few of the ideas on foreign policy that he expressed in 1914 were new to him. His sense of the significance of great power conflicts, advocacy of preparedness, scorn for pacifism and unenforced arbitration, and perception that American involvements abroad were critical—all these he had expounded many times during the preceding twenty years. Moreover, the league idea had formed the text of his Nobel Prize acceptance speech in 1910. Yet the outbreak of World War I injected a momentous quality and ensured a hearing that those views had not previously enjoyed. After the November 1914 elections Roosevelt did start to "smite the administration with a heavy hand." As a result, he frequently distorted and shifted his stands, both out of the exigencies of political conflict and in growing fury at Wilson. Not until the end of the war, in the last weeks of his life, did Roosevelt recover much of the perspective and insight he displayed in the fall of 1914.

The war's overweening significance he asserted by describing its outbreak as "on a giant scale like the disaster to the *Titanic*"—millions of people had been "hurled from a life of effortless ease back into elemental disaster; to a disaster in which baseness showed naked, and heroism burned like a flame of light." Roosevelt pointed to China and Belgium as examples of the importance of preparedness and the futility of peace schemes. Concerning American involvements abroad, he drew a defense perimeter that excluded much of South America and all of the Philippines. Outside Alaska, Hawaii, and the approaches to the Panama Canal, Roosevelt argued, the United States had no vital strategic interests; the larger nations of South America were "now so far advanced in stability and power that there is no longer any need of applying the Monroe Doctrine as far as they are concerned." Regarding the Philippines, he revealed publicly for the first time what he had thought privately for almost a decade. Inasmuch as Congress and his successors had consistently shown themselves unwilling to defend the Philippines adequately and govern them vigorously, the islands should be speedily granted independence. "Any kind of position by us in the Philippines," Roosevelt conceded, "merely results in making them our heel of Achilles if we are attacked by a foreign power."[25]

Alongside those counsels of restraint, Roosevelt laid heavy emphasis on international morality by dwelling repeatedly on two concerns—Belgium and a league of nations. He refrained from attacking Wilson's conduct toward Belgium until the Sunday following election day in November. "As regards Belgium," he charged, "the administration has clearly taken the ground that our own selfish ease forbids us to fulfill our explicit obligations to small neutral nations when they are deeply wronged." In the face of such a transparent "breach of international morality" and in spite of the United States having signed international conventions affirming Belgian neutrality, the Wilson administration had done nothing. Such inaction might serve short-run interests, but at the cost of besmirching national honor. "But I believe that I speak for a considerable number of my countrymen," stated Roosevelt, "when I say that we ought not solely to consider our own interests."[26]

Instead he urged Americans to help establish an international body to adjudicate disputes and enforce a just peace. In two articles in October 1914 Roosevelt called for creation of an "international judiciary" backed by an "international police force." That could be done when the "great civilized nations of the world which do possess force, actual or immediately potential, should combine by solemn agreement in a World League for the Peace of Righteousness." He accompanied his attack on Wilson's inaction toward Belgium with a comparison between international affairs and the old West before the law enforcement agencies arrived, and he recommended a similar remedy, "through the action of a posse comitatus of powerful and civilized nations." In the concluding article in November 1914, Roosevelt condemned old-fashioned alliances as "very shifty and uncertain" because they were "based on self-interest . . . But in such a world league as that of which we speak and dream, the test would be conduct and not merely selfish interest." Americans must be ready, therefore, "to take some chance for the sake of internationalism, that is of international morality."[27]

Those declarations placed Roosevelt at the forefront of American spokesmen for internationalism and also anticipated much of Wilson's thinking along the same lines. Roosevelt's public assertions about the need for supranational judicial and enforcement agencies mirrored Wilson's private convictions. The contrast Roosevelt made between "selfish" alliances and a "world league" based upon "international morality" forecast Wilson's later justification for membership in a league of nations, particularly when he advocated "a peace without victory" in January 1917. In January 1915 Roosevelt went still further in foreshadowing Wilson's and others' internationalist arguments when he admonished the great powers to pledge at once "their entire military force" behind an international tribunal. Although smaller nations could also participate, he argued, "no power should be admitted into the first circle, that of the contracting powers, unless it is civilized, well-behaved, and able to do its part in enforcing the decrees of the court." Roosevelt was proposing two levels of membership directed by the right-minded great powers, features that later became central both to the League of Nations after World War I and to the United Nations after World War II.[28]

The similarity in their internationalist thinking did not betoken a willingness on Roosevelt's part to cooperate with Wilson. In the fall of 1914 the ex-president also vented mounting hostility toward his successor's foreign policies. By the beginning of October Roosevelt was claiming privately that if he had been in the White House the United States would have come to Belgium's aid. "If I had been President," he told his friend British ambassador Spring Rice, "I should have acted on the thirtieth or thirty-first of July, as head of a signatory power of the Hague treaties, calling attention to the guaranty of Belgium's neutrality and saying that I accepted the treaties as imposing a serious obligation which I expected not only the United States but all other neutral nations to join in enforcing." A month later Roosevelt publicly reiterated that claim, and he maintained that timely American action "might very possibly have resulted in either putting a stop to the war or in localizing and narrowly circumscribing its area." Evidently forgotten were his own initial relativism toward the belligerents and his slowness to regard Belgium as a test case of international morality.[29]

The Wilson administration's posture about the World War rankled Roosevelt so much that he distorted his previous views and conduct even further. In his public denunciations in November 1914, he went beyond dubbing the president's policy "a timid and spiritless neutrality" to charge Wilson with having betrayed a treaty obligation to uphold Belgian neutrality under the Hague conventions signed and ratified by his, Roosevelt's, administration. "As President, acting on behalf of this government, and in accordance with the unanimous wish of our people," avowed Roosevelt, "I ordered the signature of the United States to these conventions. Most emphatically I would not have permitted such a farce to have gone through if it had entered my head that this government would not feel itself bound to do all it could to see that the regulations to which it made itself a party were actually observed when the necessity for their observance arose."[30]

That charge, which Roosevelt repeated often during the next four years, was probably not a conscious lie. It was, however, a wild distortion of the facts and a wishful fantasy of mistaken memory. Roosevelt knew only too well the American people's and Congress's unconcern about foreign affairs and their unwillingness to enter into international obligations, especially toward Europe. "Your people have been shortsighted," he told Rudyard Kipling, also in November 1914, "but they are not as shortsighted as ours in these matters. The difference, I think, is to be found in the comparative widths of the Channel and the Atlantic Ocean." The best evidence of the falseness of Roosevelt's allegation that the United States had contracted an obligation to Belgium came from Senator Lodge. Despite his renewed intimacy with Roosevelt and their passionate agreement about the war, Lodge, who had steered the Hague conventions through the Senate, never repeated those charges of betrayal against Wilson.[31]

The growing intemperance of Roosevelt's attacks on Wilson and the frequent references to what he would have done if he were president led many people to dismiss him as an embittered victim of personal jealousy. "The very extravagance and unrestrained ill feeling of what he is now writing serve to nullify any influence that his utterances could have," Wilson observed to a friend in December 1914. Private as well as public expressions lent credence to the notion that Roosevelt spoke mainly from envy, even hatred of his successor. "Wilson is, I think, a timid man physically," he told Spring Rice in November 1914. To Kipling he wrote that Wilson "comes of a family none of whose members fought on either side in the Civil War." That aspersion—which was factually incorrect—

evidently reflected an unacknowledged shame over what Roosevelt regarded as his own checkered background. Earlier in the same letter to Kipling he asserted, "I have always explained to my four sons that, if there is a war during their lifetime, I wish them to be in a position to explain to their children, why they did go to it, and not why they did not go to it." The shadow of Theodore Roosevelt, Sr.'s, not having fought in the Civil War still haunted his son.[32]

Those psychological undercurrents reached back into Roosevelt's childhood, and they revealed the depth and seriousness of his conflict with Wilson. Since Roosevelt had yearned for great events to lend historical significance to both his presidency and his reform leadership, he could hardly help feeling jealous of Wilson for sitting in the White House during such an indisputably momentous event as World War I. This was not petty jealousy, it was grand jealousy. Among contemporary observers, the one who best understood Roosevelt's attitude, while rejecting it, was Taft. In November 1914 Taft commented to a friend, "Roosevelt's view on the subject of war and peace is a sincere attitude. He loves war. He thinks it is essential to develop the highest traits in manhood, and he believes in forcible rather than peaceful methods." Publicly, Roosevelt held up "the great patriot-statesmen-soldiers like Washington, the great patriot-statesmen like Lincoln" as mankind's greatest benefactors, and he declared, "To condemn war in terms which include the wars these men waged or took part in precisely as they include the most wicked and unjust wars of history is to serve the devil and not God."[33]

Here was the heart of Roosevelt's conflict with Wilson and with everyone else who believed that America served some higher cause through remaining neutral during the World War. "The storm that is raging in Europe at this moment is terrible and evil," wrote Roosevelt in January 1915; "but it is also grand and noble. Untried men who live at ease will do well to remember that there is a certain sublimity even in Milton's defeated archangel, but none whatever in the spirits who kept neutral, who remained at peace, and dared side neither with hell nor with heaven." Americans must never, Roosevelt argued, "assume an attitude of superior virtue in the face of the war-torn nations." Europeans did not "regard us as having set a spiritual example to them by sitting idle, uttering cheap platitudes, and picking up their trade, while they have poured out their blood like water in support of ideals in which, with all their hearts and souls, they believe." To Roosevelt the warring Europeans were the true idealists. They, not his countrymen, were setting the examples that should be honored and perhaps eventually followed.[34]

For himself, Roosevelt envied Wilson the chance to play a part in events that might call forth another Washington or Lincoln. On the same grounds, he despised Wilson. Roosevelt extended their domestic differences to their foreign policies, considering his successor as the ideological heir to the viewpoint opposed to his own Hamiltonian tradition of strong, disinterested government. Wilson and Bryan were, he told Lodge in December 1914, "worse than Jefferson and Madison." Roosevelt also feared parallels with the situation leading to the War of 1812. In January 1915 he described to the British foreign secretary how "pacificists" too often "drift helplessly into a war, which they have rendered inevitable, without the slightest idea they were doing so," and he warned, "A century ago this was what happened to the United States under Presidents Jefferson and Madison."[35]

Roosevelt frequently leveled charges of weakness and drifting into war until the United States did go to war in 1917. Those charges constituted one of the two principal bases for subsequent contentions that he championed diplomatic realism. The other bases for such contentions were his denunciations of allegedly visionary and impractical peacekeeping proposals, after he largely reversed his internationalist stand later in 1915. Actually, after the first two or three months of the war, Roosevelt expressed little concern about either the nation's defense perimeter or strategic consequences of victory by one side or the other. "Personally, I think the Allies will win," he told Spring Rice in February 1915. "I know they ought to win." After the autumn of 1914 Roosevelt never again spoke of maintaining Germany as a bulwark against Russia or of any other possibly adverse effects of an Allied victory. Roosevelt's realism always remained a highly selective criterion of judgment, which he applied or ignored as he saw fit.[36]

Realism was not central to either his attitude toward World War I nor his conflict with Wilson. Rather, the war and his adversary engaged Roosevelt across the entire spectrum of his thought and emotions. The interpretation that has come closest to capturing the full range and richness of Roosevelt's engagement is Robert E. Osgood's invocation of Friedrich Nietzsche's "distinction between the Warrior and the Priest." According to Osgood, Nietzsche's Warrior "is the man of true nobility, the man of honor transcending self-interest." Osgood further observes that toward the Priest, Nietzsche's Warrior "reserves a special loathing . . . for the will of the Priest is not the frank, straightforward will of the Warrior but rather the devious influence of a crafty intellect, which compensates the Priest for his physical weakness by investing cowardice with the semblance of morality." That is a near perfect depiction of Roosevelt's attitude toward Wilson. Whether Nietzsche's other characterization should be applied to Wilson remains to be seen.[37]

Roosevelt's attacks at the end of 1914 and beginning of 1915 and Wilson's implicit reply when he squelched the preparedness agitation constituted the first round in their foreign policy conflict. Thus far it was a decidedly unequal conflict, with mixed showings by the two adversaries. Roosevelt had said far more than Wilson and had expounded his views much more fully. His newspaper and magazine articles collected in *America and the World War* had presented a well-reasoned exposition of his thinking on foreign affairs. If Roosevelt had not vitiated the impact of those pieces with increasingly fierce attacks on Wilson after November 1914, his arguments might have served better to educate Americans about involvement in world affairs. As it was, Roosevelt gathered so little support that he ruefully confessed to the British foreign secretary in January 1915, "I have no influence whatever in shaping public action and, as I have reason to believe, very little influence indeed in shaping public opinion."[38]

Wilson, in contrast, appeared to be prevailing more decisively in his foreign policy conflict with Roosevelt than in their domestic rivalry. His dismissal of the agitation for preparedness at the end of 1914 elicited outspoken support not only from Democrats but also from regular Republicans, particularly Taft, erstwhile insurgents, and some of Roosevelt's Progressives. Wilson's public statements on preparedness and his private observation about "extravagance and unrestrained ill feeling" were his only comments even indirectly about Roosevelt. There seemed no need to answer or worry about someone who was doing such a fine job of discrediting himself. As in their domestic rivalry, however, immediate appearances were misleading. The widespread public acceptance of Wilson's assurances of remoteness from the war reinforced attitudes that would hamper his diplomacy. The war was about to take a turn that would transform both the context of foreign policy and the remaining rounds of his conflict with Roosevelt.

· 18 ·

Facing War

AMERICA'S POSTURE TOWARD THE WORLD WAR changed dramatically in a few hours on the afternoon of May 7, 1915, as the news arrived of the sinking of the *Lusitania*. Ten years later the journalist Mark Sullivan found that all the people he talked with remembered exactly where they had been when they had learned of the sinking, what they had thought and felt, and what they had done for the rest of the day. The event left an indelible memory not just because it was a great disaster, comparable to the sinking of the *Titanic*. It also raised for the first time the threat of American involvement in the war. Many spokesmen, most notably Roosevelt, raised cries of outrage, yet almost no one suggested going to war. Of a thousand newspaper editors asked to telegraph their views to New York newspapers, only six called for war. Wilson expressed the dominant public reaction when he commented privately a month later, "I wish with all my heart I saw a way to carry out the double wish of our people, to maintain a firm front in respect of what we demand of Germany and yet do nothing that might by any possibility involve us in the war."[1]

Although the sinking of the *Lusitania* shocked Wilson and Roosevelt, neither man was unprepared for its impact on the United States. German submarine attacks on American vessels and on Allied merchant ships carrying American citizens had begun in March 1915, but even before then Wilson had tried to prepare public opinion for fresh strains. "The circumstances created by the war put the nation to a special test," he had warned in a message to Congress, "a test of its true character and self-control." After the

first submarine attacks, Wilson asserted in a speech in April that
"the supreme test" of a nation's greatness "is self-possession, the
power to resist excitement, to think calmly . . . to be absolutely
master of itself and of its fortunes." In another speech Wilson
declared, "Our whole duty for the present, at any rate, is summed
up in this motto: 'America First.' Let us think of America before we
think of Europe, in order that America may be fit to be Europe's
friend when the day of tested friendship comes." When the sinking
of the *Lusitania* brought that day, it was natural for him to urge
Americans to be "too proud to fight."[2]

Wilson prepared Americans perhaps too well against becoming
aroused by the threat of involvement in the war. He immediately
retracted the "too proud to fight" statement. "I did not mean that
as a declaration of policy of any sort," he told reporters the next day.
". . . I was expressing a personal attitude, that was all." Wilson was
not backing down in the face of public outrage. The statement did
draw a few denunciations although, curiously, not immediately
from Roosevelt. It attracted widespread approval, particularly from
Democrats, insurgent Republicans, and some Progressives. It was
neither praise nor blame that moved Wilson to retract "too proud
to fight." He repudiated the statement before he had any chance to
sample public reaction, and he acted for his own reasons.[3]

Wilson retracted the statement and chose his diplomatic response because he took each half of the "double wish" equally
seriously. In that attitude he differed both from Roosevelt, who was
by now his leading foreign policy critic, and from Bryan, his chief
adviser. Roosevelt, who had labeled earlier German submarine
attacks "piracy, pure and simple," now charged, "But none of these
old-time pirates committed murder on so vast a scale as in the case
of the *Lusitania*." America's response must not be to "earn as a
nation measureless scorn and contempt if we follow the lead of
those who exalt peace above righteousness," but rather "to do the
duty imposed on us in connection with the World War." A few
others, principally such Republicans as Lodge, Gardner, and Elihu
Root, voiced similar sentiments. Within the Wilson administration,
Secretary of War Lindley M. Garrison and Colonel House, who was
in Britain on one of his missions, also favored a tough line and
welcomed the prospect of intervention. As with newspaper editors
and the public at large, however, those quasi-belligerent attitudes

attracted scant support among political spokesmen, whether Democrats, Repbulicans, or Progressives.[4]

The more dangerous difference of opinion was between Bryan and Wilson. After the sinking of the *Lusitania*, as earlier, the secretary of state advocated two responses. First, the United States should take a mild tone toward Germany, and second, the government should warn Americans not to travel on Allied merchant vessels. Wilson rejected those suggestions in favor of a stiff diplomatic note of protest, which he drafted himself. The United States would not omit, he declared, "any necessary act in sustaining the rights of its citizens or in safeguarding the sacred duties of international obligation." When the Germans replied evasively to that note, Bryan once more urged conciliation, and when Wilson again rejected his suggestions, he resigned as secretary of state on June 8, 1915. Nearly every newspaper criticized Bryan's action, but Wilson privately worried that "the newspapers do not express the real feeling of the country for that strange man . . . There are deeper waters than ever ahead of us."[5]

His fears were justified. In addition to causing disunity in a diplomatic crisis, Bryan's resignation spelled trouble at home. Evidence abounded of public repugnance toward being drawn into war, and the secretary made it clear before he left that he intended, as Wilson noted, "to make a determined effort to direct public opinion in this German matter." The Great Commoner retained formidable political assets. Two leading Democrats from Capitol Hill, a representative and a senator, bolstered Bryan's stand when they told him shortly before he resigned that if Congress were called into session, the vote would be overwhelmingly against a declaration of war. For themselves, they declared in a letter for Bryan to show to Wilson, "we have not been able to reach a conclusion that war should result from any questions growing out of the destruction of the Lusitania and the incidental loss of American lives." Now that Bryan was outside the government, vowing to keep the country out of war by speaking out, and representing the strongest attitude among Americans in general and Democrats in particular, Wilson faced the severest test yet of his leadership.[6]

He met the test during the year following Bryan's resignation by pursuing foreign policy on three levels. First came diplomacy toward the belligerent nations: toward Germany over submarine warfare, toward the Allies over their dealings with the United States, and with both sides over mediation and a peace settlement. Wilson sought to assert American rights while staying out of the war through complex, frequently shifting negotiations. Those negotiations revealed both strengths and weaknesses in his diplomatic methods. He showed the greatest strength and resourcefulness in his dealings with the Germans, which he conducted himself with little significant aid or influence from anyone else. As Link has shown, Wilson did not adopt a single policy toward submarine warfare. Instead he attempted to uphold national prestige and safeguard American lives and property while allowing the Germans latitude in using their new weapon. His combination of patience, forbearance, and firmness finally paid off in May 1916. After three subsequent crises over sinkings of passenger vessels, the Germans at last agreed to moderate submarine warfare rather than face a threatened diplomatic break and likely intervention by the United States. Wilson had temporarily fulfilled his "double wish."[7]

The submarine controversy was only one aspect of Wilson's diplomacy with the belligerents. Although they were overshadowed by the recurrent crises with Germany, frictions with the Allies persisted. Ill feelings mounted as the British imposed tighter restrictions on trade and armed their merchant vessels, purportedly in self-defense against submarines. The Wilson administration dealt with those problems far less skillfully and in ways that revealed a major shortcoming in the president's approach to diplomacy—his reliance on his two chief lieutenants, House and Robert Lansing. Wilson elevated Lansing, formerly the counselor of the State Department, to the secretaryship in June 1915 as Bryan's successor. He had initially balked at promoting Lansing because, according to McAdoo, "he did not think he was big enough." Wilson relented, however, as a matter of convenience and out of frustration from his experience with Bryan. "I think the most important thing is to get a man with not too many ideas of his own and one that will be entirely guided by you without unnecessary argument," advised House, "and this, it seems to me, you would find in Lansing." Wilson made the appointment because, House recorded, "he is practically his own Secretary of State and Lansing would not be troublesome by obtruding or injecting his own views."[8]

Lansing turned out to be the worst appointment Wilson ever made. At his best, he lived up to the president's misgivings about his smallness of mind and character. At his worst, he belied House's assurances about his docility and lack of ideas. Lansing frequently attempted to pursue his own aims in ways that were at once devious and maladroit. Although he privately harbored pro-Allied views similar to Roosevelt's and House's, Lansing made his first trouble for Wilson early in 1916 by proposing a "modus vivendi" under which British merchant vessels would be disarmed in return for an agreement that German submarines would cease attacking without warning. For all its seeming reasonableness, the modus vivendi was a diplomatic blunder. It enraged the British and would have made German concessions on the submarine question dependent on British actions. When House, who was in London in February, warned of the depth of British hostility, Wilson at once withdrew the proposal. The withdrawal precipitated a showdown with Bryanite Democrats on Capitol Hill over congressional resolutions criticizing Wilson's submarine policy.[9]

The modus vivendi episode offered a foretaste of Lansing's behavior. Several times during the next four years he worked to undermine Wilson's most cherished policies, and he usually acted deliberately, not by inadvertance. In December 1916 Wilson sent a public diplomatic note to the warring nations asking them to state their peace terms and promising American participation in postwar international efforts to maintain peace. Lansing, who feared that the overture might harm Allied chances for victory, told reporters, "Neither the President nor myself regard this note as a peace note"; rather, it was sent because "we are drawing nearer the verge of war ourselves." Lansing's statement appears to have affected the Allies' response, and it certainly undermined domestic support for Wilson's move.[10]

Again in 1919 Lansing worked to weaken collective security commitments under the League of Nations. At the peace conference he drafted evasive language about security obligations under the League Covenant, which Wilson rejected. Later, when the Senate was considering the treaty, Lansing publicly aired his disagreements with the president during the negotiations and stated his opposition to the obligations incurred under Article X of the Covenant. When Wilson finally fired Lansing in February 1920,

the ostensible reason was that the secretary had convened un-
authorized cabinet meetings during the president's illness. The real
reasons stemmed from his long history of disloyalty, which had
culminated, after Wilson's stroke, in a plot to foment war with
Mexico.[11]

Wilson's other problem in dealing with the Allies involved
Colonel House. Thanks in part to his role as a consoler after Ellen
Wilson's death, House gained an ascendancy in foreign policy that
lasted until the middle of 1916. In January 1915 Wilson sent him on
his first wartime mission to Europe to ascertain prospects for mediation and possible peace terms. On that trip House cemented his
prewar acquaintance with the British foreign secretary, Sir Edward
Grey, into an intimate friendship. The colonel buttressed his entente with Grey by disclosing his own pro-Allied views, which
resembled Roosevelt's and which he normally concealed from Wilson. House did partially disclose his true sentiments when he cabled the president immediately after the sinking of the *Lusitania,*
"Our intervention will save rather than increase loss of life. America has come to the parting of the ways, when she must determine
whether she stands for civilized or uncivilized warfare." House
soon backtracked, but those expressions raised Wilson's first doubts
about him. "It *is very* interesting to find how House is getting
re-Americanized," he commented privately after the colonel's return during the summer of 1915.[12]

House soon regained much of Wilson's confidence, in part by
helping him through a difficult time during September 1915 in his
engagement to Edith Bolling Galt. As a result he departed on his
second wartime mission in December, to mount a full-fledged
peace offensive. His negotiations in London led to the House-Grey
memorandum, which was initialed by the two men on February 12,
1916. Under the terms of the memorandum, the British would have
agreed to support an American mediation attempt; if that attempt
failed, the United States would reassess its posture toward the war
with a view to intervening on the side of the Allies. The project
revealed House's characteristic deviousness. On the one hand he
misled the British by depicting the mediation overture as mainly a
pretext for entering the war. On the other hand he misled Wilson
by depicting the British as genuinely interested in mediation. Wilson scotched House's interventionist hints to the British by in-

serting the word "probably" in the portion of the memorandum that described the chances of American entry into the war. The British gave the lie to House's assurances of their interest in mediation when the cabinet's War Committee shelved the House-Grey memorandum and disdained any further communication on the subject. In all, the episode contributed to Wilson's renewed hard feelings toward the Allies and to the waning of House's influence. [13]

Ironically, although her engagement helped renew the colonel's lease on the president's favor, Mrs. Galt was the principal cause of House's decline. From the time Wilson first met and swiftly fell in love with her in the spring of 1915, she had not only obviated his emotional dependence on House, but she had become his closest confidante on public affairs. Wilson's courtship of Mrs. Galt illustrates the axiom that power is the strongest aphrodisiac. The president wooed the sometimes bashful, sexually reluctant widow by letting her read drafts of important policy statements, such as the *Lusitania* notes to Germany, and by sharing with her confidential political and diplomatic papers, including House's correspondence. Unlike Ellen Wilson, who had largely removed herself from her husband's academic and political concerns after the onset of a serious depression in 1905, Edith Bolling Galt welcomed involvement in affairs of state both before and after her marriage to Wilson in December 1915. Four years later, when his severe stroke almost totally incapacitated him for several weeks, Edith Wilson assumed some of the duties of an acting president, prompting charges of "government by petticoat." What was not known then was how well prepared she was, through acquaintance with her husband's work, to be a surrogate president. [14]

Besides displacing House in Wilson's affections, Mrs. Galt took an immediate dislike to the little Texan. Even before she met him, she confessed to Wilson, "I can't help feeling he is not a very *strong* character." Although she granted "what a comfort and staff" House was, she still thought that "he does look like a weak vessel and I think he writes like one very often." Wilson defended his confidant, but he acknowledged, "About him, again, you are no doubt partly right. You have too keen an insight and too discerning a judgment to be wholly wrong, even in a snap judgment of a man you do not know!" Knowing the colonel and appreciating his help in the troubles during her engagement did not much reconcile the second

Mrs. Wilson to House. Later she tried on at least one occasion to persuade her husband to get rid of House by sending him overseas as ambassador to Britain. By the time of the House-Grey memorandum, the colonel's star was poised for a rapid fall in Wilson's firmament. [15]

House still retained a large capacity for mischief. On his European missions he built up important contacts, particularly with the British. Starting early in 1917, he established a close relationship with a British Secret Service agent, Sir William Wiseman, and their connection became the effective diplomatic link between the two countries. That tie allowed House to continue his long established practice of trying to eliminate any other strong figures who might dispute his importance in foreign policy. Like Lansing, House tried to sabotage Wilson's peace initiative in December 1916. He secretly informed his British contacts that the overture was just another pretext for intervention. After the United States entered the war, House continually strove to counteract Wilson's efforts to maintain the nation's ideological distance from the Allies. At the peace conference he connived behind Wilson's back to stiffen British and French resistance toward less punitive treatment of Germany. His friendship with Wilson collapsed during the peace conference because the president suspected the colonel of helping the British and French to gain advantages in the settlement. Those suspicions were well-founded but belated. House had long since forfeited any claim to Wilson's trust. [16]

Wilson's reliance on Lansing and House had some short-term consequences for his policies toward the Allies. The episode with the House-Grey memorandum in early 1916 strained Anglo-American relations at an inopportune time. The Easter Rebellion in Ireland in April 1916 and its brutal suppression coincided with the relaxation of tensions between the United States and Germany. Together, those two sets of events plunged American sympathies toward the Allies to their lowest point since the outbreak of the war. Wilson's disenchantment with the British over the House-Grey memorandum reinforced his conviction that blame for the war lay on both sides. In a peace note drafted toward the end of 1916, Wilson deplored both "German militarism" and "British navalism" for having caused "this vast, gruesome contest of systematized destruction." Ironically, the activities of one of his two covertly pro-Allied advisers had strengthened Wilson's resolve to avoid involvement in the war on either side. Otherwise, mainly through good luck, Lansing's and House's doings had little immediate impact on the course of events in 1916.[17]

But their prominence in foreign policy making had a more serious effect in the longer run. By remaining in high places, Lansing and House continued to pose potential dangers through their covert views and devious methods. They became actual dangers following the peace overture of December 1916 and the United States entry into the war, and especially during and after the peace conference in 1919. The actions of both men played a part in the eventual failure of Wilson's peace settlement and his political downfall. By retaining them in responsible positions, even though he relied on them less and less as time passed, Wilson left a pair of unexploded bombs near his right hand.

Why did Wilson fail to dismiss Lansing long before 1920? Why did he use House for delicate negotiations after 1916, particularly the pre-Armistice talks in the fall of 1918? Why did he take both of them to the peace conference? These remain intriguing questions. The embarrassment of firing a secretary of state probably accounted for some of Wilson's seemingly incredible willingness to stomach Lansing. House's adroit concealment of his true opinions, his highly developed talents for ingratiation, and his well-cultivated contacts and inflated reputation abroad—those undoubtedly helped explain Wilson's continuing association with him. But none of those factors touched the basic reason for retaining that pair in high places, which reflected one of the most serious shortcomings in Wilson's political leadership. After Bryan's resignation foreign affairs was the one area in which Wilson's collegiality and his encouragement of able lieutenants consistently failed him. It became instead the province in which he indulged his long-standing penchant for excessive self-reliance.[18]

Wilson usually performed well as a single-handed diplomat, as when he dealt with Germany over submarine warfare. He also eloquently articulated sweeping international programs, as with the league of nations idea after May 1916 and with a compromise peace settlement in December 1916 and January 1917. Wilson's great shortcoming lay in the middle range, in coordinating diplomacy with several nations and in gradually implementing larger aims. Those operations would have required working through and directing trusted subordinates who shared his aims and helped to shape his methods. Earlier Wilson had acted through such subordinates and in such ways in domestic affairs. Later, in both the military and civilian aspects of the American war effort, he again acted through such men and in such ways. But in foreign affairs during the World War, Wilson's tolerance of men like Lansing and House revealed a missing dimension in his leadership. It was a lack he may have appreciated intellectually but could never emotionally bring himself to take seriously. Ultimately, that missing dimension, combined with the failure of his health, would defeat Wilson.

In 1915 and 1916, however, his politics met only success at home and abroad. Wilson's foreign policies prevailed in other ways besides gaining a diplomatic settlement of the submarine controversy. One way was in domestic politics. Wilson built support for his policies toward the World War, particularly among Democrats, by asserting his leadership mainly on military preparedness. In July 1915 administration sources began sending signals through the press that substantial increases were being contemplated in the size and strength of the army and navy. At the beginning of November the president announced a program of military and naval increases. "We have it in mind to be prepared, but not for war, but only for defense," Wilson insisted. But he also warned, "The influences of a great war are everywhere in the air. All Europe is embattled. Force everywhere speaks out with a loud and imperious voice in a titanic struggle of governments." Americans must know "what our own force is, how far we are prepared to maintain ourselves against any interference with our national action and development."[19]

Wilson's reversal of his previous stand on preparedness made many observers think he was retreating in the face of increasingly sharp attacks from such critics as Roosevelt. Some signs from the White House supported that view. A few days after he came out for increased preparedness in November 1915, Wilson released a letter to the press in which he stated, "There is a quotation from Ezekiel which I have had very much in my mind in connection with these important matters." The quotation, Ezekiel 33:2–6, included the injunction, "When he seeth the sword come upon the land he blow the trumpet, and warn the people." It was in Wilson's mind at least partly because Roosevelt had repeatedly used it in lambast-

ing the administration's defense program. Yet despite such indications, it was not primarily because of heat from Roosevelt and
other advocates of large-scale preparedness that Wilson changed
his stand. Those opponents and their views did not pose the greatest political danger for him. [20]

Wilson had far more to fear politically from the other side. In
large measure because of Bryan's influence, deep-seated opposition
to increased military spending and strength flourished among
Democrats and, to a lesser but growing extent, among insurgent
Republicans and Progressives. Since before 1900 congressional
Democrats had consistently opposed Republican administration
projects for increasing the size of the army and navy. Many rural-
based Democrats had remained steadfast in their opposition after
their own party had regained power in 1913. Claude Kitchin of
North Carolina, a close friend of Bryan's and an antipreparedness
recusant, had succeeded Underwood as House majority leader in
1915. Kitchin promptly used his post to stack the military and naval
affairs committees with like-minded representatives, who bottled
up the administration's new defense program. By the beginning of
1916 Wilson appeared to be losing on the preparedness issue to
Bryan and his Democratic followers. [21]

To regain the initiative on preparedness, Wilson responded
with the most important and impressive display of leadership of his
entire presidency. He resorted to a practice he had used earlier in
New Jersey but not yet in the White House—appealing over the
heads of his adversaries directly to the people. At the end of January and beginning of February 1916, Wilson made a nine-day tour
of the Northeast and Middle West, during which he delivered
eleven speeches about national defense. At the outset he admitted
he had changed his mind under new conditions, but he admonished, "America does not control the circumstances of the world,
and we must be sure that we are faithful servants of those things
which we love and are ready to defend them against every con-
tingency that may affect or impair them." Wilson reiterated that
message throughout the tour. "The world is on fire, and there is
tinder everywhere," he warned in another speech. "America cannot shut itself out from the rest of the world," he avowed in still
another, "because all the dangers at this present moment—and

they are many—come from her contacts with the rest of the world."[22]

That exercise in educating the public rallied support, though some antipreparedness Democrats dug in their heels. The president seemed to many Congressmen, Kitchin told Bryan, "a little too war-alarming in his speeches—they sounded too much like Roosevelt." But Wilson used a carrot as well as a stick with his opponents. On his return from the speaking tour, he bowed to criticisms of his program's most controversial feature, the plan for a national reserve force for the army, called the Continental Army. Because he had never felt strongly committed to the Continental Army, Wilson dropped the plan on February 10, which prompted Secretary of War Garrison to resign in protest. Wilson's compromise—combined with his appointment of Newton D. Baker, a noted reform Democrat and previously an opponent of increased preparedness, as Garrison's successor—defused nearly all further opposition to the administration's program.[23]

The preparedness issue marked the first time that Wilson had overcome Bryan's influence among Democrats. His policy on the German submarines soon provided another contest, and Wilson won even more decisively by using the same methods. Toward the end of February 1916 panic swept Capitol Hill after the withdrawal of the modus vivendi. Bryanite Democrats in both houses brought forward resolutions embodying their leader's earlier proposals to warn or stop Americans from traveling on Allied merchant ships. Wilson quelled the furor by assuring congressional leaders at several private meetings of his desire for peace. Then he took the offensive by publicly requesting votes on the resolutions at the beginning of March and by sending McAdoo and Burleson to the Capitol to crack the party whip. The votes on tabling the resolutions proved particularly gratifying. All but two Democratic senators and over three-quarters of the House Democrats backed the president. Wilson had established total primacy among the Democrats.

It was a remarkable feat, with profound consequences for both Wilson's presidency and the whole context of American foreign policy. For all his achievements in domestic affairs, Wilson had chiefly refined and strengthened tendencies that were already well advanced among Democrats. Not he, but Bryan, had charted their basic response to the industrial age. In his domestic triumphs Wilson played conquering Joshua to Bryan's Moses, the prophet barred from the promised land after years of leading his people in the wilderness. In foreign affairs, however, the two men played vastly different roles. There Wilson moved the Democrats in a direction they almost certainly would not otherwise have taken. Thanks in part to his background as an erstwhile expansionist, Wilson stood virtually alone among leading Democrats in believing that the United States must play a more active, involved role in world politics. His submarine and preparedness policies flowed from that belief, and they ran counter to nearly twenty years of Democratic resistance to overseas commitments and large-scale armament. By supplanting Bryan's influence in foreign affairs, Wilson set a new course for his party.

The impact of his feat extended beyond the Democrats. The votes on the congressional resolutions on submarine policy also revealed the beginning of a Republican retreat from support for greater foreign involvement. Twelve Republican senators and over half the Republicans in the House voted in favor of the resolutions. The senators included leading insurgents, such as La Follette, Albert B. Cummins of Iowa, and George W. Norris of Nebraska, while the representatives included nearly every Republican, Old Guardsman and insurgent, from outside the Northeast. In addition, five of the six Progressives in the House favored the resolutions. Those votes mortified Roosevelt and such Republicans as Lodge, Gardner, and Root, who until then had appeared to speak for their respective parties when they had attacked Wilson for not increasing preparedness still more and for not taking a tougher line on submarine warfare. These congressional votes in March 1916 offered the first sign of a reversal of the two major parties' positions on foreign policy. It was a switch that would affect much of the rest of Wilson's and Roosevelt's careers as well as the course of American foreign policy.[24]

The parties' incipient reversals went deeper than their immediate responses to the danger of involvement in the World War. Wilson also pursued his foreign policy in a way that transcended diplomacy and politics—through doctrine. He formulated general principles to guide the nation's actions in respect to the rest of the world. He did not take the lead among prominent Americans in developing foreign policy doctrines or even in publicly espousing the internationalist views he held privately. Roosevelt had proposed the establishment of and participation in a league of nations early in the war. Taft had helped organize and in June 1915 became head of the League to Enforce Peace, the principal internationalist lobbying group in the United States. On the other side, Bryan had emerged shortly after his resignation as the leading isolationist spokesman. In June 1915 he had denounced the League to Enforce Peace for seeking to compromise pacific American ideals through entanglement in power politics. Roosevelt had likewise recanted his earlier internationalism during the summer of 1915. He now attacked the League to Enforce Peace for promoting a chimerical scheme that would interfere with preparedness and willingness to fight for ideals.[25]

Growing conflict over the league idea did not deter Wilson from announcing his support on May 27, 1916. Addressing the convention of the League to Enforce Peace and sharing the speakers' platform with Senator Lodge, the President declared, "Only when the great nations of the world have reached some sort of agreement as to what they hold to be fundamental to their common interest, and as to some feasible method of acting in concert when any nation or group of nations seeks to disturb those fundamental things, can we feel that civilization is at last in a way of justifying its existence and claiming to be fully established." As fundamentals for such an agreement, Wilson laid down three principles: every people's right to choose its sovereignty, equal rights for large and small nations, and freedom from aggression. He also called for a negotiated end to the World War, free use of the seas, and an international tribunal to settle disputes and uphold national rights. Although he declined to discuss specific programs, Wilson pledged "that the United States is willing to become a partner in any feasible association of nations formed in order to realize these objects and make them secure against violation."[26]

An unwonted vagueness and circumlocution masked the boldness of Wilson's declaration. Like Roosevelt earlier, he was trying to deflect criticism by distinguishing between "selfish" alliances, which the United States had traditionally spurned, and a peace league. "I shall never, myself, consent to an entangling alliance," Wilson avowed on May 30, 1916. "But I would gladly assent to a disentangling alliance—an alliance which would disentangle the people of the world from those combinations in which they seek their own separate and private interests and unite the people of the world to preserve the peace of the world upon a basis of common right and justice." Such softpedaling did not minimize the magnitude of the step Wilson was taking. Two weeks later, when he drafted his party's platform for the 1916 election, Wilson repeated virtually word for word his statement of fundamentals and his pledge to the League to Enforce Peace, and the Democratic convention adopted his language without change or dissent. Woodrow Wilson had set forth the basis of his foreign policy for the remainder of his presidency.[27]

·19·

The Decision to Intervene

IN 1916 THEODORE ROOSEVELT would have liked nothing better than a presidential race run primarily on foreign policy issues, with himself as Wilson's main opponent. Roosevelt's public outrage over the sinking of the *Lusitania,* though sincere, had cloaked a certain satisfaction. "As a nation, we have thought very little about foreign affairs," he told one of his sons; "we don't realize that the murder of the thousand men, women, and children on the *Lusitania* is due, solely, to Wilson's abject cowardice and weakness in failing to take energetic action when the *Gulflight* [an American oil tanker] was sunk a few days previously." Wilson's strong diplomatic protests and Bryan's resignation did not mollify Roosevelt. Wilson and Bryan agreed, he argued, "that our policy should be one of milk and water. They only disagree as to the precise quantity of dilution in the mixture; and this does not seem to me to be important enough to warrant a quarrel." His own disagreement with Wilson, Roosevelt believed, did involve important differences. His denunciations of the president would, he hoped, awaken Americans to the realities of international life.[1]

Roosevelt did not underestimate the difficulty of his task. His animosity toward Wilson's foreign policies deepened as he recognized their popularity. After the sinking of the *Lusitania,* Roosevelt again likened Wilson to Jefferson. Privately he called Jefferson "one of the most mischievous enemies of democracy, one of the very weakest whom we have ever had in public life. He was politically very successful—and Wilson may very well be also—" but both of them had gained their successes by pandering to people's selfishness, sloth, and wishful thinking. "Wilson even more than Jefferson has been the apologist for and has given impetus to our very worst [tendencies]." His own criticisms had little effect, Roosevelt ruefully conceded in June 1915, "beyond making people think that I am a truculent and bloodthirsty person, endeavoring futilely to thwart able, dignified, humane Mr. Wilson in his noble plan to bring peace everywhere by excellently written letters sent to persons who care nothing whatever for any letter that is not backed up by force!"[2]

Far from daunting him, those difficulties inspired Roosevelt. The submarine controversy snapped him out of the mood of sullen resignation into which he had fallen earlier in 1915. The sinking of the *Lusitania* gave Roosevelt a fresh lease on the role of heroic agitator. The chance for intervention allowed him to take his stand, again in defiance of political expediency and on questions that concerned him most. Although Roosevelt boasted of having "always striven to be a practical politician," he avowed shortly after the sinking of the *Lusitania*, "When I have felt a fundamental issue of morals or of vital interest or honor was concerned, I have never hesitated to follow my belief even though I was certain that to do so would hurt me in the estimation of the people as a whole." That conviction—not, as critics charged, simple egotism or militarist enthusiasm—led Roosevelt to make his celebrated remark in March 1916, "It would be a mistake to nominate me unless the country has in its mood something of the heroic—unless it feels not only devotion to ideals but the purpose measurably to realize those ideals in action."[3]

In addressing foreign policy toward the World War through diplomacy, politics, and doctrine, Roosevelt seemed to resemble Wilson, but he really did not. Considering his earlier detailed treatment of American strategic interests, concrete diplomatic dealings with Germany and the Allies concerned him surprisingly little. Throughout 1915 and 1916 Roosevelt mainly repeated his strictures against inadequate preparedness and the failure to protest over Belgium; he also made frequent but vague denunciations of Wilson's "policy of milk-and-water" concerning the submarines. Roosevelt often condemned Germany and lauded the Allies, but he never issued an outright call for intervention, and he sometimes claimed that a tougher stance would keep the United States out of war. In all, Roosevelt did not present a coherent diplomatic course toward the World War.[4]

His lack of diplomatic specificity reflected his continuing concern for "devotion to ideals." Right convictions—what he accused Wilson of lacking—mattered far more to Roosevelt than specific actions. Behind his high-sounding talk the president combined, Roosevelt charged in February 1916, "mean timidity and mean commercial opportunism . . . One of the besetting sins of many of our public servants (and of not a few of our professional moralists, lay and clerical) is to cloak weakness or baseness behind insincere oratory on behalf of impractical ideals." No one, Roosevelt told Owen Wister, displayed more despicable baseness than Wilson, "the demagogue, adroit, tricky, false, without one spark of loftiness in him, without a touch of the heroic in his cold, selfish and timid soul." The Warrior was indeed flaying the Priest.[5]

For Roosevelt, politics formed the critical consideration in foreign policy. Ever since the outbreak of the war, his growing concern with military preparedness and international affairs had complemented his repugnance toward many of his Progressive followers. As a result he soon sought reconciliation with his erstwhile Old Guard foes. As early as December 1914 he was saying that he would prefer even Penrose to Wilson, while he and Lodge continued to use foreign policy to refurbish their personal and political intimacy. Roosevelt did stop short of wanting to beat Wilson at all costs. Wilson's defeat must accomplish more than merely exchanging him, Roosevelt declared in his "heroic mood" statement of March 1916, "for one equally timid, equally vacillating, equally lacking in vision, in moral integrity, and in high resolve." Yet, as in 1912 with domestic reform, who could supply such leadership except Roosevelt?[6]

In 1916, however, his heroic agitation did not leave him averse to making practical calculations. Whether Roosevelt thought he had any chance for the Republican nomination—the only one he thought worth having—remains unclear. It is clear that he strung the Progressives along in an effort to influence the Republicans. He succeeded in getting the Progressive platform to downplay domestic reform and emphasize preparedness and foreign policy, while the Republican platform made practically identical statements. Otherwise Roosevelt failed. The Republicans nominated Hughes, whom Roosevelt privately called "a man somewhat on the Wilson type" and "the bearded iceberg." The Progressives ignored his pleas to leave their nomination open so that he could bargain further with the Republicans. When the Progressives nominated him again in June 1916, Roosevelt not only spurned them, he also publicly suggested Lodge as an alternative, thereby sowing consternation among his followers. The party effectively disbanded in July after Roosevelt had already announced his support for Hughes. It was an inglorious end to his career as a reform leader, but Roosevelt had made his choice of a lesser evil.[7]

The ensuing campaign, featuring Roosevelt speaking for Hughes to sympathetic audiences in the Northeast, afforded much less of a debate over foreign policy than the 1912 race had done for domestic reform. Roosevelt hammered away at familiar charges against Wilson. "He has dulled the national conscience and relaxed the spring of lofty, national motives by teaching our people to accept high sounding words as the offset and atonement for shabby deeds," Roosevelt declared in June 1916. Just before the election Roosevelt excoriated Wilson as "only another Buchanan" in a time of "terrible world cataclysm." Instead of "a Washington or a Lincoln," the United States had a president who was renting an estate called Shadow Lawn. "There should be shadows enough at Shadow Lawn; the shadows of men, women, and children who have risen from the ooze of the ocean bottom and from graves in foreign lands; . . . the shadows of lofty words that were followed by no action; the shadows of the tortured dead." That graphic simile epitomized most of Roosevelt's campaign attacks. They cast more shadow than light.[8]

Nowhere did he cast darker shadows than over foreign policy doctrines. Almost as soon as he outlined his plan for a league of nations at the beginning of 1915, Roosevelt began to backtrack. "Frankly, I do not think that this is an opportune time to go into details about a World League for Peace," he confided to Bryce in March of that year. The founding of the League to Enforce Peace with Taft at its head moved him to declare publicly in August 1915, "Even the proposal for a world league of righteousness, based on force being put back of righteousness, is inopportune at this time." Roosevelt continued to reject internationalist proposals as foolish unless backed by preparedness and by the resolve to honor prior commitments. "National unselfishness—which is another way of saying service rendered to internationalism," he asserted in February 1916, "—can become effective only if the nation is willing to sacrifice something." During the Civil War under Lincoln, Americans had shown "willingness to face death and eager pride in fighting for ideals, which marked a mighty people led by a mighty leader." Lacking that kind of spirit and leadership, the best-laid plans to enforce peace were worthless in Roosevelt's eyes.[9]

The vagueness, repetition, and passion of his attacks on Wilson's foreign policy did not conceal their central thrust. Roosevelt's case against his rival rested on the same point in domestic and foreign affairs. Abroad as well as at home, Roosevelt believed that social good must come from rising above self-interest in sacrificial pursuit of transcendent ideals. For all his scorn of "impracticality," Roosevelt vied with Bryan as the most visionary idealist in American politics. His fundamental complaint against Wilson was that the president provided the wrong kind of leadership by serving interests rather than transcending them. As in his earlier conflict with Taft, the heart of Roosevelt's conflict with Wilson lay with himself. Beneath all his attacks and criticisms remained that one question— who in America could provide properly heroic leadership at this world-shaking time in history—who but himself? The cause of his quarrel with Wilson was Roosevelt's sublime egotism.

He did raise two valid points in his criticisms of Wilson's foreign policy. One was that the president had not sufficiently awakened Americans to their international involvement. The Democratic convention in June 1916 turned into a celebration of non-involvement in the World War. Delegates spontaneously chanted "We didn't go to war!" in response to the keynote address. They also demanded a speech by Bryan, who backhandedly praised Wilson for having stayed out of war. During the campaign the Democratic organization trumpeted the slogan, "He Kept Us Out of War," while contantly harping on Roosevelt's support for Hughes as a harbinger of war. Although Wilson reputedly disliked his party's slogan, he too wielded the peace bludgeon. "There is only one choice as against peace," Wilson avowed in a speech in September 1916, "and that is war. Some of the supporters of that [Republican] party, a very great body of supporters of that party, outspokenly declare that they want war. So that the certain prospect of the success of the Republican party is that we shall be drawn, in one form or other, into the embroilments of the European war."[10]

During the campaign Wilson reiterated both his earlier argument that the war touched Americans regardless of their wishes and his endorsement of a league of nations. "I have said, and shall say again," he declared in one speech in October, "that, when the present war is over, it will be the duty of America to join with the other nations of the world in some kind of league for the maintenance of peace." Two weeks later he asserted that the World War was "the last war of this kind or of any other kind that involves the world that the United States can keep out of." Regrettably, therefore, "I believe that the business of neutrality is over . . . that war now has such a scale that the position of neutrals sooner or later becomes intolerable." Toward the end of the campaign, however, Wilson backed off from such assertions. Meanwhile the Democrats kept up their deafening cries of "He Kept Us Out of War," and the president made further insinuations about his opponents' alleged warmongering. Roosevelt did have a point when he charged Wilson with not fully alerting the American people to foreign perils.[11]

The 1916 election did not serve as a referendum on foreign policy, particularly concerning the World War. Both sides diluted and compromised their appeals. Democratic peace slogans and Republican accusations of weakness referred more often to Mexico than to Europe. Wilson mixed his aspersions on Republican belligerency with stinging denunciations of "disloyal" German-American and Irish-American organizations that were attempting to influence the United States against the Allies. Hughes echoed some of Roosevelt's tough talk, but he kept the ex-president at arm's length. Moreover, Hughes accepted support from the ethnic organizations Wilson scorned, and he criticized the administration for not protesting against British maritime restrictions. It was small wonder that many observers saw little to choose between Hughes and Wilson on foreign policy. "There were two milk-and-water candidates," William Allen White told Roosevelt, " . . . and Hughes was a cambric tea candidate as against a kind of skimmed milk candidate." It was small wonder, too, that domestic issues made a much clearer and stronger impact on the way people voted in November 1916.[12]

The greater importance of domestic policy issues betokened failure as well as success for Wilson. The election results illustrated that neither he nor Roosevelt had yet cracked Americans' long-standing unconcern about international involvement. Those results underscored both of Roosevelt's main criticisms. Not only had the president failed to awaken people to present dangers from abroad, but also he had come nowhere near gaining the kind of popular commitment needed to support American membership in a league of nations. That was Roosevelt's second valid point against Wilson, and it was shot through with irony. Despite boastful recollections of his own presidency, Roosevelt knew that he too had signally failed at the task of arousing his countrymen to support active, self-conscious, sustained international leadership. Being out of power during World War I galled him so deeply because conditions at last seemed to favor success at that task. "My usefulness in 1912 and again this year," Roosevelt confided to a friend in September 1916, "would have been because we were facing a period when there was need of vision in both national and international matters."[13]

Roosevelt's criticism of Wilson's failure to build sufficient public support for an international peacekeeping venture contained a further irony. Those criticisms made Roosevelt sound like a realist and forced him to work against his own desires. A climactic confrontation over foreign policy occurred between the two men during the three months following the 1916 election. As soon as his reelection was certain, Wilson opened a campaign to mediate the World War, achieve an equitable and stable peace settlement, and establish a league of nations under American leadership. Immediate events hastened those moves. Pressures were mounting in Germany to reopen submarine warfare, while the Allies' growing financial dependency on the United States offered new leverage with them. A warning, orchestrated by Wilson, by the Federal Reserve Board to American banks in November 1916 against foreign loans caused consternation, particularly among the British. On December 20, 1916, Wilson published the diplomatic note he had sent two days before, in which he asked the belligerents to state their peace terms and offered American participation in "measures to be taken to secure the future peace of the world." Despite its dastardliness, Lansing's remark that "we are drawing nearer to the verge of war ourselves" was factually correct. Wilson wanted to keep the United States out by ending the war.[14]

Broader concerns also underlay the peace initiative. Wilson's distaste for the World War had turned to repugnance. As he wrote in a memorandum late in 1916, "Deprived of glory, war loses all its charm . . . The mechanical slaughter of today has not the same fascination as the zest of intimate combat of former days; and trench warfare and poisonous gases are elements which detract alike from the excitement and the tolerance of modern conflict. With maneuver almost a thing of the past, any given point can admittedly be carried by the sacrifice of enough men and ammunition. Where is any longer the glory commensurate with the sacrifice of the millions of men required in modern warfare to carry and defend Verdun?" That statement contained Wilson's answer to both Bryan and Roosevelt. Much as he hated the World War and wanted to end it, he did not act primarily as an idealistic lover of peace. Rather, Wilson had expanded his earlier practical, mainly economic objections to most wars into a rejection of the scale and the dehumanizing technology of modern total war. If he could have believed, as Roosevelt did, that meaningful sacrifice and glory were still possible, Wilson might conceivably have behaved or spoken differently. At bottom he considered the warfare practiced on the western front a repudiation of human reason and aspiration.[15]

Roosevelt attacked Wilson's peace move on two grounds. On January 3, 1917, he told reporters that the note to the belligerents was "profoundly immoral and misleading," particularly because it made the claim that both sides were fighting for the same objects. German actions in Belgium, most notably the recent forced deportation of 300,000 workers, proved that "this is palpably false. Nor is this all. It is wickedly false." But Roosevelt reserved his greatest scorn for Wilson's offer to participate in international peacekeeping activities. "If his words mean anything," he sniffed, "they would mean that hereafter we intended to embark on a policy of violent meddling in every European quarrel, and in return to invite Old World nations violently to meddle in everything American. Of course, as a matter of fact, the words mean nothing whatever." To the reporters and in a magazine article published soon afterward, Roosevelt reiterated his objections to proposals for a league of nations as premature and distracting. First, the United

States must adopt thoroughgoing preparedness, including universal military training, and it must honor diplomatic pledges already made, like those regarding Belgium.[16]

Roosevelt in turn received sharp criticism for his attack. One critic found it curious that the league idea drew opposition from "yourself as the leading advocate of Preparedness, and Mr. Bryan, our Apostle of Pacifism!" Roosevelt answered by reminding his critics that he had objected to the proposals of the League to Enforce Peace for over a year. "My position is absolutely unchanged. I have always said, and say now, that when we prepare our strength, and keep our promises, I am for such a league as I outlined two years ago," he maintained, "a league which has nothing whatever in common with the policies of Messrs. Wilson and Taft." Roosevelt undoubtedly believed that he was being consistent with his previous stands, but in fact he was making a momentous shift in his foreign policy. By alluding to European quarrels and meddling in the Americas, he was resorting to arguments he had never used before. He was appealing to the despised opposite of his own convictions—to the isolationist, anti-interventionist, and parochial sentiments he had fought against for over twenty years.[17]

Roosevelt's shift portended a significant new alignment on foreign policy. Objections by Senator William E. Borah of Idaho, a one-time Republican insurgent, postponed Senate consideration of a resolution endorsing the note to the belligerents until January 3, 1917—the same day that Roosevelt attacked the initiative. Lodge opened the Senate debate by echoing his friend's charges. Wilson was projecting the United States, Lodge asserted, "into the field of European politics." He was proposing "a departure from the hitherto unbroken policy of this country," a departure that could make "us part of the political system of another hemisphere, with the inevitable corollary that the nations of that other hemisphere will become part of our system." Borah accused Wilson of adopting the program of the League to Enforce Peace, whose war-making and supranational ideas, he charged, approached "moral treason." Roosevelt congratulated Borah but added that his criticisms "did not go nearly far enough," because such a league might act *not against the wrong doer but against the wronged party!* A more preposterous, a more wickedly preposterous absurdity could hardly be devised."[18]

The juxtaposition of Roosevelt and Lodge with Borah in criticizing the league idea offered the first evidence of an emerging coalition. The Idaho senator's objections closely resembled Bryan's. Borah declared that Wilson's proposal would serve "not to promote peace but to promote war." The allegation that Roosevelt was teaming up with Bryan against the league idea was not literally true. The Great Commoner was starting to downplay his criticisms, in support of Wilson's peace initiative and for the sake of Democratic party harmony. Ideologically, however, by cooperating with Borah, Roosevelt was joining hands with an idealistic isolationist who thought along the same lines as Bryan. Borah's alliance with Roosevelt heralded the beginning of a new anti-internationalist coalition that had little in common besides Republican partisanship and opposition to Wilson. [19]

These new political alignments on foreign policy cut both ways. Just as Wilson's Republican opponents of opposite persuasions were drawing together against the league idea, the Democrats were closing ranks behind their leader. Bryan's quiescence was not the only sign of Democratic support for Wilson. On January 5, 1917, by a vote of forty-eight to seventeen, the senate endorsed a watered-down version of the resolution commending Wilson's peace initiative, with all reference to peacekeeping activities omitted. Thirty-eight of the votes in favor came from Democrats, while only one Democrat opposed the resolution. The drawing of party lines for and against the league idea was becoming clearer still. It marked the second step in the reversal of party roles that had begun to unfold ten months earlier in the congressional votes on submarine policy. [20]

A bigger step in that party reversal soon followed. Undaunted by opposition at home and abroad, Wilson pushed forward with his campaign to mediate the World War and inaugurate a new international order. On January 22, 1917, the president delivered his "peace without victory" address to the Senate. The war must be ended on terms that would establish, declared Wilson, "not a balance of power, but a community of power; not organized rivalries, but an organized common peace." The only way to achieve that end was through "a peace without victory. It is not pleasant to say this . . . I am seeking only to face realities and to face them without soft concealments. Victory would mean peace forced upon the loser" and would therefore "rest only as upon quicksand. Only a peace between equals can last." Wilson hoped to establish such a peace through "an equality of rights" among nations. The indispensable right was self-government, he contended, "not because of any abstract principle . . . but for the same reason that I have spoken of the other conditions of peace which seem to me clearly indispensable—because I wish frankly to uncover realities. Any peace which does not recognize and accept this principle will inevitably be upset. It will not rest upon the affections and convictions of mankind."

Wilson also proposed to build lasting peace upon the free use of the seas for commerce and upon relief from the burdens and dangers of excessive armament. Above all, he pledged "that the people and government of the United States will join the other civilized nations of the world in guaranteeing the permanence of peace upon such terms as I have named." Wilson closed with an argument intended to disarm domestic critics. "I am proposing, as it were," he asserted, "that the nations should with one accord adopt the doctrine of President Monroe as the doctrine of the world . . . I am proposing that all nations henceforth avoid entangling alliances which would draw them into competitions of power; catch them in a net of intrigue and selfish rivalry, and disturb their own affairs with influences obtruded from without. There is no entangling alliance in a concert of power. When all unite to act in the same sense and with the same purpose all act in the common interest and are free to live their own lives under a common protection." These were, Wilson insisted, "American principles, American policies. We could stand for no others." Since they were also desired by "forward looking men and women everywhere," these were "the principles of mankind and must prevail."[21]

Wilson had delivered a remarkable utterance. The "peace without victory" address ranked among his three or four greatest speeches, and it disclosed his thinking on foreign policy better than any other single piece of his speaking or writing. What made the address remarkable was not new ideas. Wilson had unveiled his program of international rights—self-rule, freedom of the seas, and security against aggression—when he had endorsed the league of nations idea in May 1916. He had also tried then to forestall idealistic objections to peacekeeping commitments by distinguishing between "entangling" alliances and an international concert serving common goals.

What made the "peace without victory" address remarkable was the presentation of a single vision of lasting peace and the reasons given to support that vision. In one way Wilson was undeniably idealistic. He called for the warring nations to renounce victory in order to build a better world. He also claimed to speak not only "for liberals and friends of humanity in every nation" but also "for the silent mass of mankind everywhere." Yet Wilson repeatedly justified his proposals by appealing to "realities" and stating unpleasant truths. He contended that international order must rest upon self-government because satisfaction of that fundamental "common interest" was indispensable to the assurance of lasting peace. In foreign policy Wilson's synthesis of ideals and self-interest stood out most clearly in the "peace without victory" address.[22]

Politically, the speech appeared to blunt, but actually sharpened, domestic divisions over the war and the league idea. La Follette, who had opposed increased preparedness and all risk of intervention, led the senators' applause for Wilson and declared, "We have just passed through an important hour in the life of the world." Other peace-minded midwestern Republicans praised the address, as did nearly all the Democrats. Bryan saluted Wilson's "brave and timely appeal to the war-mad rulers of Europe," and he stated, "I rather prefer to leave the [league] question until he [Wilson] himself has presented his views more in detail in the hope that when he does so present them we may find that there is no reason for difference." Some Old Guard Republicans, following the lead of Taft and the League to Enforce Peace, lauded Wilson. The outpouring of support reflected three main considerations. One was general public approval of what seemed a disinterested gesture toward peace. Other areas of support reflected the persuasiveness of Wilson's idealistic rhetoric, which won over many anti-interventionists in both parties, at least temporarily. But the strongest support came from partisanship, as several developments swiftly demonstrated.[23]

Not all pacific critics of the league idea proved as pliant as Bryan. On January 25, 1917, Borah sparked fresh Senate debate by introducing a resolution affirming "faith and confidence in the permanent worth and wisdom" of the United States' traditional rejection of alliances and charged the administration "to conform its acts to these time-honored principles so long and so happily a part of our policy." In a speech outside the Senate, Borah warned, "Once in the maelstrom of European politics and it will be impossible to get out." Another long-time insurgent Republican senator agreed. On January 30 Albert B. Cummins of Iowa declared that if the nation followed Wilson "we will be involved either in continuous war waged all over the world or we will be engaged in almost continuous rebellion against the authority which he proposes to set over us." Although Cummins favored peaceful settlement of disputes, he maintained that attempts at supranational enforcement would "provoke war instead of suppressing it." The anti-interventionist case against the league of nations idea was in no danger of fading away.[24]

Predictably, fiercer attacks came from the other side. "Peace without victory is the natural ideal of the man who is too proud to fight," sneered Roosevelt in a statement to the press on January 28. "It is spurned by all men of lofty soul, by all men fit to call themselves fellow-citizens of Washington and Lincoln or of the war-worn fighters who followed Grant and Lee." He called Wilson a spiritual descendant of the Tories of 1776 and the Copperheads of 1864, who had also "demanded peace without victory." He accused Wilson of acting from fear of submarine warfare and from a hypocritical refusal to judge Germany's wrongdoing. Once more Roosevelt invoked Biblical sanction by quoting from the Old Testament: "Curse ye, Meroz, said the angel of the Lord, curse ye bitterly the inhabitants thereof; because they came not to the help of the Lord against the wrongdoings of the mighty." In Roosevelt's judgment, "President Wilson has earned for the nation the curse of Meroz for he has not dared to stand on the side of the Lord against the wrongdoings of the mighty."[25]

A calmer but no less stinging attack came from Lodge. On February 1 the Massachusetts senator delivered a long speech in which he rejected "peace without victory." Lasting peace, he argued, "rests upon justice and righteousness" and could be won by "victories in the field." Wilson's principles of self-government and freedom of the seas Lodge dismissed as either meaningless generalities or potential problems for future American action. He concentrated his strongest criticisms on the league of nations proposal. Lodge admitted his own earlier attraction to the idea, "but the more I have thought about it the more serious the difficulties in the way of accomplishment seem to be." Two difficulties bothered him most. First, a genuinely effective peacekeeping organization would require dangerous powers of coercion; "no amount of shouting about the blessings of peace" would obviate the need for force. Second, membership in a league of nations would mean abandoning traditional American diplomatic principles. Lodge insisted that he had "no superstition in regard to Washington's policy" against alliances, but he could find no sufficient cause for departing from it in Wilson's murky and misleading proposals. On the contrary, "I now see in this tortured and distracted world nothing but peril in abandoning our long and well-established policies."[26]

Lodge was making the same departure as Roosevelt. Both men were compromising their generation-old fight for a more active, committed foreign policy and were appealing to sentiments they had long combated. Lodge's opposition to Wilson rested on exactly the same grounds as Roosevelt's. His frosty manner and circumspect style masked an idealism of comparable order and stripe. Lodge did ask probing questions in his February speech about how international peacekeeping plans might work, and he dwelt on the vagueness of Wilson's proposals. But those "realistic" criticisms were his less important objections. Instead, as Lodge's repeated allusions to "righteousness" suggested, he was denouncing Wilson as a false prophet, a purveyor of bogus idealism. "We cannot secure our own safety or build up the lasting peace of the world upon peace at any price," Lodge avowed in closing the speech; "the peace of the world must be based upon righteousness at any cost." Roosevelt would not have put the matter any differently.[27]

The chief significance of those debates at the beginning of 1917 lay, as has often been pointed out, in providing a dress rehearsal for the conflict two years later over membership in the League of Nations. The major opponents in the Senate of Wilson's project in 1919 would be the same two men who took the lead in attacking the note to the belligerents and "peace without victory"—Borah and Lodge—and they would head another anti-internationalist coalition. Moreover, the party division over foreign policy that stood out so sharply at the end of World War I was forming in January and

February 1917. Offsetting Bryan's and other Democrats' leanings toward the league idea were equally striking Republican defections. A rash of resignations hit the League to Enforce Peace, despite Taft's leadership. The stage was set for the future conflict, and it is tempting to view the outcome of that conflict as virtually foreordained. One circumstance would be different in 1919, however, and one major actor would be removed. Roosevelt's death profoundly altered the political context of the postwar debate.[28]

Before that conflict over peacemaking could take place, the world war had to end, and the United States had to play its final part. When Lodge attacked the "peace without victory" address on February 1, he knew that events had overtaken both Wilson and himself. The day before, Germany had announced the opening of unrestricted submarine warfare against Allied and neutral shipping, to commence on February 1. Wilson promptly broke diplomatic relations. Observers on both sides of the Atlantic, particularly the German leaders, expected war to begin shortly. Yet Wilson held back for two months. He suffered an agony of conflicting desires, which culminated in what Arthur Link has called "the time of Wilson's Gethsemane." He tried several expedients to avert intervention. He sent unmistakably pacific public signals to Germany, he negotiated secretly with Germany's ally Austria, and he briefly pursued armed neutrality as a possible alternative to full belligerency. Finally, on the night of April 2, 1917, he asked Congress to declare war. The two months from February 1 to April 2 had an air of suspended reality about them, and Wilson's decision to intervene has never entirely lost a mysterious aspect.[29]

Those two months also brought agony to Roosevelt, but in a different way and with no sense of mystery. Wilson's reluctance to go to war merely reconfirmed his Nietzschean Warrior's scorn for Wilson as a Priest. "He is a very cold & selfish man," Roosevelt told Hiram Johnson; "a very timid man when it comes to dealing with physical danger . . . As for shame, he has none, and if anyone kicks him, he brushes his clothes, and utters some lofty sentence." The Republican insurgents' outspoken opposition to intervention and to arming American merchant ships further deepened Roosevelt's distaste for his former followers. Just as British liberals had displayed "incredible silliness in foreign affairs," he observed to Lodge, "our own progressives and near-progressives and progressive Republicans have tended to travel the same gait." As for himself, his political priorities could not have been clearer. "When root questions such as national self-preservation, and the upholding of the national honor, and the performance of duty in international affairs are concerned," he also informed Lodge, "the ordinary matters that divide conservative and progressive must be brushed aside." Roosevelt chafed in agony because his hopes for war seemed so near and yet so far from fulfillment. [30]

Doubts about whether the United States would enter the World War were well founded. Contrary to the hopes of Roosevelt and others like him, public pressure did not prod Wilson toward intervention. Outrage again flared as Americans died in submarine attacks on British liners and, for the first time since early in 1915, on American vessels. Some previously uncommitted politicians and newspapers came out for war at the end of February and beginning of March 1917. Interventionist sentiment rose particularly after publication of the Zimmermann Telegram, in which Germany promised Mexico restoration of the "lost provinces" of Texas, New Mexico, and Arizona if, in the event of war between Germany and the United States, Mexico fought against the United States. But most contemporary estimates and subsequent studies of public opinion have shown that substantial anti-interventionist sentiment persisted in March and April. The great majority of Americans apparently still clung to their "double wish" to uphold national honor and stay out of the war. Congressional opinion reflected the public uncertainty. Several independent observers noted that large majorities in both houses remained undecided about intervention right up to the night of April 2. [31]

The decision to go into or stay out of the World War fell upon Wilson alone. His decision has remained mysterious for three reasons. First, Wilson made it in his usual solitary way; second, he expressed doubts about the wisdom and likely consequences of entering the war; and finally, both his choice of and his justification for intervention seemed out of character. [32]

None of those considerations should cast unnecessary shadows over Wilson's thought and action. His solitariness as president was never so great a handicap as some critics claimed, and it probably affected his performance between February and April 1917 even less than at other times. Wilson frequently discussed the matters

that were uppermost in his thinking. The cabinet considered submarine issues at four meetings during February and March, and
Wilson talked about those issues several times individually with the
members most concerned, the secretaries of state, war, and the
navy. Wilson also bared some of his deepest qualms about the
choice to Frank Cobb, editor of the New York *World*. He revealed
his thoughts in public as well. On February 3 Wilson told a joint
session of Congress that a diplomatic break with Germany was the
only "alternative consistent with the dignity and honor of the
United States," but he wanted "merely to stand true alike to the
immemorial principles of our people which I sought to express in
my [peace without victory] address to the Senate only two weeks
ago." On February 26 he told another joint session that the United
States sought simply to defend "those rights of humanity without
which there is no civilization." On March 5, in his second inaugural
address, he urged Americans to persevere in bringing "calm counsel" to the issues of war and peace. "The shadows that now lie dark
upon our paths will soon be dispelled and we shall walk with the
light all about us," he maintained, "if we be but true to ourselves—
to ourselves as we have wished to be known in the counsels of the
world and in the thought of all who love liberty and justice and the
right exalted."[33]

   Wilson often sounded like a mystic when he portrayed himself
as a representative and instrument of popular opinion, but no leading politician in 1917 was better attuned to the sentiment of the
majority. It was Wilson's attunement to the pacific side of the
public's "double wish" that fostered much of the doubt he expressed about the wisdom and consequences of intervention. That
doubt has, in turn, formed the second reason for finding mystery in
his choice of war. In February and March Wilson expressed repugnance toward entering the World War on two grounds. One
was an odd combination of international concerns. At one cabinet
meeting, the president reportedly asked what effect "the depletion
of manpower" caused by American intervention might "have upon
the relations between the white and yellow races?" But Wilson's
greatest international concern was about abandoning "peace without victory." According to Frank Cobb's recollection, Wilson argued "that so long as we remained out there was a preponderance
of neutrality, but that if we joined the Allies the world would be off

a peace basis and onto a war basis." Intervention would change
everything, Cobb recalled Wilson asserting. "It means an attempt
to reconstruct a peace-time civilization with war standards, and at
the end of the war there will be no bystanders with sufficient power
to influence the terms. There won't be any peace standards to work
with. There will be only war standards." As Wilson stated in his
speeches and as others have repeatedly observed, his basic foreign
policy problem was how to pursue "peace without victory" through
war.[34]

Wilson's second ground for fearing the consequences of intervention was domestic. He also reportedly asserted to Cobb, "Once
lead this people into war, and they'll forget there ever was such a
thing as tolerance. To fight you must be brutal and ruthless, and the
spirit of ruthless brutality will enter into the very fibre of our
national life, infecting Congress, the courts, the policeman on the
beat, the man in the street." Much of that prediction did come true
after the United States went to war, and the later curtailment of
civil liberties has raised questions about whether Wilson really
feared those consequences. It is indisputable, however, that he
viewed the likely political impact of the war with misgivings. "Daniels, if this country goes into war," he reportedly also said in March
1917, "you and I will live to see the day when the big interests will
be in the saddle." Since the beginning of his presidency, Wilson
had expressed similar fears, in connection with threats of war in
Mexico, that the nation would be distracted from reform and that
conservatives and big business would gain political advantage.[35]

Wilson's fears of the foreign and domestic consequences of
intervention have helped lend the note of mystery to his choice of
war. If Wilson knew that intervention would have so many evil
consequences at home and abroad, how could he choose to fight?
Much of the mystery has stemmed from viewing those utterances
as isolated from other ideas expressed by Wilson. He gave equal
weight to the other side of the "double wish." He did not hesitate
to break relations with Germany or to arm American ships against
the submarines. "We may even be drawn on, by circumstances, not
by our own purpose or desire," he warned in March in his inaugural
address, "to a more active assertion of our rights as we see them and
a more immediate association with the great struggle itself." In
none of his doubts about entering the war did Wilson speak as a

diehard anti-interventionist. For him, evil consequences were realities to be faced and dangers to be recognized, not necessarily
insuperable obstacles. Most of his doubts amounted to factors to be
weighed in the scales of circumstance, interest, and strategy as he
decided how to address the situation.[36]

Wilson also felt deep personal anguish over his decision. In
April 1914 the deaths of American servicemen at Veracruz had
shaken him, and he had understandably recoiled from the mass
slaughter on the western front. "Think what it was they were applauding," Wilson reportedly said to Tumulty after asking Congress
for the declaration of war on April 2. "My message to-day was a
message of death for our young men. How strange it seems to
applaud that." Such evidence of emotional involvement has raised
a persistent question about Wilson's decision to intervene. If he felt
so deeply against the war and such a personal burden of guilt for the
deaths of young Americans, how could he still choose to fight? The
most common answer to that question, aside from confessions of
bewilderment, has been the contention that only an idealistic crusade to reform the world—making the world "safe for democracy"
and fighting "a war to end all wars"—could justify such sacrifices
and assuage the guilt that plagued Wilson.[37]

That interpretation, based upon two errors, is wrong. One
error is a mistaken view of Wilson's political personality; the other
is a misreading of his war address. The mistaken view of Wilson's
personality has derived from a depiction of him, albeit usually
unconsciously, as a Nietzschean Priest. From that perspective,
with its pejorative stress on a reluctance to wield power, nothing
short of a holy war involving eternal principles of right and wrong
could have reconciled Wilson to intervention in World War I.
Actually the only correct element in the Nietzschean categorization
of Wilson has been the recognition that he was not a Warrior. But
neither was he a Priest. Instead, Wilson's beliefs in self-control and
in realization of ideals through self-interest made him resemble
more the figure who embodied Nietzsche's ideal of self-overcoming
and creative expression of the will-to-power—not the Warrior, but
the Superman.[38]

A second, closely related error in interpretations of Wilson's
choice of intervention has been the misreading of his speech of
April 2 as an endorsement of an idealistic crusade. The address is

a work of somber beauty, which lays major stress on uncertainty, limitation, and inescapability. "We must put excited feeling away," Wilson declared early in the speech. "Our motive will not be revenge or the victorious assertion of the physical might of the nation, but only the vindication of right, of human right, of which we are only a single champion." For himself, Wilson added, he felt "a profound sense of the solemn and even tragical character of the step I am taking." Wilson was casting himself and his country in a tragic role.

The tragedy lay in having to pursue good ends through evil means. "I have exactly the same things in mind now that I had in mind when I addressed the Senate on the twenty-second of January last," Wilson avowed. ". . . Our object now, as then, is to vindicate the principles of peace and justice in the life of the world as against selfish and autocratic power and to set amongst the really free and self-governed peoples such a concert of purpose as will henceforth insure the observance of these principles." Yet he urged that Americans must "fight without rancor . . . without passion and ourselves observe with proud punctilio the principles of right and of fair play we profess to be fighting for." In closing, Wilson again acknowledged, "It is a fearful thing to lead this great peaceful people into war, into the most terrible and disastrous of all wars, civilization itself seeming to be in the balance. But the right is more precious than the peace, and we shall fight for the things which we have always carried nearest our hearts—" and, after reciting once more the objects that he had named earlier for the United States to pursue, he ended—"God helping her, she can do no other."[39]

Those last words, as many recognized, paraphrased and echoed Martin Luther's declaration to the Diet of Worms, "God helping me, I can do no other." The words were probably a chance combination, but it seems doubtful that Wilson did not know he was imitating Luther's declaration. Although Wilson often admitted that he was no theologian, his origins and upbringing among highly educated Protestant clergymen made it almost certain that he grasped, at least in a general way, the philosophical implication of invoking Luther. Next to his role in the Reformation, Luther's best-known contribution to Christianity was his dictum, "Sin boldly." Luther had held that inasmuch as Christians lived in a sinful world and were themselves sinners, they could not avoid sin but must, in seeking to follow God's will, "sin boldly."

Wilson's basic argument in the war address was analogous to Luther's contention. In trying to make the world freer, more just, and more peaceful, both he and the United States confronted the sin of the World War. Yet, as he argued, continued armed neutrality would result in much of the destruction of war without the advantage of being able to influence the war's conduct and aims. Wilson's choice, therefore, was not the possibly lesser, but also less promising, evil of staying out. Rather, for the sake of greater leverage in pursuing his international program, he would "sin boldly" by going into the war. He made the decision, not as a Nietzschean Priest or Superman, but as the protagonist in a Christian tragedy.[40]

In one way, Wilson's tragedy began as he delivered the war address. Applause interrupted him after his most belligerent statements, particularly when he uttered the phrase "safe for democracy." This time Lodge led the applauding senators. He rushed up afterward to shake Wilson's hand and tell him, "Mr. President, you have expressed in the loftiest manner the sentiments of the American people." La Follette, who sat grimly through the address with his arms tightly folded, led the senatorial opposition. On April 4 the Senate approved a declaration of war with six members voting against—La Follette, two other insurgent Republicans, and three Bryanite Democrats. Two days later the House followed suit, with fifty-four representatives voting or announced in opposition—thirty-five Republicans, a majority of whom were insurgents; eighteen Democrats, all Bryanite stalwarts, including Majority Leader Kitchin, and the lone Socialist. The congressional opposition reflected some likely influence from German-American constituencies and a clear sectional bias toward the Middle West and West, but its strongest characteristic was a reformist inclination. As in the preparedness and submarine policy controversies a year before, Wilson was bending his side of the political spectrum toward an uncongenial foreign policy, and he was once more accepting support from the other side. As before, he succeeded overwhelmingly for the time being, but he was sowing more seeds of future trouble.[41]

· 20 ·

The End of the Conflict

FOUR DAYS AFTER THE UNITED STATES entered World War I, Theodore Roosevelt and Woodrow Wilson met for the last time. On April 10, 1917, the ex-president made a well-publicized visit to the White House to ask permission to lead a division of volunteers on the western front. Roosevelt's pilgrimage testified to both his ardor to fight and his faith in his persuasive powers. Ever since he had left the White House eight years before, he had greeted nearly every foreign trouble with hopes and plans to lead troops in combat. By 1917 he yearned so deeply to go to war that he pledged to cease his attacks on Wilson, and he tried to tempt his rival with allurements of historical greatness. "Mr. President, what I have said and thought, and what others have said and thought," Roosevelt recounted telling Wilson, "is all dust in a windy street, if now we can make your message good. Of course, it amounts to nothing, if we cannot make it good. But, if we can translate it into fact, then it will rank as a great state paper, with the great state papers of Washington and Lincoln. Now, all that I ask is that I be allowed to do all that in me is [sic] to help make good this speech of yours—to help get the nation to act, so as to justify and live up to the speech, and the declaration of war that followed."[1]

Surprisingly, in view of their past conflicts and the implicit arrogance of Roosevelt's offer, the twenty-five-minute meeting went well. Although Wilson seemed cool at first, the two men soon loosened up and enjoyed each other. The president encouraged his predecessor to visit with members of the staff who had once served him. Wilson also lifted the rule then in force against reporters and newsreel cameramen gathering at the White House entrance. As a result, one presidential secretary recorded in his diary, "The Colonel was filmed and interviewed to his heart's content." After Roosevelt left, Wilson reportedly asked Tumulty, "Well, and how did the Colonel impress you?" Tumulty recalled remarking on Roosevelt's charm and warmth. "Yes," Wilson reportedly agreed, "he is a great big boy. I was, as formerly, charmed by his personality. There is a sweetness about him that is very compelling. You can't resist the man. I can easily understand why his followers are so fond of him."[2]

Charm availed Roosevelt little. His offer to play Grant to Wilson's Lincoln died aborning. The War Department recommended strongly against raising separate volunteer units and pointedly against giving divisional command to a fifty-eight-year-old civilian whose health was poor and whose last military experience dated back nearly two decades. In a public statement on May 19, 1917, Wilson bowed to the professional soldiers' judgment of the need for orderly mobilization under the new system of conscription. "I need not assure you," he telegraphed Roosevelt, "that my conclusions were based entirely upon imperative considerations of public policy and not upon personal or private choice." Roosevelt and his circle accused Wilson of doing just that, and their accusations had a ring of plausibility. Wilson could hardly have avoided feeling some resentment toward Roosevelt. He might understandably also have balked at bestowing a military command that would almost certainly brighten the political prospects of his greatest rival and severest critic.[3]

Actually, neither personal revenge nor political calculations weighted much in Wilson's rejection of Roosevelt's offer. Others besides the ex-president's friends and followers criticized the decision. Militant Allied spokesmen prized Roosevelt as a symbol of American commitment to their cause. The fiery French editor-politician Georges Clemenceau, soon to be premier, dispatched a public letter to Wilson in which he demanded Roosevelt's presence at the front. "He is an idealist, imbued with simple vital idealism," declared Clemenceau. "Hence his influence over the crowd, his prestige." Such comments ironically pointed to Wilson's major reasons for rejecting Roosevelt. The romantic colonel of the Rough Riders seemed out of place in the grim business of modern technological war. Worse, the War Department's experts maintained that Roosevelt's enthusiastic amateurism would hamper military efficiency, particularly because he had already hatched plans to skim off the cream of the officer corps for his volunteer division.[4]

Wilson's basic reason for rejecting Roosevelt lay in his ideological justification for intervention in the World War. From the outset of American belligerency, Wilson emphasized its special character. He spurned the appeals of the British and French as well as arguments of Roosevelt, Lodge, Lansing, and House when he declined to join the Allies formally. Wilson insisted that the United States be called an "Associated Power." In his first speech after the declaration of war he dwelled on the nation's idealistic commitment, but he added, "It is a thing one does not dare to talk about because a certain passion comes into one's thought and one's feeling as one thinks of the nature of the task." As earlier, Wilson eschewed "passion" and projected his belief in self-control onto the nation. That was his fundamental reason for rejecting Roosevelt. Wilson dismissed his rival for stirring up rather than bridling passions and for seeking total victory instead of "peace without victory."[5]

The ex-president's opposition to the military and foreign policies of Wilson's administration during most of the rest of his life appeared to vindicate the decision to keep him at arm's length. If anything, Roosevelt's attacks grew even fiercer after May 1917 than they had been before the United States entered the war. "It is not our alien enemies who are responsible for our complete unpreparedness," Roosevelt charged in a speech in July 1917. "It is the foes of our own household. The leaders who have led us wrong are these foes; and in so far as our own weakness and shortsightedness and love of ease and undue regard for material success have made us respond readily to such leadership, we ourselves have been our foes." It was not hard to guess who Roosevelt thought was the most dangerous of "the foes of our own household."[6]

The familiarity of Roosevelt's charges lulled administration supporters into unwisely continuing to dismiss them as neither serious nor threatening. In contrast to Wilson, Roosevelt favored making common cause with the Allies and pursuing total victory over not only Germany but also the other Central Powers. "A limited liability war in which we fight Germany ourselves and pay money to Italy and Russia to enable them to fight Austria and Turkey, with whom we are at peace," he asserted in October 1917, "savors of sharp practice and not of statesmanship. It is a good rule either to stay out of war or to go into it, but not to try to do both things at once." A year later, when Germany opened armistice negotiations on the basis of the Fourteen Points, Roosevelt condemned Wilson's peace settlement proposals as "muddy" and "empty competitive rhetoric." Instead, he demanded, "Let us dictate peace by the hammering guns and not chat about peace to the accompaniment of the clicking of typewriters."[7]

Although such criticisms made Roosevelt sound once more like a "realist," that posture continued to be deceptive. Militant idealism remained the basis of all his political stands, foreign and domestic. "To my fellow Americans I preach the sword of the Lord and of Gideon," proclaimed Roosevelt in September 1917. Two months later he reiterated his long-held conviction that personal and national morality were identical. "It is well that there should be some ideals so high as never to be wholly possible of realization," he argued; "but unless there is a sincere effort measureably [sic] to realize them, glittering talk about them represents merely a kind of self-indulgence which ultimately means atrophy of will power." Roosevelt's continuing condemnation of "materialism" revealed that he had by no means abandoned the cause of reform at home. Instead, fulsome wartime advocacy of service and sacrifice allowed him to integrate his views on domestic and foreign policy better than at any time since 1912.[8]

Roosevelt was able to recapture his basic political vision so well during 1917 and 1918 because he could draw upon his deepest concerns. As Wilson's reputed description of him as "a great big boy" implied, many found his ardor for the war easy to dismiss as childish love of fighting. Those dismissals misread the nature of Roosevelt's militarism. Neither his views of human conflict nor his own desire to fight reflected shallow, juvenile romanticism. As in 1898 Roosevelt appreciated and welcomed war's grim and brutal aspects. Only by passing through those, he believed, could men live to the utmost and attain full humanity. When American soldiers reached the front in the spring of 1918, Roosevelt exulted, "They are the men who have paid with their bodies for their soul's desire. Let no one pity them, whatever their fate, for they have seen the mighty days and risen level to the need of the mighty days."[9]

Nothing revealed the roots and the depth of Roosevelt's concern better than his attitude toward his sons' service in the World War. All four of them saw action. "You are having your crowded hours of glorious life," Roosevelt told the eldest when he reached France; "you have seized the great chance, as it was seized by those who fought at Gettysburg, and Waterloo, and Agincourt, and Arbella and Marathon." The father's mingled pride and envy swelled when the third son, "Archie," was wounded in March 1918. "Well, we know what it feels like to have a hero in the family!", Roosevelt told Archie. To Clemenceau he said, "One of your Generals gave him the Croix de Guerre, and I am prouder of his having received it than of my having been President!" Greater glory and loss followed in July 1918. When the youngest son, Quentin, who had become an aviator, shot down a German plane, Roosevelt observed to his younger daughter, "Whatever now befalls Quentin he has now had his crowded hour, and his day of honor and triumph." Five days later reporters called at the Roosevelt home with news that Quentin's plane had been shot down behind German lines. After three days of suspense, a telegram from President Wilson confirmed that Quentin had been killed. When Roosevelt received the first reports about his son on July 17, he was standing in his study under a portrait of his father. Theodore Roosevelt's engagement with war was ending where it had begun more than half a century before.[10]

Quentin's death hit him harder than anything since the deaths of his father and mother and his first wife. He met the blow stoically and actively. Despite the initial uncertainty about Quentin's fate, Roosevelt insisted upon going ahead with his keynote speech to the New York state Republican convention on July 18, and he stepped up his partisan activities before the elections in November. The only apparent effect of his son's death on Roosevelt's political role lay in reinforcing his determination to seek the presidency in 1920 strictly on his own terms. "Since Quentin's death the world seems to have shut down upon me," he reportedly told a friend in the fall of 1918. ". . . If I do consent [to run], it will be because as President I could accomplish some things I should like to see accomplished before I die." About the same time, in tributes to the war dead, he lauded "the torch-bearers . . . who have dared the Great Adventure" and "the young Galahads of this Great War [who] when they have found the grail have too often filled it with their own hearts' blood." Quentin's death had only hardened his father's creed.[11]

If his sons' fates in the World War did not change Roosevelt's views or conduct, outward circumstances did introduce novel features and ultimately influenced a last major shift in his foreign policy. Domestic opposition to the war stirred repressive tendencies in him that had lain dormant since the 1890s. Roosevelt advocated suppression of all German-language publications and denial of the vote to conscientious objectors, and he urged the establishment of military courts to try dissenters and others suspected of disloyalty. He praised vigilante actions against the I.W.W. and favored the application of military censorship to all publications. In November 1918 Roosevelt called for a crackdown on Bolsheviks and other radicals—along the lines of the campaign that Attorney General Palmer subsequently launched during the Red Scare. Yet Roosevelt also recognized that his own criticisms made him something of a dissenter. In April 1918 he denounced a proposed version of the Sedition Act as unconstitutional. A month later he admonished Congress to "guarantee the right of the press and people to speak the truth freely of all their public servants, including the President, and to criticize them in the severest terms of truth whenever they come short in their public duty." That limited defense of free speech brought Roosevelt as close as he ever came to sympathizing with victims of official repression.[12]

An even greater novelty in Roosevelt's role as a wartime critic came with the resurrection of his popularity and political prospects. A weekly newspaper column in the *Kansas City Star*, which started in the fall of 1917 and was widely syndicated, gave him a new journalistic platform in addition to his monthly magazine editorials. Old Guard Republican foes now sought his advice and services as a speaker, and by early 1918 he was being touted as the next Republican presidential nominee. The turnabout in Roosevelt's political fortunes stemmed from several sources. One, ironically, was Wilson's successful prosecution of the war. Despite furious attacks by Roosevelt, Lodge, and a host of Republicans, the administration ran a war effort of unprecedented honesty and efficiency. Also, despite the lack of bipartisan overtures, Wilson did not use high-ranking military or civilian appointments to advance leading Democrats or promote personal protégés. Such feats increased the Republicans' apparent need for the strongest possible candidate in 1920, and no one filled the bill better than Roosevelt.

But more than partisan need fed his renewed hold on popular affections. To Roosevelt the reason for his restored popularity was obvious—American intervention had proved him right and Wilson wrong. He had a point. Once the United States entered the war, Roosevelt lost the stigma of someone advocating unpopular views. Further, with his unassailable militarist and interventionist credentials, he enjoyed the luxury of unbridled criticism without suspicion of disloyalty. Perhaps most important, the kind of war Wilson fought could not help but enhance Roosevelt's standing with the people. Because he lacked the governmental machinery for a highly coercive approach, Wilson had to rely upon exciting popular sentiment. The administration employed the latest techniques of advertising and public relations, particularly through its sophisticated new propaganda agency, the Committee on Public Information, which did a spectacular job of selling the war to the American public. To Wilson that success was a mixed blessing, because it undermined the limited, critical commitment he wished to maintain. To Roosevelt it was an unalloyed boon, because greater popular excitement boosted the all-out idealistic crusade he advocated. [13]

The growing likelihood of another Roosevelt presidency underlay his final foreign policy shift, which came at the end of 1918 on the league of nations issue. Intervention had brought a moratorium on debate about postwar peacekeeping plans during the first year of American belligerency. Wilson had initiated the moratorium when he told a member of the League to Enforce Peace in May 1917 that the organization had "a very much too definite programme which I myself have been very careful not to subscribe to. The general idea of the League I have publicly endorsed . . . but further than that I cannot go and I think it would be very unwise to go at the present time." In January 1918, however, Wilson reopened the debate by outlining his peace program in the Fourteen Points address. The last point read, "A general association of nations must be formed under specific covenants for the purpose of affording mutual guarantees of political independence and territorial integrity to great and small nations alike." Wilson also declared that "such arrangements and covenants" would inaugurate "a just and stable peace such as can be secured only by removing the chief provocations to war, which this program does remove."[14]

Roosevelt scorned all talk of a compromise peace in January 1918 as "high-sounding speech to cloak ignoble action" and a "Judas kiss," but for several months he held his fire against both the league idea and the Fourteen Points. Privately, Roosevelt continued to condemn the ideas of the League to Enforce Peace as premature and misleading. He also gave encouragement to his erstwhile imperialist and Progressive cohort, Albert J. Beveridge, who had emerged as a leading critic of internationalist proposals. "As you say, nationalism is the keynote of your attitude and mine," Roosevelt told Beveridge in July 1918. ". . . As you say, it may well be that this will be the issue which we shall have to force against Wilson." At the same time Roosevelt publicly scorned "professional internationalists" as "a sorry crew" who appealed to "weaklings, illusionists, materialists, lukewarm Americans and faddists of all the types that vitiate sound nationalism." A month later he demanded the application of "horse-sense" to internationalist schemes and argued that unless plans for a league of nations meant maintaining and broadening the present cooperation between America and the Allies, they rested "on a doctrine of fatal sterility."[15]

Those public and private utterances made Roosevelt appear to be gearing up for a new assault on the league idea. He gave other signs as well that he contemplated a renewal of his earlier flirtation with the isolationists. Earlier in 1918 Roosevelt had buried the hatchet with Taft, and in August he agreed to back the proposals of the League to Enforce Peace "as an *addition to*, but not as *a substitute for*, our preparing our own strength for our own defense." In a speech in September 1918 Roosevelt announced his willingness to accept a league of nations "as a supplement to, and not a substitute for, the preparation of our own strength." But Roosevelt reiterated so many familiar strictures about national self-reliance and the untrustworthiness of other nations, particularly Germany, that his endorsement sounded less than wholehearted. The lukewarmness was deliberate. "I am insisting upon Nationalism as against Internationalism," Roosevelt assured Beveridge. His gesture toward the league idea was "merely a platonic expression, designed to let Taft and his followers to get over without too much trouble, and also to prevent any accusation that we are ourselves merely Prussian militarists."[16]

Roosevelt was playing a canny political game on foreign policy in the fall of 1918. By talking out of one side of his mouth to Taft and out of the other side to Beveridge, he was attempting to hold together Republicans with conflicting views on the league issue. Lodge, who self-consciously carried on for Roosevelt after his death, performed the same task with Republicans inside and outside the Senate during the debate over membership in the League of Nations in 1919 and 1920. The similarity in their approaches did not mean, however, that Roosevelt was preparing to consort with a revived isolationist coalition, as Lodge later did. Roosevelt's statements about preserving and extending ties with the Allies showed that his thinking ran counter to isolationist policies. He favored broader participation in the war than almost any other American. During 1917 and 1918 he publicly advocated sending troops to fight in virtually every theater of World War I, including the Balkans against Austria-Hungary and the eastern Mediterranean against Turkey, as well as intervention in Russia against the Bolsheviks. Privately, Roosevelt repeatedly told British friends that he wanted postwar security pacts with them and with the French, and in July 1918 he told an Australian leader, "I am quite prepared to say now that Australia and the United States must stand together as absolutely in international relations as the several states of our own Union now stand." Such declarations rang true to his generation-old desire to expand America's involvement in world politics. They also showed how eager he was to seize upon the World War as the occasion to extend and make permanent his country's role as a leading world power.[17]

Important though the war was in restoring Roosevelt's bearings in foreign affairs, however, the reason for the biggest shift in his views resulted from his revived political prospects. Roosevelt's conciliation toward Taft on the league of nations proposals and his attempts to hold Republicans together on this issue coincided with the growing talk of his being the party's next presidential nominee. Despite his continued pose of heroic defiance, Roosevelt was reverting to his original preference for intraparty manipulation and diplomacy. The likelihood of another chance at the presidency was restoring a better balance between his political roles of principled agitator and professional operator than he had achieved at any time since he had left the White House nearly a decade before.

The clearest sign of this salutary effect came after the Republicans won congressional majorities in November 1918. When he delivered the main rebuttal to Wilson's appeal for a Democratic Congress, Roosevelt enhanced his standing as the party's leading contender. He hastened to assert his newfound primacy by issuing public demands for an advanced reform program at home and sweeping postwar commitments abroad, including membership in a league of nations. "The United States cannot again completely withdraw into its shell," Roosevelt declared two weeks after the elections. "We need not mix in all European quarrels nor assume all spheres of interest everywhere to be ours, but we ought to join the other civilized nations of the world in some scheme that in a time of great stress would offer a likelihood of obtaining settlements that will avert war." Roosevelt proposed that the United States join with the Allies and the new nations of eastern Europe in a general peacekeeping organization. "Then it would probably be best for certain spheres of interest to be reserved to each nation or group of nations," he added, and he specified the Caribbean as an American sphere, eastern Asia for Japan, and Africa for the European Allies. [18]

In December 1918 Roosevelt praised Taft for proposing a plan for "a league under existing conditions and with such wisdom in refusing to let adherence to the principle be clouded by insistence upon improper or unimportant methods of enforcement that we can speak of the league as a practical matter." That renewed endorsement of the league idea contained plenty of qualification. Privately, Roosevelt continued to doubt Americans' will to sustain foreign commitments. "Any treaty adopted under the influence of war emotions would be like the good resolutions adopted at mass meetings," he confided to a newspaper editor in December 1918. "We have an anti-vice crusade. Everybody is aroused. The movement culminates in a big meeting and we adopt resolutions abolishing vice. But vice isn't abolished in that way." [19]

In his last pronouncement on foreign policy, which he dictated on January 3, 1919, Roosevelt once more attacked the Fourteen Points as the basis for a peace settlement, and he expressed further doubts about a league of nations. "Finally make it perfectly clear," Roosevelt declared, "that we do not intend to take a position of international Meddlesome Matty." Americans must not send "our gallant young men to die in obscure fights in the Balkans or in central Europe," nor could they compromise the Monroe Doctrine. "Let civilized-Europe and Asia introduce some kind of police system in the weak and disorderly countries at their thresholds," as the United States had done in parts of the Western Hemisphere. That would lay a foundation for real peace and stability. But Roosevelt's last words about a league of nations expressed a qualified hope: "I believe that such an effort made moderately and sanely, but sincerely and with utter scorn for words that are not made good by deeds, will be productive of real and lasting international good." Two days later, death took away his chance to help build a new world order.[20]

As in domestic politics, one should not make too much of what might have happened if Roosevelt had lived. The later attitudes of both Republicans and Democrats toward collective security, as well as the actions of the countries that did join the League of Nations, make it questionable that anyone could have established lasting international stability after World War I. In his previous terms as president, Roosevelt himself had failed to awaken Americans to foreign responsibilities, and the behavior of his party during the debates over peacemaking in 1919 and 1920 and then during the 1920s, when the Republicans were back in power, did not bode well for his chances of doing much better.

Nor is it clear that Roosevelt would have eased the work of the peacemakers if he had lived longer. For several months before his death, he urged Allied leaders to seek a punitive settlement, and after the 1918 elections he reminded them of Wilson's weak support at home. "At the peace conference England and France can get what they wish, so far as America is concerned," Roosevelt wrote Bryce in November, "if, while treating Wilson with politeness, they openly and frankly throw themselves on the American people for support in any vital matter." In the newspaper column in December 1918 in which he endorsed Taft's ideas for a league of nations, Roosevelt also maintained, "The American envoys must not sit at the table as umpires between the Allies and the conquered Central Powers, but as loyal brothers of the Allies, as loyal members of the league of free peoples, which has brought about peace by overthrowing Turkey, Bulgaria, and Austria, and beating Germany to her knees." As matters transpired at the peace conference, Wilson was able to moderate the territorial, financial, and colonial demands of Britain, France, Italy, and Japan and to win acceptance of the Covenant of the League of Nations largely because the Allied leaders saw no alternative if they wished to gain American adherence to the settlement. If Roosevelt had lived, the Allies would have had an attractive alternative, and Wilson's task at the conference would have become much more difficult, perhaps impossible.[21]

Although Roosevelt's death may have removed foreign complications for Wilson, it also ruined an opportunity for building a domestic consensus, bridging ideological and partisan divisions, and taking a larger role in the maintenance of international peace and security. Lodge's strongest reason for cooperating with the isolationists during the debates of 1919 and 1920 and for seeking to limit commitments under the League Covenant was his mistrust of Wilson. If Roosevelt had been waiting in the wings to lead the nation and the world, Lodge and others would have viewed American membership in a different light. Partisan conflict and the personal animus that Roosevelt bore toward Wilson might still have prevented approval of the peace treaties and participation in the League in 1919, but the debates would almost certainly have taken a different and more promising direction. A foreign policy debate between Roosevelt and Wilson in the 1920 presidential campaign might have replicated their domestic debate in 1912. Whatever the outcome, the result might have fostered a better approach to America's role in world affairs.[22]

Other misfortunes besides Roosevelt's death precluded a constructive debate over peacemaking in the United States after World War I. Even greater harm flowed from the major stroke Wilson suffered on October 2, 1919, at a critical point in the Senate's consideration of the peace treaty. For a week the president lay near death, and he remained almost completely isolated from outside contacts for over three months. The stroke left Wilson permanently paralyzed on his left side, with limited vision, tenuous control of his emotions, and reduced concentration and capacity for work. Given the severity of the stroke, Wilson made a remarkable recovery. He was able to devote some attention to domestic and foreign affairs and to do a little reading and writing, and he lived another four years. But after October 1919 Wilson was clearly a broken man. He never again adequately filled his office, much less functioned anywhere near his own exalted level of presidential leadership.[23]

The debate over the peace treaty and League membership would almost certainly have gone better if Wilson had died in the fall of 1919. At the time and later, observers commented that if he had died then—when he had just made an extended speaking tour to arouse public support—a wave of national remorse might have compelled reluctant senators to approve the treaty with few restrictions. Instead, in November 1919 and again in March 1920, the stricken president ordered Democratic senators to vote against the treaty with the reservations, principally on participation in the League, that had been drafted by Lodge and were supported by the Republicans. Deadlock ensued. The treaty failed to muster the necessary two-thirds either with Lodge's reservations or under Wilson's virtually unrestricted terms, and the United States never joined the League of Nations. The deadlock stemmed mainly from Wilson's refusal to accept Lodge's reservations, and questions have persisted about whether he would have acted the same way if he had not suffered his stroke.[24]

Speculation about the probable effects of Wilson's stroke on the failure of peacemaking can be misleading apart from a broader consideration of his wartime leadership and other likely influences of his health. The postwar deadlock between the president and the Republican senators culminated an estrangement that had begun soon after intervention. In addition to declining Roosevelt's offer of military service, Wilson had made few attempts to enlist prominent Republicans on the civilian side of the war effort. His main overtures had been appointing Taft to the National War Labor Board and selecting Root to head a diplomatic mission to Russia in May 1917. Neither appointment made a major impact on domestic or foreign policy. Wilson's failure to practice bipartisanship largely reflected a lack of precedent; no previous president had tried to make the opposition party a partner in waging war. With his background as a student of politics and parties, Wilson did recognize the need for such partnership, but he failed to translate thought into action.[25]

War leadership brought out some of Wilson's greatest strengths and weaknesses as president. The strengths included a firm grasp of diplomatic and strategic goals, a willingness to delegate authority to able lieutenants, such as Baker, Daniels, and McAdoo, and an ability to pick gifted men from outside the political arena for key jobs in economic mobilization, most notably Bernard M. Baruch and Herbert Hoover. Wilson's chief contribution to the strictly military side of the war lay in allowing the professional soldiers to run the show with little meddling from civilian politicians. Not everything went well, particularly on the industrial front, but when all the shortcomings are accounted for, economic mobilization and support for the military effort rank among Wilson's greatest successes as president.[26]

His wartime diplomacy, against considerable odds, formed another area of achievement. One of the biggest ironies in Wilson's historical reputation has been the way that realist critics, especially in the 1940s and 1950s, used his prosecution of World War I as an example of the pitfalls of idealistic foreign policy. According to such writers as Walter Lippmann and George F. Kennan, Wilson gave a classic demonstration of failing to recognize security interests and limit objectives while becoming swept up in a messianic crusade. What Wilson really demonstrated was the difficulty of waging a war of limited commitments and objectives. During 1917 and 1918 he maintained a precarious balance between aid to the Allies and emphasis on separate American aims. "Peace without victory" remained his overriding goal. "You will realize how unfortunate it would be," Wilson warned House on the eve of an inter-Allied meeting in December 1917, "for the conference to discuss peace terms in a spirit antagonistic to my January address to the Senate." Nor did Wilson relax his suspicions of the war aims of the Allies, even Britain. "He questioned the desirability of drawing the two countries too closely together," Taft recorded Wilson telling him in December 1917. "He said that there were divergences of purpose and that the United States must not be put in a position of seeming, in any way, involved in British policy."[27]

Attacks from outside and subversion from within hampered Wilson's pursuit of his objectives. Roosevelt's sneer at "a limited liability war" typified the criticisms of pro-Allied stalwarts, who demanded total commitment and crushing victory. Anti-interventionist sentiment likewise persisted in many quarters, and the Socialists made impressive gains in various elections during 1917 as a vehicle for protest against the war. Liberal and socialist criticism also presented problems abroad, particularly after the Bolshevik revolution in November 1917. The strongest impetus for enunciation of the Fourteen Points in January 1918 came from an effort to counter Bolshevik antiwar propaganda. Wilson strove to rally labor and socialist elements in the Allied countries and to woo their German counterparts toward peace. The enemy's actions provided no help, either. The settlement the Germans imposed upon the Bolsheviks at Brest-Litovsk in February 1918 disclosed their harsh and grandiose war aims. Wilson was learning how hard it was to wage war for "peace without victory."[28]

His top diplomatic lieutenants added to his difficulties by their disloyalty. Secretary of State Lansing persisted in occasional open dissent from Wilson's policies and more frequent covert attempts to sabotage his pursuit of moderate war aims. During 1917 and 1918 Lansing found himself increasingly isolated from major decisions. Colonel House also enjoyed less influence than earlier, but Wilson continued to send him abroad for critical negotiations, during which House tried to compromise the president's separate war effort and peace program. At the Paris peace conference during the first half of 1919, Wilson lacked the diplomatic experience and well-trained, trustworthy lieutenants that the Allied leaders, Clemenceau and David Lloyd George, the British prime minister, possessed. He also differed with them on most of the major issues of the peace settlement. Wilson did not stand completely alone. In setting up the League of Nations, Wilson received indispensable assistance from the British diplomat Lord Robert Cecil and the South African leader Jan Christian Smuts. On the critical issue of allowing Germany to remain a strong, undivided power, he found an occasional ally in Lloyd George. Otherwise Wilson got little help as he struggled for a nonpunitive settlement based on the Fourteen Points and for ways to prevent future wars. The wonder was not that he fell short of complete success but that he, more than any other leader, shaped the peace.[29]

Wilson's performance at Paris was equally impressive because of other handicaps he had to overcome. The defeated Germans worsened the prospects for a "peace without victory" by immediately disbanding their armies and plunging into near revolutionary chaos. Without a credible threat from a resurgent Germany, Wilson lost one of his two strongest bargaining points with the Allies in seeking a moderate settlement. The other bargaining point, American commitment to a settlement, was weakened by reports of domestic opposition. Especially damaging was the round robin signed by thirty-seven Republican senators in February 1919, opposing membership in the League of Nations as then presented. Wilson had to compromise his diplomatic position by getting the Monroe Doctrine, tariffs, and immigration restriction explicitly exempted from League jurisdiction, in an effort to mollify opponents at home.[30]

Wilson's greatest handicap at Paris was his own failing health. Contrary to some later views, intervention and the burdens of belligerency had not subjected him to undue strain. With his usual discipline and capacity for delegating work, Wilson had fitted the business of mobilization and military strategy into his presidential routine, and he had found adequate time for rest and relaxation, particularly through golf games and automobile rides. In his wartime diplomacy, however, he had grown even more solitary and self-reliant than before. Moreover, according to contemporary accounts and later recollections, Wilson had begun to show signs of irritability, suspicion, and rigidity during the summer of 1918, particularly over questions involving peacemaking.[31]

The most glaring and politically costly manifestation of his growing isolation at the end of 1918 arose with his selection of delegates to the peace conference. Previously, Wilson had planned to include at least one prominent Republican, most likely Taft or Root. Now, however, he refused to appoint either of those men or anyone who did not strike him as totally sympathetic to his peace program. Wilson not only gave a spectacular demonstration of apparent partisanship by not naming any leading Republican, he also chose a weak delegation. The delegates included, besides Lansing and House, the retired diplomat Henry White as the token Republican and General Tasker H. Bliss as the military representative. In addition, by appointing no senators, Wilson failed to follow McKinley's precedent from the peace negotiations of 1898 after the Spanish-American War. That omission seemed more defensible. The Republican victory in November had made Lodge chairman of the Foreign Relations Committee, and it would have been an insult to invite anyone from the Senate without also inviting him.[32]

How much Wilson's health affected his behavior before the peace conference must remain a matter of speculation. Both his age—sixty-two at the end of 1918—and the progressive arteriosclerosis that soon caused the major stroke do seem to have had psychological ramifications. His solitariness and self-reliance appear to have hardened. During the peace conference Wilson's health made a demonstrable impact on his actions. Early in April 1919 he suffered a serious illness, which was reported to the press as influenza. Some writers have contended that the illness was really a minor stroke, and the changes in Wilson's behavior support their view. But it seems more probable, as Edwin A. Weinstein has argued, that Wilson did fall victim to influenza, which was then epidemic in Europe and America, and that the illness probably had neurological complications. Either way, Wilson's behavior changed. He became still more isolated, he gave unprecedented displays of anger and arbitrariness toward his staff, and he entertained fantasies about spies. Most important, he blamed House and broke with him for allegedly making concessions to the French during his illness. In fact, Wilson made those concessions himself in a euphoric mood immediately following his recovery.[33]

Between his return to the United States in July 1919 and his stroke three months later, Wilson's health apparently had further effects on his behavior. He acted toward the Senate with none of his old collegiality. Instead, he took a peremptory tone and missed opportunities to negotiate with sympathetic Republicans. In his address of July 10, presenting the peace treaty, Wilson called the League "the only hope for mankind," and he demanded of the senators, "Dare we reject it and break the heart of the world?" Failure to cultivate the handful of Republican senators who favored League membership with "mild reservations" was a serious tactical error. Together, those Republicans and Democratic loyalists would not have supplied the necessary two-thirds, but such a coalition would have conferred a measure of bipartisanship and constituted a majority. The onus of opposition on Lodge and his followers would thereby have been much heavier. Nor did Wilson conduct himself well when, at the senators' request, he met with the Foreign Relations Committee at the White House on August 19. The three-hour meeting featured a mutually unedifying, often testy discussion, mainly about obligations to enforce peace under the League Covenant.[34]

Rather than try to negotiate further with senators, Wilson plunged into a three-week tour through the Middle West and West during September 1919. He delivered forty speeches advocating full-fledged membership in the League of Nations, but he did not complete his original schedule. Severe headaches and exhaustion—warning symptoms of a stroke—forced him to cancel the last few engagements and rush back to Washington. Many observers at the time doubted Wilson's wisdom in making the speaking tour, because many critical or opposing senators announced that they would not be swayed by public opinion. After the stroke and revelations of his earlier poor health, a number of writers have speculated about whether his decision to make the tour revealed impaired judgment or a wish for martyrdom. None of those contemporary doubts and later questions have much validity. The speaking tour apparently did stir public support, and it is interesting to speculate about what might have happened if Wilson had completed the tour and had been able to exploit his improved bargaining advantage.[35]

Wilson's precedent for the speaking tour and for his dealings with the Senate in 1919 was the preparedness controversy three years earlier. Whether he might again have followed his arousal of public support with a strategic compromise can never be answered. Some students of the League controversy have contended that Wilson's rigid stand and unwillingness to consider objections would not have allowed him to meet his critics halfway, even if he had remained in perfect health. Other signs indicated, however, that the stroke did prevent a happier outcome. Wilson's speeches on the tour did not reveal a would-be messiah seeking martyrdom in a holy cause—that would have been Roosevelt's style. Rather, Wilson was trying once more to educate opinion through reasoned argument, especially by repeated assertions that America's fundamental self-interest lay in preventing another world war.[36]

Not just the stroke but, even more, Wilson's psychological mechanism for dealing with disability left him unable to appreciate the political reality of the situation. For nearly forty years, as Weinstein has shown, Wilson had responded to illness through denial—a practice that reinforced his tendencies toward relying only on himself and minimizing difficulties. The clearest previous example of such denial had been his advocacy of the quad plan at Princeton after the stroke in 1906. In 1919 a more severe stroke intervened at a different stage in the controversy. Its chief effect was to make him stand firm in a final showdown rather than, as before, to push a visionary plan at the outset. Wilson's recovery of collegiality after the quad plan dispute, his long practice of patient persuasion, and his sense of momentous stakes in the League controversy—all these factors indicate that he would have tried to find some basis for American membership, if the stroke had not so badly skewed his emotional outlook. Like Roosevelt's death in January 1919, Wilson's collapse nine months later had far-reaching consequences for the nation and the world.[37]

The failure of peacemaking in 1919 extended further. The outcome of the wrangles at Paris over peace terms and in the United States over League membership ultimately constituted tragedy. Doubts remain about whether the later breakdown of international order could have been prevented if Wilson had led his country into the League in 1919. The tragic flaw for Americans lay in their unwillingness to play a larger, more committed role in world politics. All Wilson's labors in 1919 at Paris and in the United States had not overcome that flaw. Roosevelt's basic criticism still applied. Wilson was asking his people to make commitments that they were not about to sustain. Roosevelt's death deepened the tragedy by transforming his legacy, through Lodge and others, into an instrument for thwarting Wilson's effort.

Like Roosevelt, Wilson owed at least a measure of his final failure to flaws in his leadership and character. Ironically, those flaws involved the area in which he had displayed his greatest talents—education of the public. Wilson failed to lead the United States to greater international commitment for two major reasons. One was that during the war he had not sufficiently awakened Americans to their involvement in world affairs. When he finally did take his case to the people in September 1919, he gave another brilliant display of his persuasive powers, but unfortunately his educational campaign came too late and did too little to instill sufficient popular awareness. The second major reason for Wilson's failure was that he had permitted unrealistic and conflicting expectations to arise about the purposes and prospects of his diplomacy. During 1917 and 1918 he had neglected to counteract expressions of excessively militant idealism, like Roosevelt's, or fantastic hopes for a universal reign of peace, freedom, and justice. The activities of his own administration, particularly propaganda by the Committee on Public Information, had compounded the problem. Wilson's first failure—insufficient elucidation of his aims—led to the public and politicians becoming rapidly sick of the whole business of peacemaking and League membership, once the deadlock developed between him and the Republican senators. His second failure—permissiveness toward excessive expectations— fed a more slowly developing disillusionment among idealists with all international commitments.

It would be hard to imagine a less constructive outcome to the domestic debate over the peace treaty than what occurred in 1920. Popular revulsion toward an invalid president whose administration seemed to be, and often was, out of control quickly erased support for League membership and also eroded much of the political base of Democrats and other reformers. The massive victory of Harding and the Old Guard Republicans in the 1920 elections not only inaugurated a new era of domestic conservatism, but it also closed off possibilities for most international commitments. In 1921 the Harding administration negotiated separate peace treaties that embodied the same terms laid down at Paris, except for the League Covenant and the administrative machinery for enforcing the settlement. Also scrapped was a security pact with Britain and France, to which Wilson had agreed at Paris and which Lodge and other former Roosevelt followers had deeply desired. By either set of guiding lights, Wilsonian or Rooseveltian, the commitment to a larger American role in world affairs lost badly in the political debacle at the end of World War I.[38]

Wilson and Lodge both died in 1924. Although their circumstances appeared totally different, each was a repudiated man. Lodge remained a senator and chairman of the Foreign Relations Committee for the rest of his life. He played a part as a power broker at the 1920 Republican convention, and he later aided the sometimes impressive diplomatic initiatives of Charles Evans Hughes, who became secretary of state in 1921. After 1920 Lodge talked like an isolationist. He frequently appealed to America's traditional avoidance of alliances. He also claimed that such Republican actions as Hughes's accomplishments with the Washington

Conference of 1921, which negotiated naval disarmament and Far Eastern security agreements, offered a much better basis for international order than the League of Nations or other schemes for the enforcement of peace. Even at their most resourceful, however, those actions were a far cry from Lodge's and Roosevelt's visions of American world leadership. The basic drift of foreign policy in the 1920s represented as great a repudiation of them as of Wilson. Lodge himself fared little better. Narrowly reelected to the Senate in 1922, he had already lost control of the Massachusetts Republicans. In 1924 he sat as an ignored, rank-and-file delegate to his last national convention, which nominated Calvin Coolidge, a despised home state rival, for president. Lodge died suddenly four days after Coolidge's sweeping victory in the November election.[39]

When Wilson died on February 3, 1924, his failures were not masked by outward appearances. His physical condition had ruled out a bid for a third term in 1920, although he did try to make some moves in that direction. As in 1912, the 1920 Democratic convention featured another prolonged deadlock among leading contenders, and domestic issues again dominated, especially those involving the party's widening urban-rural split. Unlike the situation eight years earlier, however, none of the main contenders got the nomination. Governor James M. Cox of Ohio emerged as a compromise choice, principally because he had no connection with the Wilson administration. The president's followers received a consolation prize with the vice-presidential nomination of Assistant Secretary of the Navy Franklin D. Roosevelt. The thirty-eight-year-old New Yorker was an administration loyalist and an enthusiastic advocate of League membership. As both a distant cousin and husband of the niece of Theodore Roosevelt, he also enjoyed a politically attractive name and family ties. Cox's efforts to establish his independence and to downplay international concerns proved unavailing. Wilson and the League issue hung like a pall over the Democratic campaign. The 1920 election did not, as several scholars have pointed out, constitute a foreign policy referendum, but it was an unmistakable repudiation of Wilson. The election closed out most of his domestic and foreign policies as viable political options, even if Harding had had any desire to pursue them.[40]

Physical deterioration followed political defeat for Wilson. He outlived his apparently healthy successor and made one of his last public appearances to ride in Harding's funeral procession in October 1923. But it was clear that he did not have long to live after he left the White House. Wilson regarded both political repudiation and approaching death with a serenity that amazed his family and friends. His accepting attitude flowed from several sources. His religious faith, which had become warmer but still less sectarian in his later years, had always inclined him toward an optimistic fatalism about himself. Physical decline and psychological denial combined to shield him from harsh realities. At various times during the last year of his life, Wilson stated that he had done his most important work before entering politics and that as president he had accomplished the most in domestic affairs during his first term. Those judgments served in part to rationalize his failure in foreign affairs and his political downfall.[41]

Yet Wilson's last thoughts about his public career revealed that he gained perspective and insight as he neared the end of his life. Nothing indicated his understanding better than his final reflections on the events of 1919. Wilson's assertion to his brother-in-law that it was better that he had not won "a mere personal victory" on League membership showed that he had regained his conception of leadership through representation and education of popular opinion. Those thoughts about the peacemaking controversy also disclosed that Wilson had apprehended the underlying reasons for his failure. To his oldest daughter he similarly confided, "I think it was best after all that the United States did not join the League of Nations." When she asked why, he explained that instead of registering "only a personal victory" for him, "Now, when the American people join the League it will be because they are convinced it is the right thing to do, and then will be the *only right* time for them to do it." With a smile he added, "Perhaps God knew better than I did after all."[42]

Woodrow Wilson was implicitly acknowledging that Theodore Roosevelt had known better, too. Within twenty years an aroused and remorseful public and the chastened political heirs of both men would form a deeply based bipartisan consensus for an American role in world affairs that fulfilled both men's dreams. When he went to his grave with serene acknowledgment of his own failure, Wilson grasped a major aspect of his place in history.

· 21 ·
Legacies

THE COUNTRY'S REACTION against the political legacies of Theodore Roosevelt and Woodrow Wilson did not last long. For the Republicans much of the politics of the 1920s reverted to pre-1912 patterns. Once more the Old Guard bosses and their big business allies, backed by electoral majorities in the Northeast and Middle West, prevailed. The Republican insurgents drew upon much the same following and often the same leaders as earlier. La Follette, Norris, Borah, and others resumed their previous struggles within the party and in Congress. Postwar dissidence against the Republicans also spawned such separatist movements as the Non-Partisan League on the Great Plains, the Farmer-Labor Party in Minnesota, and La Follette's presidential candidacy on a Progressive ticket in 1924. Nearly all the Republican insurgents of the 1920s, except La Follette, held Roosevelt's memory dear, and two of his most prominent Progressive lieutenants joined their ranks. Hiram W. Johnson, who had entered the Senate in 1917, became another leading maverick on Capitol Hill. Gifford Pinchot beat the remnants of Penrose's machine to become governor of Pennsylvania and to contest Coolidge's nomination in 1924.[1]

Even the national convention, the bastion of Republican pro-business conservatism, did not remain immune to a leader who drew upon Roosevelt's methods, policies, and appeals. In 1928 the party forsook its prior devotion to Harding's genial complacency and Coolidge's masterly inactivity to nominate a dynamic presidential candidate from outside regular channels. Herbert Hoover had risen to the top both through the immense personal popularity he had gained through his services during World War I and his shrewdly publicized activities as secretary of commerce under Harding and Coolidge. A one-time Progressive, Hoover pursued governmental policies in the 1920s of fostering business consolidation, rationalizing markets, and improving wages and working conditions—all of which harked back to elements of the New Nationalism. When he won a smashing victory in the 1928 election, Hoover reopened the road to the White House that Roosevelt had built.[2]

Hoover's rise owed even more to Wilson. Hoover's appointments by the president during the World War had kicked off his public career, and economic mobilization had supplied much of the precedent for his promotion of cooperation between government and business. As president, Hoover softened the Republicans' repudiation of Wilson's foreign policies. He opened contacts with the League of Nations, and he sought a coordinated response with the European powers to the Japanese conquest of Manchuria in 1931. Yet Hoover's policies at home and abroad represented at best a selective adaptation of Roosevelt's and Wilson's legacies, squarely within the Republican mainstream of the 1920s. His domestic policies departed from Roosevelt's by stressing voluntarism and equality between government and business, not governmental direction and primacy. Those policies differed still more from Wilson's in that they eschewed an adversarial relation between government and business and rejected promotion of the interests of less advantaged groups and areas. In foreign policy Hoover ruled out virtually all use of force, either as a primary instrument of American diplomacy, along Rooseveltian lines, or as a last resort in maintaining international order, after the Wilsonian design. At home and abroad Hoover's echoes of Roosevelt and Wilson were consistently muted.

It fell to the Democrats to reclaim more fully and directly the political estates of both men. For the Democrats, the 1920s also resurrected earlier patterns. Their 1924 convention topped the 1920 one for the urban-rural deadlock, which had first surfaced in 1912. Again in 1924 they failed to nominate a strong contender who could bridge the factional chasm as Wilson had done. The party deadlock ended in 1928 with the nomination of Alfred E. Smith. As a Catholic, opponent of Prohibition, and governor of New York,

Smith had emerged as the leader of the urban, ethnic-based faction. His nomination transferred to the electoral arena much of the hitherto internal party conflict. Large numbers of southern and western rural-based Protestant Democrats either bolted or tended to stay home on election day, thereby swelling Hoover's margin of victory. Not until the nomination of Franklin Roosevelt in 1932 did the Democrats choose a candidate who filled Wilson's shoes by overcoming intraparty divisions and by emphasizing economic concerns and reform. Ironically, one of the prices Roosevelt paid for the nomination in 1932 was repudiation of his previous advocacy of League membership. That year the Democrats dropped all mention of the League from their platform and ended what had been one of their few gestures toward Wilson's memory.[3]

Personal and political circumstances combined uncannily to make Franklin Roosevelt inherit the mantles of both Theodore Roosevelt and Woodrow Wilson. As a distant cousin, his family ties with the earlier Roosevelt had begun at birth. Those ties had grown much closer with his marriage in 1905 to Eleanor Roosevelt in a ceremony at which the president had given away the bride, his niece. From the beginning of his political career in 1910 Franklin self-consciously trod in Theodore's footsteps. First he battled the bosses in the New York legislature, then he served from 1913 to 1920 as assistant secretary of the Navy, and finally he ran for vice-president—all following his kinsman's example. In his early years at the Navy Department, the younger Roosevelt often acted as an undercover agent for "Uncle Ted" and Senator Lodge. He leaked damaging information to them about preparedness and covertly tried to undermine his chief, Secretary Daniels. On the issues of preparedness and the Allies, he was a Rooseveltian in the Wilson camp. After the United States entered the war, however, he came to admire Daniels, and he also became personally devoted to Wilson and emerged as an ardent supporter of the League of Nations.[4]

Those experiences, together with his party allegiance, also made Franklin Roosevelt the political heir of Wilson. Why he originally joined the Democrats, aside from loosely held family tradition and personal opportunity, is unclear, but after the war and the 1920 campaign he remained a Wilson loyalist. The crippling attack of poliomyelitis that Roosevelt suffered in 1921 removed him from the worst of the party infighting of the next few years. He supported Smith, but he also helped found the Woodrow Wilson Foundation and organized an effort to revive "progressivism" among Democrats. When Roosevelt won the New York governorship in 1928, he automatically gained the launching point toward the presidency enjoyed formerly by Smith, Hughes, and the earlier Roosevelt. When he sought the Democratic nomination in 1932, he garnered support from his state party and some old-line Wilsonians such as Colonel House, who had continued his high-level political dabbling. For the most part, however, Roosevelt had to prevail over opposition from hard-core urban-ethnic elements—who backed a futile comeback bid by Smith—and from diehard Wilsonians—who supported Newton D. Baker as the true keeper of their flame.[5]

Roosevelt's first administration initially was much less of a Wilsonian restoration than might have been expected. In part the administration's break with the past reflected Roosevelt's previous lack of support from the Wilsonian faction of the Democratic party. Cabinet posts did go to two southerners who revered Wilson's memory. Cordell Hull became secretary of state, and Daniel C. Roper was named secretary of commerce. Neither man acquired great influence in administration policy, however. In foreign affairs Roosevelt bowed for nearly five years to swelling isolationist sentiment in Congress and among the public. He also conferred major ambassadorial appointments on William C. Bullitt, a bitterly outspoken critic of Wilson. In foreign trade policy Roosevelt gave no encouragement for nearly two years to Hull's cherished project of lowering tariffs in line with Wilson's achievement twenty years before. Meanwhile, from his seat on the Supreme Court, Brandeis, the second-ranking architect of the New Freedom, viewed the administration's most important domestic initiatives during 1933 and 1934 with skepticism and scorn.[6]

The ostensible reason for the discontinuity with the last Democratic administration was the economic crisis Roosevelt faced in 1933. The Great Depression, which had brought Hoover's downfall, presented Roosevelt's greatest challenge. He responded from the beginning by stressing novelty and experimentation. He ostentatiously flouted the custom of both major parties by imitating Theodore Roosevelt's appearance before the Progressives in 1912. Immediately after his nomination in July 1932, Roosevelt flew in an airplane to Chicago and addressed the Democratic convention. "Let it also be symbolic that in so doing I broke traditions," he declared in his speech. "Let it be from now on the task of our Party to break foolish traditions." Roosevelt lauded "the great indomitable, unquenchable, progressive soul of our Commander-in-Chief, Woodrow Wilson," but he dwelled mainly on Republican failures and coined the slogan of his campaign and administration. "I pledge you, I pledge myself," he concluded, "to a new deal for the American people."[7]

Yet as Roosevelt's imitation of his kinsman suggested, his appeal to newness was borrowed from the earlier Progressives. Two former party activists joined his cabinet and ranked among the most influential figures in the New Deal. Harold Ickes served as secretary of the interior during Roosevelt's entire presidency and also headed the Public Works Administration. Henry A. Wallace spent nearly eight years as secretary of agriculture before he was elected vice-president during Roosevelt's third term. Another ex-Progressive, Donald Richberg, was second in command and later head of the spearhead agency of early New Deal industrial policy, the National Recovery Administration. The NRA pushed a program of cooperative planning with business, suspension of antitrust laws, and control of production and working conditions—all of which drew upon New Nationalist ideas. More broadly, national self-sufficiency and centralized economic direction characterized the views of Roosevelt's most important advisers in 1933 and 1934. In personnel and inspiration the New Deal at its outset marked something of a Theodore Rooseveltian restoration.[8]

The influence of his kinsman ran deeper than policies and appointments. Roosevelt's basic approach to the Depression was what William E. Leuchtenburg has called "the analogue of war." Roosevelt drew the analogy explicitly in his inaugural address on March 4, 1933, when he admonished, "If we are to go forward we must move as a trained and loyal army willing to sacrifice for the good of a common discipline . . . pledging that the larger purposes will bind upon us all with a unity of duty hitherto evoked only in time of armed strife." Roosevelt left little doubt about the source of his vision of united action and transcendent purpose. "The money-changers have fled from their high seats in the temple of our civilization," he declared. Americans recognized "the falsity of material wealth as the standard of success," and they were learning that happiness "lies not in the mere possession of money; it lies in the joy of achievement, in the thrill of creative effort." Not only Roosevelt's upper-class New York accent but also his phrases and underlying viewpoint recalled the earlier president with the same name.[9]

National leadership to transcend self-interest, after Theodore Roosevelt's model, remained Franklin Roosevelt's favorite political role throughout twelve years in the White House. His election to four consecutive terms has obscured the division of his presidency into two distinct phases. The first phase, dominated by the domestic concerns of the Depression, ended midway through his second term. A convergence of setbacks—defeat of his plan to enlarge the Supreme Court in 1937, severe recession also that year, and political deadlock stemming from his unsuccessful party purge and the Republican resurgence in 1938—largely undid Roosevelt's domestic presidency. Fortuitously, international crises in Asia in 1937 and in Europe in 1938 and the outbreak of World War II in 1939 allowed him to shift his major concern to foreign affairs. Without that shift, Roosevelt would almost certainly have neither sought nor won a third term in 1940 and a fourth in 1944. The shift also allowed him to resume the Theodore Rooseveltian role of national leader, which he had played during the early days of the New Deal.[10]

Between those efforts at national leadership fell a period of party leadership after the Wilsonian model. By early 1935 a combination of circumstances—slowness of economic recovery, defections by business and conservative spokesmen, and especially, mounting pressures from radical elements within and outside the Democratic party—forced Roosevelt to alter his political stance. How self-conscious was the shift of roles, Roosevelt disclosed in March 1935. Wilson's biographer, Ray Stannard Baker, wrote to urge him to follow Wilson's example by explaining his larger purposes to the public, but the president responded by invoking, as a contrary example, the earlier Roosevelt, whom Baker had not mentioned. "Theodore Roosevelt lacked Woodrow Wilson's appeal to the fundamental," he claimed, "and failed to stir, as Wilson did, the truly profound moral and social convictions. Wilson, on the other hand, failed where Theodore Roosevelt succeeded in stirring people to enthusiasm over specific individual events, even though these specific events may have been superficial in comparison with the fundamentals."[11]

That statement revealed what vivid models Roosevelt's predecessors formed in his mind. Moreover, by reversing their actual political roles, his invocation of them exposed his reluctance to abandon transcendent national leadership. The lesser contribution he ascribed to Theodore Roosevelt came closer to describing both Wilson's basic approach and the one Franklin Roosevelt himself pursued in domestic politics during the next three years. Historians have disagreed about how substantial a shift occurred in 1935 from previous New Deal policies. They have also differed over whether the initiatives of those years—often called the "Second New Deal"—were fundamentally Wilsonian, either inspired by New Freedom ideas or influenced by devotees of those ideas, particularly Brandeis. Those debates have failed to grasp the main point. Between 1935 and 1938 Roosevelt completed the task Wilson had begun. He aligned a majority coalition of disadvantaged interest groups—economic, social, and sectional—behind the Democratic party. It was one of his two most lasting and significant political achievements.[12]

In part by railing against "economic royalists" and "stealing the thunder" from Huey Long's call to redistribute wealth, Roosevelt triumphed in the 1936 election. He won more than 60 percent of the popular vote and carried every state but two. More important, Roosevelt forged the majority status that the Democrats would enjoy for more than forty years. His true accomplishment became clear during the next four years. In 1938, despite Democratic dissension and Republican resurgence, his party retained control of both houses of Congress by comfortable, though greatly reduced, majorities. In 1940, despite the unpopularity of Roosevelt's seeking a third term, the divisiveness of foreign policy issues, and the attractiveness of his Republican challenger, he won another reelection with a respectable popular margin and a large majority in the electoral college. His winning coalition drew primarily upon ethnic and poorer voters in the Northeast and Middle West. During the following four decades the Democrats won the presidency five out of eight times and lost control of Congress for only four years.[13]

Franklin Roosevelt's establishment of an enduring Democratic majority produced the supreme irony of his career. The international crisis at the end of the 1930s, which renewed his lease on the Theodore Rooseveltian role of transcendent national leader, was what furnished his opportunity to fulfill the Wilsonian role of party leader. Roosevelt's performance in that role repeated much of Wilson's earlier experience, with both similar and different consequences.

The chief similarity lay in the relationship between partisanship and ideology. Just as had happened twenty years before, when Wilson had appropriated "progressivism" for the Democrats, the Republicans took a clear-cut stand in opposition. As early as the 1932 campaign, when Hoover stated his deeply held beliefs in voluntarism and at least implicitly excused his presidential failures, he stressed governmental limitation and the indispensability of private economic initiative. In 1936 the Republicans tried to take a different tack. They adopted an outspokenly though vaguely "progressive" platform and nominated a national ticket of erstwhile followers of Theodore Roosevelt. Presidential candidate Alfred M. Landon had been an active Progressive in Kansas; vice-presidential candidate Frank Knox had fought with the Rough Riders and had published Progressive-affiliated newspapers. But the Republicans' grab at a "progressive" mantle proved unavailing. The 1936 campaign witnessed a shift into the Republican camp of state-rights, limited-government Democrats, particularly through their organization, the American Liberty League. A combination of organizational and financial support by the Liberty League and the difficulty of attacking Roosevelt except from an antistatist, pro-business standpoint pushed the Republicans inexorably to the right. The 1936 election featured the clearest ideological division between the two major parties since Wilson's reelection in 1916. The division endured to provide the basis of party alignment through five decades.[14]

After 1936 ideological nonconformists in both parties found themselves in increasingly uncomfortable positions. For the Democrats, party success and Roosevelt's popularity helped keep more conservative southerners in line for a while. But with the reemergence of racial justice as a major political issue starting in the late 1930s, southern white Democrats became a dissident faction. From the 1940s through the 1960s, white southerners would play much the same role in the Democratic party as middle western and western insurgents had previously played with the Republicans. Every election from 1944 through 1968 occasioned either separatist southern presidential efforts or refusals by prominent white southern Democrats to support the national ticket. Southern Democrats in Congress formed a bloc in opposition to many of the party's programs, particularly the growing commitment of the power of the federal government to promote civil rights of black Americans. The South's anomalous position within the Democratic party did not end until the 1960s and 1970s, when political realignment in the region brought newly reenfranchised blacks into the party and pushed out the more conservative whites. By the middle of the 1970s two-party competition along the same lines as in the rest of the country prevailed in the South.[15]

Ideological dissidents among Republicans fared worse. The two bases for earlier nonconformity—middle western and western groups and Theodore Roosevelt's urban, upper-middle-class followers—met varying fates. In the late 1930s and early 1940s middle western and western Republican insurgency withered. Domestic issues, particularly Roosevelt's "court-packing" plan in 1937, combined with foreign policy concerns to bring most, though not all, of the leading Republican insurgents on Capitol Hill into greater harmony with their party than at any time since Theodore Roosevelt's presidency. The third-party movements, the Minnesota Farmer-Laborites and the Progressives in Wisconsin, collapsed during World War II. They repeated the earlier Progressives' experience not only of disbanding during a war but also of scattering their subsequent loyalties. Their leading politicians returned to the Republicans, but a majority of their followers eventually became Democrats. "Moderate" Republicans from the Middle West and West still sometimes attained prominence, but for the most part the erstwhile heartland of insurgency became the party's most stalwart conservative base.[16]

A generation after his death, Theodore Roosevelt's political legacy enjoyed greater acceptance in his home region and among his social and political peers than it had during his lifetime. Among Republicans after 1940, views favorable to a larger governmental role in economic and social affairs and a more active, committed foreign policy flourished mostly among educated, socially elite groups, principally in the Northeast. Because Franklin Roosevelt also appealed to members of those groups, prominent figures from such backgrounds sometimes became Democrats, most notably Averell Harriman and Dean Acheson. Moreover, the twentieth-century presidency most closely modeled, albeit largely unconsciously, on Theodore Roosevelt's was also Democratic. When he put greatest stress on world leadership, advocated domestic reforms for the sake of strength and image abroad, and purveyed quasi-aristocratic cultural patronage, John F. Kennedy came closer to duplicating Theodore Roosevelt's viewpoint and approach than did any of his successors, even Franklin Roosevelt. Kennedy's exploitation of the public dimensions of his office, the retrospectively legendary aura surrounding his presidency, and his factional and family political legacies—those, too, recalled the first Roosevelt.

The true home of the Theodore Rooseveltian viewpoint remained, however, among Republicans in the Northeast, particularly New Yorkers. Two Republicans with expansive views of the role of government at home and abroad, Thomas E. Dewey and Nelson A. Rockefeller, between them held the New York governorship for nearly thirty years and played leading roles in the national party. Even before he was elected governor, Dewey made a strong bid for the Republican presidential nomination in 1940. After he entered the statehouse, Dewey did become the party's standard bearer in 1944 and 1948. Rockefeller was a major contender for the presidential nomination in 1960, 1964, and 1968, and he served as vice-president from 1974 to 1977. Their breed of northeastern Republicans exerted the greatest influence through foreign affairs. In 1940 they used international concerns to win the nomination for Wendell Willkie; during and after World War II they promoted bipartisan agreement for international commitments, and in 1952 they appealed to such bipartisanship to persuade Dwight D. Eisenhower to seek the nomination and win the presidency. A major figure in the later bipartisan efforts was Henry Cabot Lodge, Jr., the grandson and political heir of Roosevelt's friend and cohort.

The influence of those Republicans waned after 1960 as the party moved consistently to the right. Several promising younger "liberal" Republicans switched to the Democrats in the 1970s, while defeat thinned the ranks of their elders. Rockefeller's vice-presidency was the last national recognition accorded that wing of the party; despite being the incumbent, he was dumped from the ticket in 1976. Four years later the separate presidential candidacy of Representative John B. Anderson of Illinois marked a final, forlorn gasp from both the old bases of Republican insurgency. It came at a time when the party elected the most "conservative" candidate since Harding. The victory of Ronald W. Reagan—the most deeply committed antigovernmental devotee of private enterprise to enter the White House in a century—completed the Republican ideological alignment that had begun to take shape in 1936. Some of Reagan's political appeal has derived from a nostalgic nationalism that has been occasionally and mistakenly associated with Theodore Roosevelt. In fact, Reagan's fondness for private wealth and his vows to "get government off our backs" offer a fundamental rejection of Roosevelt's approach to politics.

Much of the ideological differentiation of the two major parties since the 1930s has stemmed from the ways in which Franklin Roosevelt fulfilled the legacies of Theodore Roosevelt and Woodrow Wilson in domestic and foreign affairs. In domestic affairs one of the two dominant concerns was governmental power. During Roosevelt's first term, fears of excessive concentration of, and inadequate checks on, federal power under New Deal programs alienated not only state-rights Democrats and Old Guard Republicans but also long-standing reformers from insurgent Republican, Progressive, and Democratic backgrounds. But the most important turning point in the public's concern over governmental power and, indeed, of his entire domestic presidency occurred in 1937, with the court-packing controversy.

When he proposed to enlarge the Supreme Court, Franklin Roosevelt followed once more in Theodore Roosevelt's footsteps by attempting to limit judicial obstruction of reform measures supported by popular and legislative majorities. Like the earlier Roosevelt nearly thirty years before, he laid himself open to charges of usurpation, and he appeared to confirm his critics' worst suspicions. Franklin Roosevelt's almost incredible tactical blunders and the resourceful opposition of Hughes, who had earlier succeeded Taft as chief justice, hurt the court-packing plan badly, but the main reason for its failure was widespread fear of tampering with basic constitutional safeguards. In Congress the plan drew opposition

from a broad coalition, including not only conservatives from both
parties but also nearly all insurgent Republicans and a number of
"radical" southern and western Democrats. For many of those
erstwhile reformers, the court-packing fight of 1937 marked the
start of a permanent swing to the right. Ideologically, the controversy served further to enshrine limitation of governmental power
as a fundamental tenet of the right wing in American politics. In
that way Franklin Roosevelt confirmed and extended his kinsman's
heritage. [17]

The other major concern arising from the domestic side of his
presidency reflected his Wilsonian legacy. One of the major anom-
alies that struck observers at the time and that has been noted by
historians since was the opposition to the New Deal by former
adherents of the various schools of "progressivism." Even at a
discount for differences of age, personal circumstance, and partisanship, the break between the two reform eras remains striking.
Some of the opposition sprang from concern over governmental
power. Even under Wilson a number of southern Democrats had
only grudgingly accepted greater governmental intervention in
economic and social affairs. Wilson's own southern credentials and
the overwhelming inattention of northern whites to issues of racial
justice had served to allay their restiveness. In the 1930s, however,
several developments—including the renewed concern of northern
whites over civil rights issues, shifts of black voters in northern
cities to the Democrats, and sympathetic gestures toward racial
equality by certain New Dealers, most notably Eleanor Roosevelt
and Harold Ickes—undermined white southern acceptance of governmental activism. From a different perspective, such earlier reformers as Amos Pinchot and Oswald Garrison Villard had grown to
fear a strong, unchecked state because they had opposed intervention in World War I and had deplored the administration's
repression of civil liberties in 1917 and 1918. For them and for
others, particularly former Republican insurgents, opposition to
intervention in World War II further heightened their antistatist
convictions. [18]

Even those concerns did not account, however, for some of the
most noteworthy opposition to the New Deal, from former
Progressives and admirers of Theodore Roosevelt, who still shared
their idol's relish for greater and more concentrated governmental
power. Their opposition reflected the other concern that domi-

nated domestic politics in the 1930s—lack of transcendent national purpose. Such men as Henry L. Stimson and Donald Richberg opposed the New Deal after 1935 on the same grounds on which Theodore Roosevelt had earlier rejected the New Freedom—that it failed to rise above parochial interests and serve higher ideals. Despite his name, social background, and unmistakable echoes of his kinsman, Franklin Roosevelt attracted even less support from their upper-class peers. The main reason why northeastern Republicans became the principal repository of Theodore Roosevelt's political legacy was that Franklin Roosevelt repeated Wilson's accomplishment of forging a coalition of disadvantaged interest groups behind the Democrats. The repeated calls of moderate, northeastern Republicans for a "national purpose" and their condemnations of both the Democrats and their own party for serving narrow interests leavened the main ideological conflict between the two parties. But Theodore Roosevelt's Republican heirs followed their mentor as prophets without honor among their own kind. They found their greatest utility in foreign affairs and their greatest appreciation from such Democrats as Franklin Roosevelt and John Kennedy.[19]

Partisan and ideological alignments over foreign policy likewise reflected Franklin Roosevelt's fulfillment of his predecessors' legacies. The second of his two lasting political achievements was to build a broad and deep bipartisan consensus behind American leadership in world affairs. Roosevelt not only succeeded where Wilson had failed, but he also owed at least a portion of his success to learning from Wilson's mistakes. Almost as soon as World War II broke out, Roosevelt started cultivating bipartisan ties. In 1940 he brought Henry Stimson and Frank Knox into his cabinet as secretaries of war and the navy. He also cooperated with the principal pro-Allied organization, the Committee to Defend America by Aiding the Allies, headed by another Republican, William Allen White, and after the election he sent Wendell Willkie to Britain as his special emissary. When the United States entered the war, Roosevelt pursued a low-keyed approach to war aims and allowed the drive for a new international peacekeeping organization to originate with members of both parties on Capitol Hill.

Wilsonian precedents and overtones did stand out in Roosevelt's policies. His proclamation of the "Four Freedoms" in January 1941 unmistakably recalled the Fourteen Points, as did his joint declaration with the British prime minister, Winston Churchill, of the Atlantic Charter the following August. After the United States entered World War II a massive upsurge occurred in popular regard for the memory of Wilson. Books, magazines, and even a motion picture harped on the need to atone for the country's failure to heed Wilson's warnings and adopt his policies. Such sentiments aided the efforts to enlist public opinion in support of foreign policy commitments. The precipitate conversion of leading Republicans to a larger international role also fostered bipartisan cooperation. The two parties agreed to exempt war aims and peacekeeping plans from debate in the 1944 campaign. Republicans and members of both houses of Congress participated in the conferences that led to the establishment of the United Nations in May 1945. Three months later the Senate gave its consent to American membership with only two dissenting votes. Unfortunately, Franklin Roosevelt had died on April 12, 1945, and did not witness his completion of Wilson's work.[20]

At heart, however, Roosevelt did not subscribe to a Wilsonian model in his foreign policy. Instead, as several scholars have pointed out, his wartime diplomacy followed more traditional notions of great-power leadership, and he regarded what he considered Wilson's excessive idealism as a pitfall to be avoided. Except for his enthusiasm for the League of Nations at the end of World War I and his willingness to bow to the isolationist upsurge in the mid-1930s, Franklin Roosevelt always drew his greatest inspiration in foreign affairs from Theodore Roosevelt. His foreign policies from late 1937 until America's entry into World War II at the end of 1941 did not resemble Wilson's course from 1914 to 1917, but the line his kinsman might have pursued if he had been in power at either of those times. Franklin Roosevelt made no secret of his sympathies for Britain and France. In 1939 he committed the United States to differential neutrality in favor of the Allies, and from the summer of 1940 he moved steadily toward quasi-belligerency on their side. Some of Theodore Roosevelt's admirers, however, castigated the president for not moving more boldly toward intervention, as they somewhat inaccurately remembered his kinsman having done before 1917.[21]

The path of heroic defiance did not lie open to Franklin Roosevelt. Pro-Allied sympathies in the United States coexisted uneasily with even stronger anti-interventionist sentiments. Neither political party showed the slightest inclination toward promoting intervention in World War II. Like Wilson before him, Roosevelt was almost certainly pushing his party much further toward a more assertive foreign policy than any other leading Democrat would have done. Conversely, the great bulk of the Republicans took anti-interventionist stands. Roosevelt's appointment of Stimson and Knox and his attempts to invoke his kinsman's legacy did little to dampen Republican opposition to his foreign policies. Despite his own views, Willkie charged Roosevelt with "warmongering" during the 1940 campaign. Roughly seven-eighths of the Republicans in both houses of Congress repeatedly voted against measures to aid the Allies in 1940 and 1941. Theodore Roosevelt's daughter Alice and his one-time Progressive protégé, Representative Hamilton Fish of New York, became outspoken isolationists. Under conditions like those, no one would have understood better than "Uncle Ted" the need for caution, manipulation, and often deviousness in seeking to play the right American role in the world.

Franklin Roosevelt's establishment of a lasting foreign policy consensus was the greatest fulfillment of Theodore Roosevelt's political legacy. That achievement embodied both the salutary and the potentially dangerous sides of his kinsman's approach to politics. The United States emerged from World War II as a world leader and then commenced a twenty-year career of global involvement and intervention, with virtually no effective dissent or questioning at home. Especially in the early 1960s, America bestrode the world as a colossus. It bent other peoples and powers to its will and justified its actions in militantly idealistic language. Not until the disasters of intervention in Vietnam after 1965 did questions about the necessity and wisdom of such globalism become respectable. Then, ironically, much of the questioning came from self-styled realists, who blamed overreaching policies since World War II on an overblown idealism, supposedly Wilson's main legacy.

Actually, Wilson's greatest influence on policymakers in foreign affairs from Franklin Roosevelt onward was as an example to be shunned. As his remark to Ray Stannard Baker in 1935 indicated, the chief lesson Roosevelt drew from Wilson was not to pitch his appeals to people too high or to expect too much in the way of educating the public. The deviousness and self-deception in his policies toward the warring powers from 1939 through 1941 reflected that lesson. The main lessons that Roosevelt's successors have drawn from his foreign policies have been that the public usually has to be either hoodwinked or inflamed into pursuing the right course and that attempting to educate the people only invites trouble. The much-discussed and frequently condemned "imperial presidency" of the middle of the twentieth century has been Franklin Roosevelt's chief legacy to his presidential successors. Inasmuch as Theodore Roosevelt was his alternative model to Wilson, he derived the "imperial presidency" from a genuinely imperialist source.[22]

Franklin Roosevelt's death in 1945 ended the last direct personal link with the political legacies of Theodore Roosevelt and Woodrow Wilson. For nearly all his successors, he himself became the great positive or negative model. Domestic and foreign policy debates in succeeding decades have flowed largely from the precedents of the New Deal and World War II. Wilson and the earlier Roosevelt have receded into the realm of historical curiosity, albeit often a lively and controversial curiosity. The Rough-Rider-as-President has continued to evoke a fond but misplaced nostalgia in a time of frustratingly complex international affairs. To some the preacher of world peace has offered inspiration, but more often he has served as an object lesson of unwise "idealism." Both men deserve better from posterity, and in deeper, unacknowledged ways, they have received better at the hands of their political descendants. The approaches that they opened to foreign and domestic affairs in an industrial age have persisted, even as their ideas and policies have undergone repeated metamorphoses. Recent adherents to their positions in domestic and foreign affairs often have not recognized the origins of those inclinations. Yet, as with the earlier influences of Jefferson and Hamilton, their ideological legacies remain to be rediscovered, pondered, and applied anew. Theodore Roosevelt and Woodrow Wilson still stand as the principal architects of modern American politics.

Notes
Acknowledgments
Index

Abbreviations

EA(W)	Ellen Axson (Wilson)
RSB	Ray Stannard Baker
WJB	William Jennings Bryan
EBG(W)	Edith Bolling Galt (Wilson)
EMH	Edward M. House
MAH(P)	Mary Allen Hulbert (Peck)
HCL	Henry Cabot Lodge
TR	Theodore Roosevelt
WHT	William Howard Taft
WW	Woodrow Wilson

Works

RSB MSS	Ray Stannard Baker Papers, Library of Congress
TRA	*Presidential Addresses and State Papers by Theodore Roosevelt*, ed. Albert Shaw, 8 vols. (New York, 1910)
TRL	*The Letters of Theodore Roosevelt*, ed. Elting E. Morison, 8 vols. (Cambridge, Mass., 1951–1954)
TRW	*The Works of Theodore Roosevelt*, national edition, ed. Hermann Hagedorn (New York, 1925)
WWP	*The Papers of Woodrow Wilson*, ed. Arthur S. Link, 42 vols. to date (Princeton, 1966–)
WWPP	*The Public Papers of Woodrow Wilson*, ed. Ray Stannard Baker and William E. Dodd, 6 vols. (New York, 1925–1927)

Notes

1. Knickerbocker and Gray

1. Lewis Einstein, *Roosevelt: His Mind in Action* (Boston, 1930), 8–9. For examples of Roosevelt's downplaying his advantages and gifts, see TR to Richard Watson Gilder, Aug. 20, 1903, quoted in Joseph B. Bishop, *Theodore Roosevelt and His Times* (New York, 1920), I, 2; and TR, *Autobiography, TRW*, XX, 54–55.

2. *TRW*, XX, 30. On his adolescent transformation, see the comment in Corrinne Roosevelt Robinson, *My Brother Theodore Roosevelt* (New York, 1922), 94. Excellent accounts of his family and youth are in Carleton Putnam, *Theodore Roosevelt: The Formative Years* (New York, 1958); Edmund Morris, *The Rise of Theodore Roosevelt* (New York, 1978); and David McCullough, *Mornings on Horseback* (New York, 1981).

3. On Roosevelt's tastes in sports, see TR to Walter Camp, Mar. 11, 1895, *TRL*, VIII, 1434; and Alexander Lambert, "Roosevelt the Companion," *TRW*, II, 386. Except for tennis, he never cared for or was good at games that primarily required skill and coordination.

4. Roosevelt quoted in Owen Wister, *Roosevelt: The Story of a Friendship* (New York, 1930), 331; TR, *Autobiography, TRW*, XX, 55. The self-created aspect of Roosevelt's character has been remarked upon variously by a number of writers. The most perceptive comments are in Edward Wagenknecht, *The Seven Worlds of Theodore Roosevelt* (New York, 1958), 2, 3, 23, 157; Einstein, *Roosevelt*, v–vi; and Nicholas Roosevelt, *Theodore Roosevelt: The Man as I Knew Him* (New York, 1967), 62–63.

5. Robinson, *My Brother*, 50; TR to Edward S. Martin, Nov. 26, 1900, *TRL*, II, 1443. His father's few surviving letters to Theodore usually have an admonitory aspect. "It is a very important year in your

life, those embryo whiskers at which your mama laughs are an evidence of approaching manhood," he wrote when Theodore was sixteen. "As I saw the last of the train bearing you away the other day I realized what a luxury it was to have a boy in whom I would place perfect trust and confidence who was leaving me to take his first independent position in the world," he wrote when TR left for Harvard. TR Sr. to TR, Oct. 16, 1874, Sept. 28, 1876, Theodore Roosevelt Papers, Houghton Library, Harvard University. Roosevelt adopted the same stance, at once loving and pushing, toward his own sons (but not his daughters).

6. TR to Josephine Shaw Lowell, Feb. 24, 1882, *TRL*, VIII, 1425; Robinson, *My Brother*, 206–207. On his memories of his father, see also TR to Sarah B. Leavitt, Oct. 7, 1901, *TRL*, III, 161–162; TR to Robert B. Roosevelt, Mar. 6, 1906, *TRL*, IV, 1131; and Jacob Riis, *Theodore Roosevelt the Citizen* (New York, 1904), 36–37, 445–446. The view of his mother's abdication is disputed in McCullough, *Mornings on Horseback*, 114.

7. On Elliott, who was the father of Eleanor Roosevelt, see chapters in Joseph P. Lash, *Eleanor and Franklin* (New York, 1971); Morris, *Rise of Roosevelt*, 429–440, 444–446; and McCullough, *Mornings on Horseback*, 143–148.

8. TR, *Autobiography*, *TRW*, XX, 26.

9. Ibid.; TR Sr. to TR, Oct. 27, 1876, TR Papers, Houghton.

10. TR diary, Aug. 18, 1879, quoted in Putnam, *Roosevelt*, 178; ibid., 178, 238–239. On Theodore, Sr.'s political involvements, see McCullough, *Mornings on Horseback*, 750–752, 156–158, 164–180.

11. TR to Eleonora K. Kinnicutt, June 28, 1901, *TRL*, III, 102; Riis, *Roosevelt the Citizen*, 48–49. Roosevelt's attitude anticipated an incisive distinction drawn by E. Digby Baltzell between an "aristocracy," which discharges obligations to govern and serve its society, and a "caste," which merely enjoys its privileged economic and social status. See Baltzell, *The Protestant Establishment: Aristocracy and Caste in America* (New York, 1968), especially 7–10, 78–88.

12. TR, *Autobiography*, *TRW*, XX, 223–224; Anna Roosevelt Cowles reminiscence, July 15, 1925, Corinne Roosevelt Robinson Papers, Houghton Library, Harvard University; Archie Butt to Clara Butt, Oct. 21, 1908, in Lawrence F. Abbott, ed., *The Letters of Archie Butt* (Garden City, N.Y., 1924), 146; TR speech, Feb. 23, 1907, *TRW*, XIII, 564. Most Roosevelt biographers make some comment on his father's lack of war service, but the only comment on any of Roosevelt's later statements (the one from the *Autobiography*) is in Einstein, *Roosevelt*, 2. Among Roosevelt's intimates, Jacob Riis commented briefly and apologetically in his 1904 campaign biography on the father's lack of war

service: Riis, *Roosevelt the Citizen*, 436. Roosevelt's younger sister Corinne later privately believed that the father's failure to flock to the colors had had a lasting effect on the son. According to Putnam, she told her daughter that in retrospect she "felt strongly that her elder brother's aggressive personal passion for active military service in any national emergency was in part compensation for an unspoken disappointment in his father's course in 1861." Putnam, *Roosevelt*, 48–49.

13. TR, *The Naval War of 1812, TRW*, VII, xxv, 24 n. 2, 377, 404.

14. Hermann Hagedorn, *The Boy's Life of Theodore Roosevelt* (New York, 1918), 63–64. In the last year of his life Roosevelt told his sister Corinne that he had decided at twenty-one to live "up to the hilt" until he was sixty and did not care what happened after that. Morris, *Rise of Roosevelt*, 793 n. 41.

2. Manse and World

1. Grover Cleveland, the only other Democrat elected president during Wilson's lifetime, was also a Presbyterian minister's son, while Wilson's opponent for reelection in 1916, Charles Evans Hughes, was a Baptist minister's son.

2. Margaret Axson Elliott, *My Aunt Louisa and Woodrow Wilson* (Chapel Hill, N.C., 1944), 5, 30. On James Woodrow, see the entry by John E. Pomfret, *Dictionary of American Biography*, XX (New York, 1936), 495–496.

3. WW to EA, Oct. 12, 1884, *WWP*, III, 349–450. On James Woodrow's tutelage of Wilson, see WW speech Mar. 12, 1908, *WWP*, XVIII, 32–33.

4. John M. Mulder, *Woodrow Wilson: The Years of Preparation* (Princeton, 1978), 15–17, 40–41. For Wilson's own recollection, see RSB interview with Gary T. Grayson, Feb. 18–19, 1926, RSB MSS, Box 109; for his early political interests, see Douglas McKay to WW, June 25, 1875, *WWP*, I, 66–67.

5. On Joseph R. Wilson's beliefs and habits, see especially RSB interviews with Stockton Axson, Feb. 8–11, 1924, RSB MSS, Box 99; with Joseph R. Wilson, Jr., Feb. 19, 1926, ibid., Box 124; Elliott, *My Aunt Louisa*, 126–128; and Mulder, *Wilson*, chap. 1.

6. On Wilson's mother see especially Harriet W. Welles to RSB, Sept. 28 [1925], RSB MSS, Box 124; Edith Gittings Reid, *Woodrow Wilson: The Caricature, the Myth and the Man* (New York, 1934), 5–7; Mulder, *Wilson*, 30–31; Edwin A. Weinstein, James William Anderson, and Arthur S. Link, "Woodrow Wilson's Political Personality: A Reappraisal," *Political Science Quarterly* 93 (Winter, 1978–79), 592–593; and

Edwin A. Weinstein, *Woodrow Wilson: A Medical and Psychological Biography* (Princeton, 1981), 10–13.

7. On Wilson's religious outlook, see especially Winthrop M. Daniels memoir, summer 1924, RSB MSS, Box 105; RSB interview with Axson, Feb. 8–11, 1925, ibid., Box 99; interview with Jessie Wilson Sayer, Dec. 1, 1925, ibid., Box 121; Eleanor Wilson McAdoo, *The Woodrow Wilsons* (New York, 1937), 41–42.

8. Mulder, *Wilson*, 27–28, 89; WW to Robert Bridges, Nov. 7, 1879, *WWP*, I 583; Janet W. Wilson to WW, Aug. 23 [1880], ibid., 674. On his name change, see also WW to Emma C. Spenser, Jan. 19, 1903, *WWP*, XIV, 328. Jessie Wilson was also a loyal wife, however. When her brother failed to gain a second term as moderator of his synod, she told her son, "I confess I am glad he was defeated—he has had too much success for his own good—and besides his voice unfits him for such a position." Janet W. Wilson to WW, [May 23, 1877], *WWP*, I, 265. Joseph R. Wilson, on his side, evidently supported and encouraged his son's identification with the Woodrow connection. At one point during his law studies at the University of Virginia his father complimented him for facing up to adversity "like a man (may I add, like a Woodrow Wilson?)": Joseph R. Wilson to WW, June 7, 1880, ibid., 660.

9. Stockton Axson comments on manuscript of RSB biography, circa 1926, RSB MSS, Box 100; WW to EAW, Mar. 9, 1889, *WWP*, VI, 139. On his slowness to read, see also RSB interview with Grayson, Feb. 18–19, 1926, RSB MSS, Box 109; Isabella H. Jordan memorandum, Oct. 1927, ibid., Box 113; anonymous, "The Man from Georgia," enclosure with Pleasant A. Stovall to Baker, June 8, 1925, RSB MSS, Box 122; McAdoo, *The Wilsons*, 40.

10. Weinstein, *Wilson*, 14–20; WW to Edith G. Reid, June 18, 1897, *WWP*, X, 272. On his memory, see also editorial note, *WWP*, XXVIII, 452 n. 4.

11. WW to J. Edwin Webster, July 3, 1878, *WWP*, I, 384–385.

12. Wilson's recollection of his intellectual awakening is in RSB interview with Grayson, Feb. 18–19, 1926, RSB MSS, Box 109.

13. On Wilson's class standing, see *WWP*, I, 175 n. 1, 444 n. 1; Henry W. Bragdon, *Woodrow Wilson: The Academic Years* (Cambridge, Mass., 1967), 48–49, 420 n. 4. Unlike Roosevelt, Wilson did not become intimate with his wealthy, socially prominent contemporaries at Princeton, several of whom were later trustees. In April 1877, Roosevelt mentioned to his father that the visiting Princeton contingent for the football game with Harvard included "a good many of my friends," among whom were Cleveland H. Dodge and M. Taylor Pyne. TR to TR, Sr., Apr. 29, 1877, *TRL*, I, 28.

14. "Junius"[pseudonym for WW], "Some Thoughts on the Present State of Public Affairs," circa Jan. 30, 1878, *WWP*, I, 347–354.

15. On the article's acceptance, see Joseph R. Wilson to WW, Apr. 10, 1879, ibid., 476.

16. WW, "Cabinet Government in the United States" ibid., 493–510; WW to William Milligan Sloane, circa Dec. 5, 1883, *WWP*, II, 567. On other influences on the article, see "Editorial Note: 'Cabinet Government in the United States,' " *WWP*, I, 492–493.

17. On Bagehot, see Alastair Buchan, *The Spare Chancellor: The Life of Walter Bagehot* (London, 1959). On his inspiration for Wilson, see also Bragdon, *Wilson*, 60–61.

18. Joseph R. Wilson to WW, Jan. 10, 1878, *WWP*, I, 338. On the senior debate, see "Editorial Note: Wilson's Refusal to Enter the Lynde Competition," ibid., 480–481. I disagree with the editors' conclusion that Wilson himself was still completely opposed to universal suffrage.

19. WW to Charles A. Talcott, July 7, 1879, ibid., 487.

3. Paths of Glory

1. "Dude" was first used in 1883, evidently to denote a fancy dresser, and in 1885, to denote an easterner and city-bred person vacationing on a ranch: Mitford M. Mathews, ed., *A Dictionary of Americanisms on Historical Principles* (Chicago, 1951), I, 530.

2. TR quoted in entry, Apr. 6, 1898, in David Shannon, ed., *Beatrice Webb's American Diary, 1898* (Madison, Wis., 1963), 15. On Choate's patronage, see TR to Joseph H. Choate, Nov. 10, 1881, *TRL*, I, 55; on his entry into politics, see Carleton Putnam, *Theodore Roosevelt: The Formative Years* (New York, 1958), 240–248.

3. TR to Robert M. La Follette, Sept. 29, 1911, *TRL*, VII, 348; TR, *Autobiography*, *TRW*, XX, 88.

4. *TRW*, I, 329; Edmund Morris, *The Rise of Theodore Roosevelt* (New York, 1978), 286–287, 294–295.

5. On his changed appearance, see Putnam, *Roosevelt*, 528–530.

6. On TR's role in 1884, see especially Putnam, *Roosevelt*, 425–450, 463–471, 490–506. Interestingly, "dude" was used as a term of derision in 1884 by Republican regulars against their fastidious brethren who bolted in protest over Blaine's nomination. Mathews, *Dictionary of Americanisms*, I, 530.

7. TR to Anna Roosevelt, Apr. 22, 1886, *TRL*, I, 98.

8. Roosevelt's friendship with Owen Wister is both charmingly recounted and insightfully analyzed in Wister, *Roosevelt: The Story of a Friendship* (New York, 1930). On the meaning of the West to them and

their mutual friend, the painter Frederic Remington, see G. Edward White, *The Eastern Establishment and the Western Experience: The West of Frederic Remington, Theodore Roosevelt, and Owen Wister* (New Haven, 1968).

9. Stewart H. Holbrook, "Frank Merriwell at Yale Again—and Again and Again," *American Heritage* 12 (June 1961), 25.

10. John M. Blum, "Theodore Roosevelt: The Years of Decision," *TRL*, II, 1491. On Roosevelt's conservatism, one of the ablest analyses, curiously neglected, is Elting E. Morison, "Introduction," *TRL*, V, xiii–xxiv.

11. *TRW*, XIII, 81–82; TR to HCL, Oct. 27, 1894, *TRL*, I, 408; TR to Brander Matthews, Dec. 9, 1894, ibid., 412.

12. *TRW*, X, 450; Edith Roosevelt quoted in Henry F. Pringle, *Theodore Roosevelt: A Biography* (New York, 1931), 167.

13. TR to *Harvard Crimson*, Jan. 2, 1896, *TRL*, I, 506. "Baboo" was a term for Hindus who superficially aped British ways in India. For a perceptive discussion of Roosevelt's and Brooks Adams's antimaterialism in relation to their militarist views, see John P. Mallan, "Roosevelt, Brooks Adams, and [Homer] Lea: The Warrior Critique of Business Civilization," *American Quarterly* 8 (Fall 1956), 218–230.

14. TR to HCL, Dec. 27, 1895, *TRL*, I, 504. I am one of the writers who has mistakenly asserted that Roosevelt placed primary importance on foreign affairs. See John Milton Cooper, Jr., "Progressivism and American Foreign Policy: A Reconsideration," *Mid-America* 51 (Oct. 1969), 261–262.

15. TR to HCL, May 18, 1895, *TRL*, I, 457; TR to Anna R. Cowles, June 28, 1896, ibid., 545.

16. On Roosevelt's work in the Navy Department, see Walter R. Herrick, Jr., *The American Naval Revolution* (Baton Rouge, La., 1966), especially 196–198, 219–221.

17. HCL to Corinne R. Robinson, Apr. 24, 1898, Corinne Roosevelt Robinson Papers, File 831, Houghton Library; TR to Alexander Lambert, Apr. 1, 1898, *TRL*, II, 808. For the comparisons with Parkman and Hemingway, see also Edward Wagenknecht, *The Seven Worlds of Theodore Roosevelt* (New York, 1958), 23.

18. Lewis Einstein, *Roosevelt: His Mind in Action* (Boston, 1930), 70–71, 73. On TR's publicity efforts, see Morris, *Rise of Roosevelt*, 629, 845 n. 66.

19. Hanna quoted in Pringle, *Roosevelt*, 223.

20. Thomas C. Platt to TR, May 6, 1899, *TRL*, II, 1004 n. 1; TR to Platt, May 8, 1899, ibid., 1006. The fullest study of Roosevelt's governorship is G. Wallace Chessman, *Governor Theodore Roosevelt: The Albany*

Apprenticeship, 1898–1900 (Cambridge, Mass., 1965); another excellent treatment is in Richard L. McCormick, *From Realignment to Reform: Political Change in New York, 1893–1910* (Ithaca, N.Y., 1981), 157–164.

21. TR speech, May 30, 1899, *TRW*, XIV, 333.

22. TR, *Gouverneur Morris* (1887), *TRW*, VII, 327.

23. The best treatments of Lodge, largely sympathetic, are John A. Garraty, *Henry Cabot Lodge: A Biography* (New York, 1953), and William Widenor, *Henry Cabot Lodge and the Search for an American Foreign Policy* (Berkeley, 1979).

24. On Boies Penrose, see the entry by Robert C. Brooks, *Dictionary of American Biography*, XIV (New York, 1934), 448–449. For an interesting comparison of Lodge and Penrose, which favors Lodge, see E. Digby Baltzell, *Puritan Boston and Quaker Philadelphia: Two Protestant Ethics and the Spirit of Class Authority and Leadership* (New York, 1979), 406–414. For a sprightly description of Penrose, who is summed up in the arresting though probably philosophically inaccurate phrase, "a gutter Nietzschean," see Francis Russell, *The Shadow of Blooming Grove: Warren G. Harding and His Times* (New York, 1968), 330–331.

25. Viscount Lee of Fareham, "Cromwell and Roosevelt," *TRW*, X, 169–170; TR, *Oliver Cromwell* (1899), ibid., 215.

4. Groves of Academe

1. WW to EA, Oct. 30, 1883, *WWP*, II, 500–501.

2. WW, "Congressional Government," circa Oct. 1, 1879, *WWP*, I, 548–549; "John Bright," Mar. 1880, ibid., 618–619; Joseph R. Wilson to WW, Dec. 22, 1879, ibid., 589.

3. WW to Robert Bridges, Mar. 21, 1883, *WWP*, II, 322.

4. WW to Bridges, May 13, 1883, ibid., 358. On his stay in Atlanta see also "Editorial Note. Wilson's Practice of Law," ibid., 144–145.

5. WW To EA, Mar. 21, 1885, *WWP*, IV, 394; WW to EA, Dec. 1, 1884, *WWP*, III, 504.

6. WW to Albert Bushnell Hart, June 3, 1889, *WWP*, VI, 243. Wilson wrote "Mere Literature" evidently in rebuttal to the use of the phrase by a philologist at Johns Hopkins, yet it seems hardly coincidental that his father had earlier used almost the same words to pooh-pooh his son's ambitions. On the essay, see "Editorial Note: 'Mere Literature,' " *WWP*, VIII, 238–240.

7. WW to EA, Nov. 27, 1883, *WWP*, II, 552. On the beginnings of Johns Hopkins, see Hugh Hawkins, *Pioneer: A History of the Johns Hopkins University 1874–1899* (Ithaca, N.Y., 1960); for another young man's discontent there, see John Milton Cooper, Jr., *Walter Hines Page:*

The Southerner as American, 1855–1918 (Chapel Hill, N.C., 1977), 31–41.

8. [Arthur S. Link], "Editorial Note: *Congressional Government,*" *WWP,* IV, 6–13; WW to EA, Jan. 1, 1884, *WWP,* II, 641; WW to Bridges, Nov. 19, 1884, *WWP,* III, 465.

9. WW, *Congressional Government, WWP,* IV, 168.

10. Edward S. Corwin, comment on interview with Henry W. Bragdon, June 9, 1939, Henry W. Bragdon Collection, Princeton University Library.

11. WW to EA, Feb. 13, 1885, *WWP,* IV, 245; Winthrop M. Daniels memoir, summer 1924, RSB MSS, Box 105.

12. WW, *Congressional Government, WWP,* IV, 114.

13. Ibid., 172. Perhaps the best estimate of the book is by Corwin, who called *Congressional Government* "the earliest work by an American writer to consider American governmental institutions from a pragmatic rather than a juristic point of view and—what is perhaps of even greater importance—to compare them with the governmental institutions of another country." Edward S. Corwin, "Departmental Colleague," in William Starr Myers, ed., *Woodrow Wilson: Some Princeton Memories* (Princeton, 1946), 25–26.

14. WW, *The State, WWP,* VI, 253, 288–289, 311, 279. Once at Princeton, when Wilson spoke to a faculty group on "sovereignty," McCosh, who had by then retired, protested that sovereignty rested with God. "So it does, Dr. McCosh," answered Wilson, "but I did not go quite so far back in my discussion." Ray Stannard Baker, *Woodrow Wilson: Life and Letters* (Garden City, N.Y., 1927), II, 18–19. On Wilson's separation of his religious and political views, see Mulder, *Wilson,* 106–107.

15. Corwin called Wilson's *History* a "gilt-edged potboiler." Bragdon interview with Corwin, June 9, 1939, Bragdon Collection.

16. WW to EA, Nov. 9, 1884, *WWP,* III, 418; WW to Frederick Jackson Turner, Jan. 21, 1902, *WWP,* XII, 240; WW memorandum, May 5, 1902, *WWP,* XII, 365.

17. WW, "Edmund Burke: The Man and His Times," circa Aug. 31, 1893, *WWP,* VIII, 342; "Edmund Burke: A Lecture," Feb. 23, 1898, *WWP,* X, 421; *Constitutional Government in the United States* (1908), *WWP,* XVIII, 105–106. On Wilson's reading of Burke, see also "Editorial Note: Wilson's First Lecture on Burke," *WWP,* VIII, 313–318; and on his insight in *Constitutional Government,* see Louis Martin Sears, "Woodrow Wilson," in William T. Hutchinson, ed., *The Marcus W. Jernegan Essays in American Historiography* (Chicago, 1937), 114.

18. Edward Graham Elliott memorandum of conversation with WW, Jan. 5, 1903, *WWP*, XIV, 322. For his reliance on Bradford, see Arthur S. Link, *Wilson: The Road to the White House* (Princeton, 1947), 17–18; and on Ford, see *WWP*, XVIII, 208 n. 5.

19. Wilson said of Bagehot in 1898, "There is everywhere the same close intimacy between the fact and the thought. What he writes seems always a light playing in affairs, illuminating their substance, revealing their fibre": WW, "Walter Bagehot—A Lecture," Feb. 24, 1898, *WWP*, X, 439–440.

20. WW, "Burke" (1893), *WWP*, VIII, 342; "Burke" (1898), *WWP*, X, 421. On Wilson's primary interest in how politics worked, see Patrick Devlin, *Too Proud to Fight: Woodrow Wilson's Neutrality* (New York, 1975), 49–50.

21. The failure with the Bryn Mawr graduate students was recounted by Lucy M. Salmon, who later became a distinguished historian and herself felt the distaste for him. See Salmon to RSB, Jan. 6, 1926, RSB MSS, Box 121. Wilson's experience at Bryn Mawr was far from completely happy, but he was hardly antifeminist, as some writers have charged. Actually, he supported women's higher education, although his wife did not. His greatest unhappiness stemmed from the imperiousness of Bryn Mawr's dean and real power, M. Carey Thomas. Wilson's daughters all went to college and one of them, Jessie, once contemplated transferring to Bryn Mawr, with her father's approval. Neither of Roosevelt's daughters attended college but followed the traditional upper-class practice of making a debut after a finishing school education. Interestingly, William Howard Taft's daughter Helen not only graduated from Bryn Mawr but also took a Ph.D. in history and became a professor and dean at her alma mater.

22. WW to EAW, Feb. 4, 1898, *WWP*, X, 374–375; RSB interview with Stockton Axson, Mar. 12, 1925, RSB MSS, Box 99.

23. On Wilson's likely stroke, see *WWP*, IX, 507 n. 2; Edwin A. Weinstein, "Woodrow Wilson's Neurological Illness," *Journal of American History* 57 (Sept. 1970), 333; and Edwin A. Weinstein, *Woodrow Wilson: A Medical and Psychological Biography* (Princeton, 1981), 140–149. Axson made his observations on several occasions; see Axson, "Mr. Wilson As Seen by One of His Family Circle," circa 1916, RSB MSS, Box 99; RSB interview with Axson, Feb. 8–11, 1925, ibid.; Axson notes on manuscript of RSB biography of WW, Sept. 1931, RSB MSS, Box 100.

24. John M. Mulder, *Woodrow Wilson: The Years of Preparation* (Princeton, 1978), 274, 276–277; WW lecture, Richmond, Va., Nov. 4,

1889, *WWP*, XI, 71; speech, Chicago, Jan. 14, 1899, ibid., 94; speech, Waterbury, Conn., Dec. 14, 1899, ibid., 299. According to Axson, Wilson avidly followed war news and "regretted he was not free to enlist in the Armed Forces and fight." Axson notes on manuscript of RSB biography, Sept. 1931, RSB MSS, Box 100.

25. WW to Harriet W. Welles, June 27, 1902, *WWP*, XII, 462. On McCosh's earlier work see J. David Hoeveler, Jr., *James McCosh and the Scottish Intellectual Pattern: From Glasgow to Princeton* (Princeton, 1981), pt. 3. On Patton's downfall and Wilson's succession, see "Editorial Note: The Crisis in Presidential Leadership at Princeton," *WWP*, XII, 289–293; Henry W. Bragdon, *Woodrow Wilson: The Academic Years* (Cambridge, Mass., 1967), 269–270, 274–276; Thomas Jefferson Wertenbaker, *Princeton, 1746–1896* (Princeton, 1946), 345–347, 368, 388–389.

5. Acquaintances

1. WW to Munroe Smith, Jan. 7, 1889, *WWP*, VI, 45; James Bryce, *The American Commonwealth* (New York, 1888), I, 516. Publicly Wilson gave the book an enthusiastic but carefully reserved review, "Bryce's American Commonwealth," *Political Science Quarterly* (Mar. 1889), *WWP*, VI, 61–76. Privately he said many times that he greatly preferred Tocqueville's *Democracy in America* to Bryce's work. See W. M. Daniels memoir, summer 1924, RSB MSS, Box 105. Boies Penrose received a commendation similar to Roosevelt's in the first edition of *The American Commonwealth;* all mention of him disappeared from subsequent editions.

2. *TRW*, XII, 303; EAW to WW [July 13, 1902], *WWP*, XIV, 8.

3. WW to EAW, Mar 15, 1900, *WWP*, XI, 515; WW speech, Oct. 13, 1899, ibid., 253; TR to Cleveland H. Dodge, June 16, 1902, *TRL*, III, 275; TR to WW, June 23, 1902, *WWP*, XII, 454. Axson's comment about Wilson's possibly changing parties is in his comments on manuscript of RSB biography, Sept. 1931, RSB MSS, Box 100. That recollection is supported by a private note WW wrote around the time of TR's accession in which he declined to be considered for a state senatorial nomination in New Jersey because "I find myself so far from sympathizing with the general attitude of the national Democratic party upon many of the chief articles of its creed, as the country understands it." WW to _____, circa Oct. 1, 1901, *WWP*, XII, 189.

4. WW, "Democracy and Efficiency," *Atlantic* (Mar. 1901), written circa Oct. 1, 1900, *WWP*, XII, 11.

Introduction to Part II

1. TR's listing of his accomplishments is in TR to Sydney Brooks, Dec. 28, 1908, *TRL*, VI, 1444–46.

6. Public Performer

1. The son's remark is quoted in Nathan Miller, *The Roosevelt Chronicles* (Garden City, N.Y., 1979), 248.

2. Oscar King Davis, *Released for Publication: Some Inside Political History of Theodore Roosevelt and His Times, 1898–1918* (Boston, 1925), 131–133; Henry F. Pringle, *The Life and Times of William Howard Taft* (New York, 1939), I, 415–416, For his advice to Taft on golf, see TR to WHT, Sept. 14, 1908, *TRL*, VI, 1234–1235.

3. TR to Albert Shaw, Dec. 26, 1902, *TRL*, III, 397.

4. TR to George Otto Trevelyan, Nov. 30, 1903, ibid., 662–663.

5. TR messages to Congress, Dec. 3, 1901; Dec. 2, 1902; Dec. 6, 1904, *TRW*, XV, 115, 151, 257.

6. TR message to Congress, Dec. 6, 1904, ibid., 255–256; speech at San Francisco, May 13, 1903, *TRA*, I, 395–396.

7. TR message to Congress, Dec. 6, 1904, *TRW*, XV, 253–254.

8. On TR's Venezuela actions, see Howard K. Beale, *Theodore Roosevelt and the Rise of America to World Power* (Baltimore, 1956), 395–431; and Frederick W. Marks, III, *Velvet on Iron: The Diplomacy of Theodore Roosevelt* (Lincoln, Neb., 1979) 37–48.

9. On his actions in the Russo-Japanese War, see Beale, *Roosevelt and the Rise of America*, 157–158.

10. TR to HCL, Jan 28, 1909, *TRL*, VI, 1498. Likewise, in 1916, shortly after Hay's biography was published, TR detailed to its author, William Roscoe Thayer, how he had handled the Venezuelan affair in 1902: TR to Thayer, Aug. 21, 1916, *TRL*, VIII, 1101–1105.

11. On the Alaskan boundary dispute, see Marks, *Velvet on Iron*, 61–64, 105–111.

12. Senate amendments in William Malloy, ed., *Treaties, Conventions, International Acts, Protocols, and Agreements between the United States of America and Other Powers, 1776–1909* (Washington, 1919), II, 2183, 2247; HCL statement, *Congressional Record*, 59th Cong., 1st Sess., 1470 (Jan. 24, 1906).

13. TR messages to Congress, Dec. 3, 1901, Dec. 6, 1904, *TRW*, XV, 87–89, 221.

14. TR to Douglas Robinson, Oct. 4, 1901, *TRL*, III, 160.

15. John M. Blum, *The Republican Roosevelt* (Cambridge, Mass., 1954), 39–54.

16. Ibid., 73–105; TR speech at Chautauqua, N.Y., Aug. 11, 1905, *TRA*, IV, 455; TR to William Allen White, July 31, 1906, *TRL*, V, 341; speech at Washington, Apr. 14, 1906, *TRW*, XVI, 416.

17. Blum, "Theodore Roosevelt and the Legislative Process: Tariff Revision and Railroad Regulation, 1904–1906," *TRL*, IV, 1333–1342; TR to John St. Loe Strachey, Feb. 12, 1906, *TRL*, V, 152.

18. TR to Nicholas Murray Butler, Aug. 12, 1902, *TRL*, III, 312–313; TR to HCL, Sept, 27, 1906, *TRL*, V, 427; Albert J. Beveridge, "The Statesmanship of Theodore Roosevelt," *TRW*, VII, xvi.

19. New York *Sun,* quoted in Mark Sullivan, *Our Times: The United States, 1900–1925* (New York, 1927), II, 460.

20. TR message to Congress, Dec. 5, 1905, *TRW*, XV, 272.

21. Joseph B. Bishop, *Theodore Roosevelt and His Times* (New York, 1920), I, 184–185; TR speech at Chicago, May 10, 1905, *TRA*, IV, 373; message to Congress, Dec. 2, 1902, *TRW*, XV, 149.

22. TR speech at Washington, Nov. 22, 1904, *TRW*, XIII, 531; message to Congress, Dec. 5, 1905, *TRW*, XV, 288.

23. TR speech at Washington, Apr. 14, 1906, *TRW*, XVI, 420; speech at Berkeley, Calif., May 14, 1903, *TRA*, II, 407; speech at Washington, Feb. 19, 1902, *TRA*, I, 15; speech at Brooklyn, N.Y., May 30, 1905, *TRA*, IV, 385.

24. TR to Philander C. Knox, Nov. 10, 1904, *TRL*, IV, 1023; TR to Spring Rice, Dec. 27, 1904, ibid., 1083.

25. TR speech at Denver, May 9, 1905, *TRA*, III, 351–352; speech at Ocean Grove, N.J., July 7, 1905, *TRA*, IV, 425–426; William Henry Harbaugh, *Power and Responsibility: The Life and Times of Theodore Roosevelt* (New York, 1961); TR to Wister, Nov. 19, 1904, *TRL*, IV, 1036–1037.

26. TR, *Autobiography, TRW*, XX, 411.

27. Owen Wister, *Roosevelt: The Story of a Friendship* (New York, 1930), 124. On TR's various cultural activities, see Willard W. Gatewood, *Theodore Roosevelt and the Art of Controversy* (Baton Rouge, La., 1970), 213–235.

28. Lewis Einstein, *Roosevelt: His Mind in Action* (Boston, 1930), v–vi; Jacob Burckhardt, *The Civilization of the Rennaissance in Italy* (New York, reprint ed., 1954), pt. 1.

29. Wister, *Roosevelt,* 149.

7. Academic Reformer

1. Laurence R. Veysey, "The Academic Mind of Woodrow Wilson," *Mississippi Valley Historical Review* 44 (Mar. 1963), 613–634;

Veysey, *The Emergence of the American University* (Chicago, 1965), especially 194, 197, 233, 241–251; Henry W. Bragdon, *Woodrow Wilson: The Academic Years* (Cambridge, Mass., 1967), especially 308–310; WW, "Princeton in the Nation's Service," *WWP*, X, 30.

2. RSB interview with Henry B. Fine, June 10, 1925, RSB MSS, Box 108; WW speech at Newark, May 16, 1903, *WWP*, XIV, 462; speech at Pittsburgh, Nov. 5, 1903, *WWP*, XV, 35.

3. WW to EAW, July 19, 1902, *WWP*, XIV, 27.

4. Ibid. On the new curriculum, see "Editorial Note: The New Princeton Course of Study," *WWP*, XV, 277–92; and Bragdon, *Wilson*, 288–94.

5. WW, "Report to the Board of Trustees," Oct. 21, 1902, *WWP*, XIV, 150–161. For Wilson's prediction of the three reforms in his Princeton presidency, see RSB interview with Stockton Axson, Mar. 15–16, 1927, RSB MSS, Box 99.

6. WW, "Report to Trustees," *WWP*, XIV, 157.

7. Bragdon interview with William F. Magie, June 12, 1939; with Charles H. McIlwain, Jan. 2, 1940, Bragdon MSS. Among the thirty-seven doctorates held by preceptors, seven came from Harvard, five from Johns Hopkins, five from German universities, and four from Chicago: Bragdon, *Wilson*, 306.

8. Robert K. Root, "Wilson and the Preceptors," in William Starr Myers, ed., *Woodrow Wilson: Some Princeton Memories* (Princeton, 1946), 15; Samuel Shellabarger, *Tolbecken* (Boston, 1956), 112–113; Hardin Craig, *Literary Study and the Scholarly Profession* (Seattle, 1944), 72.

9. WW, "Statement of the Tutorial System," circa Feb. 18, 1905, *WWP*, XVI, 6; WW to Ralph Barton Perry, Mar. 4, 1905, ibid., 19; Bragdon interview with C. H. McIlwain, Jan. 2, 1940; interview with Charles Grosvenor Osgood, Apr. 14, 1939, Bragdon MSS.

10. WW, speech at East Orange, N.J., Nov. 9, 1905, notes and newspaper report, *WWP*, XVI, 214, 218; notes, Feb. 17, 1906, ibid., 314–315.

11. WW, supplementary report to trustees, circa Dec. 13, 1906, ibid., 519–525; speech to trustees, June 10, 1907, *WWP*, XVII, 199. The April 1907 meeting is described in RSB interview with Harry A. Garfield, May 18, 1925, RSB MSS, Box 109, and in Bragdon interview with Garfield, Feb. 14, 1940, Bragdon MSS. The June 1907 trustees' meeting is described in Stockton Axson, "The Princeton Controversy," RSB MSS, Box 99; and Henry B. Thompson to RSB, May 31, 1927, RSB MSS, Box 122. Wilson's surprise is noted in Hardin Craig, *Woodrow Wilson at Princeton* (Norman, Okla., 1960), 123.

12. Bragdon, *Wilson*, 326; WW speech at Harvard, June 26, 1907, *WWP*, XVII, 226. Two observations on the dual nature of Wilson's confidence were given by Bliss Perry, who had taught at Princeton in the 1890s, and by Fine. Referring to Wilson, Perry noted that, in accord with Aristotle's concept of the tragic flaw flowing from an excess of virtue, "The line between superb confidence and tragic overconfidence is often hidden from the hero himself." Perry, *And Gladly Teach: Reminiscences* (Boston, 1935), 158. In observing that Wilson's confidence accounted for his success as well as his failures, Fine stated, "To be certain of anything in a world of doubt is to have one of the most powerful weapons that ever comes to the hand of man." RSB interview with Fine, June 18, 1925, RSB MSS, Box 108.

13. On Wilson's 1906 stroke, see Edwin Weinstein, "Woodrow Wilson's Neurological Illness," *Journal of American History* 54 (Sept. 1970), 334–336; and Weinstein, *Woodrow Wilson: A Medical and Psychological Biography* (Princeton, 1981), 165–180.

14. WW to Cleveland H. Dodge, Sept. 16, 1906, *WWP*, XVI, 453; RSB interview with H. A. Garfield, Mar. 18, 1925, RSB MSS, Box 109.

15. Edith Gittings Reid, *Woodrow Wilson: The Caricature, the Myth, and the Man* (New York, 1934), 108; Bragdon interview with W. F. Magie, June 13, 1939, Bragdon MSS; WW speech at New York, Dec. 9, 1902, *WWP*, XIV, 275. West expressed that theme of the opposition when he told WW, "If the spirit of Princeton is to be killed, I have little interest in the details of the funeral." West to WW, July 10, 1907, *WWP*, XVII, 271.

16. On Wilson's faculty recruitment and building, see Bragdon, *Wilson*, 360–361; and John M. Mulder, *Woodrow Wilson: The Years of Preparation* (Princeton, 1978), 164. When Conklin and Capps first met in the fall of 1908, Capps asked, "What brought you here?" "Woodrow Wilson," Conklin replied, "and what brought you here?" Capps rejoined, "The same." Edwin Grant Conklin, "As a Scientist Saw Him," in Myers, *Princeton Memories*, 59. On "captains of erudition" see Thorstein Veblen, *The Higher Learning in America: A Memorandum on the Conduct of Universities by Business Men* (New York, 1918), especially 83–85, 115.

17. WW speech at Jersey City, Mar. 25, 1910, *WWP*, XX, 290; RSB interview with Fine, June 18, 1925, RSB MSS, Box 108.

18. Veblen plainly caricatured Chicago's often egregious William Rainey Harper, but David Reisman has pointed out that the term can and should be applied to other presidents, and he uses Harper's respected Chicago successor Robert Maynard Hutchins as an example. See Reisman, *Thorstein Veblen: A Critical Interpretation* (New York, 1953), 102–103.

19. WW, speech at Harvard, June 26, 1907, *WWP*, XVII, 227.

20. Axson, "Princeton Controversy," Feb. 1925, RSB MSS, Box 99. Another version of the story states that Wilson said grimly, "I could lick a half-million, but I'm licked by ten million." Margaret Axson Elliott, *My Aunt Louisa and Woodrow Wilson* (Chapel Hill, N.C., 1944), 242. On West and his work, see Thomas Jefferson Wertenbaker, *Princeton, 1746–1896* (Princeton, 1946), 381–383; Bragdon, *Wilson*, 270–272. West left his own account of the conflict with Wilson, a 117-page typescript, written in 1920 and revised in 1929: "A Narrative of the Graduate College of Princeton University from Its Proposal in 1896 until Its Dedication in 1913," Princeton University Archives.

21. Axson, "Princeton Controversy," RSB MSS, Box 99; Henry van Dyke to M. Taylor Pyne, Jan. 6, 1910, *WWP*, XIX, 739.

22. J.H. Jeans to WW, Mar. 20, 1909, *WWP*, XIX, 115–116; WW, speech at St. Louis, Mar. 26, 1910, *WWP*, XX, 293.

23. Edmund Wilson made the assertion in a review of the first two volumes of Ray Stannard Baker, *Woodrow Wilson: Life and Letters* (Garden City, N.Y., 1927); it is reprinted in Wilson, *The Shores of Light: A Literary Chronicle of the 1920s and 1930s* (New York, 1952), 322. Two intimates and Princeton colleagues of Wilson's had earlier privately drawn similar parallels. See Axson, "Princeton Controversy," Feb. 1925, RSB MSS, Box 99; and RSB interview with George McLean Harper, Nov. 12, 1925, RSB MSS, Box 111. For a critical review and re-examination of the drawing of such psychological parallels, see Edwin A. Weinstein, James William Anderson, and Arthur S. Link, "Woodrow Wilson's Political Personality: A Reappraisal," *Political Science Quarterly* 93 (Winter 1978–79), 585–598.

24. WW to MAHP, Nov. 2, 1908, *WWP*, XVIII, 480; EAW to WW, Feb. 28, 1910, *WWP*, XX, 189.

25. For versions of the interpretation that stress the political spillover of the academic controversies, see Arthur S. Link, *Wilson*, I (Princeton, 1947), 123; Bragdon, *Wilson*, 349–352, and Mulder, *Wilson*, 252.

26. For a comment on how Fitzgerald inverted Wilson's values at Princeton, see John W. Davies, "Scott Fitzgerald and Princeton: A New Look at Old Legends," *Princeton Alumni Weekly* (Feb. 8, 1966), 6.

27. WW to MAHP, Feb. 12, 1911, *WWP*, XXII, 426; Raymond B. Fosdick to RSB, June 23, 1926, RSB MSS, Box 108. Wilson's letter to Mrs. Peck, in which he describes the hurt of Hibben's lost friendship, contains a statement that has often been quoted out of context: "Perhaps it is better to love men in the mass than to love them individually!" *WWP*, XXII, 426.

8. Stalemate and Departure

1. TR to G. O. Trevelyan, June 19, 1908, *TRL*, VI, 1087.

2. Butt to Mrs. _____ Butt, May 15, 1908, in Lawrence F. Abbott, ed., *The Letters of Archie Butt* (Garden City, N.Y., 1924), 7; TR to Paul Morton, Mar. 2, 1909, *TRL*, VI, 1541.

3. TR, speech at Canton, Ohio, Jan. 27, 1903, *TRW*, XI, 236. The interpretation of crisis-fomenting leadership was first laid against John F. Kennedy in Henry Fairlie, *The Kennedy Promise: The Politics of Expectation* (Garden City, N.Y., 1973).

4. TR to William Kent, Feb. 4, 1909, *TRL*, VI, 1503; TR, *Autobiography*, *TRW*, XX, 536–537.

5. TR to WHT, Aug. 21, 1907, *TRL*, V, 762; TR speech at Newport, R.I., July 22, 1908, *TRW*, XVI, 256.

6. TR, speech at Washington, May 2, 1907, *TRA*, VI, 1232–1233, 1236.

7. TR to Arthur Lee, Dec. 26, 1907, *TRL*, VI, 874; TR speech at Cairo, Ill., Oct. 3, 1907, *TRW*, XVI, 17.

8. TR to Sydney Brooks, Nov. 20, 1908, *TRL*, VI, 1369.

9. Cecilia M. Kenyon, "Alexander Hamilton, Rousseau of the Right," *Political Science Quarterly* 73 (June 1958), 161–178; quote, 167.

10. TR, *Autobiography*, *TRW*, XX, 416; TR to Lyman Abbott, Sept. 22, 1908, *TRL*, VI, 1248.

11. TR to F. S. Oliver, Aug. 9, 1906, *TRL*, V, 351.

12. TR, speech at Cambridge, May 26, 1910, *TRW*, XIII, 575. For observations on the change after the African venture, see Oscar King Davis, *Released for Publication: Some Inside Political History of Theodore Roosevelt and His Times, 1898–1918* (Boston, 1925), 309–310; and Lewis Einstein, *Roosevelt: His Mind in Action* (Boston, 1930), 176–177.

13. TR, speech at New York, June 18, 1910, *TRW*, XVII, 3. For an observation on the foreboding, see Archie Butt to Clara Butt, June 19, 1910, in Butt, *Taft and Roosevelt: The Intimate Letters of Archie Butt, Military Aide*, I (Garden City, N.Y., 1930), 403–404.

9. Spokesman and Critic

1. WW statement, July 15, 1910, *WWP*, XX, 581; WW to Robert Garrett, July 9, 1910, ibid., 569.

2. WW, speech at Montclair, N.J., Jan. 22, 1904, *WWP*, XV, 143; speech at New York, Nov. 30, 1904, ibid., 547–548.

3. WW, speech at New Rochelle, N.Y., Feb. 27, 1905, *WWP*, XVI, 14; speech at Detroit, Mar. 31, 1905, ibid., 43; speech at New York, Apr. 16, 1906, ibid., 360–362; WW to Adrian F. Joline, Apr. 29, 1907, *WWP*, XVII, 124; WW, "A Credo," ibid., 336–337.

4. On Harvey's activities, see Arthur S. Link, *Wilson*, I (Princeton, 1947), 97–106, 140–145; and "Editorial Note: Colonel Harvey's Plan for Wilson's Entry into Politics," *WWP*, XX, 146–148.

5. On Holmes, see Mark De Wolfe Howe, *Justice Holmes: The Proving Years, 1870–1882* (Cambridge, Mass., 1963); and Fasal Rogat, "The Judge as Spectator," *University of Chicago Law Review* 31 (Winter 1963), 213–256.

6. WW, speech at New York, Apr. 16, 1906, *WWP*, XVI, 360, 362; *Constitutional Government, WWP*, XVIII, 71.

7. WW, speech at Chicago, Feb. 12, 1909, *WWP*, XIX, 39.

8. Corwin, "Departmental Colleague," in William Starr Myers, ed., *Woodrow Wilson: Some Princeton Memories* (Princeton, 1946), 27–28. On the meeting, see also entry for May 8, 1907, William Starr Myers diary, *WWP*, XVIII, 293–294. On WW's sympathies for people outside northeastern metropolitan areas, see also Henry W. Bragdon, *Woodrow Wilson: The Academic Years* (Cambridge, Mass., 1967), 349.

9. WW, *Constitutional Government, WWP*, XVIII, 79; speech at New York, Apr. 16, 1906, *WWP*, XVI, 367.

10. WW, speech at Chicago, Mar. 14, 1908, *WWP*, XVIII, 40–41; speech at Denver, Sept. 30, 1908, ibid., 426–427; speech at Pittsfield, Mass., Oct. 8, ibid., 441, 443.

11. WW, speech at Chicago, Nov. 2, 1909, *WWP*, XIX, 477; Link, *Wilson*, I, 122–123; WW, speech at Cleveland, Nov. 16, 1907, *WWP*, XVII, 500.

12. WW to MAHP, Sept, 5, 1909, *WWP*, XIX, 358. On WW's involvement in the short ballot movement, see Link, *Wilson* I, 124–126.

13. WW, "The Tariff Make-Believe," Sept. 5, 1909, *WWP*, XIX, 377; speech at New York, Dec. 9, 1908, *WWP*, XVIII, 537; speech at Chicago, Feb. 12, 1909, *WWP*, XIX, 45; speech at Elizabeth, N.J., *WWP*, XX, 298.

14. WW, speech at Baltimore, Feb. 19, 1909, *WWP*, XIX, 60–61; speech at New York, Jan. 18, 1910, *WWP*, XX, 24; "Platform suggestions" [circa Apr. 4, 1910], ibid., 315–317.

15. WW to Alfred Hayes, Jr., May 23, 1910, *WWP*, XX, 467; speech at Atlantic City, N.J., May 6, 1910, ibid., 419.

16. WW to David B. Jones, June 27, 1910, ibid., 543–544.

10. Adversaries

1. TR to WW, Dec. 6, 1902, *WWP*, XIV, 265; WW, speech at Morristown, N.J., Feb. 23, 1903, *WWP*, XIV, 374; J. Duncan Spaeth, "Wilson as I Knew Him and View Him Now," in William Starr Myers, ed., *Woodrow Wilson: Some Princeton Memories* (Princeton, 1946), 84.

2. WW, speech at Oberlin, Ohio, Mar. 22, 1906, *WWP*, XVI, 340; J. V. Badley memorandum [Apr. 1925], RSB MSS, Box 125; WW, "Credo," *WWP*, XVII, 338; WW interview, *New York Times*, Nov. 24, 1907, ibid., 519, 521.

3. TR to Wister, Dec. 31, 1907, *TRL*, VI, 880; TR to Lyman Abbott, Aug. 29, 1908, ibid., 1201; Cleveland H. Dodge to WW [circa Dec. 13, 1908], *WWP*, XVIII, 546.

4. WW, speech at St. Louis, Mar. 9, 1909, *WWP*, XIX, 82; speech at Philadelphia, Mar. 13, 1909, ibid., 99; speech at Lancaster, Pa., Jan. 7, 1910, ibid., 746; "Hide-and-Seek Politics" [circa Mar. 2, 1909], *WWP*, XX, 202.

5. TR to F. S. Oliver, Aug. 9, 1906, *TRL*, V, 352.

6. WW, speech at Cleveland, Nov. 16, 1907, *WWP*, XVII, 498, 504; speech at Chicago, Feb. 12, 1909, *WWP*, XIX, 45.

7. WW, *Constitutional Government*, *WWP*, XVIII, 108, 114.

8. WW, speech at New York, Apr. 7, 1910, *WWP*, XX, 339–340. Wilson's brother-in-law remembered that he had liked Oliver's book more than any other recent work. RSB interview with Axson, Feb. 8–11, 1925, RSB MSS, Box 99. A Princeton faculty colleague recalled Wilson telling him, "I have just been reading one of the greatest books sent me by a friend, and by a British shopkeeper of whom I never heard. The work is the life of Alexander Hamilton, by Frederick Scott Oliver." William Starr Myers, "Wilson in My Diary," in Myers, *Princeton Memories*, 42.

9. Lyman Abbott to WW, Apr. 8, 1910, *WWP*, XX, 350.

Introduction to Part III

1. WW speech at Springfield, Ill., Oct. 9, 1912, *WWP*, XXV, 395; TR speech at Chicago, June 17, 1912, *TRW*, XVII, 231.

2. WW to George Howe III, July 6, 1912, *WWP*, XXIV, 542.

11. Insurgent

1. TR to HCL, May 5, 1910, *TRL*, VII, 80; TR to Ethel Roosevelt, Dec. 12, 1909, *TRL*, VIII, 1448; Gifford Pinchot diary entry, Apr. 11, 1910, *TRL*, VII, 51 n. 3.

2. TR to HCL, Apr. 11, 1909, *TRL*, VII, 69–74.

3. TR to Percy Girouard, July 21, 1910, *TRL*, VII, 104; TR to Arthur Lee, Aug. 16, 1910, ibid., 112; TR to Pinchot, Aug. 17, 1910, ibid., 113.

4. For a description, by a journalist who was present, of the disparity between the commonplace content of one of Roosevelt's speeches in 1910 and the electrifying impression he made, see Oscar King Davis, *Released for Publication: Some Inside History of Theodore Roosevelt and His Times, 1898–1918* (Boston, 1925), 223–225. On the disparity between what he said in 1910 and its public reception, see also Lewis Einstein, *Roosevelt: His Mind in Action* (Boston, 1930), 188–189.

5. TR speech at Osawatomie, Kansas, Aug. 31, 1910, *TRW*, XVII, 6, 9, 14, 19. He called for expansion of the navy and fortification of the canal in a speech at Omaha, Sept. 2, 1910, in TR, *The New Nationalism* (New York, 1910), 144–157.

6. TR speech at Osawatomie, *TRW*, XVII, 18; speech at Freeport, Ill., Sept. 8, 1910, *TRW*, XVI, 162–163; speech at Columbus, Ohio, Sept. 10, 1910, *New Nationalism*, 219.

7. TR speech at Denver, Aug. 29, 1910, *New Nationalism*, 42–43; speech at Osawatomie, *TRW*, XVII, 18.

8. TR speech at Denver, Aug. 29, 1910, *New Nationalism*, 55; speech at Osawatomie, *TRW*, XVII, 19; speech at Fargo, N.D., Sept. 5, 1910, *New Nationalism*, 137; speech at Syracuse, N.Y., Sept. 17, 1910, ibid., 244.

9. TR speech at Syracuse, *New Nationalism*, 231: On TR's influence on Croly, see John M. Blum, *The Republican Roosevelt* (Cambridge, Mass., 1954), 107, 122; and Croly, *The Promise of American Life* (New York, 1909), 86, 167–175.

10. Croly, *Promise of American Life*, 45, 358–359.

11. Ibid., 5–6, 22, 399.

12. Ibid., 454. On, Croly see Charles Forcey, *The Crossroads of Liberalism: Croly, Weyl, Lippmann and the Progressive Era, 1900–1925* (New York, 1961), especially 3–52; and the observations of Edmund Wilson, who knew him later on the *New Republic*, in " 'H.C.' " [July 16, 1930], in Wilson, *The Shores of Light* (New York, 1952), 476–484; and Wilson to Arthur M. Schlesinger, Jr. [June 10], 1964, in Elena Wilson, ed., *Edmund Wilson: Letters on Literature and Politics, 1912–1972*, (New York, 1977), 197–198.

13. TR to TR, Jr., Sept. 21, 1910, *TRL*, VII, 133.

14. TR speech at Denver, *New Nationalism*, 35–41. The *Lochner* decision had prompted Justice Holmes's celebrated remark in dissent that "the Fourteenth Amendment does not enact Mr. Herbert Spencer's *Social Statics.*"

15. TR to HCL, Sept. 12, 1910, *TRL*, VII, 122–123. On the press mishap, see Davis, *Released for Publication*, 208–211, and on the conservatives' reaction, see Einstein, *Roosevelt*, 188–190.

16. Archie Butt to Clara Butt, May 5, 1910, in Butt, *Taft and Roosevelt: The Intimate Letters of Archie Butt, Military Aide* (Garden City, N.Y., 1930), I, 345–346; WHT to Charles P. Taft, Sept. 10, 1910, quoted in Henry F. Pringle, *The Life and Times of William Howard Taft* (New York, 1939), II, 573.

17. Archie Butt to Clara Butt, Aug. 15, 1910, in Butt, *Taft and Roosevelt*, II, 479.

18. TR speech at New Haven, Dec. 13, 1910, *TRW*, XVI, 88–89; WHT to Charles P. Taft, Sept. 10, 1910, quoted in Pringle, *Taft*, II, 573.

19. TR to Jonathan Bourne, Jr., Jan. 2, 1911, *TRL*, VII, 197. For Root's assessment, see Elihu Root to TR, Feb. 12, 1912, quoted in Philip C. Jessup, *Elihu Root* (New York, 1938), II, 173–176.

20. See TR *Outlook* columns, "Nationalism and Popular Rule," Jan. 21, 1911, and "Nationalism and the Judiciary," Feb. 25, Mar. 4, Mar. 11, 1911, *TRW*, XVII, 53–66, 74–100; TR speech at New York, Oct. 20, 1910, *TRW*, XVI, 197–202.

21. TR, "The Peace of Righteousness," *Outlook*, Sept. 9, 1911, *TRW*, XVI, 311–312; WHT to Otto Bannard, Sept. 10, 1911, quoted in Pringle, *Taft*, II, 748. On the treaty controversy, see John P. Campbell, "Taft, Roosevelt, and the Arbitration Treaties of 1911," *Journal of American History* 52 (Sept. 1966), 279–298.

22. TR to Henry White, Apr. 2, 1910, *TRL*, VII, 65; TR address at Christiana, Norway, May 5, 1910, *TRW*, XVI, 305–309; speech at Harvard, Dec. 14, 1910, *TRW*, XIII, 609; TR to HCL, June 12, 1911, *TRL*, VII, 284.

23. George E. Mowry, *Theodore Roosevelt and the Progressive Movement* (Madison, Wis., 1946), 197–198; William Henry Harbaugh, *Power and Responsibility: The Life and Times of Theodore Roosevelt* (New York, 1961), 404–405; Butt to Clara Butt, Dec. 31, 1911, Jan. 15, 1912, in Butt, *Taft and Roosevelt*, II, 804, 813.

24. Robert Grant to James Ford Rhodes, Mar. 22, 1912, *TRL*, VIII, 1458; Corinne Roosevelt Robinson note on Charles G. Washburn to Corinne R. Robinson, Jan. 12, 1924, Robinson MSS, File 1454; William Roscoe Thayer, *Theodore Roosevelt: An Intimate Biography* (Boston, 1919), 353.

25. TR speech at New York, Mar. 20, 1912, *TRW*, XVII, 169; speech at Louisville, Apr. 3, 1912, ibid., 184.

26. TR and WHT statements quoted in *TRL*, VII, 541 n. 3; WHT to Otto Bannard, Jan. 22, 1912, quoted in Pringle, *Taft*, II, 764; WHT to Horace D. Taft, Apr. 14, 1912, quoted in ibid., 772.

27. The losses were a narrow one to Taft in Massachusetts and a more substantial one in North Dakota to La Follette, who had not withdrawn from the race and who denounced Roosevelt as a usurper and betrayer of the progressive cause. On the campaign, see Mowry, *Roosevelt and Progressive Movement*, 220–236.

28. On the convention, see ibid., 237–253; on the conservatives and their thinking, see Norman M. Wilensky, *Conservatives in the Progressive Era: The Taft Republicans of 1912* (Gainesville, Fla., 1965).

29. WHT to Myron Herrick, June 20, 1912, quoted in Pringle, *Taft*, II, 808.

30. TR to H. H. Kohlsaat, Mar. 16, 1912, *TRL*, VII, 527; TR to Chase S. Osborn, Apr. 16, 1912, ibid., 534.

31. TR statement, Mar 9, 1916, *TRW*, XVII, 410.

32. TR to Hiram Johnson, Oct. 27, 1911, *TRL*, VII, 420; TR to Benjamin Ide Wheeler, Dec. 21, 1911, ibid., 462; TR to William B. Howland, Dec. 23, 1911, ibid., 467.

33. Kermit Roosevelt, quoted in Link, *Wilson*, I, (Princeton, 1947), 422. For the story of Bryan's conversations with Roosevelt, see Davis, *Released for Publication*, 316–317.

34. TR speech at Chicago, June 17, 1912, *TRW*, XVII, 204–231. For estimates of the speech by journalists who knew Roosevelt well and covered him for years, see Mark Sullivan, *Our Times: The United States, 1900–1925* (New York, 1932), IV, 508–509; and William Allen White, *Autobiography* (New York, 1946), 464.

35. For the observation about balance and qualification spoiling TR's oratory, see Davis, *Released for Publication*, 213. Unlike Wilson and Bryan, Roosevelt had not been trained in school and college as a debater and speaker, and he later scorned education in such arts as a form of trickery. See TR, *Autobiography, TRW*, XX, 25. After the Armageddon speech, William Allen White discussed it with Senator William E. Borah, who had also been present. "Borah was an orator, and he knew how Roosevelt did it. He was tremendously impressed with it; but he was a little frightened, as I was." White, *Autobiography*, 466.

36. Blum, *Republican Roosevelt*, 145, 149.

12. Frontrunner

1. James Kerney, *The Political Education of Woodrow Wilson* (New York, 1926), 52. On Wilson's gubernatorial nomination, see ibid., 51–54; and Arthur S. Link *Wilson*, I (Princeton, 1947), 155–166.

2. WW speech at Trenton, Sept. 15, 1910, *WWP*, XXI, 91–94; newspaper report, Sept. 17, 1910, ibid., 118–120. For press reaction to his nomination and appearance, see Link, *Wilson*, I, 170–172.

3. Tumulty quoted in Dan Fellows Platt to WW, Sept. 19, 1910, *WWP*, XXI, 142. On the New Idea Republicans, see Ransom E. Noble, Jr., *New Jersey Progressivism before Wilson* (Princeton, 1946).

4. Kerney, *Political Education of Wilson*, 61–64; WW to David B. Jones, Sept. 25, 1910, *WWP*, XXI, 163. On WW's campaign expenses, see Link, *Wilson*, I, 187–188.

5. WW speech at Trenton, Oct. 3, 1910, *WWP*, XXI, 229–230.

6. WW speech at Trenton, Sept. 15, 1910, ibid., 92; interview, Sept. 17, 1910, ibid., 126–127; speech at Jersey City, Sept. 20, 1910, ibid., 147.

7. George L. Record to WW, Oct. 17, 1910, *WWP*, XXI, 338–347; WW to Record, Oct. 24, 1910, ibid., 406–411; Record, quoted in Link, *Wilson*, I, 195. On Record's attitude toward Wilson and motives in posing his questions, see also RSB interview with Record, Apr. 6, 1928, RSB MSS, Box 120.

8. WW to Harvey, Nov. 15, 1910, *WWP*, XXII, 47–48. On the result, see *WWP*, XXI, 584 n. 1.

9. WW speech at Elizabeth, Oct. 28, 1910, *WWP*, XXI, 462; speech at Newark, Nov. 5, 1910, ibid., 575.

10. WW interview, Oct. 2, 1910, ibid., 223; WW to E. A. Van Valkenburg, Sept. 25, 1910, ibid., 165; WW speech at Newark, Sept. 30, 1910, ibid., 205.

11. The differences between the progressive followings and their national leaders are discussed in George E. Mowry, *Theodore Roosevelt and the Progressive Movement* (Madison, Wis., 1946), and *The Era of Theodore Roosevelt and the Birth of Modern America, 1900–1912* (New York, 1958).

12. On Record's distrust of Wilson, which persisted after his governorship and presidency, see RSB interview with Record, Apr. 6, 1928, RSB MSS, Box 120.

13. WW speech to American Bar Association, Chattanooga, Tenn., Aug. 31, 1910, *WWP*, XXI, 65.

14. Ibid., 81. In this assessment I disagree with Richard Hofstadter, who compared the two as conservatives, dubbing Roosevelt "the conservative as progressive," and Wilson "the conservative as liberal." See Hofstadter, *The American Political Tradition and the Men Who Made It* (New York, 1948), chaps. 9, 10.

15. WW speech at Jersey City, Sept. 28, 1910, *WWP*, XXI, 191.

16. Robert Bridges, *Woodrow Wilson: A Personal Tribute* ([Princeton?], 1924), 5.

17. WW speech at Flemington, Oct. 20, 1910, *WWP*, XXI, 371–376.

18. WW speech at Elizabeth, Oct. 28, 1910, ibid., 462; speech at Perth Amboy, Nov. 4, 1910, ibid., 551.

19. On Wilson's effort to get Smith to withdraw in favor of a compromise candidate, see *WWP*, XXII, 73 n. 3.

20. WW to MAHP, Jan. 29, 1911, ibid., 392; Watterson to G. B. M. Harvey, Jan. 29, 1911, ibid., 435 n. 1. On the senatorial nomination fight, see Link, *Wilson*, I, 211–237.

21. Link, *Wilson*, I, 249; WW to MAHP, Apr. 23, 1911, *WWP*, XXII, 581–582.

22. Frank P. Glass memo, Jan. 1926, RSB MSS, Box 109. For the criticism of Wilson's personal dealings, see Charles O'Connor Hennessy to RSB, RSB MSS, Box 111.

23. WW to MAHP, Apr. 2, 1911, *WWP*, XXII, 532.

24. Link, *Wilson*, I, 298, 307.

25. WW to Henry S. Breckinridge, Dec. 21, 1910, *WWP*, XXII, 237. On the second presidential drive, see Link, *Wilson*, I, 392–393; and Breckinridge to WW, Dec. 17, 1910, *WWP*, XXII, 213–214.

26. WW to Walter Hines Page, Feb. 10, 1911, *WWP*, XXII, 413–414. On Page's involvement, see John Milton Cooper, Jr., *Walter Hines Page: The Southerner as American, 1856–1918* (Chapel Hill, N.C., 1977), 235–241; and on McCombs and McAdoo, see Link, *Wilson*, I, 313–314, 329–331, 336–337.

27. WW speech at Philadelphia, Feb. 21, 1911, *WWP*, XXII, 441–443, 444.

28. Ibid., 449–450; WW speech at Indianapolis, Apr. 13, 1911, ibid., 559; speech at Minneapolis, May 25, 1911, *WWP*, XXIII, 94.

29. WW speech at Los Angeles, May 12, 1911, *WWP*, XXIII, 33–36; speech at Columbia, S.C., June 2, 1911, ibid., 120–121; speech at Harrisburg, Pa., June 16, 1911, ibid., 157.

30. WW to MAHP, Apr. 9, 1911, *WWP*, XXII, 545; WJB to WW, Jan. 5 [1911], ibid., 307. On Bryan's influence in the party, see Paul W. Glad, *The Trumpet Soundeth: William Jennings Bryan and His Democracy, 1896–1912* (Lincoln, Neb., 1960).

31. On the break with Harvey see Link, *Wilson*, I, 359–378, which reproduces most of the relevant contemporary documents, and RSB interview with Stockton Axson, Mar. 12, 1925, RSB MSS, Box 99; RSB interview with Dudley Field Malone, Nov. 1, 1927, RSB MSS, Box 116.

32. WW to MAHP, Apr. 30, 1911, *WWP*, XXII, 598.

33. On the Underwood movement in the South, see Link, *Wilson*, I, 408, 415–417; and Evans C. Johnson, *Oscar W. Underwood: A Political Biography* (Baton Rouge, La., 1980), 170–183.

34. On the Clark movement and the forces behind it, see Link, *Wilson,* I, 380–382, 400–402.

35. WW to Cleveland H. Dodge, May 16, 1912, *WWP*, XXIV, 402.

36. WW speech at Nashville, Feb. 24, 1912, ibid., 204; speech at Chicago, Feb. 12, 1912, ibid., 156; speech at Springfield, Ill., Apr. 6, 1912, ibid., 295; speech at New York, May 23, 1912, ibid., 415.

37. WW speech at Atlanta, Apr. 17, 1912, ibid., 337; speech at New York, Apr. 14, 1912, ibid., 331–332; speech at Boston, Apr. 27, 1912, ibid., 365; speech at Buffalo, Apr. 10, 1912, ibid., 314.

38. The best account of the Baltimore convention is Link, *Wilson,* I, 433–463. On Wilson's telegram releasing his delegates, see also *WWP*, XXIV, 524 n. 3.

39. Link, *Wilson,* I, 450–451, 459. On the Underwood forces, see also Johnson, *Underwood,* 189–192.

40. *New York Times,* July 3, 1912, in *WWP*, XXIV, 522; WW to MAHP, July 6, 1912, ibid., 541; Luke Lea to WW, July 13, 1912, ibid., 546.

13. On the Hustings

1. WW to Edith G. Reid, May 26, 1912, *WWP*, XXIV, 446; WW to MAHP, Dec. 17, 1911, *WWP*, XXIII, 597; William Starr Myers, "Wilson in My Diary," in William Starr Myers, ed., *Woodrow Wilson: Some Princeton Memories* (Princeton, 1946), 42–43; *Newark Evening News,* May 28, 1912, *WWP*, XXIV, 448–449.

2. William Allen White, *Autobiography,* (New York, 1946), 482–484. On the Progressive convention, see also George E. Mowry, *Theodore Roosevelt and the Progressive Movement* Madison, Wis., 1946), 262–266; and for an assessment of their activists, see Alfred D. Chandler, Jr., "The Origins of Progressive Leadership," *TRL*, VIII, 1462–1465.

3. Among Roosevelt's youthful supporters, Acheson, then fresh out of Yale, recalled his involvement in accents reminiscent of Wordworth's ecstasy over the French Revolution: "Bliss it was to be alive in that dawn, / But to be young was very heaven." Forty years later Acheson wrote, "At the beginning of the second decade of this century, when the world seemed young and I certainly was, I thrilled to every bugle call to action blown by the 'Young Turks,' the 'Progressives,' and most of all by 'T. R.,' the most ebullient of them all, in the revolt against the 'Old Guard,' the 'malefactors of great wealth,' against 'reaction' in the person of Uncle Joe Cannon and inaction in the benign and ineffective figure of

President William Howard Taft. It was springtime and 'T. R.' rode again." Acheson, *A Democrat Looks at His Party* (New York, 1955), 13. Lippmann similarly recalled that from 1898, when as a boy of nine he had first seen Roosevelt, until 1912, "I was his unqualified hero-worshipper. He became for me the image of a great leader and the prototype of Presidents. The impression is indelible and, if I wished, I could not even now erase it. So persistent is it that in any complete confession, I think I should have to say that I have been less than just to his successors because they were not like him." Lippmann, TR memorial address, Oct. 27, 1935, in Gilbert A. Harrison, ed., *Public Persons by Walter Lippmann* (New York, 1976), 126.

4. Mowry, *Roosevelt and Progressive Movement*, 263; Blum, *TR*, 149. For a contrasting view, which stresses the presence and contributions of professionals, see John Allen Gable, *The Bull Moose Years: Theodore Roosevelt and the Progressive Party* (Port Washington, N.Y., 1978), especially 76–77.

5. *New York Times*, Aug. 7, 1912, quoted in Mowry, *Roosevelt and Progressive Movement*, 265.

6. TR speech at Chicago, Aug. 6, 1912, *TRW*, XVII, 258, 273; TR to Arthur Lee, Aug. 14, 1912, *TRL*, VII, 598.

7. On the antitrust plank, see Mowry, *Roosevelt and Progressive Movement*, 269–272.

8. TR speech at Chicago, Aug. 6, 1912, *TRW*, XVII, 272–283.

9. Ibid., 255, 276–277, 292; TR to Sir Horace Plunkett, Aug. 3, 1912, *TRL*, VII, 591–593. For TR's reaction to his nomination, see Mowry, *Roosevelt and Progressive Movement*, 273.

10. On the notification ceremony and Wilson's backing, see Link, *Wilson*, I, (Princeton, 1947), 472–473, 478–479.

11. WW speech at Sea Girt, N.J., Aug. 7, 1912, *WWP*, XXV, 3–4, 5–6, 8, 11.

12. Ibid., 6, 7.

13. Ibid., 6, 14.

14. WW to MAHP, Aug. 25, 1912, ibid., 55; Eleanor Wilson McAdoo, *The Woodrow Wilsons* (New York, 1937), 172.

15. *New York Times*, Aug. 29, 1912, in *WWP*, XXV, 57–58.

16. Link, *Wilson*, I, 488–489; RSB interview with Brandeis, Mar. 3, 1929, RSB MSS, Box 102; WW to Brandeis [Nov. 13, 1912], *WWP*, XXV, 545. On Brandeis's role in 1912 and his economic thought, see Alpheus T. Mason, *Brandeis: A Free Man's Life* (New York, 1946), 375–383; and Melvin I. Urofsky, *A Mind of One Piece: Brandeis and American Reform* (New York, 1971), especially 45–92.

17. WW speech at Buffalo, Sept. 2, 1912, *WWP*, XXV, 75.

18. Ibid., 77–78. For one criticism of Wilson's denunciation of "government of experts," see Richard Hofstadter, *Anti-Intellectualism in American Life* (New York, reprint ed., 1966), 209–210.

19. TR speech at Fargo, N.D., Sept. 6, 1912, *Outlook* 2 (Sept. 14, 1912), 105–107.

20. WW speech at New York, Sept. 9, 1912, *WWP*, XXV, 124. In this incident, as John Wells Davidson has pointed out, Wilson was paying a price for his extraordinary skill at extemporaneous speaking. Davidson, ed., *A Crossroads of Freedom: The 1912 Campaign Speeches of Woodrow Wilson* (New Haven, Conn., 1956), 122–123. Roosevelt, who did not have the same gift, had learned from painful experiences, like the one at Denver in 1910, to dictate advance texts of his speeches and supply them to the press. Later in the campaign Wilson quizzed reporters accompanying him who had covered Roosevelt about the ex-president's practice. "I wish I could do that," he confessed. "I've tried to do it over and over again, but I can't." Charles Willis Thompson to Bernice M. Thompson, Oct. 6, 1912, *WWP*, XXV, 361. Except for the most formal addresses, such as his acceptance speech and state occasions later as president, when he read from prepared texts, Wilson persisted in speaking either from sketchy notes or none at all.

21. TR speech at San Francisco, Sept. 14, 1912, *TRW*, XVII, 306, 307, 313, 314.

22. Oscar King Davis, *Released for Publication: Some Inside History of Theodore Roosevelt and His Times, 1898–1918* (Boston, 1925), 360–361. On TR's campaign style and performance, see also Mowry, *Roosevelt and Progressive Movement*, 276–277.

23. WW speech at Sioux City, Iowa, Sept. 17, 1912, *WWP*, XXV, 152; speech at Boston, Sept. 27, 1912, Davidson, *Crossroads of Freedom*, 291–292. On Brandeis's further influence, see Brandeis to WW, Sept. 30, 1912, with accompanying memoranda, *WWP*, XXV, 287–304; and Link, *Wilson*, I, 491–492.

24. WW speech at Scranton, Pa., Sept. 23, 1912, *WWP*, XXV, 222, 224–225; Davidson, *Crossroads of Freedom*, 233.

25. WW speech at Springfield, Ill., Oct. 9, 1912, *WWP*, XXV, 395; speech at Lincoln, Neb., Oct. 5, 1912, ibid., 348; speech at Dover, Del., Oct. 17, 1912, ibid., 425.

26. WW speech at Sioux City, Iowa, Sept. 17, 1912, ibid., 154; speech at Boston, Sept. 27, 1912, Davidson, *Crossroads of Freedom*, 293, 295.

27. WW speech at Indianapolis, Oct. 3, 1912, *WWP*, XXV, 327; speech at Lincoln, Neb., Oct. 5, 1912, ibid., 350, 354, 359; speech at Cleveland, Oct. 11, 1912, ibid., 412.

28. TR speech at Chicago, Oct. 12, 1912, quoted in TR to WJB, Oct. 22, 1912, *TRL*, VII, 630–631.

29. TR speech at Milwaukee, Oct. 14, 1912, *TRW*, XVII, 320, 322–323.

30. Ibid., 328; TR telegram, Oct. 16, 1912, ibid., 331. For a detailed eyewitness account of the incident, see Davis, *Released for Publication*, 375–390; and for TR's own recollection, see TR to Sir Edward Grey, Nov. 15, 1912, *TRL*, VII, 649–650. Whether Roosevelt really thought he was dying when he went on with his speech is open to dispute. He privately claimed soon afterward that he knew at once he was not badly wounded because when he coughed on his hand no blood appeared (ibid.). At the time, however, stunned by the shot and starting to suffer from shock, he could not know that for sure. Fundamentally, it did not matter whether Roosevelt really thought he was dying or not. He had been wounded, apparently seriously, and others were fearing for his life. His purpose in carrying on with the speech was to demonstrate the right qualities and to embody the right values before others, like a commander before his troops. His performance at Milwaukee offered an example of Roosevelt the showman at his best.

31. For Roosevelt's October 19 trust statement, see Davidson, *Crossroads of Freedom*, 480; and for Harbaugh's observation see *Power and Responsibility: The Life and Times of Theodore Roosevelt* (New York, 1961), 448. In point of fact, Roosevelt was not reconciled to Wilson, and he delivered one other short address, on the day before the election, that contained an attack on Wilson over the trusts. See TR speech at Oyster Bay, Nov. 2, 1912, *TRW*, XVII, 341–348.

32. TR speech at New York, Oct. 30, 1912, *TRW*, XVII, 334–335, 336, 339.

33. Davidson, *Crossroads of Freedom*, 511. On Wilson's decision to suspend campaigning, see entry for Oct. 15, 1912, EMH diary, *WWP*, XXV, 421–422, and McAdoo, *The Wilsons*, 173.

34. WW speech at Clarksburg, W. Va., Oct. 18, 1912, Davidson, *Crossroads of Freedom*, 449; speech at West Chester, Pa., Oct. 28, 1912, *WWP*, XXV, 463–464; speech at Philadelphia, Oct. 28, 1912, Davidson, *Crossroads of Freedom*, 489.

35. WW speech at Philadelphia, Oct. 28, 1912, Davidson, *Crossroads*, 491; speech at Long Branch, N.J., Nov. 2, 1912, *WWP*, XXV, 505.

36. For treatments of the 1912 vote, see Link, *Wilson*, I, 525; and Mowry, *Roosevelt and Progressive Movement*, 280–282. The six states Roosevelt won were California (eleven of thirteen electoral votes), Michigan, Minnesota, Pennsylvania, South Dakota, and Washington.

37. In 1920 Debs polled a slightly larger number of votes, 919,799,

but it was a smaller share, 3.4 percent as compared with 6.0 percent in 1912. On Deb's and the Socialists' showing, see James Weinstein, *The Decline of Socialism in America, 1912–1925* (New York, 1967). On Roosevelt's weakness in one part of the Rockies, see James C. Wright, *The Politics of Populism: Dissent in Colorado* (New Haven, Conn., 1974), 258–264. Roosevelt placed third in eighteen states—Arkansas, Connecticut, Delaware, Idaho, Kentucky, Massachusetts, Missouri, New Hampshire, New Mexico, New York, Ohio, Rhode Island, Tennessee, Texas, Utah, Virginia, Wisconsin, and Wyoming.

14. The New Nationalism versus the New Freedom

1. *New York Times*, Nov. 7, 1912, *WWP*, XXV, 524; WW to WJB, Nov. 9, 1912, ibid., 533; WHT to Otto Bannard, Nov. 10, 1912, quoted in Henry F. Pringle, *The Life and Times of William Howard Taft* (New York, 1939), II, 840; WHT to C. H. Kelsey, Nov. 8, 1912, quoted in ibid., 841; TR to Gifford Pinchot, Nov. 13, 1912, *TRL*, VII, 642. For Roosevelt's analysis, see also TR to Amos Pinchot, Dec. 5, 1912, ibid., 665.

2. See George E. Mowry, *Theodore Roosevelt and the Progressive Movement* (Madison, Wis., 1946), 282–283.

3. TR to Gifford Pinchot, Nov. 13, 1912, *TRL*, VII, 642.

4. The two men evidently subscribed to different philosophies of public speaking. Roosevelt does seem to have followed an approach of deliberate simplification for public consumption. He frequently declared himself "no orator," and he often asserted that literary finesse was incompatible with effective public speech. Wister recounts that when Roosevelt was president he once grew annoyed when Wister and Alice Roosevelt joked about "bromides." After having the term defined to him, Roosevelt answered, "All the same, I have to use bromides in my business." Wister, *Roosevelt: The Story of a Friendship* (New York, 1930), 93. Wilson, in contrast, appears to have had great confidence in his ability to convey complicated ideas to the public. Later, the Democratic national chairman once objected to a party appeal of Wilson's as too elaborate in its phrasing, but Wilson answered with a grin, "I think that is all right because you see the people have gotten used by this time to having a highbrow President." Homer S. Cummings memorandum, Nov. 21, 1928, RSB MSS, Box 104.

5. William Allen White, *Woodrow Wilson* (Boston, 1924), 264.

6. Apparently, no single personal element poisoned Roosevelt's view of Wilson more than jealousy of his rival's gifts as a writer and a speaker. Bainbridge Colby, a leading New York Progressive who later

served as Wilson's last secretary of state and still later was briefly his law partner, believed that envy of Wilson's articulateness underlay much of Roosevelt's feeling. RSB interview with Colby, June 19, 1930, RSB MSS, Box 104.

7. *TRL*, VII, 593 n. 3; Link, *Wilson*, V (Princeton, 1965), 94; Link, *Woodrow Wilson and the Progressive Era, 1910–1917* (New York, 1954), 239–240.

8. For statements of their respective views on woman suffrage, see TR to Mary E. Swift, Mar. 7, 1911, *TRL*, VII, 240; WW to Eugene N. Foss, Aug. 17, 1912, *WWP*, XXV, 42.

9. On Roosevelt's racial thinking, see Thomas G. Dyer, *Theodore Roosevelt and the Idea of Race* (Baton Rouge, La., 1980). On the race-related controversies during Roosevelt's presidency, see Willard B. Gatewood, Jr., *Theodore Roosevelt and the Art of Controversy* (Baton Rouge, La., 1970), chaps. 2–4. On Roosevelt's wooing of southern whites, see George E. Mowry, "The South and the Progressive Lily White Party of 1912," *Journal of Southern History* 6 (May 1940), 237–247, and John Allen Gable, *The Bull Moose Years: Theodore Roosevelt and the Progressive Party* (Port Washington, N.Y., 1978). Roosevelt also made a respectable showing in Georgia, where he had the support of the racist demagogue Tom Watson, who remained unreconciled to Wilson.

10. On Wilson's racial attitudes and policies as president, see Morton P. Sosna, "The South in the Saddle: Racial Politics during the Wilson Years," *Wisconsin Magazine of History* 54 (Autumn 1970), 30–49; and Kathleen L. Wolgemuth, "Woodrow Wilson's Appointment Policy and the Negro," *Journal of Southern History* 24 (Nov. 1958), 457–471.

11. On Wilson administration antitrust policies, see Melvin I. Urofsky, *Big Steel and the Wilson Administration: A Study in Government-Business Relations* (Columbus, Ohio, 1969); and Alan L. Seltzer, "Woodrow Wilson as 'Corporate Liberal': Toward a Reconsideration of Left Revisionist Historiography," *Western Political Quarterly* 30 (June 1977), 183–212. Lippmann stressed businessmen's "disinterestedness" in *Drift and Mastery* (New York, 1914), and later in his newspaper column and in talks at the outset of the Depression. See Ronald Steel, *Walter Lippmann and the American Century* (Boston, 1980), 78–79, 276–277, 289–290.

12. See Galbraith, *American Capitalism: The Concept of Counter-vailing Power* (Boston, 1956). Mowry, who argues that "in the polemics [of 1912] over two divergent philosophies of government, Roosevelt was calling the tune of the times," labels his position "a new paternalism." Mowry, *Roosevelt and Progressive Movement*, 269, 276. For an eluci-

dation of the term "tory" by a commentator who proudly applies the label to himself, see George F. Will, *The Pursuit of Virtue and Other Tory Notions* (New York, 1981).

13. For an opposite view of their respective influences in twentieth-century American politics, see the introductions by William E. Leuchtenburg to his editions of TR, *The New Nationalism*, and WW, *The New Freedom* (both, Englewood Cliffs, N.J., 1961).

14. WW speech at New York, Oct. 19, 1912, *WWP*, XXV, 447.

15. Wilson was not the only nonconservative spokesman to deplore a potential undermining of self-reliance. Eugene Debs once declared, "If you are looking for a Moses to lead you out of the . . . wilderness you can stay right where you are. I would not lead you into this promised land if I could, because if I could lead you in, someone else could lead you out." Debs quoted in Emmet John Hughes, *The Ordeal of Power: A Political Memoir of the Eisenhower Years* (New York, 1963), 349.

16. TR to Gifford Pinchot, Nov. 13, 1912, *TRL*, VII, 641. Roosevelt conceded his admiration for aristocracies when he wrote privately soon after the election, "There is something to be said for government by a great aristocracy which has furnished leaders to the nation in peace and war; even a democrat like myself must admit this." TR to Sir Edward Grey, Nov. 15, 1912, ibid., 648.

17. For a discussion of marketplace behavior as a social and economic ideal, see James Willard Hurst, *Law and the Conditions of Freedom in the Nineteenth Century United States* (Madison, Wis., 1956).

18. Fittingly, Wilson praised Jefferson more often and more ardently during the 1912 campaign than at any other time in his life. That did not indicate any lessening of his admiration for Hamilton. In May 1913 he again publicly lauded Hamilton. WW speech at Jersey City, May 2, 1913, *WWP*, XXVII, 391. In April 1914 Colonel House recorded, "I asked whom he considered the greatest man in early days of the Republic. He thought Alexander Hamilton was easily the ablest." Entry, Apr. 15, 1914, EMH diary, *WWP*, XXIX, 448.

19. On Roosevelt's conservatism and social views, compare Lewis Einstein, *Roosevelt: His Mind in Action* (Boston, 1930); John M. Blum, *The Republican Roosevelt* (Cambridge, Mass., 1954), especially 4–5, 106–107; and Elting E. Morison, "Introduction," *TRL*, V, xiii–xiv.

20. On Jeffersonian persuasions among Democrats, see Merrill D. Peterson, *The Jefferson Image in the American Mind* (New York, 1960), especially 254–265, 330–331. For a discussion of Wilson's views of human nature, see William McCleery interview with Arthur S. Link, "What Carter Could Learn from Wilson," *Princeton Alumni Weekly*, Sept. 25, 1978, 12–17.

21. WW speech at Wheeling, W.Va., Oct. 18, 1912, Davidson, *A Crossroads of Freedom: The 1912 Campaign Speeches of Woodrow Wilson* (New Haven, Conn., 1956), 458.

22. TR to Henry White, Nov. 12, 1912, *TRL*, VII, 639; TR to Benjamin Ide Wheeler, Nov. 20, 1912, ibid., 652.

23. RSB interview with Edwin Grant Conklin, June 19, 1925, RSB MSS, Box 104. Conklin amplified on Wilson's remark in Conklin to DeWitt Clinton Poole, Nov. 7, 1933, DeWitt Clinton Poole Papers, State Historical Society of Wisconsin, Box 1.

15. Party Leader

1. Entry, Jan. 8, 1913, EMH diary, *WWP*, XXVII, 23. On the Democratic party situation, see Link, *Wilson*, II (Princeton, 1956), 158; and *Woodrow Wilson and the Progressive Era* (New York, 1954), 35. On the administration's southern flavor, see Morton P. Sosna, "The South in the Saddle: Racial Politics during the Wilson Years," *Wisconsin Magazine of History* 54 (Autumn 1970), 30–49.

2. WW to A. Mitchell Palmer, Feb. 5, 1913, *WWP*, XXVII, 99–100; WW speech to New Jersey electors, Jan. 13, 1913, ibid., 40; entry, Mar. 18, 1913, Josephus Daniels diary, ibid., 194.

3. RSB interview with Albert Sidney Burleson, Mar. 17–19, 1927, RSB MSS, Box 103.

4. For an account of Wilson's dealings with the Democratic party that stresses more his bowing to regularity, see Link, *Wilson*, II, 48–53, 152–175.

5. WW statement, May 26, 1913, *WWP*, XXVII, 473. For an account of the tariff revision fight, see Link, *Wilson*, II, 177–197.

6. WW to MAH, June 22, 1913, *WWP*, XXVII, 556; Carter Glass to H. Parker Willis, Dec. 29, 1912, *WWP*, XXV, 644.

7. WW press conference, June 16, 1913, *WWP*, XXVII, 522; WW speech to Congress, June 23, 1913, ibid., 572–573. For Brandeis's advice, see Brandeis to WW, June 14, 1913, ibid., 520–521; on the whole struggle for banking reform, see Link, *Wilson*, II, 199–240.

8. WW speech to Congress, Jan. 20, 1914, *WWP*, XXIX, 155. On the labor exemption, see Link, *Wilson*, II, 433.

9. WW to Henry F. Hollis, June 2, 1914, *WWP*, XXX, 134. On Wilson's shift and the combination of the two acts, see Link, *Wilson*, II, 433–436, 439–440.

10. On the Panama canal tolls exemption repeal, see Link, *Wilson*, II, 309–314. Some analysts have tended to downgrade Wilson's legis-

lative accomplishments in 1913 and 1914 because the Democrats enjoyed a majority of 73 seats in the House, including 112 first-termers, most of whom owed their election to the 1912 Republican split. Actually, such a large majority, containing so many inexperienced members, could have made party discipline harder to maintain (as happened to the Democrats in 1937 and 1938, following Franklin D. Roosevelt's landslide reelection). Ideological coherence offered Wilson a much greater advantage. Appropriately, in the next Congress, elected in 1914, in which the Democrats' House majority fell to 25, he had no trouble in getting his legislation passed. In the Senate the Democrats held only small majorities during Wilson's first term, and he had a consistently harder job winning approval of his programs there.

11. WW speech at Trenton, Jan. 13, 1913, *WWP*, XXVII, 41; WW to MAH, Sept. 21, 1913, *WWP*, XXVIII, 311; WW press conference, Nov. 3, 1913, ibid., 487.

12. WW message to New Jersey legislature, Jan. 14, 1913, *WWP*, XXVII, 46–47.

13. WW to MAH, Mar. 16, 1913, ibid., 190; WW speech at Washington, Mar. 20, 1914, *WWP*, XXIX, 363–364.

14. Entries, Feb. 14, Dec. 22, 1913, EMH diary, *WWP*, XXVII, 114, XXIX, 59; Helen W. Bones to Jessie B. Brower, Apr. 12, 1913, *WWP*, XXIX, 556. After Wilson's dismissal of Roosevelt and men on horseback, House noted in his diary, "I took the opposite ground." *WWP*, XXVII, 114.

15. John Reed, unpublished article, June 1914, *WWP*, XXX, 232–233; entry, May 12, 1916, RSB diary, *WWP*, XXXVII, 32. The editors of the *Wilson Papers* speculate that Reed's article did not appear in print because Wilson had spoken too frankly about Mexican policy in the interview and therefore refused permission to publish, *WWP*, XXX, 231 n. 2. Interestingly, except for House and occasional writers, few observers compared Wilson with Cleveland, the last Democratic president. The absence of such comparisons no doubt reflected the contrast between the deadlock and frustration of Cleveland's second term and the accomplishment and fulfillment of Wilson's first term.

16. See Link, "The South and the 'New Freedom': An Interpretation," *American Scholar* 20 (Summer 1951), 314–324. In "Woodrow Wilson and the Southern Congressmen, 1913–1916," *Journal of Southern History* 22 (Nov. 1956), 417–437, Richard M. Abrams argues that southern congressional forces were neither so radical nor so influential with Wilson as Link maintains, but he does not deny the presence and leanings of those spokesmen. On the Democratic party situation, see also note 10 above.

17. I have discussed the comparison of Roosevelt and Wilson separately in "The Warrior and the Priest: Toward a Comparative Perspective on Theodore Roosevelt and Woodrow Wilson," *South Atlantic Quarterly* 80 (Autumn 1981), 419–428.

18. Josephus Daniels, *The Wilson Era: Years of Peace, 1910–1917* (Chapel Hill, N.C., 1944), 137. The best source for cabinet discussions is Daniels's diary, whose entries bear out this later description. Unfortunately, Daniels stopped keeping a full diary in September 1913. Occasional accounts of later cabinet discussions can be gleaned from memoranda kept by other members, particularly Robert Lansing and Lindley M. Garrison, and published in the *Wilson Papers*, as well as from a few descriptions in cabinet members' memoirs. On the freedom Wilson gave his cabinet members, see also Link, *Wilson*, II, 76–77.

19. Entry, Aug. 10, 1913, EMH diary, *WWP*, XXVIII, 139; WW press conference, Oct. 9, 1913, ibid., 380. For an assessment of the complaints as they relate to charges that Secretary of the Interior Franklin K. Lane leaked information about cabinet discussions to the press, see Keith W. Olson, *Biography of a Progressive: Franklin K. Lane, 1864–1921* (Westport, Conn., 1979), 121–124. Olson is mistaken, however, in accepting the view that Wilson did not consult with the cabinet.

20. On the Wilsons' personal life in the White House, see Link, *Wilson*, II, 85–91.

21. On Wilson's working habits and health, see Edwin A. Weinstein, *Woodrow Wilson: A Medical and Psychological Biography* (Princeton, 1981), 251–252.

22. Entry, Nov. 14, 1914, EMH diary, *WWP*, XXXI, 319. The best and most extended criticism of Wilson's solitariness is Patrick Devlin, *Too Proud to Fight: Woodrow Wilson's Neutrality* (New York, 1974). I have discussed my partial disagreement with Devlin's view in "Woodrow Wilson through Alien Eyes," *Reviews in American History* 3 (Sept. 1975), 359–364.

23. Wilson reserved his reading mainly for the heavy traffic of official papers that crossed his desk, together with detective stories for relaxation. But he also reread certain classic political biographies, particularly John Morley's life of Gladstone, at times of stress, and he evidently made some efforts to keep abreast of important recent books on politics. A list of his overdue books from the Library of Congress in 1914 included Walter Lippmann's *A Preface to Politics* and Graham Wallas's *Human Nature in Politics*, along with books on Jefferson and Hamilton, John Stuart Mill's *Principles of Political Economy*, and a variety of lighter works. See William W. Bishop to WW, Nov. 14, 1914, *WWP*, XXXI, 316–317.

24. On Tumulty's contributions, see John M. Blum, *Joe Tumulty and the Wilson Era* (Boston, 1951), especially 60–67, 72–87.

25. Entries, EMH diary, Feb. 28, Dec. 22, 1913, *WWP*, XXVII, 140–141, XXIX, 59. The other nonfamily members with whom Wilson maintained frank, intimate relations were his physician, Dr. Cary T. Grayson, with whom he rarely discussed affairs of state, and three women, with whom he did. They were Mary Allen Hulbert (formerly Mrs. Peck), with whom he had had a brief love affair in 1909 or 1910; Nancy Saunders Toy; and Edith Giddings Reid. Of those women, Mrs. Toy and Mrs. Reid occasionally visited Wilson in the White House. Wilson maintained relations with them and Mrs. Hulbert mainly through frequent, revealing letters. On his affair with Mrs. Peck, see Francis W. Saunders, "Love and Guilt: Woodrow Wilson and Mrs. Hulbert," *American Heritage* 30 (Apr.–May 1979), 68–77; and Weinstein, *Wilson*, 181–94. For another statement of a president's need for disinterested friendship, compare Franklin Roosevelt's comment to Wendell Wilkie about Harry Hopkins in January 1941: "You'll be looking at that door over there and knowing that practically everybody who walks through it wants something out of you. You'll learn what a lonely job this is, and you'll discover the need for somebody like Harry Hopkins who asks for nothing except to serve you." FDR quoted in Robert E. Sherwood, *Roosevelt and Hopkins: An Intimate History* (New York, 1948), 3.

26. WW to EBG, Aug. 28, 1915, *WWP*, XXXIV, 352–353. This is apparently Wilson's only surviving comment about House outside the colonel's diary. That circumstance points up the biggest obstacle to an accurate assessment of House's role and influence. For over half a century his diary— first in its highly selective, misleading published edition and later in its manuscript versions—has led historians astray in two ways. First, the diary contains inaccuracies and misrepresentations, making it necessary for one to use its entries with considerable caution and skepticism. Second, even when it is accurate, the diary consistently magnifies House's role in events and his influence over Wilson. Unfortunately, too little independent evidence remains to assess their personal relationship as closely as one might wish, but House's role and influence are now undergoing reassessment and revision. Inga Floto, *Colonel House in Paris: A Study of American Policy at the Paris Peace Conference, 1919* (Princeton, 1980), presents an incisive account and interpretation of his role in the negotiations at the end of the war and of his break with Wilson. The first full, critical biography of House is now being written by Charles E. Neu. On the relationship, see also Weinstein, *Wilson*, 265–278.

27. Entry, Sept. 28, 1914, EMH diary, *WWP*, XXXI, 95. For a similar reference to Philip Dru, see EMH diary entry, Oct. 30, 1913, *WWP*, XXVIII, 477. The full title of the novel was *Philip Dru, Administrator: A Story of Tomorrow, 1920–1935* (New York, 1911).

28. For other examples of House's dreaming and working through others, see John Milton Cooper, Jr., *Walter Hines Page: The Southerner as American, 1855–1918* (Chapel Hill, N.C., 1977) 268–273; and Christopher Lasch, "Lincoln Colcord and Colonel House," in *The New Radicalism in America, 1889–1963: The Intellectual as a Social Type* (New York, 1965), 225–250.

29. The best account of Wilson's press conferences is in Robert C. Hilderbrand, *Power and the People: Executive Management of Public Opinion in Foreign Affairs, 1897–1921* (Chapel Hill, N.C., 1981), 95–104.

30. Roosevelt had not had completely smooth sailing with the press during his presidency. He had often resented statements and charges, particularly those by Democratic newspapers. Allegations in the New York *World* about the Panamanian revolution—always a sore point with Roosevelt—had so infuriated him at the end of 1908 that he had begun an ill-advised libel suit against that paper. See Wiliam Henry Harbaugh, *Power and Responsibility: The Life and Times of Theodore Roosevelt* (New York, 1961), 366–367; and *TRL*, VI, 1415–1416 n. 1.

31. WW speech at Washington, Mar. 20, 1914, *WWP*, XXIX, 362; WW speech at Washington, Nov. 11, 1914, *WWP*, XXXI, 561–562. The nickname "Teddy" was strictly for public consumption. None of Roosevelt's family or friends called him that after his teenage years, and it was once remarked that if someone called Roosevelt Teddy it was a sure sign that the person did not know him.

32. Among contemporary observers, Ray Stannard Baker grasped the difference in their public appeals best when he wrote, "Wilson himself inspires people with confidence. He is *safe*. We trust him. He is not magnetic, he does not awaken emotion as T.R. does." Entry, May 12, 1916, RSB diary, *WWP*, XXXVII, 35.

16. Crossroads of Politics

1. TR to Arthur Lee, Dec. 31, 1912, *TRL*, VII, 684.

2. TR to HCL, Feb. 27, 1913, ibid., 710; TR to Arthur Lee, June 29, 1914, ibid., 769. Roosevelt's commitment to the Progressives has raised considerable controversy among historians. Pringle quoted him as saying right after the 1912 election, "The fight is over. We are beaten.

There is only one thing to do and that is to go back to the Republican Party." Henry F. Pringle, *Theodore Roosevelt* (New York, 1931), 570–571. Actually, as John Gable has noted, Pringle omitted part of Roosevelt's statement. The omitted part makes it appear less a desire to abandon the Progressives than a pessimistic reflection on the party's likely fate. Further, as John Gable observes, Roosevelt's behavior over the next two years proved that he had no wish to abandon the party. See John Allen Gable, "The Bull Moose Years: Theodore Roosevelt and the Progressive Party, 1912–1916" (Ph.D. dissertation, Brown University, 1972), 378–379, 396 n. 53. On the other hand, as Mowry and Einstein have commented, Roosevelt's actions and his private statements did betray lack of enthusiasm for the party and growing distaste for what Einstein calls its "freakish radicalism." See George E. Mowry, *Theodore Roosevelt and the Progressive Movement* (Madison, Wis., 1946), 284; and Lewis Einstein, *Roosevelt: His Mind in Action* (Boston, 1930), 217.

3. TR speech at Portsmouth, R.I., July 2, 1913, *TRW*, XVII, 385; TR, "The Living Wage and the Living Rate," *Outlook* (July 5, 1913), *TRW* (memorial edition: New York, 1925), XIX, 121–122; TR to W. A. White, July 6, 1914, *TRL*, VII, 773.

4. TR to Ethel R. Derby, Nov. 4, 1914, *TRL*, VIII, 831–832; TR to White, Nov. 7, 1914, ibid., 836.

5. WW to Nancy Toy, Nov. 9, 1914, *WWP*, XXXI, 290; WW press conference, Nov. 10, 1914, ibid., 292. On the 1914 results, see Link, *Wilson*, II (Princeton, 1956), 468–469; on the western votes, see David Sarasohn, "The Election of 1916: Realigning the Rockies," *Western Historical Quarterly* 2 (July 1980), 285–305.

6. WW speech to Congress, Aug. 29, 1916, *WWP*, XXXVIII, 101. On the 1916 measures, see Link, *Wilson*, IV (Princeton, 1964), 321–323, 348, 360–361, V, 58–59, 64–65.

7. WW to Burleson and McAdoo, Mar. 2, 1916, *WWP*, XXXVI, 239. On the preparedness and armed ships controversies, see Link, *Wilson* IV, 50–54, 186–194; and John Milton Cooper, Jr., *The Vanity of Power: American Isolationism and World War I, 1914–1917* (Westport, Conn., 1969), 87–98, 106–117.

8. Draft of Democratic party platform with WW corrections [circa June 10, 1916], *WWP*, XXXVI, 190–201; TR to Arthur Lee, June 7, 1916, *TRL*, VIII, 1055; Lippmann, "The Case for Wilson," *New Republic* 8 (Oct. 14, 1916), 263.

9. WW speech at Washington, July 4, 1916, *WWP*, XXXVII, 357. The best and strongest statements of the interpretation of Wilson's belated, opportunistic conversion come in Link, "The South and the New Freedom," *American Scholar* 20 (Summer 1951), 314–324; and Link,

Woodrow Wilson and the Progressive Era (New York, 1954), especially 80, 224–225. By the time Link treated the first of these events in the full-scale biography, however, the interpretation had been modified; see *Wilson* II, 241–242, 444, 471. By the time he treated the 1916 shift, it had been downplayed in *Wilson* IV, 322–323, and absent from volume V (Princeton, 1965).

10. WW speech at Washington, July 20, 1916, *WWP*, XXXVII, 442; WW speech at Washington, Nov. 18, 1916, *WWP*, XXXVIII, 673. During the 1916 campaign Wilson also made as bold an assertion as Roosevelt ever had of the primacy and power of government. "The business of government is to see that no other organization is as strong as itself," he declared in September; "to see that no body or group of men, no matter what their private interest is, may come into competition with the authority of society": WW speech at Shadow Lawn, N.J., Sept. 23, 1916, *WWP*, XXXVIII, 214.

11. WW speech at Washington, July 4, 1916, *WWP*, XXXVII, 355; speech at Shadow Lawn, N.J., Oct. 21, 1916, *WWP*, XXXVIII, 501–502.

12. WW speech at Atlantic City, Sept. 8, 1916, *WWP*, XXXVIII, 314–315.

13. EMH, "The Memoirs of Colonel House," George Sylvester Viereck MSS, Yale University Library; Sarasohn, "The Election of 1916," *Western Historical Quarterly* 2, 285–305. On Wilson's farmer support and on the Socialist shift, see Link, *Wilson*, V, 127, 162.

14. On labor support for Wilson, see Link, *Wilson*, V, 91, 126–127.

15. Ibid., 124.

16. TR speech at Battle Creek, Mich., Sept. 30, 1916, *New York Times*, Oct. 1, 1916; speech at Wilkes-Barre, Pa., Oct. 14, 1916, *New York Times*, Oct. 15, 1916. On the weakness of progressivism in 1916, see Link, "What Happened to the Progressive Movement in the 1920's?" *American Historical Review* 64 (July 1959), 833–851.

17. TR speech at New York, Nov. 3, 1916, *TRW*, XVIII, 447–448. Roosevelt quoted Wilson accurately. In an address to farmers, Wilson had used those sentences to preface his familiar observation that the Lord's Prayer begins with a plea for bread. WW speech at Shadow Lawn, N.J., Oct. 21, 1916, *WWP*, XXXVIII, 508.

18. TR to James Bryce, Nov. 26, 1917, *TRL*, VIII, 1253; TR, *National Strength and International Duty* (Princeton, 1917), 97–98; TR column, June 5, 1918, in Ralph Stout, ed., *Roosevelt in the Kansas City Star: War-Time Editorials by Theodore Roosevelt* (Boston, 1921), 160. For his condemnation of La Follette and former Progressives, see TR to TR, Jr., Nov. 29, 1917, *TRL*, VIII, 1257.

19. TR statement to Joseph B. Bishop, fall 1918, in Bishop, *Roose-*

velt and His Times, II, 468–469; TR to Medill McCormick, Oct. 30, 1918, *TRL,* VIII, 1384; TR, "The Men Who Pay with Their Bodies for Their Souls' Desire," *Metropolitan* (Oct. 1918), *TRW,* XIX, 258–259; TR, "The Romanoff Scylla and the Bolshevist Charybdis," *Metropolitan* (Dec. 1918), *TRW,* XIX, 345.

20. Harding quoted in Wesley M. Bagby, *The Road to Normalcy: The Presidential Campaign and Election of 1920* (Baltimore, 1962), 23. For assessments of the Republican repudiation of Roosevelt's legacy and how little he might have changed events, see George E. Mowry, *Theodore Roosevelt and the Progressive Movement* (Madison, Wis., 1946), 381; and William Henry Harbaugh, *Power and Responsibility: The Life and Times of Theodore Roosevelt* (New York, 1961), 509–510. The contrast in public images between Harding and Wilson is nicely caught in this description: "modest mediocrity rather than arrogant genius; party government rather than one-man government; consultation rather than dictation; warm humanity rather than austere intellectualism; genial realism rather than strenuous idealism." Bagby, *Road to Normalcy,* 101. In most of those terms, Harding was equally the antithesis of Roosevelt.

21. TR speech at Syracuse, N.Y., July 18, 1918, *TRW,* XIX, 363.

22. WW public letter to New Jersey Democrats, Mar. 20, 1918, *WWPP,* V, 194–195.

23. On Wilson's wartime economic policies, see Charles Gilbert, *American Financing of World War I* (Westport, Conn., 1970).

24. On Wilson's labor policies, see Valerie Jean Conner, *The National War Labor Board, 1918–1919: Stability and Social Justice in the Voluntary State* (Chapel Hill, N.C., 1983).

25. WW, "The Road away from Revolution," *Atlantic Monthly* (Aug. 1923), *WWPP,* VI, 538; WW message to Congress, Dec. 2, 1919, *WWPP,* VI, 437.

26. On wartime and postwar repressions, see Harry N. Scheiber, *The Wilson Administration and Civil Liberties, 1917–1921* (Ithaca, N.Y., 1960).

27. WW speech to Congress, May 27, 1918, *WWPP,* V, 219. On wartime politics, see Seward W. Livermore, *Politics Is Adjourned: Woodrow Wilson and the War Congress, 1916–1918* (Middletown, Conn., 1966).

28. WW statement, Oct. 25, 1918, *WWPP,* V, 286. On the background and drafting of the appeal, see Homer S. Cummings memorandum, Nov. 21, 1928, RSB MSS, Box 104; RSB interview with Vance C. McCormick, July 15, 1928, RSB MSS, Box 116. The 1918 elections did not go so badly for the Democrats as previous pro-Republican trends had suggested they might. The returns also pointed to two particularly

bright spots for the Democrats. One was in New York, where Al Smith was elected governor for the first time. The other was in Massachusetts, where David I. Walsh became the first popularly elected Democratic senator. Both men defeated Republican incumbents, and their victories heralded major inroads in the Northeast based upon the rising urban, ethnic following that would play a critical part in future Democratic majorities.

29. WW public letter to Democrats, Jan. 8, 1920, *WWPP*, VI, 455. On Wilson's party purge, see Livermore, *Politics Is Adjourned*, 138–142, 160–165.

30. RSB interview with Stockton Axson and George Howe, Feb. 24, 1925, RSB MSS, Box 99; WW cable to Congress, May 20, 1919, *WWPP*, V, 486–487.

31. RSB interview with S. Axson, Aug. 28, 1931, RSB MSS, Box 99; William Gorham Rice notes of talk with WW, May 2, 1922, RSB MSS, Box 120. For a nearly identical statement by Wilson that he was glad he had not won the League fight, which he reportedly made to his daughter Margaret, see Edith Gittings Reid, *Woodrow Wilson: The Caricature, The Myth and The Man* (New York, 1934), 235–236.

17. Designs of Diplomacy

1. Entry, Jan. 17, 1913, EMH diary, *WWP*, XXVII, 63. The once nearly universally accepted view of Wilson's unpreparedness and disinclination for foreign affairs is attacked in Arthur S. Link, *Woodrow Wilson: Revolution, War and Peace* (Arlington Heights, Ill., 1979, especially 2–7); and John Milton Cooper, Jr., " 'An Irony of Fate': Woodrow Wilson's Pre-World War I Diplomacy," *Diplomatic History* 3 (Fall 1979), especially 429.

2. WW statement, Mar. 12, 1913, *WWP*, XXVII, 172.

3. On Wilson's working methods, see Cooper, "An Irony of Fate," *Diplomatic History* 3, 430–431.

4. Entry, Feb. 14, 1913, EMH diary, *WWP*, XXVII, 113. On the Veracruz affair, see Link, *Wilson*, II (Princeton, 1956), 393–404; and Robert E. Quirk, *An Affair of Honor: Woodrow Wilson and the Occupation of Vera Cruz* (Lexington, Ky., 1962).

5. WW to Lindley M. Garrison, Aug. 8, 1914, *WWP*, XXX, 362.

6. WW speech at Brooklyn, N.Y., May 11, 1914, ibid., 15; speech at Philadelphia, May 10, 1915, *WWP*, XXXIII, 149. For accounts of Wilson's agitation over the Veracruz casualties, see H. J. Forman to RSB, quoted in Ray Stannard Baker, *Woodrow Wilson: Life and Letters*

(Garden City, N.Y., 1931) IV, 330; Henry Cabot Lodge, *The Senate and the League of Nations* (New York, 1925), 17–18.

7. Helen Woodrow Bones to Jessie Bones Brower, Feb. 23, 1913, *WWP*, XXIX, 554; WW speech at Mobile, Ala., Oct. 27, 1913, *WWP*, XXVIII, 450–451. It was the outbreak of violence in Mexico that evidently prompted Wilson to make his "irony of fate" remark to Edwin Grant Conklin. See Conklin to DeWitt Clinton Poole, Nov. 7, 1933, DeWitt Clinton Poole Papers, State Historical Society of Wisconsin, Box 1.

8. *WWP*, XXVIII, 448–449; WW speech at Washington, May 29, 1914, *WWP*, XXX, 107–108.

9. The literature of the idealist-realist debate is extensive. For a discussion of its application to Wilson in relation to World War I, see Daniel M.Smith, "National Interest and American Intervention, 1917: An Historical Appraisal," *Journal of American History* 54 (June 1965), 5–24. The best work, which draws upon that debate and also transcends it, is Robert E. Osgood, *Ideals and Self-Interest in America's Foreign Relations: The Great Twentieth-Century Transformation* (Chicago, 1953), which pays special attention to Roosevelt and Wilson. For an excellent recent reexamination of the applicability of idealism and realism to Roosevelt and his circle, see William C. Widenor, *Henry Cabot Lodge and the Search for an American Foreign Policy* (Berkeley, 1980).

10. TR to HCL, Sept. 9, 1913, *TRL*, VII, 747. Lodge, who was on the scene during Wilson's first year in office, eagerly used foreign policy to rebuild his friendship with Roosevelt. But he also gave the new administration the benefit of the doubt, refraining from public attacks on Wilson's Mexican policy and supporting repeal of the canal tolls exemption. For Lodge the breaking point came with Wilson's reaction to the Veracruz casualties. When members of the Senate Foreign Relations Committee visited the president soon after the occupation, his emotional state disgusted Lodge. "What struck me most in the conversation was the President's evident alarm and his lack of determination as to his policy," Lodge later recalled (HCL, *Senate and League of Nations*, 18). On Lodge's initial forbearance and his reactions to the Veracruz affair, see Widenor, *Lodge*, 173–174, 176–177, 181–183. It is not known whether Lodge told Roosevelt about Wilson's reactions. Even if he did not, he was anticipating a similar attitude toward Wilson on Roosevelt's part.

11. TR to William Joel Stone, July 11, 1914, *TRL*, VII, 778–779. On the Colombian treaty, see Link, *Wilson*, II, 322; and WW to T. A. Thompson, Feb. 18, 1915, *WWP*, XXXII 245. Thanks largely to Lodge's opposition, the treaty twice failed to gain the Senate's consent during Wilson's presidency. In 1921, after Roosevelt's death, the Harding ad-

ministration negotiated another treaty with Colombia that included the $25 million indemnity but no expression of regret. Lodge supported and helped persuade the Senate to approve that treaty.

12. WW press conference, Aug. 3, 1914, *WWP*, XXX, 332; public statement, Aug. 18, 1914, ibid., 394.

13. WW speech to Congress, Dec. 8, 1914, *WWP*, XXXI, 423. When he uttered those words, Wilson reportedly looked Gardner straight in the eye. See Gus J. Karger to WHT, July 27, 1915, WHT MSS, Box 316.

14. WW remarks, Nov. 12, 1914, *WWP*, XXXI, 305–306; Daniels to Franklin D. Roosevelt, June 10, 1933, quoted in ibid., 309 n. 2.

15. Entry, Sept. 30, 1914, EMH diary, ibid., 109. The remark also betrays Wilson's perhaps surprising but deep-seated superstitious streak. He carried a lucky piece for years and avoided certain numbers for fear of their being unlucky for him.

16. RSB interview with Stockton Axson, Feb. 8, 10, 11, 1925, RSB MSS, Box 99; Herbert B. Brougham, "Memorandum of Interview with the President, Dec. 14, 1914, *WWP*, XXXI, 458–459.

17. Entry, EMH diary, Sept. 28, 1914, *WWP*, XXXI, 95. See entry, EMH diary, Oct. 22, 1914, EMH MSS, Yale University Library.

18. WW to Nancy S. Toy, Nov. 9, 1914, *WWP*, XXX, 289. Wilson also revealed his emotional state at the meeting with the black spokesmen when he declared, "God knows that any man that would seek the presidency of the United States is a fool for his pains. The burden is all but intolerable, and the things that I have to do are just as much as a human spirit can carry." WW remarks, Nov. 12, 1914, ibid., 301.

19. TR to Hugo Münsterberg, Aug. 8, 1914, *TRL*, VII, 795; TR, *Outlook* 107 (Aug. 22, 1914), 1011–1015.

20. TR to Arthur Lee, Aug. 1, 1914, *TRL*, VII, 790. On this early distrust of Wilson, see also Hermann Hagedorn, *The Bugle That Woke America: The Story of Theodore Roosevelt's Last Fight for His Country* (New York, 1940), 16.

21. TR to Arthur Lee, Aug. 22, 1914, *TRL*, VII, 811–812. On Roosevelt's mixed attitudes toward both sides, see also William Henry Harbaugh, *Power and Responsibility: The Life and Times of Theodore Roosevelt* (New York, 1961), 466–467.

22. E. A. van Valkenberg to _____, Sept. 8, 1914, quoted in Joseph B. Bishop, *Theodore Roosevelt and His Times* (New York, 1920), II, 370; TR to Arthur Lee, Sept. 4, 1914, *TRL*, VIII, 817; TR, "The Belgian Tragedy," *Outlook* (Sept. 23, 1914), *TRW*, XVIII, 19.

23. TR to HCL, Dec. 8, 1914, *TRL*, VIII, 862. On the Progressives' foreign policy views in 1914, see John Allen Gable, *The Bull Moose*

Years: Theodore Roosevelt and the Progressive Party (Port Washington, N.Y., 1979), 203.

24. TR, "Belgian Tragedy," *TRW*, XVIII, 19, 20, 29–30.

25. TR, "The Duty of Self Defense," *New York Times*, Sept. 27, 1914, *TRW*, XVIII, 3–4; "Our Peacemaker, the Navy," *New York Times*, Nov. 22, 1914, ibid., 109.

26. TR, "An International Posse Comitatus," *New York Times*, Nov. 8, 1914, *TRW*, XVIII, 74, 79.

27. TR, "Unwise Peace Treaties a Menace to Righteousness," *New York Times*, Oct. 4, 1914, *TRW*, XVIII, 40; "How to Strive for World Peace," *New York Times*, Oct. 18, 1914, ibid., 55; "An International Posse Comitatus," *New York Times*, Nov. 8, 1914, ibid., 73; "Summing Up," *New York Times*, Nov. 29, 1914, ibid., 170, 172–173.

28. TR, "Utopia or Hell?" *Independent* (Jan. 14, 1915), *TRW*, XVIII, 159–160.

29. TR to Spring Rice, Oct. 3, 1914, *TRL*, VIII, 821; TR, "Summing Up," *New York Times*, Nov. 29, 1914, *TRW*, XVIII, 169.

30. *TRW*, XVIII, 167; "An International Posse Comitatus," *New York Times*, Nov. 8, 1914, ibid., 75.

31. TR to Rudyard Kipling, Nov. 4, 1914, *TRL*, VIII, 830.

32. WW to Dudley Field Malone, Dec. 9, 1914, *WWP*, XXXI, 429; TR to Spring Rice, Nov. 11, 1914, *TRL*, VIII, 841; TR to Kipling, Nov. 4, 1914, ibid., 829–830. The expression Roosevelt used to Kipling was a variation of the statement Roosevelt had often used, most recently in his autobiography, to explain his service in the Spanish-American War. Equally revealingly, he made several similar references during World War I. Under universal military service, he wrote in January 1915, "no man could buy a substitute; no man would be excepted because of his wealth; all would serve in the ranks on precisely the same terms side by side." TR, "Preparedness against War," *Everybody's* (Jan. 1915), *TRW*, XVIII, 140. Later in 1915 he reiterated, "A democracy should not be willing to hire somebody else to do its fighting . . . The much praised 'volunteer' system means nothing but encouraging brave men to do double duty and incur double risk in order that cowards and shirks and mere money-getters may sit at home in a safety bought by the lives of better men." TR, "Uncle Sam's Only Friend Is Uncle Sam," *Metropolitan* (Nov. 1915), ibid., 334. In 1917, after the United States had entered the war, he argued in favor of sending American armies to the western front, "for the sake of our honor and our future world usefulness we must ourselves fight and not merely hire others to fight for us. If we do not follow this course, our children's heads will be bowed with humiliation." TR newspaper column, Oct. 23, 1917, in Ralph Stout, ed.,

Roosevelt in the Kansas City Star: Wartime Editorials by Theodore Roosevelt (Boston, 1921), 31.

33. WHT to Edwin P. Parker, Nov. 16, 1914, WHT MSS, Series VIII, Letterbook 23; TR, "Self-Defense without Militarism," *New York Times,* Nov. 15, 1914, *TRW,* XVIII, 99.

34. TR, *America and the World War, TRW,* XVIII, 185. Privately, he made his attitude clear when he wrote an Englishman, "My dear fellow, you and those like you are playing heroic parts; I admire and respect you; I bitterly regret that my own people are not at this time rising to the same level." TR to John St. Loe Strachey, Feb. 22, 1915, *TRL,* VIII, 903.

35. TR to HCL, Dec. 8, 1914, *TRL,* VIII, 863; TR to Sir Edward Grey, Jan. 22, 1915, ibid., 879.

36. TR to Spring Rice, Feb. 18, 1915, ibid., 890.

37. Osgood, *Ideals and Self-Interest,* 144–145.

38. TR to Sir Edward Grey, Jan. 22, 1915, *TRL,* VIII, 879.

18. Facing War

1. WW to WJB, June 7, 1915, *WWP,* XXXIII, 349. For the account of memories of the *Lusitania* sinking, see Sullivan, *Our Times: The United States, 1900–1925* (New York, 1932), V, 120 n. 5. For the breakdown of the thousand editors' reactions, see David Lawrence, *The True Story of Woodrow Wilson* (New York, 1925), 197–198.

2. WW message to Congress, Mar. 4, 1915, *WWP,* XXXII, 316; speech at Washington, Apr. 19, 1915, *WWP,* XXXIII, 15; speech at New York, Apr. 20, 1915, ibid., 38.

3. WW press conference, May 11, 1915, *WWP,* XXXIII, 153–154. Wilson also confided to a friend, "That was just one of the foolish things a man does. I have a bad habit of thinking out loud. That thought occurred to me while I was speaking, and I let it out. I should have kept it in, or developed it further, of course." Frank Parker Stockbridge memorandum, RSB MSS, Box 11. Wilson may have been distracted by his newfound love for Edith Bolling Galt. "If I said what was worth saying to that great audience last night it must have been because love had complete possession of me," he told Mrs. Galt. "I did not know before I got up very clearly what I was going to say, nor remember what I had said when I sat down; but I knew that I had left the speech in your hands and that you needed me as I needed you." WW to EBG, May 11, 1915, *WWP,* XXXIII, 162. Privately, Roosevelt was quick to scorn the statement. "President Wilson's delightful statement about the nation being 'too proud to fight' seemed to me to reach the nadir of cowardly infamy,"

he confided to a British friend. "But as a whole our people did not especially resent it." TR to Arthur Lee, June 17, 1915, *TRL*, VIII, 938. Roosevelt made his scorn public later in the summer of 1915.

4. TR statement, *New York Times*, May 4, 1915; press statement, May 11, 1915, *TRW*, XVIII, 377, 379. For an analysis of reactions to the *Lusitania* sinking, see Link, *Wilson*, III (Princeton, 1960), 372–376.

5. WW draft of *Lusitania* note [May 11, 1915], *WWP*, XXXIII, 158; WW to EBG, June 8, 1915, ibid., 366. Some evidence indicates that Wilson wrote his stiff protest to Germany before he made the "too proud to fight" speech, but other evidence suggests that he wrote the note at roughly the same time that he retracted the statement. See WW to EBG [May 9–10, 1915], May 11, 1915, ibid., 145, 162. After the first *Lusitania* note, Wilson also made conciliatory overtures to the Germans, both through their ambassador and, apparently, through a Dutch intermediary. See ibid., 280 n. 1.

6. WW to EBG, June 8, 1915, *WWP*, XXXIII, 366; Thomas S. Martin and Hal D. Flood to WJB, June 5, 1915, WJB MSS, Library of Congress. See also WJB to WW, June 4, 1915, *WWP*, XXXIII, 337. For accounts of Bryan's resignation, see Link, *Wilson*, III, 419–425; Paolo E. Coletta, *William Jennings Bryan* (Lincoln, Neb., 1969), II, 329–344.

7. For the best characterization of Wilson's submarine policies, see Link, *Woodrow Wilson: Revolution, War and Peace* (Arlington Heights, Ill., 1979), 40–46.

8. Entries, June 14, 24, 1915, EMH diary, *WWP*, XXXIII, 397, 449; EMH to WW, June 16, 1915, ibid., 409.

9. On the modus vivendi, see Link, *Wilson*, IV (Princeton, 1964), 142–164. It might be argued that Wilson's first Supreme Court justice, James C. McReynolds, and his last attorney general, A. Mitchell Palmer, vied with Lansing for the dubious honor of being his worst appointment. After an undistinguished year as attorney general, McReynolds was elevated to the Supreme Court, where he commenced a twenty-three-year career as a reactionary jurist and a prejudiced, nasty, divisive presence among his judicial brethren. Wilson soon regretted his choice of McReynolds and was doubly determined to name Brandeis to the Court to rectify that mistake. Palmer, a man of Quaker background who had been a humanitarian, pro-labor representative from Pennsylvania, seized upon the anti-Bolshevik hysteria at the end of World War I to mount a series of raids on radical organizations, deportations of aliens, and scare pronouncements, spearheading the Red Scare of 1919–1920. Clearly, the appointments of both McReynolds and Palmer were disasters, but for sheer incompetence and consistent underhandedness in dealing with momentous events, Lansing still wins the prize. On Palmer, see Stanley

Coben, *A. Mitchell Palmer: Politician* (New York, 1963). Lansing awaits a biographer who will portray his truly low stature. Daniel M. Smith, *Robert Lansing and American Neutrality* (Berkeley, Calif., 1958), is incredibly favorable to Lansing. The best brief portrait of him is in Patrick Devlin, *Too Proud to Fight: Woodrow Wilson's Neutrality* (New York, 1974), 304–306, 522–523.

10. *New York Times*, Dec. 22, 1916, *WWP*, XL, 307 n. 1. On the incident, see also Link, *Wilson*, V (Princeton, 1965), 221–225.

11. On Lansing's intrigues in Mexico and his firing, see Clifford W. Trow, "Woodrow Wilson and the Mexican Interventionist Movement of 1919," *Journal of American History* 58 (June 1971), 46–72.

12. EMH to WW [May 9, 1915], *WWP*, XXXIII, 134; WW to EBG, Aug. 9, 1915, *WWP*, XXXIV, 151.

13. For the text of the House-Grey memorandum, see *WWP*, XXXVI, 180 n. 2. On the memorandum, see Link, *Wilson*, IV (Princeton, 1964), 102–141; and John Milton Cooper, Jr., "The British Response to the House-Grey Memorandum: New Evidence and New Questions," *Journal of American History* 59 (March 1973), 958–971. The British strung House along by appearing considerably more sympathetic than they were. They had tapped the American embassy's cables and cracked the American diplomatic codes, so they were also reading House's communications back to Wilson. See John Milton Cooper, Jr., *Walter Hines Page: The Southerner as American, 1855–1918* (Chapel Hill, N.C., 1977), 329.

14. Wilson's correspondence with Mrs. Galt reveals probably better than anything else his passionate, highly sexed temperament. The letters are in *WWP*, XXXIII and XXXIV; they have also been published in a selected edition, in Edward Tribble, ed., *A President in Love: The Courtship Letters of Woodrow Wilson and Edith Bolling Galt* (Boston, 1981).

15. EBG to WW, Aug. 26, 1915, *WWP*, XXXIV, 338; WW to EBG, Aug. 28, 1915, ibid., 352.

16. On House's later activities, see Inga Floto, *Colonel House in Paris: A Study of American Policy at the Paris Peace Conference, 1919* (Princeton, 1980); and on the break with Wilson, see Edwin A. Weinstein, *Woodrow Wilson: A Medical and Psychological Biography* (Princeton, 1981), 338–340, 347–348.

17. WW draft "prolegomenon" to peace note, circa Nov. 25, 1916, *WWP*, XL, 67–68.

18. Other evidence also supports the contention that foreign affairs after 1915 formed a special sphere in which Wilson tolerated or ignored disagreement and shoddy performance in key subordinates. On the one

hand, in other areas he did not hesitate to force the dismissal of top lieutenants. The most notable case came in February 1916, when he overruled and precipitated the resignation of Secretary of War Garrison, who had pushed too far in the direction of Roosevelt-style large-scale preparedness. On the other hand, Wilson retained ambassadors in the two most important belligerent capitals, Berlin and London, who were either vocally out of sympathy with his policies or distinctly inferior diplomats. On Wilson's failure to remove his old acquaintance Page, who espoused pro-Allied and interventionist views like Roosevelt's, see Cooper, *Page*, 354–356.

19. WW speech at New York, Nov. 4, 1915, *WWP*, XXXV, 168–169.

20. WW to Seth Low, Nov. 8, 1915, *WWP*, XXV, 180–181. Wilson's appropriation of Ezekiel was not lost on Roosevelt; see TR to John Carter Rose, Nov. 12, 1915, *TRL*, VIII, 978–979.

21. On Democratic opposition to Wilson's preparedness program, see Link, *Wilson*, IV, 27–33. As recently as February 1915, 155 House Democrats had voted to cut the Wilson administration's proposal for new battleship construction from two ships to one. See *Congressional Record*, 63rd Cong., 3rd Sess., 3152 (Feb. 5, 1915).

22. WW speech at New York, Jan. 27, 1916, *WWP*, XXXVI, 12; speech at Pittsburgh, Jan. 29, 1916, ibid., 32; speech at Des Moines, Feb. 1, 1916, ibid., 79.

23. On dropping the Continental Army and Garrison's resignation, see Link, *Wilson*, IV, 48–54, and George C. Herring, Jr., "James Hay and the Preparedness Controversy, 1915–1916," *Journal of Southern History* 30 (Nov. 1964), 383–404. In the House, however, Democratic opposition to any increases beyond the Wilson administration program, for either the army or the navy, persisted. On that later opposition, see John Milton Cooper, Jr., *The Vanity of Power: American Isolationism and the First World War, 1914–1917* (Westport, Conn., 1969), 98, 226–229.

24. In retrospect, especially after the part the Republicans played at the end of World War I and the beginning of World War II, it is difficult to appreciate how radical a shift of roles the two parties underwent. In February 1915 a leading political scientist had written that the Democrats were the party that "would hold aloof from Europe, would continue to pursue a policy of conciliation with the countries to the south of us, and would not be aggressive in matters pertaining to the Orient," whereas the Republicans "must favor an aggressive policy of interest, participation, and often interference in affairs beyond our borders and in every corner of the globe." E. E. Robinson, "A Future for the Democratic Party," *New Republic* 1 (Feb. 13, 1915), 47.

25. On Taft and his organization, see Ruhl J. Bartlett, *The League to Enforce Peace* (Chapel Hill, N.C., 1944). On Bryan and isolationism, see Cooper, *Vanity of Power*, especially 55–59.

26. WW speech at Washington, May 27, 1916, *WWP*, XXXVII, 114–116. Wilson ignored the advice of House and Lansing, both of whom opposed the ideas of the League to Enforce Peace. See EMH to WW, May 19, 1916, ibid., 77; Lansing to WW, May 25, 1916, ibid., 107–108.

27. WW speech at Arlington, Va., May 30, 1916, ibid., 126. For the statement in the platform, see WW draft [circa June 10, 1916], ibid., 195–196. Wilson further downplayed his move by squelching plans for a congressional resolution endorsing his internationalist commitment. According to Taft, Wilson said, "It was most unwise to give those opposed to the principle and [*sic*] opportunity to enlarge upon their objections now." WHT to Theodore Marburg, June 6, 1916, WHT MSS, Series VIII, Letterbook 49.

19. The Decision to Intervene

1. TR to Archibald Roosevelt, May 19, 1915, *TRL*, VIII, 922–923; TR to Arthur Lee, June 17, 1915, ibid., 937.

2. TR to A. B. Hart, June 1, 1915, ibid., 927; TR to Arthur Lee, June 17, 1915, ibid., 937.

3. TR to Raymond Robins, June 3, 1915, ibid., 931; TR statement, Mar. 9, 1916, *TRW*, XVII, 410.

4. See, for example, TR, "Peace Insurance by Preparedness against War," *Metropolitan* (Aug. 1915), *TRW*, XVIII, 308. On Roosevelt's diplomatic inconsistencies, see also Edward Wagenknecht, *The Seven Worlds of Theodore Roosevelt* (New York, 1958), 276–282.

5. TR, introduction to *Fear God and Take Your Own Part* (Feb. 1916), *TRW*, XVIII, 204; TR to Owen Wister, Feb. 5, 1916, quoted in Wister, *Roosevelt: The Story of a Friendship* (New York, 1930), 355.

6. TR statement, Mar. 9, 1916, *TRW*, XVII, 411.

7. TR to Arthur Lee, June 7, 1916, *TRL*, VIII, 1055; TR to W. Austin Wadsworth, June 23, 1916, ibid., 1078. On Roosevelt's behavior toward the nominations in 1916, see George E. Mowry, *Theodore Roosevelt and the Progressive Movement* (Madison, Wis., 1946), 345–360.

8. TR to William Furnell Jackson, June 8, 1916, *TRL*, VIII, 1059; TR speech at New York, Nov. 3, 1916, *TRW*, XVIII, 442, 451–452.

9. TR to James Bryce, Mar. 31, 1915, *TRL*, VIII, 913; TR, introduction to *Fear God and Take Your Own Part*, *TRW*, XVIII, 454. Roosevelt started qualifying his internationalist proposal almost as soon as he

presented it. He carefully differentiated his ideas from peace ideas discussed by Wilson, Taft, and Bryan in TR to Lewis Einstein, Feb. 19, 1915, quoted in Einstein, *Roosevelt: His Mind in Action* (Boston, 1930), 249–250.

10. WW speech at Shadow Lawn, N.J., Sept. 30, 1916, *WWP*, XXX-VIII, 306. On the Democrats' use of the peace issue, see Link, *Wilson*, V (Princeton, 1965), 108–112.

11. WW speech at Indianapolis, Oct. 12, 1916, *WWP*, XXXVIII, 418; speech at Cincinnati, Oct. 26, 1916, ibid., 531.

12. White to TR, Dec. 27, 1916, in Walter Johnson, ed., *Selected Letters of William Allen White, 1899–1943* (New York, 1947), 173. On the role of foreign policy in the 1916 election, see also John Milton Cooper, Jr., *The Vanity of Power: American Isolationism and the First World War, 1914–1917* (Westport, Conn., 1969), 122–123.

13. TR to E. A. Van Valkenberg, Sept. 5, 1916, *TRL*, VIII, 1114. For another statement of what he would have done if he had been president during World War I, see TR to A. B. Hart, Sept. 28, 1916, Theodore Roosevelt Papers, Library of Congress, Letterbook 96.

14. WW, note to Belligerent Governments, Dec. 18, 1916, *WWP*, XL, 273–276. For the fullest account of the complicated maneuvering surrounding the peace note, see Link, *Wilson*, V, 162–219. For British perceptions, see also V. H. Rothwell, *British War Aims and Peace Diplomacy, 1914–1918* (Oxford, 1971), 59–64. On economic aspects of the initiative, see John Milton Cooper, Jr., "The Command of Gold Reversed: American Loans to Britain, 1915–1917," *Pacific Historical Review* 45 (May, 1976), 222–226.

15. WW, "prolegomenon" to peace note, [circa Nov. 1916], *WWP*, XL, 70–71.

16. *New York Times*, Jan. 4, 1917. See also, TR, "The League to Enforce Peace," Metropolitan 55 (Feb. 1917), 15–16, 66–67.

17. Henry Sturgis Drinker to TR, Jan. 16, 1917, TR MSS, Series I, Box 318; TR to William R. West, Jan. 31, 1917, TR MSS, Series 3A, Vol. 304.

18. HCL speech, *Congressional Record*, 64th Cong., 2nd Sess., 792–797 (Jan. 3, 1917); Borah speech, ibid., 892–895 (Jan. 5, 1917); TR to Borah, Jan. 15, 1917, TR MSS, Letterbook 101.

19. Borah speech, *Congressional Record*, 64th Cong., 2nd Sess., 895 (Jan. 5, 1917). On Borah's position, see Cooper, *Vanity of Power*, 135–142.

20. *Congressional Record*, 64th Cong., 2nd Sess., 896–897 (Jan. 5, 1917). The lone Democratic dissident was James Martine, whose election Wilson had assured in 1911 by defying the New Jersey bosses.

Martine had been defeated the previous November. On the senatorial alignment, see also Cooper, *Vanity of Power*, 145–146.

21. WW speech at Washington, Jan. 22, 1917, *WWP*, XL, 533–539.

22. Ibid., 538.

23. La Follette statement, *Congressional Record*, 64th Cong., 2nd Sess., 1743 (Jan. 22, 1917); WJB to WW, Jan. 26, 1917, Woodrow Wilson Papers, Library of Congress, File VI–A, Folder 2400; WJB speech, Feb. 2, 1917, *The Commoner* 17 (Mar. 1917), 8. On support for Wilson's address, see Link, *Wilson*, V, 269–271; and Cooper, *Vanity of Power*, 150–151, 159–160.

24. Borah resolution, *Congressional Record*, 64th Cong., 2nd Sess., 1950 (Jan. 25, 1917); Borah speech, *New York Times*, Jan. 27, 1917; Cummins speech, *Congressional Record*, 64th Cong., 2nd Sess., 2231–2235 (Jan. 30, 1917).

25. TR statement, *New York Times*, Jan. 29, 1917. The Bible verse he quoted was Judges 5:23.

26. HCL speech, *Congressional Record*, 64th Cong., 2nd Sess., 2364–2370 (Feb. 1, 1917).

27. Ibid., 2370. On Lodge's position, see also William C. Widenor, *Henry Cabot Lodge and the Search for an American Foreign Policy* (Berkeley, 1980, 254–260).

28. On Republican abandonment of the League to Enforce Peace, see Cooper, *Vanity of Power*, 156–158.

29. Link, *Woodrow Wilson and the Progressive Era* (New York, 1954), 275. For the best brief account of Wilson's actions during this period, see Link, *Woodrow Wilson: Revolution, War and Peace* (Arlington Heights, Ill., 1979), 64–71.

30. TR to Johnson, Feb. 17, 1917, *TRL*, VIII, 1153–1154; TR to HCL, March 18, 1917, ibid., 1162; TR to HCL, March 10, 1917, Henry Cabot Lodge Papers, Massachusetts Historical Society.

31. On public and congressional opinion, see Link, *Wilson*, V, 415–419; Cooper, *Vanity of Power*, 191–192.

32. The first writer to grasp the centrality of Wilson's personal role was Winston Churchill in his often-quoted remark: "It seems no exaggeration to pronounce that the action of the United States with its repercussions on the history of the world depended, during the awful period of Armageddon, upon the workings of this man's mind and spirit to the exclusion of almost every other factor; and that he played a part in the fate of nations incomparably more direct and personal than any other man." Churchill, *The World Crisis* (London, 1923), III, 229.

33. WW speech, Feb. 3, 1917, *WWP*, XLI, III; speech, Feb. 26, 1917, ibid., 286; speech, March 5, 1917, ibid., 333–335. Almost the only

important adviser with whom Wilson did not discuss the decision before he made it was House. Here as elsewhere, much of Wilson's reputation for solitariness derives from House's complaints, which by this time reflected the colonel's diminished influence.

34. William B. Wilson to RSB, Sept. 17, 1932, RSB MSS, Box 58; John L. Heaton, ed., *Cobb of the World* (New York, 1924), 269. Fears about the war's racial impact were common in Europe and America, although this was apparently one of the few times Wilson voiced such fears. The date and the substance of the conversation with Cobb have been the subject of extensive questioning and discussion. Questions about the date are raised in Link, *Wilson*, V, 399 n. 33, and about the substance in Jerold S. Auerbach, "Woodrow Wilson's 'Prediction' to Frank Cobb: Words Historians Should Doubt Ever Got Spoken," *Journal of American History* 54 (Dec. 1967), 608–617.

35. Heaton, *Cobb*, 270; Katherine E. Brand interview with Daniels, Aug. 8, 1936, RSB MSS, Box 105. For other predictions about political consequences of the war, see Ray Stannard Baker, *Woodrow Wilson: Life and Letters* (Garden City, N.Y., 1937), VI, 506. Doubts about the civil liberties portion of the conversation are raised in Auerbach, "WW's 'Prediction,' " *Journal of American History* 54, 612–613.

36. WW speech, March 5, 1917, *WWP*, XLI, 333.

37. Tumulty, *Woodrow Wilson as I Know Him* (Boston, 1921), 256. Link effectively demolishes Tumulty's further assertion that Wilson broke down and cried after the speech (ibid., 259); see Link, *Wilson*, V, 427. For surprising examples of the "crusade" view of Wilson's decision in otherwise admirable treatments, see Robert E. Osgood, *Ideals and Self-Interest in America's Foreign Relations: The Great Twentieth Century Transformation* (Chicago, 1951), 256–259; and Patrick Devlin, *Too Proud to Fight: Woodrow Wilson's Neutrality* (New York, 1974), 686–687. The actual sentence in the war address is, "The world must be made safe for democracy" (*WWP*, XLI, 525). That is different from Wilson saying that the United States would make the world safe for democracy. Wilson never uttered the phrase "war to end all wars."

38. On Nietzsche's concepts of the Warrior, Priest, and Superman, see Walter Kauffman, *Nietzsche: Philosopher, Psychologist, Anti-Christ* (New York, 1956), 165–171, 272–274.

39. WW speech, April 2, 1917, *WWP*, XLI, 519–527.

40. For an incisive interpretation of Wilson's decision, stressing his desire to promote a liberal peace program, see Link, *Revolution, War and Peace*, 69–71. Elsewhere, Link has also compared Wilson's basic Christian philosophy of conduct to Luther's. See McCleery, "What Carter Could Learn from Wilson," *Princeton Alumni Weekly* (Sept. 25, 1978), 17.

41. For descriptions of the scene in the House chamber, see Link, *Wilson*, V, 423, 426; and Eric F. Goldman, *Rendezvous with Destiny: A History of Modern American Reform* (New York, 1952), 238, 250–251. On the opposition to intervention, see Cooper, *Vanity of Power*, 196–208, 235.

20. The End of the Conflict

1. TR to J. Callan O'Laughlin, April 13, 1917, *TRL*, VIII, 1173.

2. Entry, April 10, 1917, Thomas W. Brahany diary, *WWP*, XLII, 31–32; Tumulty, *Woodrow Wilson as I Know Him* (Boston, 1921), 286–288. Roosevelt's offer contained an even sharper barb, inasmuch as he also compared Wilson to Jefferson and himself to "Light-Horse Harry" Lee during the maritime troubles with Britain in the early 1800s: see TR to O'Laughlin, April 13, 1917, *TRL*, VIII, 1173–1174. The only other first- and second-hand accounts of the meeting are John J. Leary, *Talks with TR* (Boston, 1920), 95–98; and Alice Roosevelt Longworth, *Crowded Hours* (New York, 1933), 246.

3. WW to TR, May 19, 1917, *WWP*, XLII, 346. On the War Department's role, see Frederick Palmer, *Newton D. Baker: America at War* (New York, 1931), I, 194–206; Daniel R. Beaver, *Newton D. Baker and the American War Effort, 1917–1919* (Lincoln, Neb., 1966), 28–30.

4. Clemenceau public letter, quoted in William Henry Harbaugh, *Power and Responsibility: The Life and Times of Theodore Roosevelt* (New York, 1961), 502.

5. WW speech at Washington, May 2, 1917, *WWP*, XLII, 186.

6. TR speech at Oyster Bay, July 4, 1917, *TRW*, XIX, 6. The day his offer was refused, he told his sister, "It is exactly as if we were fighting the Civil War under Buchanan—and Wilson is morally a much worse man, and much less patriotic, than Buchanan." TR to Anna R. Cowles, May 17, 1917, *TRL*, VIII, 1192.

7. TR newspaper column, Oct. 18, 1917, in Ralph Stout, ed., *Roosevelt in the Kansas City Star: Wartime Editorials by Theodore Roosevelt* (Boston, 1921), 23–24; newspaper column, Oct. 17, 1918, *TRW*, XIX, 376; TR to HCL, Oct. 24, 1918 (public telegram), *TRL*, VIII, 1380.

8. TR, "Must We Be Brayed in a Mortar before Our Folly Depart from Us?" *Metropolitan* (Sept. 1917), *TRW*, XIX, 27; *National Strength and International Duty* (Princeton, 1917), 33. Roosevelt made the latter statement in November 1917 in a series of lectures that he delivered at Princeton at the invitation of West and Hibben.

9. TR newspaper column, April 2, 1918, in Stout, *Roosevelt in Kansas City Star*, 129. Roosevelt's devoted follower and sympathetic biographer Hermann Hagedorn has argued that Wilson's calling him a "great big boy" betrayed a fundamental misunderstanding of Roosevelt. "Roosevelt was no Tom Sawyer, begging to go on an adventure, but a Peter asking for the ultimate privilege of drinking the Master's cup," wrote Hagedorn. ". . . But the President saw only the boy who liked to play with a gun." Hagedorn, *The Bugle That Woke America: The Story of Theodore Roosevelt's Last Fight for His Country* (New York, 1940), 129–130. Whether or not Wilson saw beyond Roosevelt's juvenile facade, that appearance was not Wilson's basic reason for turning down Roosevelt's offer of service.

10. TR to TR, Jr., Oct. 20, 1917, *TRL*, VIII, 1245; TR to Archibald B. Roosevelt, March 13, 1918, ibid., 1301; TR to Clemenceau, March 22, 1918, ibid., 1303; TR to Ethel R. Derby, July 12, 1918, ibid., 1351. The story of Roosevelt's standing beneath his father's portrait is recounted in Hagedorn, *Bugle That Woke America*, 184.

11. Joseph B. Bishop, *Theodore Roosevelt and His Times* (New York, 1920), II, 468; TR, "The Great Adventure," *Metropolitan* (Oct. 1918), *TRW*, XIX, 247; "The Men Who Pay with Their Bodies for Their Souls' Desire," *Metropolitan* (Nov. 1918), ibid., 251.

12. TR newspaper column, May 7, 1918, in Stout, *Roosevelt in Kansas City Star*, 147–148.

13. On the Wilson administration's propaganda efforts, see Stephen L. Vaughn, *Holding Fast the Inner Lines: Democracy, Nationalism, and the Committee on Public Information* (Chapel Hill, N.C., 1980).

14. WW to Braxton D. Gibson, May 5, 1917, *WWP*, XLII, 221. WW speech at Washington, Jan. 5, 1918, *WWPP*, V, 161. See also Ruhl J. Bartlett, *The League to Enforce Peace* (Chapel Hill, N.C., 1944), 90–91.

15. TR, "This Is the People's War: Put it Through," *Metropolitan* (Jan. 1918), *TRW*, XIX, 261; TR to Beveridge, July 18, 1918, *TRL*, VIII, 1352–1353; TR, *Metropolitan* (July 1918), *TRW*, XIX, 324–325; TR newspaper column, Aug. 4, 1918, ibid., 319, 321. On Beveridge's opposition to internationalist ideas, see John Milton Cooper, Jr., *The Vanity of Power: American Isolationism and the First World War, 1914–1917* (Westport, Conn., 1969), 121–122, 158, 191; and John Braeman, *Albert J. Beveridge: American Nationalist* (Chicago, 1971), 259–260.

16. TR to WHT, Aug. 15, 1918, *TRL*, VIII, 1362; TR speech at New York, Sept. 6, 1918, *TRW*, XIX, 374; TR to Beveridge, Oct. 31, 1918, *TRL*, VIII, 1385.

17. TR to James Ashton, July 26, 1918, *TRL*, VIII, 1356. For the comparison between Lodge's and Roosevelt's partisan roles and Lodge's

belief that he was following in Roosevelt's footsteps, see William C. Widenor, *Henry Cabot Lodge and the Search for an American Foreign Policy* (Berkeley, 1980), 311–312, 322.

18. TR newspaper column, Nov. 17, 1918, *TRW*, XIX, 400–403. Privately, Roosevelt took credit for the Republican victory by answering Wilson's appeal to elect a Democratic Congress. "This gave me my chance," he told a British friend, "and in the last week of the campaign we did the seemingly impossible—carried the House by a substantial and the Senate by a bare majority." TR to Arthur Lee, Nov. 19, 1918, *TRL*, VIII, 1397.

19. TR newspaper column, Dec. 2, 1918, *TRW*, XIX, 403; Ralph Stout, "Introduction," *Roosevelt in Kansas City Star,* xlvi. For a similar account of Roosevelt's attitude in December 1918 see Leary, *Talks with TR*, 319–321.

20. TR newspaper column, Jan. 13, 1919, *TRW*, XIX, 406–408. Roosevelt's last known written words were a brief memorandum to himself about the Republican national chairman, Will Hays, probably jotted down the day before he died: "Hays see him; he must go to Washington for 10 days; see Senate and House, prevent split on domestic policies," TR memorandum [circa Jan. 4, 1919], *TRL*, VIII, 1422.

21. TR to Bryce, Nov. 19, 1918, *TRL*, VIII, 1400; TR newspaper column, Dec. 2, 1918, *TRW*, XIX, 406.

22. On the difference Roosevelt's death made to Lodge's objectives, compare Widenor, *Lodge,* 310–311.

23. For the best account and diagnosis of the stroke and its effects, see Edwin A. Weinstein, *Woodrow Wilson: A Medical and Psychological Biography* (Princeton, 1981), 353–362, 371–378.

24. On the second vote, twenty-one Democrats broke ranks to vote for approval with the Lodge reservations. Twenty-three Democrats stood by the president, however, and their votes, together with those of the twelve "irreconcilables," who opposed League membership under any conditions, prevented the treaty from receiving the necessary two-thirds.

25. On Taft's work with the War Labor Board, see Henry F. Pringle, *The Life and Times of William Howard Taft* (New York, 1939), II, 915–925; and Valerie Jean Conner, *The National War Labor Board, 1918–1919: Stability and Social Justice in the Voluntary State* (Chapel Hill, N.C., 1983).

26. On the War Industries Board, see Robert D. Cuff, *The War Industries Board: Business-Government Relations during World War I* (Baltimore, 1973); and on Baruch, see Jordan A. Schwartz, *The Speculator: Bernard M. Baruch in Washington, 1917–1965* (Chapel Hill, N.C.,

1981), especially 50–108. On military management, see Edward M. Coffman, *The War to End All Wars: The American Military Experience in World War I* (New York, 1968).

27. WW to EMH [Dec. 1, 1917], EMH MSS; notes of WHT interview with WW, Dec. 12, 1917, copy in Robert A. Taft MSS, Library of Congress. For the realist critique of Wilson, see Lippmann, *U. S. Foreign Policy: Shield of the Republic* (Boston, 1943), 33–39, and *U. S. War Aims* (Boston, 1944), 170–182; Kennan, *American Diplomacy, 1900–1950* (New York, reprint ed., 1952), 56–65.

28. On Socialist votes as an expression of antiwar sentiment, see James Weinstein, *The Decline of Socialism in America, 1913–1925* (New York, reprint ed., 1967), chap. 3. On the efforts to woo European socialists and liberals, see especially Lawrence W. Martin, *Peace without Victory: Woodrow Wilson and the British Liberals* (New Haven, Conn., 1958); and Inga Floto, *Colonel House in Paris: A Study of American Policy at the Paris Peace Conference, 1919* (Princeton, 1980), chaps. 1 and 2.

29. On Cecil's and Smuts's roles in the drafting of the Covenant, see George N. Egerton, *Great Britain and the Creation of the League, 1917–1918: Strategy, Politics and International Organization* (Chapel Hill, N.C., 1978), chap. 6. For the best general account of Wilson's role and accomplishments at Paris see Link, *Woodrow Wilson: Revolution, War and Peace* (Arlington Heights, Ill., 1979), 88–102.

30. On House's efforts, see Floto, *House in Paris*, chap. 3. On the early opposition, see Widenor, *Lodge*, 300–316.

31. On Wilson's wartime routine and changes in his behavior, see Weinstein, *Wilson*, 320–325.

32. On the appointment of Republicans to the delegation, see ibid., 331.

33. On the illness at Paris, changes in Wilson, and break with House, see ibid., 334–348. On the break see also Floto, *House in Paris*, chap. 4.

34. WW speech to the Senate, July 10, 1919, *WWPP*, V, 548. Doubt remains as to how far those Republican Senators, called "mild reservationists," could have gone in meeting Wilson. For a detailed account of the efforts and thinking of one of the most important of them, see Herbert F. Margulies, *Senator Lenroot of Wisconsin: A Political Biography, 1900–1929* (Columbia, Mo., 1977), especially 264–294. Another example of Wilson's poor performance with the Foreign Relations Committee was his denial of any knowledge of the Allies' "secret treaties." Whether that denial was a conscious lie or an example of either Wilson's impaired health or his lack of quickness in a tight situation cannot be answered. It

did, however, bear a resemblance to his performance at the January 1910 meeting of the Princeton trustees, when Pyne had sprung the plan for two graduate colleges on him. For a transcript of the meeting with the Foreign Relations Committee, see *Treaty of Peace with Germany: Hearings before the Committee on Foreign Relations, United States Senate, Sixty-First Congress, First Session* (Washington, 1919), 499–556.

35. For an account of the tour, see Link, *Revolution, War and Peace*, 113–121.

36. Those two arguments do not exhaust the possibilities for speculation about the possible effects of Wilson's stroke. One historian has argued that only the president's incapacity, which prevented him from actively fighting against compromise efforts, gave the treaty a chance of approval. See David M. Kennedy, "The Wilson Wars," *New Republic* 186 (March 17, 1982), 38.

37. On the major stroke and Wilson's methods of dealing with disability, see Weinstein, *Wilson*, 355–363.

38. On Lodge's objectives and the security pact, see Widenor, *Lodge*, 304, 331–332.

39. On Lodge's later attitudes and career, see ibid., 346–348; and John A. Garraty, *Henry Cabot Lodge: A Biography* (New York, 1953), chap. 22.

40. On the campaign and election, see Wesley M. Bagby, *The Road to Normalcy: The Campaign and Election of 1920* (Baltimore, 1962).

41. On Wilson's physical and psychological condition during his last years, see Weinstein, *Wilson*, 369–378.

42. RSB interview with Stockton Axson, Aug. 28, 1931, RSB MSS, Box 99; Margaret Wilson recollection, quoted in Edith Gittings Reid, *Woodrow Wilson: The Caricature, the Myth and the Man* (New York, 1934), 236.

21. Legacies

1. On Republican insurgency in the 1920s see especially Le Roy Ashby, *The Spearless Leader: Senator Borah and the Progressive Movement in the 1920's* (Urbana, Ill., 1972); and Patrick J. Maney, *"Young Bob" La Follette: A Biography of Robert M. La Follette, Jr., 1895–1953* (Columbia, Mo., 1978), chaps. 3–5.

2. On Hoover's pre-presidential years, see Joan Hoff Wilson, *Herbert Hoover: Forgotten Progressive* (Boston, 1975), chaps. 1–4; and David Burner, *Herbert Hoover: The Public Life* (New York, 1979).

3. On the Democrats in the 1920s, see David Burner, *The Politics of Provincialism: The Democratic Party in Transition, 1918–1932* (New

York, 1968). On Roosevelt's repudiation of the League, see Frank Freidel, *Franklin D. Roosevelt: The Triumph* (Boston, 1956), 248–254, 308–311.

4. The best account of Roosevelt's relationship with Daniels and his political education during the Wilson years is the incisive half-history, half-memoir by Jonathan Daniels, *The End of Innocence* (Philadelphia, 1954).

5. While an undergraduate at Harvard in 1904, Franklin had headed a student group favoring Theodore's reelection. When Franklin ran for vice-president in 1920, however, the Republicans sent Theodore Roosevelt, Jr., after him on the campaign trail to inform audiences that Franklin was a family maverick. For an account of Democratic preconvention maneuvering in 1932, see Arthur M. Schlesinger, Jr., *The Crisis of the Old Order, 1919–1933* (Boston, 1957), 273–314.

6. Roosevelt also offered the secretaryship of the Treasury to Senator Carter Glass of Virginia, an old-line Wilsonian who had held the post after McAdoo during Wilson's second term, but Glass declined. For Brandeis's view of early New Deal measures, see Schlesinger, *The Politics of Upheaval* (Boston, 1960), 219–225.

7. FDR speech at Chicago, July 2, 1932, in Samuel I. Rosenman, ed., *The Public Papers and Addresses of Franklin D. Roosevelt* (New York, 1938), I, 647, 659.

8. Roosevelt evidently viewed the Interior secretaryship as a Progressive seat in the cabinet. He offered it to two other former party members, Senators Hiram W. Johnson of California and Bronson Cutting of New Mexico, before Ickes. For an analysis of the economic nationalism of the early New Deal, see Schlesinger, *The Coming of the New Deal* (Boston, 1959), 179–194, and *Politics of Upheaval*, 214–219.

9. William E. Leuchtenburg, "The New Deal and the Analogue of War," in John Braeman, Robert H. Bremner, and Everett Walter, eds., *Change and Continuity in Twentieth Century America* (Columbus, Ohio, 1964), 81–143; FDR inaugural address, March 4, 1933, *FDR Public Papers*, II, 12, 14.

10. On the two distinct phases of Roosevelt's presidency, compare James MacGregor Burns and Michael R. Beschloss, "The Forgotten FDR," *New Republic* 186 (April 7, 1982), 19–22.

11. FDR to RSB, March 20, 1935, in Elliott Roosevelt, ed., *F.D.R., His Personal Letters, 1928–1945* (New York, 1950), I, 467. Wilson was much on Roosevelt's mind that day, since he also wrote letters to Brandeis and House. See ibid., 466, 467–468.

12. The debate over policy shifts and Wilsonian influences has spawned a historiography of its own. See Otis L. Graham, Jr., "The

Historian and the Two New Deals: 1944–1960," *Social Studies* 54 (April, 1963), 133–140; and William H. Wilson, "The Two New Deals: A Valid Concept?" *Historian* 28 (Feb. 1966), 268–288.

13. Roosevelt's huge 1936 margin was actually somewhat more narrow but obviously much more deeply based than his showing four years before. In 1936 his average state margin went up by only slightly more than one half of one percentage point (.51%), and he carried 85 *fewer* counties than in 1932. Roosevelt's mean state percentages (derived by totaling his percentage in each state and dividing by the number of states carried) were 65.22 in 1932 and 65.73 in 1936. The greater depth and decreased breadth of Roosevelt's 1936 victory can be seen more clearly when his county showings are broken down by region. In the Northeast (New England and Middle Atlantic) he carried 39 counties he had not won in 1932. In the Middle West (East North Central and West North Central) he lost 106 counties he had won in 1932. Those two sections accounted for nearly all the county-level variation between the elections. In the remaining regions, his showings by counties were:

South Atlantic	−8
East South Central	−7
West South Central	−3
Mountain	+8
Pacific	+2

For individual state percentages, see Svend Petersen, *A Statistical History of the American Presidential Elections* (New York, 1963), 93, 95; for numbers of counties carried by election and by regions, see Edgar Eugene Robinson, *They Voted for Roosevelt: The Presidential Vote, 1932–1944* (Stanford, Calif., 1947), 47.

14. On Hoover's campaign themes in 1932, see Schlesinger, *Crisis of the Old Order*, especially 435–437.

15. On the Liberty League and its influence in 1936, see George Wolfskill, *The Revolt of the Conservatives: A History of the American Liberty League, 1934–1940* (Boston, 1962); and Schlesinger, *Politics of Upheaval*, 123–125.

16. At the same time that conservative southern whites were switching parties, the two southern white Democratic presidents since Roosevelt, Lyndon B. Johnson and Jimmy Carter, were emerging as the strongest champions of racial justice since the Civil War. In 1976, despite outspoken appeals to fellow white southerners, Carter actually lost a majority of white votes in the South. He won such overwhelming margins among black voters, however, that he carried every state in the

South except Virginia and Oklahoma—a feat unmatched by any other Democrat since Roosevelt.

17. The exceptions among the one-time Republican insurgent senators were the two who had formally left the party—George W. Norris of Nebraska, who called himself an Independent, and Robert M. La Follette, Jr., of Wisconsin, who had helped organize the Wisconsin Progressives in 1934. On those senators and their colleagues, see Ronald L. Feinman, *Twilight of Progressivism: The Western Republican Senators and the New Deal* (Baltimore, 1981). The court-packing fight still awaits its historian. On aspects of the controversy, see William E. Leuchtenburg, "The Origins of Franklin D. Roosevelt's 'Court-Packing' Plan," *Supreme Court Review* 8 (1966), 347–400; and James T. Patterson, *Congressional Conservatism and the New Deal: The Growth of the Conservative Coalition in Congress, 1933–1939* (Lexington, Ky., 1967).

18. On Amos Pinchot and other antistatists, see Richard Polenberg, "The Committee to Uphold Constitutional Government, 1937–1941," *Journal of American History* 52 (Dec. 1965), 582–598.

19. The discontinuity between the two eras and the bases for the former progressives' opposition to the New Deal are discussed in Richard Hofstadter, *The Age of Reform: From Bryan to F.D.R.* (New York, reprint ed., 1960), 302–328; and Otis L. Graham, Jr., *An Encore for Reform: The Old Progressives and the New Deal* (New York, 1967), 166–186.

20. The two dissenting votes represented an irreducible minimum of agrarian-based, insurgent Republican isolationism. They came from William L. Langer of North Dakota, a Non-Partisan Leaguer, and Henrik Shipstead of Minnesota, a former Farmer-Laborite. Another implacable isolationist, Hiram W. Johnson of California, announced against the treaty but was unable to vote because he lay dying in a hospital. On the upsurge in feeling for Wilson, see Robert A. Divine, *Second Chance: The Triumph of Internationalism in America during World War II* (New York, 1967), especially 56–57, 167–174, 212–213, 311.

21. For a discussion of Roosevelt's departures from Wilsonian models, see Robert A. Divine, *Roosevelt and World War II* (Baltimore, 1969), 49–71. For a criticism of Roosevelt for not being more boldly interventionist, as well as a comparison with his kinsman, see Henry L. Stimson and McGeorge Bundy, *On Active Service in Peace and War* (New York, 1948), 373–374.

22. For recollections and opinions of a White House intimate about how much Wilson's "ghost" haunted Roosevelt, see Robert E. Sherwood, *Roosevelt and Hopkins: An Intimate History* (New York, 1948),

especially 227, 263, 359–360, 697, 756–757, 855, 876. The view of Wilson as a tragic figure who expected too much from his people did not originate with Roosevelt. Hoover viewed him in a similar light and wrote a sympathetic memoir of their association, *The Ordeal of Woodrow Wilson* (New York, 1958). The most extended critique of the methods of Roosevelt and his successors is Arthur M. Schlesinger, Jr., *The Imperial Presidency* (Boston, 1973). But the most biting and often pertinent criticisms have been in unfavorable views of the president under whom Schlesinger served and whose legacy he still celebrates—John F. Kennedy. The best of such criticisms are in Henry Fairlie, *The Kennedy Promise: The Politics of Expectation* (Garden City, N.Y., 1973); and Garry Wills, *The Kennedy Imprisonment: A Meditation of Power* (Boston, 1982). For the most pointed observations about eschewing education of the public, see Bruce Miroff, *Pragmatic Illusions: The Presidential Politics of John F. Kennedy* (New York, 1976), especially 288–293.

Acknowledgments

IN THE COURSE of seven years of work on this book, I have incurred
many debts, which it is my pleasure to acknowledge here. Several
institutions have been generous in providing financial and scholarly
support. In the fall of 1976 the Institute for Research in the Humanities
of the University of Wisconsin and its director, Robert M. Kingdon,
furnished a semester of research in extremely pleasant and intellectually
stimulating surroundings, while I was at an early stage in the work. The
Graduate School of the University of Wisconsin supplied grants and,
from 1978 to 1982, a Romnes Faculty Fellowship. A Guggenheim fellowship in 1978–1979 permitted me to spend a year and a half working
exclusively on this book. For nearly thirteen years the Department of
History of the University of Wisconsin has been a generous and efficient
scholarly home base for me. The office staff, particularly Jane Mesler,
Judith Cochran, Karen Delwiche, Anita Olson, Karen Radke, and Mar-
cia Marshall, proved unfailingly prompt in meeting repeated requests
for typing, checking, and copying. I thank these people and institutions
for making my work proceed much more quickly and easily than it could
have gone otherwise.

Libraries and archives have likewise facilitated my work. The Library of Congress, especially the Manuscript Division, furnished the
excellent services that have made it the godfather of nearly all scholarship in American history. The State Historical Society of Wisconsin has
always been, an accessible, well-organized facility for research, as well
as a resourceful locator and borrower of materials. At Princeton University, both the University Archives and the John Foster Dulles Library,
were extremely courteous and helpful. The staff of *The Papers of Woodrow Wilson,* also at Princeton, not only opened their files but also
provided a number of services far beyond the call of friendship and

scholarship. The staff of the Houghton Library at Harvard University, particularly Marte Shaw, made my visits there high points of research. Wallace Finley Dailey, curator of the Theodore Roosevelt Collection in the Houghton Library, supplied expert advice and unstinting aid. To these repositories and individuals I want to offer my thanks.

As I have indicated in the notes, a number of books have proved important to my interpretations of Theodore Roosevelt and Woodrow Wilson. Robert E. Osgood's study of the intellectual basis of twentieth-century American foreign policy supplied the inspiration for both the subject and the title of this book. Despite some disagreements with Osgood's interpretations, I continue to find his book a rich source of reflection and intellectual provocation on American foreign policy.

Of my two subjects, Roosevelt was the more fortunate in the contemporaries who published their memories and observations about him. Two memoirs in particular, by Owen Wister and Lewis Einstein, provide special insights into Roosevelt's thought, personality, and social background. These books deserve a wider readership than they have received. None of Wilson's contemporaries published comparably incisive observations. The Ray Stannard Baker Papers at the Library of Congress contain many manuscript memoirs and interviews that offer important perspectives on Wilson, as do similar materials in the Henry W. Bragdon Collection at the Dulles Library, Princeton. The most significant of those are the reminiscences, interviews, and notes in the Baker collection by Wilson's brother-in-law, Stockton Axson. A recently discovered memoir of Wilson by Axson is to be published as a supplemental volume to *The Papers of Woodrow Wilson*.

Both Roosevelt and Wilson have been blessed by the quality and extensiveness of scholarly writing about them. As the notes indicate, for Roosevelt I have relied particularly on the books by John M. Blum, William H. Harbaugh, Edmund Morris, George E. Mowry, and Carleton Putnam. William Widenor's excellent study of Henry Cabot Lodge sheds almost as much light on Roosevelt as it does on its principal subject. In the Wilson literature the magisterial five-volume biography by Arthur S. Link, along with his study of Wilson's diplomacy and his other essays, stands preeminent. Besides wise judgment and intellectual depth, he displays a comprehensiveness and imagination in research that are truly awesome. Three other books that also helped me, especially on personal and prepolitical aspects of Wilson's life, are Henry W. Bragdon's account of his academic career, John M. Mulder's study of his early years, and Edwin A. Weinstein's medical and psychological biography. Certain recent attacks on Weinstein's work should not deter anyone from reading and profiting from this pioneering study. One other book requires special mention for the perhaps ironic reason that it has not influenced my approach and interpretations. D. H. Elletson, *Roosevelt and Wilson: A Comparative Study* (London, 1965), tells the story of the two men's lives and political careers, concentrating mainly on the period after 1912. The narrative is based upon familiar published materials, and it did not come to my attention until long after I had begun work on this book.

Three sets of books deserve special mention as truly indispensable to my research and to all scholarship on Roosevelt and Wilson. *The Works of Theodore Roosevelt*, edited by Hermann Hagedorn, contains much of his published writing and many of his speeches, but at several points these volumes need to be supplemented. The *Works* contains only a small number of Roosevelt's presidential speeches, but most can be found in *The Addresses of Theodore Roosevelt*, edited by Albert Shaw. His 1910 speeches are found in *The New Nationalism*, and his later addresses and newspaper columns often have to be consulted in separate published volumes, in manuscripts in the Theodore Roosevelt Papers (Library of Congress—also available on microfilm), and sometimes from newspaper accounts. *The Letters of Theodore Roosevelt*, edited by Elting E. Morison and associates, contains an excellent selection of his correspondence and omits few important aspects of his views or activities. The *Letters* also includes some highly regarded supplemental interpretive essays by John M. Blum and by Alfred D. Chandler, Jr., as well as the undeservedly neglected introductory essay to Volume V by Elting E. Morison, which presents a penetrating analysis of Roosevelt as a conservative. In certain cases, principally Roosevelt's early literary activities, his World War I involvements, and his relationship with Lodge, it is necessary to consult the Roosevelt Papers and the Henry Cabot Lodge Papers (Massachusetts Historical Society).

By far the most important set of books for this work is *The Papers of Woodrow Wilson*. Inasmuch as it includes much of Wilson's private correspondence (often incoming as well as outgoing), most of his published writings, and a number of collateral contemporary materials (including, for example, nearly all relevant portions of the diary of Edward M. House), the *Papers* misses virtually no primary materials of importance about Wilson and the events in which he was involved. The comprehensiveness and, even more, the rigorous standards of accuracy and unmatched scholarship of these volumes make the *Papers* one of the great editorial achievements of this or any century. Only in three areas does the *Papers* require supplementation. Because the volumes published to date reach only to mid-1917, for later material it is necessary to use the earlier collection, *The Public Papers of Woodrow Wilson*, edited by Ray Stannard Baker and William E. Dodd, and to consult the Woodrow Wilson Papers (Library of Congress and also available on microfilm). Some of Wilson's 1912 presidential campaign speeches, not in the *Papers*, are in John Wells Davidson's edition, *The Crossroads of Freedom*. Finally, because the *Papers* includes only strictly contemporary materials, the collections of Baker and Bragdon must be used for reminiscences, manuscript memoirs, and interviews.

The following people have generously responded to questions about research problems and pointed me in promising directions: Joseph Alsop, James MacGregor Burns, John A. Gable, William H. Harbaugh, Carleton Putnam, and Arthur M. Schlesinger, Jr. Two friends who have repeatedly gone beyond the bounds of personal affection and scholarly dedication to answer my questions, direct my inquiries, and supply me with material are David W. Hirst and Arthur S. Link, the associate editor and the editor of *The Papers of Woodrow Wilson*. Peerless experts on Wilson and his times, they lightened and shortened my labors far more than they know.

My deepest personal debts are to those friends and scholars who took the time and effort to read all or part of the manuscript and offer sage counsel and criticism. E. Digby Baltzell of the University of Pennsylvania shared his unsurpassed knowledge of the upper classes in America. Charles E. Neu of Brown University gave me the benefit of his knowledge of Colonel House. John A. Gable of the Theodore Roosevelt Association aided me with his broad acquaintance with all aspects of Roosevelt's life and career. David Herbert Donald of Harvard University provided me with perspectives from his superb work as a biographer. Robert H. Ferrell of Indiana University shared his keen appreciation of statecraft and diplomacy. Margaret Douglas Link of *The Papers of Woodrow Wilson* read the manuscript with the penetrating eye and sympathetic insight that have made her a renowned editor. Paul K. Conkin of Vanderbilt University read successive versions of the manuscript with the deep reflection, probing questioning, and unrelenting demands for clarity that have made him the foremost intellectual critic among American historians. Arthur Link has been a tower of strength and encouragement. In addition to extending scholarly aid, warm hospitality, and personal friendship over many years, he has consistently refined and deepened my views and interpretations.

My good fortune in writing this book extends to my publisher, Harvard University Press. Aida D. Donald has shown once again her unmatched talents as an editor and publisher. From the time she first read my preliminary paper on this subject through all the stages of editing and production, she has invested enthusiasm and faith in this book that have been nothing short of inspirational. Peg Anderson has given this book the kind of editorial care and literary counsel that I have seen equaled only once and have never seen exceeded.

I must conclude with indispensable but inescapably awkward thanks to my family. My wife, son, and daughter have put up with me and tolerated my moods with good humor and grace. They have lived with this book and helped me in innumerable ways that they and I know well. They also know how deep are my thanks to them.

Illustration Credits

The following have kindly granted permission to reproduce photographs and artwork:

The White House Historical Association, portrait of Theodore Roosevelt by John Singer Sargent (copyright by the White House Historical Association; photograph by the National Geographic Society).

The National Gallery of Ireland, portrait of Woodrow Wilson by Sargent.

The Bettmann Archive, Inc., photo of Wilson at Princeton, 1910.

Princeton University Library, all other photos of Wilson and drawing by Max Beerbohm.

The Jay Norwood Darling Foundation for cartoons by J. N. "Ding" Darling.

Theodore Roosevelt Collection, Harvard College Library, all photos of Roosevelt, including the doctored photo with Wilson.

Index

Abbott, Frank Frost, 100
Abbott, Lyman, 131, 134–136
Acheson, Dean, 188, 355, 388n3
Adams, Brooks, 36, 73
Adams, Henry, 36, 73, 87
Adams, Herbert Baxter, 48
Adams, John Quincy, 73
Addams, Jane, 188, 210
Africa, TR's safari in, 65, 117–118
Alaska boundary dispute, 75
Aldrich, Nelson W., 127, 143, 144
Algeciras conference (1906), 65, 74, 76
Allies: World War I, 275, 277–278, 285, 290, 295, 299, 304, 309, 317, 319, 325, 326, 332, 333–335, 337, 338; World War II, 358–359
America and the World War (TR), 279, 286
American Bar Association, 171
American Commonwealth (James Bryce), 54, 59
American Federation of Labor, 215, 234, 261–262
American Liberty League, 353
Amherst College, 101
Anderson, John B., 356
"Armageddon" speech (TR), 161–162, 202
Atlantic Charter, 359
Atlantic Monthly, 61

Augusta, Ga., 15, 45
Australia, United States' relations with, 332
Austria-Hungary, United States' relations with, 317, 327, 332
Axson, Stockton (WW's brother-in-law), 57, 60, 92

Bagehot, Walter, influence on WW, 24–25, 49, 54
Baker, Newton D., 240, 337, 349
Baker, Ray Stannard, 238, 351
Balfour, Arthur James, 91
Ballinger, Richard A., 143
Baruch, Bernard M., 337
Belgium, neutrality of in World War I, 277–283, 304, 310–311
Beveridge, Albert J., 81, 152, 188–190, 256, 331–332
Big business: TR's attitudes and policies toward, 34–35, 40–41, 76–78, 82–84, 113, 148, 156, 188, 190, 194–196, 200, 208–209, 211–213, 215–216, 249, 347; WW's attitudes and policies toward, 120, 126, 128–129, 167, 174, 180, 192–194, 198–199, 211–213, 215–216, 231, 261, 347
Blacks, *see* Race relations
Blaine, James G., 30, 114
Bliss, Tasker H., 339

Blum, John Morton, 34, 78, 80, 147, 163, 189

Bolshevik revolution: TR's attitudes toward, 258, 332; WW's attitudes and policies toward, 262, 264, 268, 338

Borah, William E., 189, 311–312, 314–315

Boys' Life of Theodore Roosevelt (Hermann Hagedorn), 14

Bradford, Gamaliel, 54

Bragdon, Henry W., 1, 90, 97

Brandeis, Louis D., 202, 209, 211, 215–216, 233–235; as advisor to WW, 193–195, 198; appointment to Supreme Court, 251, 257, 408n9; attitudes toward New Deal, 349, 352

Brazil, TR's expedition in, 8, 248–249

Brest-Litovsk, treaty of (1918), 338

Bridges, Robert, 23, 45–46, 49, 173

Britain, see Great Britain

Brown, John, 145

Brownsville, Tex., 210

Bryan, William Jennings, 19, 37, 40, 55, 78, 109, 115, 120–125, 127, 129–130, 154, 160–161, 170, 171, 175, 189, 194, 196, 205–207, 235–236, 285, 307, 323; relations with WW, 181, 183–186, 200, 217, 220, 233–235, 244, 298–300, 307, 310–312, 314; as secretary of state, 230, 232, 240, 245, 252, 267–276, 289–291, 296, 303

Bryce, James, 54, 59, 306

Bryn Mawr College, 56, 373n21

Buchanan, James, 306

Bullitt, William C., 349

Bulloch, Irvine (TR's uncle), 13

Bulloch, James (TR's uncle), 13

Burkhardt, Jacob, 88

Burke, Edmund, 84; influence on WW, 53–56, 172, 185, 265

Burleson, Albert S., 231–232, 234, 252, 299

Business, see Big business

Butt, Archie, 156

"Cabinet Government in the United States" (WW), 24–25, 45

California, 111, 152, 170, 189

Calvinism, influence of on WW, 19

Cambridge University, 90, 96, 100, 102

Canada, United States' relations with, 75

Cannon, Joseph G., 144

Capps, Edward, 100, 104

Caribbean, United States' intervention in, 70–71, 267, 333

Carlyle, Thomas, 134

Carter, Jimmy, 421n16

Cecil, Lord Robert, 338

Central Powers (World War I), 326–327

Chicago, 76, 157, 161, 185, 190

Chicago, University of, 100, 101

China, United States' relations with, 267

Choate, Joseph H., 28

Churchill, Winston S., 359

Civil Service Commission, 34, 36

Civil War, 3, 6, 8, 15, 16, 28, 34, 39, 51; TR's attitudes toward, 12, 13, 33, 84–85, 111, 113, 115, 145, 148, 202, 215, 219, 282–284, 306–307, 315; WW's attitudes toward, 45, 47, 200

Clark, Champ, 235; and 1912 Democratic presidential nomination, 161, 183, 185–186

Clayton, Henry D., 234

Clayton Anti-Trust Act, 232, 234–235, 251

Clemenceau, Georges, 325, 328, 338

Cleveland, Grover, 232, 238

Cobb, Frank I., 319–320

Colombia, United States' relations with, 71, 226, 272, 404 n. 11

Columbia, S. C., 16, 17, 22

Columbia Theological Seminary, 16, 17, 46

Columbia University, 28, 101

Committee on Public Information
(CPI), 330, 343
Committee to Defend America by
Aiding the Allies, 358
Confederate States of America, 13,
15, 16, 45, 47
"Congressional Government" (WW),
45, 49
Congressional Government (WW),
48–51, 52, 54–55, 59, 134–135
Conklin, Edwin Grant, 100, 104
Conkling, Roscoe, 11
Conservation, TR's championship of,
66, 78–79, 143
Conservatism: TR's espousal of,
41–42, 82–84, 114, 115, 212,
216–217, 230, 259–260; WW's re-
lationship to, 121–122, 203; Taft's
espousal of, 230; Republican
party's embrace of, 256–257,
353–354, 356. *See also* Toryism
Conservative party (Britain), 212. *See
also* Tory party
*Constitutional Government in the
United States* (WW), 52–54,
123–125, 131, 134–135
Coolidge, Calvin, 259, 344, 346–347
Copperheads (Civil War), 315
Corwin, Edward S., 50, 124
Courts, TR's attitudes toward, 144,
150–151, 153–154, 156. *See also*
Supreme Court
Cowles, Anna Roosevelt (TR's sister),
8, 12, 29, 31, 37, 87
Cox, James M., 344
Croly, Herbert, 135–136, 145, 188,
211, 253; relationship with TR,
147–149, 194
Cromwell, Oliver, 43
"Cross of Gold" speech (Bryan),
161–162
Crum, William D., 210
Cummins, Albert B., 41, 76, 78,
170, 189, 300, 315

Dakota Territory, TR's sojourn in,
27, 29–31, 35, 38, 87

Daniels, Josephus, 240, 245, 274,
320, 337, 348
Dartmouth College, 101
Darwin, Charles, 16–17
Davidson, John Wells, 198, 203
Davidson College, 22
Debs, Eugene V., 205, 262
Democratic party, 34, 37, 78, 85,
109, 114, 115, 250, 333, 355,
421n16; WW's first involvement
in, 106, 119–129; in 1910 elections, 152–153, 168; in 1912 election, 140–141, 153, 156, 160–162,
168, 174, 177–186, 189–196, 200,
204–207, 210, 217, 260; in New
Jersey, 164–165, 168, 171,
176–177, 180, 232, 243; WW's
leadership of, 225–226, 230–239,
244, 248, 251–258, 262–264, 333,
395n10, 396n16; during 1920s,
240, 343–344, 347–348; foreign
policy inclinations of, 268–269,
289–290, 292, 297–300, 302,
307–308, 311, 314, 323, 328–330,
334, 336, 359–360, 410n24; during
1930s, 351–353
Dewey, Thomas E., 355
Divine Comedy (Dante), 156
Division and Reunion (WW), 52
Dixon, Joseph M., 189
Dodge, Cleveland H., 131–132
Du Bois, W. E. B., 211
"Dude," as applied to Roosevelt, 1,
27, 42

Einstein, Lewis, 5, 39, 87
Eisenhower, Dwight D., 355
Elections, congressional: (1914), 248,
250, 275–276, 278, 280; (1918),
263, 333–334, 339, 402n28; (1938),
352
Elections, presidential: (1800), 141;
(1856), 215; (1860), 140; (1896), 37,
158, 181, 191, 207, 256; (1900),
39–40, 61; (1904), 78–79, 82, 85,
110, 114, 120; (1908), 204–205;
(1912), 139–141, 147, 153,

Elections, presidential—*Cont.*
156–164, 174–175, 177–221, 225,
256, 266, 305–306, 309; (1916),
153, 158–159, 252–256, 305–309,
353; (1920), 186, 227, 259,
263–264, 333, 343–344; (1924),
186, 344, 346–347; (1928),
347–348; (1932), 348–350; (1936),
352–353, 421n13; (1940), 351–352,
355, 360; (1944), 351, 359
Eliot, Charles W., 89–90, 101
Ely, Richard T., 48
Emergence of the American University
(Laurence Veysey), 89–90
English Constitution (Walter
Bagehot), 49
Espionage Act (1917), 262
Essays in the Public Philosophy (Walter Lippmann), 149

Farmer-Labor Party (Minnesota),
346, 354
Federalist party, 13, 33, 47
Federal Reserve Act, 232–234, 236,
251
Federal Reserve Board, 309
Federal Trade Commission, 235
Fine, Henry B., 63, 90, 94–95,
100–101, 104
Fish, Hamilton, Jr., 360
Fitzgerald, F. Scott, 107
Ford, Henry Jones, 54
Foreign Relations Committee (Sen-
ate), 339–340, 343
Fosdick, Raymond B., 96, 107
"Four Freedoms" declaration (Frank-
lin D. Roosevelt), 358
Fourteen Points statement (WW),
275, 330–331, 333, 338, 358
France, United States' relations
with, 74; during World War I,
295, 332; at Paris peace confer-
ence, 335, 340, 343
Frankfurter, Felix, 188
French revolution, 157, 268

Galbraith, John Kenneth, 212
Gardner, Augustus Peabody,
273–274, 300
Garrison, Lindley M., 289
George, Henry, 34
George Washington (WW), 52
German-Americans, 308, 323
Germany: United States' relations
with, 70, 74, 251–252, 269; during
World War I, 275–278, 288–290,
292–293, 295–297, 300, 304, 309,
317–323, 326–339
Gilman, Daniel Coit, 89
Gladstone, William Ewart, 22
Glasgow University, 16
Glass, Carter, 233
Gompers, Samuel, 215, 234,
261–262
Good Society (Walter Lippmann),
149
"Government by Debate" (WW),
45–46, 49
Grant, Ulysses S., 202, 315, 325
Great Britain: United States' re-
lations with, 35–36, 43, 57, 70,
74–75, 154, 232, 266, 274; during
World War I, 278, 291–295, 332,
335, 337, 343
Great Society (Lyndon B. Johnson),
229
Gregory, Thomas W., 240
Grey, Sir Edward, 293–294
Gulflight (oil tanker), 303

Hague conferences and treaties, 76,
282–283
Hale, William Bayard, 267
Hamilton, Alexander, 41, 361; TR's
attitude toward, 33, 115–117,
135–136, 148, 217–218; WW's attitude toward, 127, 148, 217–219,
394n18
Hanna, Mark A., 40, 77–78, 114
Harbaugh, William H., 85, 155
Harding, Warren G., 152, 259,
343–347, 356

Harper's Weekly, 121
Harriman, Averell, 355
Harvard University, 3, 8, 9, 11, 13, 16, 24, 27–28, 31, 41–42, 89–90, 92, 95, 101–102, 155; TR at, 1, 9, 11, 13, 16
Harvey, George B. M., 121, 129, 132, 165–166, 168, 175, 178–179, 181, 230
Hay, John, 36, 75
Hayes, Rutherford B., 11
Hay-Pauncefote treaty, 43
Hearst, William Randolph, 88, 183–184
Heidelberg University, 16
Hemingway, Ernest, 38
Hepburn Act (1906), 79–80
Hibben, John Grier, 57, 96, 98, 107, 243–244, 379n27
Hill, James J., 77
History of the American People (WW), 52, 274
Hobart, Garret A., 39
Holmes, Oliver Wendell, Jr., 122–123, 133, 383n14
Holt, Laurence James, 257
Hoover, Herbert, 261, 346–348, 353
Houghton, Mifflin & Company, 48
House, Edward M., 57, 230, 237–238, 255, 268, 272, 275, 349; as WW's confidant, 240–245, 293–295, 398n26; WW's opinion of, 243, 294; involvement in foreign policy, 244, 267, 275–289, 291–293, 295–297, 326, 339
House-Grey Memorandum, 293–295
Houston, David F., 245
Huerta, Victoriano, 268–270
Hughes, Charles Evans, 88, 253, 256–257, 305–308, 343, 349, 356
Hull, Cordell, 349

Ickes, Harold, 350, 357
Idealism: TR's espousal of, 115–117, 148–149, 162, 171, 218–219, 254, 258, 260, 271, 278, 285, 307, 316, 325, 327, 330, 343; WW's espousal of, 133–134, 169, 171–174, 254, 258, 260, 271, 307, 310, 314, 337; isolationists' espousal of, 312
Ideals and Self-Interest in America's Foreign Relations (Robert Endicott Osgood), 223
Industrial Workers of the World (IWW), 262, 329
Intellectuals, TR and WW as, 61, 134
Internationalism: WW's espousal of, 274–275, 282, 299–301, 330–331; TR's relationship to, 279, 281–282, 306–307, 310–312, 331–334; Taft's espousal of, 279, 301, 317; Lodge's relationship to, 279, 301, 311, 315–316; attacks on, 311–312, 314–316
International Review, 24
Interstate Commerce Commission, 79, 190
Iowa, 76, 152, 170
Irish-Americans, 308
Isolationism, 312, 332, 343, 349, 359

Jackson, Andrew, 13, 229
Japan, United States' relations with, 71, 74, 109–112, 267, 278, 335
Jeans, James, 100, 104
Jefferson, Thomas, 41, 141, 225, 229, 361; TR's attitude toward, 13, 115, 217–218, 285, 303–304; WW's attitude toward, 122–123, 127, 136, 180–181, 184–185, 198, 217–219, 394n18
Johns Hopkins University, 46–49, 58, 89–90
Johnson, Hiram W., 189, 256, 317, 346
Johnson, Lyndon B., 229, 236, 421n16
Jordan, David Starr, 12
Jungle, The (Upton Sinclair), 80
Jusserand, Jules J., 261

Kansas City Star, 329
Kennan, George F., 337
Kennedy, John F., 355, 358
Kenyon, Cecilia, 115
Kettle Hill, Cuba, 39
Kipling, Rudyard, 283–284
Kitchin, Claude, 298–299, 323
"Knickerbocker," as applied to TR's family, 6
Knox, Frank, 353, 358, 360

Labor, organized: TR's attitude toward, 85, 146, 209; WW's attitude toward, 209, 251, 254–257, 261–262
Laffan, William M., 121
La Follette, Robert M., 19, 41, 76, 78, 123–124, 165, 170, 257, 300, 323, 346; TR's attitude toward, 80, 82, 152–153, 156, 258–259; attitude toward TR, 149, 186, 189; attitude toward WW, 186, 191; WW's attitude toward, 200, 209
Laissez-faire, 197, 213–214
Landon, Alfred M., 188, 353
Lansing, Robert, 291–293, 295–297, 309–310, 326, 337, 339
Lasswell, Harold, 54
League of Nations, 282, 334–335, 347–348, 357; parallels with Princeton controversies, 98–99, 105–106, 342; conflict over American membership in, 226–227, 242, 263–264, 292, 316–317, 335, 339–345
League to Enforce Peace, 279, 301–302, 306, 311, 314, 317, 330–331
Lee, Robert E., 202, 313
Letters of Theodore Roosevelt, 209
Leuchtenburg, William E., 350
Lewis, Vivian, 153, 166–168
Liberal Debating Club (Princeton), 23
Liberal party (Britain), 212, 317
Lincoln, Abraham, 5, 33, 41, 140,

148, 219; TR's attitude toward, 81–82, 86, 111, 114–116, 118, 153–154, 157, 159–160, 284–285, 306–307, 315; WW's attitude toward, 184, 204
Lind, John, 267
Link, Arthur S., 49, 126, 176, 186, 239, 256–257, 291, 317
Lippmann, Walter, 54; relationship with TR, 149, 188, 211, 388n3; attitudes toward WW, 253, 337
Lloyd George, David, 338
Lochner v. *New York* (1905), 150, 383n14
Lodge, Henry Cabot, 24, 60, 143–144, 150, 273–274, 278, 285, 300, 323, 326, 343–344, 348, 355; friendship with TR, 30–31, 36, 38, 41–42, 74, 87, 118, 152–155, 158, 249, 271–272, 283, 317–318, 404n10; opposition to WW over League of Nations, 105, 316, 332, 335, 339–340, 342; and internationalism, 311, 315–317
Lodge, Henry Cabot, Jr., 355
Long, Huey, 352
Longworth, Alice Roosevelt (TR's daughter), 29–30, 69, 360
Longworth, Nicholas, 69, 118
Louisville Courier-Journal, 121
Lusitania, sinking of, 269, 288–290, 293–204, 303–304
Luther, Martin, 322–323

McAdoo, William Gibbs, 79, 185, 240, 291; as secretary of treasury under Wilson, 240–241, 243, 252, 262, 299, 337
McCombs, William F., 179, 181–182, 185
McCosh, James, 17, 22, 58, 93, 98
McKinley, William, 37–38, 70, 75–78, 114, 256, 339
Madison, James, 274, 285
Mahan, Alfred Thayer, 73
Marryat, Frederick, 8

Martine, James E., 175
Merriam, Charles E., 54
Merriwell, Frank, 32
Mexico: United States' relations with, 35, 318; WW's policies toward, 226, 239–240, 251, 254–255, 267–270, 278, 293, 308, 320
Military preparedness, controversies over (1914–1916), 251–252, 273, 277, 297–299
Modus vivendi proposal (Robert Lansing), 292, 299
Monroe Doctrine, 70–73, 277, 280, 313, 334, 339. See also Roosevelt Corollary
Moody, William H., 150
Morgan, J. Pierpont, 77, 83, 196
Moroccan crisis (1906), 65, 74, 76, 79
Morris, Edmund, 30
Mowry, George E., 155
"Muckraking" (term coined by TR), 80, 83
Mugwumps, 30, 59, 71, 154, 208
Mulder, John M., 17, 19, 57
Munsey, Frank, 209

Nationalism, 32, 85, 115, 145–147, 191, 213, 217
National Recovery Administration (NRA), 350
National War Labor Board, 336
Naval War of 1812 (TR), 9, 13, 28, 32, 35
Negroes, see Race relations
New Deal, 229, 350–353, 356–358
New Freedom, 174, 185, 194–195, 200, 203, 208, 211, 220, 229–235, 253, 271, 349, 352, 355
"New Idea" Republicans, 166–167, 170–172
New Jersey, 91, 106, 119, 121, 129, 140, 152, 164–174, 176–178, 180, 187, 190–191, 232, 242–243, 245, 298
New Nationalism, 145, 147, 174,

187, 201–202, 208, 211–220, 253–254, 261, 350
New Nationalism (TR), 145, 147–148, 279
New York City, 6, 11, 31, 34, 36–37
New York Evening Post, 45
New York Herald, 28
New York legislature, 9, 27–29, 31
New York state, 37–39, 76–77, 80, 88, 164, 347–348, 355
New York Sun, 82, 85, 120–121
New York Times, 279
New York World, 319
Nietzsche, Friedrich, 223, 286, 317
Nobel Prize (Peace), 74, 154–155
Non-Partisan League, 255, 346
Norris, George W., 189, 257, 300, 346
Northern Securities Company, 77, 83

Oliver, Frederick S., 116, 135
Osawatomie, Kans., 145–146
Osgood, Robert Endicott, 223, 286
Outlook, 136, 153–154, 279
Oxford University, 90, 96, 102

Pacifism: TR's attitude toward, 12, 74, 154–155, 280, 285; WW's relationship to, 269–270
Page, Walter Hines, 179, 267
Palmer, A. Mitchell, 262, 329, 408n9
Panama, United States' relations with, 70–71, 73, 119, 272
Panama Canal, 65, 71, 75, 88, 145, 270, 280; tolls exemption controversy, 232, 235, 266–267
Paris peace conference (1919), 335, 338–340, 342–343
Parker, Alton B., 114, 122
Parkman, Francis, 32–33, 38, 61
Patton, Francis Landey, 58, 91
"Peace without victory" speech (WW), 275, 278, 312–314, 317, 319–320, 337–338
Pennsylvania, University of, 100
Penrose, Boies, 42, 259, 305, 346

People's party (Populists), 34
Perkins, George W., 190, 209
Phi Beta Kappa, 14
Philip Dru, Administrator (Edward
  M. House), 244–245
Philippines: United States' policies
  toward, 57–58, 61, 112, 266; TR's
  advocacy of independence for, 112,
  280–281
"Philosophy of Politics" study (WW),
  53–54, 58
Pilgrim's Progress, 80
Pinchot, Amos, 357
Pinchot, Gifford, 78, 143–144, 151,
  153, 206, 346
Platt, Thomas Collier, 37–40, 78, 80
Poe, Edgar Allan, 87
Porcellian Club (Harvard), 13
Presbyterian church, 15–22, 52, 93
Priest, concept of, 223, 286, 317
Princeton Alumni Weekly, 96
Princetonian, 23
Princeton University, 3, 17, 42, 50,
  58, 60, 63, 130–131, 179, 181,
  274; WW as student, 21–26, 44;
  WW as faculty member, 52–53,
  56–58; WW as president, 53, 58,
  66, 89–108, 119, 122–124, 173,
  210–211, 217, 237, 342; graduate
  school controversy, 66, 98,
  102–106, 122; "quad" plan, 66, 92,
  95–102, 122, 342; preceptorial system, 66, 90–95, 97, 102
Pringle, Henry, 70
Procter, William C., 103
Progressive party, 214, 230, 239,
  254, 331, 349, 350, 356; in 1912
  election, 139–141, 161–163,
  188–192, 194–207, 209–210, 215,
  217–218; decline after 1912 election, 225, 237, 248–250, 258; in
  1916 election, 253, 255–257; foreign policy attitudes of, 278, 286,
  289, 305, 307–308, 332; TR's relationship to after 1912, 305–306,
  317–318, 399n2; attitudes and ac-

tivities of former members in
  1930s, 350, 353, 357–358
Progressive party (Wisconsin), 354
Progressive Republican League,
  152–153, 156
Progressivism, 41, 78, 114; WW's relationship to, 121–122, 124–125,
  168–172, 179–180, 185, 198, 200,
  206, 231, 253, 257, 353; TR's relationship to, 123, 125, 153, 155,
  160, 162, 170, 189–191, 257–259;
  in 1930s and after, 353–354,
  356–358
Promise of American Life (Herbert
  Croly), 135–136, 145, 147–149
Public Works Administration, 350
Pure Food and Drug Acts (1906),
  79–80
Putnam's, G. P., Sons (publishers),
  31–32, 45–46
Pyne, M. Taylor, 97, 103–105, 107,
  173

Quay, Matthew S., 42

Race relations, 353–354, 357,
  421n16; TR's attitudes toward, 47,
  210; WW's attitudes toward,
  210–211, 273–274, 319
Railroad regulation, 80–81, 110, 145
Reagan, Ronald W., 356
Realism; TR's relationship to, 113,
  118, 220, 278, 285–286, 309, 316
Record, George L., 167–168,
  171–172, 176
Red Scare (1919), 262, 329, 408n9
Reed, John, 238
Reinsch, Paul S., 267
Remington, Frederick, 87
Renaissance ideal, 87–88
Renick, 45–46, 60
Republican party, 11, 27–28, 30–31,
  33, 34, 37, 39–40, 42, 88,
  127–128, 143–144, 151, 160–163,
  164, 167, 170, 180, 200, 210,
  214–215, 227, 257–258, 261,

Republican party—*Cont.*
 262–263, 343–344, 346–347;
 354–356; TR's relationship to,
 76–85, 109, 113–115, 117, 144,
 153, 216–217, 219, 226, 230, 239,
 249, 259–260, 305, 328–329, 333,
 336; in 1910 elections, 144–146,
 149–153; in 1912 election,
 139–140, 156–163, 184, 185,
 189–191, 197, 199, 205–207, 209,
 256; in New Jersey, 166–167,
 172–173, 178; in 1916 election,
 253, 256–258; foreign policy inclinations of, 268, 286, 289–290, 300,
 311, 314, 323, 334, 339–340, 343,
 357–360, 410n24
Rhodes, Cecil, 90
Rhodes, James Ford, 87
Richardson, Owen W., 100
Richberg, Donald, 350, 358
Riis, Jacob, 11, 37
Robinson, Corinne Roosevelt (TR's
 sister), 9, 156
Robinson, Edwin Arlington, 87
Rockefeller, Nelson A., 355–356
Roosevelt, Alice Hathaway Lee (TR's
 first wife), 9, 29–30
Roosevelt, Archibald Bulloch (TR's
 son), 328
Roosevelt, Edith Kermit Carow (TR's
 second wife), 31, 69
Roosevelt, Eleanor (TR's niece, wife
 of Franklin D. Roosevelt), 348,
 357
Roosevelt, Elliott (TR's brother), 9
Roosevelt, Franklin Delano, 229,
 236, 358–361; and political legacies of TR and WW, 348–353,
 355–358, 360, 361
Roosevelt, Martha Bulloch (TR's
 mother), 6, 8, 10, 13, 29
Roosevelt, Quentin (TR's son),
 328–329
Roosevelt, Theodore, 19, 21, 46, 58,
 63, 88, 123, 125, 137, 165–169,
 171–173, 179–180, 183, 229, 234,
 270, 276, 341, 344–345; youth, 3,
 5–14; asthma, 6–7; entry into politics, 11–12, 27–29, 32–34, 59;
 early domestic political attitudes,
 10–11, 29, 33–35, 40–42, 61;
 early attitudes toward war, 12,
 35–36, 38, 71–72, 85–86,
 154–155; western experiences, 27,
 29–32, 35, 38; early foreign policy
 views, 35–36; assistant secretary of
 the Navy, 37–38; in Spanish-
 American War, 38–39; governor of
 New York, 38–41, 164–165; vice-
 president, 39–40, 42–43; early acquaintance with WW, 59–62,
 130–135; as president, 65, 69–88,
 109–118, 238–240, 241, 245–247,
 255, 261, 263, 334; foreign policies
 as president, 70–76, 79, 109–112;
 domestic policies as president,
 76–86, 109–117; cultural patronage as president, 86–88, 241; retirement from presidency, 66–67,
 117–118; relationship with Taft,
 70, 74–75, 109, 113–114, 139,
 143–144, 151, 152, 154, 156–157,
 191, 196, 221, 240, 259, 271–272,
 284, 306–307, 331–333; in 1910
 elections, 144–147, 149–153; later
 domestic views, 145–155, 160,
 162, 170, 189–191, 212, 216–217,
 230, 257–260; relationship with
 Herbert Croly, 147–149; in 1912
 election, 139–141, 147, 153,
 156–164, 174–175, 184, 186–221,
 225, 256, 391n30; later foreign policy views, 154–155, 221, 226,
 266–268, 271–272, 274–275, 279,
 281–282, 306–307, 331–334; attitudes toward WW, 130–136, 160,
 187, 189, 191, 195–197, 201,
 208–209, 220–221, 225–226, 253,
 257–258, 262, 266–268, 271–274,
 277, 283–284, 297–298, 303–304,
 310–312, 315–318, 324–326,
 392n6; Progressive party lead-

Roosevelt, Theodore—*Cont.*
  ership after 1912, 248–250,
  305–306, 317–318, 399n2; attitudes toward World War I, 226,
  250, 276–286, 288–289, 300,
  304–310, 324–328; later relationship to Republican party,
  230, 239, 249, 253, 257–260, 328;
  later attitudes toward war,
  284–285, 288, 327–328, 406n32;
  death, 226, 247, 259–260, 317,
  335, 342; political legacy, 227,
  346–361; as historian and writer,
  32–33, 43; religious views, 88; oratory, 161–162, 385n35, 392n4;
  racial views, 210
Roosevelt, Theodore, Sr. (TR's father), 6, 8–13, 29, 284, 328,
  365n5, 366n12
Roosevelt: The Story of a Friendship
  (Owen Wister), 63
Roosevelt Corollary (Monroe Doctrine), 71–73, 79, 266
Root, Elihu, 300, 336, 339; relationship with TR, 75, 86,
  153–154, 158–159, 240, 259
Roper, Daniel C., 349
Rough Riders, 37–39, 325, 353, 361
Russia, United States' relations with,
  71, 74. *See also* Bolshevik revolution
Russian revolution, *see* Bolshevik
  revolution
Russo-Japanese War, 65, 74, 79

Saint-Gaudens, Augustus, 86–87
Sarasohn, David, 255
Scotland, 16–17
Sedition Act (1918), 329
Shaw, Albert, 46, 70
Sherman Anti-Trust Act, 77, 150,
  202
Sinclair, Upton, 80
Smith, Alfred E., 347–349
Smith, James, Jr., 121, 165–167,
  171, 175–177, 184, 230
Smithsonian Institution, 86

Smuts, Jan Christian, 338
Socialism: TR's attitude toward, 113,
  260; WW's attitude toward, 120,
  172, 264; Taft's attitude toward,
  172
Socialist party (United States), 205,
  207, 255, 262, 323, 338
Sorel, Georges, 54
South, 25; WW's attitudes toward,
  45, 47, 217; and backing for WW's
  presidential candidacy (1912), 168,
  178, 181, 186; opposition to WW's
  candidacy, 182–183; relationship
  to WW's administration, 230, 232,
  357; relationship to Democratic
  party since 1930s, 353–354, 357,
  421n16. *See also* Race relations
South Carolina, University of, 16
Southwestern University, 46
Spanish-American War, 12, 27,
  38–39, 339
Spring Rice, Cecil Arthur, 36, 74,
  85, 267, 282
Square Deal, 77, 79
State, The (WW), 51–52, 55
Stimson, Henry L., 152–153, 158,
  358, 360
Submarine controversy (World War
  I), 251–252, 269, 288–290,
  292–293, 296–297, 300, 304,
  317–323
Sullivan, Mark, 288
Sumner, William Graham, 131–133,
  203
Supreme Court: TR's attitude to-
  ward, 150–151, 156; Franklin
  Roosevelt's attack on, 351, 354,
  356–357

Taft, William Howard, 112,
  127–128, 187, 189, 336–337, 339,
  356; relationship with TR, 70,
  74–75, 109, 113, 191, 196, 221,
  240, 259, 271–272, 306–307,
  331–333; as president, 114, 118,
  139, 143–144, 183, 230, 232, 238,
  241, 263; in 1912 election, 140,

Taft, William Howard—*Cont.*
  147, 157–159, 161, 204–207, 256;
  views of TR, 151–152, 154,
  156–157, 284; foreign policy
  views, 267–268, 286, 279, 301,
  306, 314
Talcott, Charles A., 23, 25
Tammany Hall, 120, 133, 161,
  185–186, 230, 232
Tariff, as political issue, 80–81, 110,
  114, 120, 127–128, 209, 232–233,
  236, 251, 349
Tariff Commission, 251
Taxes, income and inheritance, 145,
  232, 251, 262
Tennessee Coal and Iron Company,
  109, 155
Tennyson, Alfred, 88
Thomas, Norman M., 96
Titanic, sinking of, 280, 288
"Too proud to fight" speech (WW),
  269, 276, 289, 407n3
Tories (American Revolution), 315
Toryism, 190–191, 208, 212, 393n12
Tory party (Britain), 260
Trotter, William Monroe, 273–274,
  276
Tumulty, Joseph P., 166, 242–243,
  246, 321
Turkey, United States' relations
  with, 327, 332
Turner, Frederick Jackson, 33, 53

Underwood, Oscar W., 182–183,
  185–186, 232, 235, 298
Underwood-Simmons Tarriff,
  232–233, 236
United Nations, 282, 359
United States Steel Corporation,
  109, 155–156
United States v. *E. C. Knight Company* (1896), 150

Vardaman, James K., 182
Veblen, Thorstein, 100, 101, 378n18
Venezuela, United States' relations
  with, 36–37, 57, 70

Veracruz, United States' intervention
  in, 268–271, 321
Verdun, seige of, 310
Veysey, Laurence, 89–90
Villard, Oswald Garrison, 357
Virginia, University of, 44–45, 56

Wallace, Henry A., 188, 350
Walters, Alexander, 211
War of 1812, 13, 274, 285
Warrior, concept of, 223, 286, 317
Washington, Booker T., 210
Washington, George, TR's attitudes
  toward, 284–285, 306, 315, 324
Washington conference (1921), 344
Washington state, 170, 189
Watson, Thomas E., 182–184
Watterson, Henry, 121, 176
Weber, Max, 54
Weinstein, Edwin A., 20, 340–342
Wesleyan University, 56
West, Andrew F., 58, 91, 96,
  102–105
West: TR's experiences in, 27,
  29–32, 35, 38; WW's attitudes to-
  ward, 217, 250; in 1916 election,
  255–256
Whig Hall (Princeton), 23
Whig party (United States), 160
White, Edward Douglas, 42
White, Henry, 339
White, William Allen, 188, 249, 358;
  view of 1912 election, 208, 211
White House, 69, 86, 324–325
Williams College, 101
Willkie, Wendell, 355, 358, 360
Wilmington, N. C. 17, 22
Wilson, Edmund, 105
Wilson, Edith Bolling Galt (WW's
  second wife), 243, 293–295
Wilson, Ellen Louise Axson (WW's
  first wife), 48, 60, 52–53, 58, 60,
  244, 276, 293–294
Wilson, Janet Woodrow (WW's
  mother), 16, 18, 21
Wilson, Joseph Ruggles (WW's fa-
  ther), 15–22, 25, 46

Wilson, Margaret (WW's daughter),
99
Wilson, Woodrow, 63, 76, 137, 147,
277, 281, 283, 284; youth, 3,
15–25; probable dyslexia, 20–21;
early political attitudes, 21–25,
47–56, 61; study and practice of
law, 44–46; graduate study in political science, 46–49; professor at
Bryn Mawr, 56, 373–21; professor
at Wesleyan, 56; professor at
Princeton, 56–58; early foreign
policy views, 59–62, 71, 119–120,
132; acquaintance with Roosevelt,
59–62, 120, 124, 130–136,
167–168, 173–174; president of
Princeton, 66, 89–108, 119,
122–124, 173, 210–211, 237; pre-
figurations of later political career,
98–99, 105–106; involvement in
politics, 66–67, 106, 119–129; domestic political attitudes, 106–107,
122–124–129, 169–184; governor
of New Jersey, 140, 152, 164–174,
187, 191, 236, 245, 298; in 1912
election, 139–141, 160–161, 164,
174–175, 177–187, 189–221, 225;
attitudes toward TR, 187, 193,
199–200, 208–209, 221, 234,
237–238, 325; as president,
225–227, 229–248, 250–258,
260–276, 282–287, 289–327,
329–344; domestic policies as
president, 229–240, 242–247,
251–258, 260–265, 319–320; leadership of Democratic party, 225,
231–239, 244, 248, 251–258,
262–264, 297–300, 335; foreign
policies as president, 221,
226–227, 229, 239–240, 242, 251,
254, 255, 260–264, 266–276,
286–287, 299–301; policies toward
World War I, 229, 251, 254–255,
260–261, 272–275, 287, 288–301,
303–343; peacemaking efforts,
335–343; fight to join League of
Nations, 343–345; major stroke,

227, 242, 260, 263, 335–336,
341–342; last years and death,
344–345; 262, 265; political legacy
of, 227, 346–361; religious beliefs,
19, 123–124, 171, 322–323; family
life, 52–53, 241, 276; as teacher,
56; health, 57, 98–99, 105, 227,
242–244, 276, 339–340; on race
relations, 210–211; views of war,
268–269; as administrator,
239–247; relationship with press,
245–247; oratory, 390n20, 392n4
Winning of the West (TR), 32–33,
255
Wisconsin, 152, 165–166, 170, 189,
354
Wiseman, Sir William, 295
Wister, Owen, 31, 63, 131, 305
Woman suffrage, 209–210, 255
Wood, Leonard, 263
Woodrow, Harriet (WW's cousin), 45,
58
Woodrow, James (WW's uncle), 16,
17, 20, 46
Woodrow, Thomas (WW's grandfather), 16, 20
Woodrow Wilson: The Academic
Years (Henry W. Bragdon), 1
World War I, 211–212, 218–219,
221, 268, 271; outbreak, 226, 239,
244, 247, 272–274; entry of United
States, 226, 258, 260, 317–323,
357; WW's policies toward, 229,
251, 254–255, 260–261, 272–275,
287–301, 303–343; TR's attitudes
toward, 226, 250, 276–286,
288–289, 300, 304–310, 324–328;
American public opinion toward,
289–290, 318, 337–338, 343;
American belligerency in, 324–343
World War II, 282, 351, 357–360

Yale University, 32, 42, 92, 95, 101
Young Men's Christian Association
(YMCA), 178

Zimmermann Telegram, 318